The Salad Days

THE SALAD DAYS

Douglas Fairbanks, Jr.

COLLINS
8 Grafton Street, London W1
1988

William Collins Sons & Co. Ltd
London · Glasgow · Sydney · Auckland
Toronto · Johannesburg

ISBN 0 00 216332 2

First published in Great Britain 1988
Copyright © 1988 by Douglas Fairbanks, Jr.

Made and Printed in The United States of America

To my wondrous Mary Lee

I would like to thank Joan Pollack for her special research and editorial contribution to this book.

D.F., Jr.

Acknowledgments

Fiction retains attention only in proportion to the skill of its teller. Total credibility is not essential provided the author's talents for entertaining the reader are adequate. But a biography—an account of a life—should be dependably authentic. To defray any doubts that may shadow this record and to verify details, I have turned not only to such sometimes retouched recollections as I happen still to have on file but also to my wife and daughters, who have contributed valuable bits and pieces. After my family's rememberings, I am bound to offer thanks to the following—warmly, gratefully, and in most cases affectionately—for their contributions, large and small, but all important, to this record. They are, in alphabetical order:

Helen Adeane
Fred Astaire
Pat Sully Ballad
Betty Barker
Countess Helen Beckendorf
Col. Joseph Bryan III
Carter Burden
Shirley Burden
Genie Chester
Mary Margaret Burden Childs
Brian and Esme Connell
Leslie Crawford
Owen and Lucile Crump

Sir Edward Ford
Harold French
Lisa Garriss
Greer Garson
Milton Goldman
Arthur Greene
Dr. Mason Hicks
John Hundley
Kay Brainard Hutchins
Alexandra Metcalfe
Elizabeth Noll
Sir Laurence Olivier
Joan S. Pollack

Charles (Buddy) Rogers   Letitia Fairbanks Smoot
Richard Schickel

I am particularly grateful for the initial suggestion and constant encouragement of Kenneth McCormick and the vital research and assistance of Caleb Gray.

I sometimes feel a little uneasy about that imagined self of mine—the Me of my daydreams—who leads a melodramatic life of his own, out of all relation with my real existence. So one day I shadowed him down the street. He loitered along for a while, and then stood at a shop window and dressed himself out in a gaudy tie and yellow waistcoat. Then he bought a great sponge and two stuffed birds and took them to lodgings, where he led a shady existence. Next he moved to a big house in Mayfair, and gave grand dinner parties, with splendid service and costly wines. His amorous adventures among the High-up Ones of this Earth I pass over. He soon sold his house and horses, gave up his motors, dismissed his retinue of servants, and went—saving two young ladies from being run over on the way—to live a life of heroic self-sacrifice among the poor.

I was beginning to feel encouraged about him, when in passing a fishmonger's he pointed at a great salmon and said, "I caught that fish."

from *All Trivia*
by Logan Pearsall Smith

My salad days,
When I was green in judgment.

Shakespeare, *Antony and Cleopatra,* I, v, 73

Prologue

It was the eleventh of December, 1939. I was barely—by two days—thirty years old. And suddenly there I was, trying to persuade myself that a major crisis affecting many lives, but principally my own, was at hand. Up to that time I know I was in no way prepared to face up to the imminent probability of my father's death.

It was early in the afternoon when I tiptoed up the stairs to his bedroom overlooking the Pacific in the elegant Santa Monica beach house he had bought in the late twenties as a weekend place for himself and my first stepmother, Mary Pickford. The male nurse beckoned me in, and the gentle bull mastiff, (Marco) Polo, sprawled in the middle of the darkened room, welcomed me with no more than a considerately slow tail-wag. My father was lying listlessly in bed. Few people had seen this fabulously famous, indefatigably vital man like this.

As I reached his bedside I uttered a muffled "Hello." Out of habit, he tried to smile, but it was unconvincing on his sallow-tan, prematurely aged fifty-six-year-old face. He turned his blue-gray eyes (still dramatic in contrast to his dark hair) and raised a feeble hand just enough to accompany his husky "Hello . . ." We had so seldom been demonstrative with each other, so seldom at ease that although in recent years we had enjoyed extended spells of camaraderie and sometimes seemed almost contemporaries it was never easy for us to be completely natural. But, now, as he lay there, weak and dependent, it seemed as though we had exchanged relationships. I was the parent and he the child—the very ill child. I was hale, hearty, and involved in the world. He had resigned. He appeared relieved to see me; he mumbled-grumbled something about how unaccustomed he was to serious illness. What he thought was indigestion had been diagnosed as a serious heart attack. The doctor had told him he must rest his heart as if it were a broken leg and let time heal it. He was forbidden ("Can you *imagine?*" *"Dammit to hell!"*) to read about the progress of the three-month-old war in Europe or even to listen to the news on the radio. Nothing, he'd been told, must be allowed to excite him. He'd rather die, he said, than be an invalid. He'd said that before, but this time the words had new meaning.

What to do then? "Shall I," I asked, "read you something?"

"Yes, fine . . . great!"

"Poetry?"

"Sure!"

"What?"

"Anything!"

Most people never knew that Douglas Fairbanks's earliest literary and theatrical interests were in the classics and were surprised by his love of reciting long passages from them. I saw one of the small Oxford anthologies of verse in his bookcase and I picked out bits of Byron and Shakespeare to read aloud.

I read, and stopped, glanced over at him, and read on. Sometimes he reacted agreeably; sometimes he dozed. I wondered if he'd be in any way disturbed if I patted his hand. I did so, but the doctor's sedative (and possibly the monotony of my voice and the gentle breaking surf outside) had done its work. He was asleep.

I watched him for a long while. I knew no one downstairs in the large living room would disturb us while we were alone. Not Mary Lee, my wife of seven months; not Robert Fairbanks—my dear Uncle Bob who was my father's only surviving brother and his closest friend and adviser (and to whom I felt closer than to my own unpaternal parent). Nor would the others below interrupt us—not my four darling cousins and surrogate sisters; not my father's company manager, Clarence Erickson; his accountant, Art Fenn; not Chuck Lewis, his trainer, secretary, and traveling companion; not my more recent stepmother of about three and a half years, Sylvia (just urgently summoned from her hairdresser), nor Sylvia's ever-present sister, Vera Bleck; none of them, grouped together whispering below, would think of coming into the room when I was there. They knew how special this visit was.

I found my normally detached self disconcertingly moved. I stared and stared at my father, and now and then I glanced between the partly drawn curtains at the restless sea outside. I remember thinking that I was beholden to this very ill man for my existence. I contemplated his life (insofar as I then knew it). This led me to thoughts of my mother as well, her fascinating and complex, spoiled but outwardly charming personality, and of *her* origins. Whatever they both were, whatever had caused *them* to *be,* contributed to my being whatever I was. Or am. Or will be.

All these conjectures, and more, rambled through my head and when I drifted back full circle to look at my half-sleeping father I did something I had never done before in my life. I leaned over and very gently kissed him on the forehead. Then, with a thin fog of tears threatening to betray my self-control, I slipped as quietly as I could out of the room and down the stairs. I never saw him alive again. At the time I didn't know exactly why I had been so moved by my father's two-day illness and his subsequent quiet (too quiet for his liking, I'm sure) death. When my father died, I became—possibly subconsciously—more "my own man." Certainly for the time being I was less challenging and less challenged, freer and more self-assured but I had lost the one I had always wished most to please.

Just before midnight, the nurse, having heard Polo growl softly and briefly, came into the bedroom and saw that his patient had died in his sleep. Sylvia and her sister awakened me by phone, crying hysterically, "He's dead! *He's dead!"*

Mary Lee and I threw on some clothes and rushed back. When I saw my father he was looking much as when I'd left him a few hours earlier, except that this time when I leaned down I whispered a loving good-bye, and then gently kissed his forehead for the second and last time.

1

Many, if not all of my mother's family—the Sullys, Ballantines, Proctors, Grenvilles, Thompsons, et al.—have been buried for generations in the same Providence, Rhode Island, cemetery, *Swan's Point.*

The old colonial capital city of Providence, Rhode Island, had so prospered and grown by the middle of the nineteenth century that plans for its expansion were authorized. Helping to design it was my maternal great-grandfather, Colonel David Moulton Thompson. He was the wealthy owner-operator of the D. B. R. Knight Cotton Mills, since the early 1830s reputed to be the world's largest and makers of the once-famous Fruit of the Loom cotton cloth. The city's most imposing residence belonged to the colonel and his lady. Both were of Scottish descent: the Thompsons were a sept of the Campbells of Argyll clan and Anne was a Ballantine. Old Colonel Thompson owed his military rank to his Civil War service. He wrote a horrifying account of his long incarceration and eventual escape from the Confederacy's infamous Andersonville prison camp.

Shortly after the war's end, the Thompsons had a daughter whom they named Emma Frances. With red hair that began to turn gray in her late teens, she was considered a budding beauty. In the course of many years she would become my maternal grandmother whom I loved very much. I called this grandmother Munnie.

Young Providence society, in the last third of the nineteenth century, enhanced by the local Brown University, was as sprightly as those more decorous times allowed. Among the presentable young men around town was handsome, charming, young Dan Sully. Dan's widowed father had brought him up single-handedly and intended him to go to Yale. But because of limited finances and his father's premature death, young Dan decided to go into business, starting as a clerk in a Providence clothing company.

Dan fell, as did so many other young swains, for the ravishing Emma Frances Thompson. Not only did he sweep Emma off her dainty feet, he also impressed canny old Colonel Thompson. It therefore followed that Emma, not yet quite eighteen, married the poor but promising young Dan Sully in 1885.

Being the boss's son-in-law was no handicap. My lovingly remembered grandfather Dan left his clerkship in the clothing company and, at the old colonel's instigation, spent a good part of the next two years in the South studying every phase of cotton's cultivation. In the meantime, Emma, to everyone's delight, produced a son, christened Kenneth Moulton Sully. Dan had further cause to glow when he won a partnership in a Boston cotton brokerage firm (in which the colonel of course had a piece of the action). He soon added even more to his knowledge of the world's cotton market.

On Sunday, June 20, 1888, at four o'clock in the afternoon Emma gave birth to her second child—my mother, Anna Beth Sully. Kenneth, her oldest child, was then three. Five years later, another daughter, Gladys, arrived. At the age of twelve Kenneth contracted an undiagnosed fever and died. A marble bust and a painting of the boy were commissioned, and the family's huge, rambling summer house in Watch Hill was from then on named Kenneth Ridge. My grandmother, from that time to the end of her own long and graceful life, affected the color purple in mourning. How beautiful she must have been can only be glimpsed from faded photographs, letters of friends, and jottings in the social columns of the New York and Providence press. Still in her twenties, Emma's hair was nearly snow white, and she always dressed in shades of mauve, lavender, or violet. As her carriage drove through New York's Central Park or along Fifth Avenue, she became known to the press of her day as "the Purple Lady."

About ten years later my grandmother's fourth and last child was born— a partial compensation for the loss of Kenneth. It was another boy—also to be named after kinfolk: Grenville Proctor. His arrival filled out the Sully family of that generation.

Dan's destiny was manifesting itself rapidly and without question, deservedly. In Providence he moved up to another, more important partnership in the nationally known cotton brokerage firm of F. W. Reynolds & Co. His knowledge of every phase of the cotton business had by now equaled and perhaps even surpassed that of his most experienced associates. Dan Sully built up a big trade in the hitherto little-known business of Egyptian cotton. The firm expanded phenomenally and at the age of thirty-nine he bought the controlling interest in it. Two years later, he moved his home and headquarters to New York and formed his own new setup: D. J. Sully & Co.

Within a year or two, Daniel J. Sully, not yet forty, had become an honest-to-goodness millionaire. In 1903 he made financial history by organizing a corner of the world's cotton market. He forced up cotton market prices from 8.8 cents to 11.15 cents a pound—in less than a month! And still he went on buying. A year or so later the price had reached 18 cents a pound! This would be legally impossible to so much as attempt today—as, indeed, would the child labor that he may hardly have known was used in his mills and factories.

Sully did not limit his energies to speculation. He persuaded Southern cotton farmers that they could correct their wasteful methods of cultivation and increase the value of their crops by improving the means of cotton seed selection. Years ahead of his time, he advocated government support of farmers. "The Cotton King" bought himself a seat on the New York Stock Exchange, then a membership on the Chicago Board of Trade, the New Orleans Cotton Exchange, and the Liverpool Cotton Association in England. Almost predictably after a few years there came a slump. But Dan Sully's firm kept on buying—even though the losses mounted—and they were immense. Neither Dan Sully nor his empire of companies could withstand the reverses for long.

In order to refresh his energies and get some perspective on what was clearly predicted as imminent disaster, Grandfather Sully took my Grandmother, Emma, on a short cruise. On his return he learned that he had been outmaneuvered by a rival and that his partners had, in his absence and without prior notification, sold him out. The Sully firm was a bust and the news made worldwide front pages. On March 18, 1904, his principal company reported liabilities of well over $4 million—the equivalent of $50 or $60 million or more today. But Dan Sully was a man of considerable character, courage, and resilience. His hero was Napoleon and he considered this sudden, shocking defeat as no more than a setback. He would, he confidently assured the financial world, come back—"strong!"

The Sullys' large Rhode Island seaside estate, Kenneth Ridge, continued through that summer at full blast. Their stately old home in Providence and the fine New York town house, on Sixty-second Street off Fifth Avenue, near the present Knickerbocker Club, were similarly maintained.

There is, somewhere, a charming photograph of my mother, at sixteen, sitting in the driver's seat of a small, smart, open carriage, drawn by a fine bay pony, about to clip-clop off to Central Park, just up and across the street. I often had occasion to pass my mother's—that is, my grandparents' —old house and was tempted to look inside to see if all I'd heard in my youth was true. Were the dining and reception rooms as large and impressive as I'd been told, and was the ballroom as grand as I'd imagined? But I never had the nerve to ring the bell. Now the house has been gutted and rebuilt, and its ghosts presumably exorcized.

When Mother was seventeen, she was given a magnificent Debutante Ball at Kenneth Ridge. Her beau then was Jim Evans, from Pittsburgh, a distant cousin of the legendary Mellon family. He went to Andover and the University of Pennsylvania. Jim dropped out of mother's life not long after the ball, but his devotion to her continued. It would be almost fifteen years before their paths would cross again.

The Sullys were not about to let at least the appearance of settled prosperity be changed, and so, shortly after the social bang of mother's "coming out," she was sent on the traditional Grand Tour of Europe: midseason Edwardian London, Paris, Venice, Rome and Naples.

It is essential for an understanding of this story to find out how and why I was born with the name of Fairbanks. Of course, it was also my father's name—but it was not the name *he* was born with!

I called my Fairbanks grandmother Tu-Tu, a name of my own invention having no connection with the classic ballet skirt. I remember her only faintly, as I was seven when she died. But her impact on my parents was considerable. She and my mother were very jealous of each other and of the relative influence each had over my father. I gather that whenever a bluff was called, Tu-Tu won. Likewise, my mother was as difficult to cope with as a New England nor'easter, but she was terrified of Tu-Tu, who, to me, was just a loving grandmother.

There were some good reasons, I was told, for my mother's antipathy toward my paternal grandmother, the most outstanding of which was that my aggressively masculine father was a devoted "mother's boy." He was the youngest, handsomest, most talented, and eventually most successful (though not the brightest) of my grandmother's four sons.

Tu-Tu's maiden name was Ella Adelaide Marsh. Her father, a Roman Catholic, had been fairly prosperous "in trade" in New York. Her mother's name had been Finch and she came from Virginia. It appealed to Ella's sense of "magnolia romance" to claim that she herself also stemmed from

Virginia. However, she was born outside of New York City, and her younger sister, Belle, was born near Boston. Life for Ella was initially a bit too comfortable to prepare her for the vicissitudes awaiting her.

The Civil War had been over for about six or seven years when John Fairbanks, a handsome, and wealthy young planter and heir to a fine sugar mill, swaggered into Yankee territory from New Orleans. That he happened to be a Roman Catholic venturing into a New England black forest of Protestants must have made his welcome to the Marsh family even warmer. John presumably got on well with both Ella and Belle, but Ella was his favorite. In no time at all, it seemed, John wooed and won her. Everyone agreed it was a fine match. The delicately raised Ella would be in very good hands because, though young John's immediate life and fortune were rooted in the Confederacy, his family was, after all, Fairbanks of Massachusetts. Young John Fairbanks shared with his bride and New England in-laws a strong sense of regional identification. In his case it was because of the proximity of what is still called the "Fairbanks House" (or "Homestead"), the oldest inhabited frame house in North America.

The house, which I commend to the historically minded, still stands on East Street, near Willow Road, in Dedham, Massachusetts, near Boston. It was built in 1636 by a spunky Yorkshireman, one Jonathan Fayerbanke, who had gathered up his wife and six children and sailed from England in about 1631. Jonathan had apparently been skeptical about the New World's timber. He brought the entire timber frame of the house he intended to build with him. Then, after buying some surrounding farmland, he conned some local Puritan handymen into helping him build the house in the current style. It is now a national monument and museum, and is the headquarters of the Society of the D.A.R., who helped restore the building in the late nineteenth century. Nine generations of the family lived there until Miss Rebecca Fairbanks (spinster) died in the early 1900s.

Ella was as proud as John of this tangible proof of their early American roots. The name *Fayerbanke* continued to be spelled that way until some probably cloddish fellow in the mid-eighteenth century couldn't tell *e* from *s* and the whole name eventually became mildly corrupted to *Fairbanks.* One of the original Jonathan's sons and a grandson were killed by Indians in 1675. A great-grandson served a century after that in Washington's ragtag regular army, while another was a Minuteman. One served well and truly in the Civil War and another became Governor of Massachusetts and a Lincoln supporter. Another was elected Vice President (under Theodore Roosevelt), but achieved greater fame by having the city of Fairbanks, Alaska, named after him.

In 1873, Ella Fairbanks brought forth her first son—another John (later my Uncle Jack), named after his father. Ella's happiness proved cruelly brief because her beloved young husband died of tuberculosis that same year. Ella was poorly equipped to hold up a world which had so suddenly come crashing down around her. Just before he died her husband was swindled out of his fortune by his financial partners. Virtually penniless, Ella turned to her late husband's distinguished older friend and New York-based lawyer, H. Charles Ulman, for help and advice, but he failed to recover anything at all for the young widow Fairbanks and her infant son.

Sister Belle, however, had married more securely. Her husband, a Mr. Weeks, had made a small fortune out of whalebone corset stays. The Weekses lived in Georgia, near Atlanta, and they sent for Ella to come and live with them.

There was little reason to doubt contemporary descriptions of Ella in her early twenties as being very pretty. It must have been no surprise that a prominent neighbor, Judge Edward Wilcox, took a fancy to Ella and persuaded her to marry him. It was too late when Ella realized that he was abrasive, abusive, and habitually hit the bottle. Still, she must have recalled those brief happier days past and closed her eyes long enough to become pregnant once again.

Ella's second son was named Norris. Shortly after his birth she turned once more to the loyal, older (by twenty years or so) distinguished friend and lawyer, H. Charles Ulman, for help. She wanted a divorce from the intolerably drunken Judge Wilcox, even though it meant disobeying her Church and the prevailing sentiments of society. It was not easy getting divorces in those days, but this time Ulman's efforts on her behalf were more successful. Not only did he succeed in obtaining Ella's divorce from Wilcox, but by the time the decree became final he had fallen in love with his client. Shortly after Ulman declared himself, they jointly defied ecclesiastical and social disapproval and publicly reported their marriage.

Ulman must have seemed an uncommonly good catch. She had long known of his fine reputation: that as a very young man he had left a promising legal career to become a Union Army officer at the outbreak of the Civil War; that as a partially disabled hero he then returned to legal practice; and that having had a major part in the creation of the United States Law Association (the precursor of the American Bar Association), he became its first president. Ella had also heard of his quiet prominence in the social and cultural life of New York, Philadelphia, and Washington, where his friends and clients ranged from government officials to commercial and industrial leaders, and also to the worlds of arts and letters. Indeed, he was enthusiastically attached to the dazzling world of the theater. Ulman's splendid looks were, to his unabashed pleasure, frequently mistaken by passersby for those of his greatly admired friend Edwin Booth—at the time, America's most famous classical actor (and, of course, brother to Lincoln's infamous assassin, John Wilkes Booth). It also impressed Ella that Ulman was the senior partner in one of New York's most substantial law firms.

H. (for Hezekiah) Charles Ulman was born, the eldest of two brothers, near Philadelphia in 1833. Their father, Lazarus, then forty-nine, had been born in Gemmingan, Baden, in 1784, and with his wife, Lydia (Abrahams), also of Baden, emigrated and settled comfortably among the Pennsylvania Dutch in the Quaker State. He prospered modestly and died in 1869. Lydia died in Philadelphia in 1883, the year her grandson, my father, was born. Young Charles was admitted to the Bar at the age of twenty-three and practiced law until the outbreak of the Civil War in 1861. Responding with rugged enthusiasm to a call for volunteers, H. Charles personally enlisted a company of 184 men for the Pennsylvania Reserve Corps and was elected their Captain. He was wounded and when he finally recovered he resigned from the army and resumed his practice of law.

If Ella hesitated at all (which I doubt) it might have been because sister Belle Weeks and her in-laws mentioned that H. Charles (everyone called him that) was of Jewish origin; whether entirely or partly, none of the family was ever quite sure. I doubt if it mattered very much to Ella. She appreciated his kindness and protection, and returned his love.

Soon after their marriage, he was attracted by a lawyer friend in Denver, Colorado, who wrote and invited him to share in the opportunities for great wealth that abounded in the Rocky Mountains. The swarms of gold and silver prospectors needed their diggings financed and coordinated. H. Charles jumped at the idea and prepared to move to what seemed in those days literally the Golden West. Bursting with self-confidence and natural vitality, H. Charles and Ella moved, in the year 1880, to the raw, growing city of Denver.

Ella's older son, John, came with them, but for some unexplained reason little Norris Wilcox, her second-born, was left behind to be brought up by the family of Lottie Barker, a paternal aunt. In fact, so completely was he abandoned that even his name would be an unlikely entry in this story had not his three half brothers rescued him from near-obscurity many years later. They brought him into my father's New York offices, where he did extremely well in an executive position and, as it were, reentered the family.

When Ella decided to marry a third time, there was gossip that not only had H. Charles been married a long time before to someone in New Orleans but that, being unacquainted with that state's blending of the Common Law with the Napoleonic Code, he did not trouble to confirm the legality of his divorce. Therefore, there was a strong suggestion that his marriage to the innocent, unknowing Ella was bigamous and their children would be illegitimate. Certainly this may have been another reason to abandon New York and his law firm. Records were not strictly kept in the American hinterlands of that period, but even so it seems a strange oversight for such a reputable lawyer.

Once in Colorado, H. Charles turned his back on his law career, absenting himself from home for weeks at a time, traveling all about with his associates, enthusiastically exploring the prospective mines that they intended to finance.

My grandmother made no pretense of liking her new home. Ella was accustomed to more genteel surroundings, scarcely to be found in the rough city of Denver. In addition, little nine-year-old John Fairbanks and his step-father had come to dislike each other so much that the boy got himself a job with a local store and moved in with the owner's family.

Good lawyers are not necessarily the best businessmen (although many act as if they are), and the fortune that H. Charles expected and so energetically sought eluded him utterly. The drain on his once robust finances began to tell. Before the year of 1882 was out, the strains on Ella became even more formidable with the arrival of their first (Ella's third) child. Another boy. This time the given names were Robert Payne, after some kin of Ella's.

Despite the stress of her new home, and H. Charles's constant, wearying travels, Ella was still a fine-looking woman of thirty-six. Her wasp waist had thickened a bit with the arrival of two more sons. Just a year after baby Robert arrived, another son, my father, was born to them on May 23, 1883.

When she named her new son, Ella confessed a sentimental liking for a poem by Robert Burns that began "Douglas, Douglas, tender and true . . ." Thus with her remote Scottish ancestry in mind and the addition of a middle name from a nearly forgotten English relative, she called my father Douglas Elton Ulman. Both my Uncle Robert and my father were whisked off to church and formally baptized as Roman Catholics.

Ella, while trying to appear prosperous without adequate support, made no effort to conceal her dislike of the brown, parched land around her, always contrasting it with the gentler past from which she had strayed. The unquestioning confidence she had happily invested in H. Charles was also dissolving. She blamed him for the glaring misjudgment that led to their

present plight. He rebutted by blaming her and saying that it was his concern for their life together that obliged him, in his middle years, to give up
his hard-won reputation and career and "to risk all in an unknown world of
mining finance."

In addition, Ella's hands were well occupied with the care of her two
littlest boys. (The eldest, John, now eleven, still helped relieve the pressure
by continuing to work and room elsewhere.) It seems also that Ella was
afflicted by a burden of guilt. She loved her children—in time, excessively—
but now she appeared to resent them. Son Robert, one year older than
Douglas, was quiet and well behaved, and generally self-sufficient. To Ella, a
natural worrier, baby Douglas became a problem. His skin was noticeably
darker than his brothers', and Ella would cover the infant's cot with a
shawl.

Modern child psychologists say that the child could well have subconsciously sensed this fuss, because he was unusually glum—an uncommunicative, ungurgling baby—who seldom attempted to speak and hardly ever
smiled. (He more than made up for that when he grew up. One early film
critic wrote: "I like Fairbanks but I do wish he would stop smiling so darned
much!")

Ella used to confide that some neighbors whispered that her "little boy is
mentally retarded." But as he grew he became very active indeed—climbing
walls, drainpipes and, on one occasion, trying (but failing) to fly, *à la* Peter
Pan, off the roof! He bumped his head badly on landing and carried the scar
of a gash above his left eye all his life.

The accident must have had a great therapeutic effect on the boy because,
instead of crying, he is said to have burst out laughing. That curious reaction *could* have confirmed the neighbors' diagnosis of his mental state; but
fortunately—for millions as it turned out—from that time on he was reported as bright, cheerful—even boisterous.

The unlucky, unsuccessful H. Charles did occasionally manage to participate in his family's life. But only occasionally. He took them on a few
summer camping holidays in the Rockies on the sites of his most promising
claims. The boys loved it. Ella loathed it.

H. Charles's name was still recognized in many Eastern professional circles and he took special pleasure in being host to visiting friends and colleagues. It had been rumored that if he had stuck to the law, it was likely
he'd have been nominated to the U.S. Supreme Court—but he'd failed "by a
whisker of his sideburns" because of the technicalities of his marriage to
Ella. H. Charles also delighted in entertaining old theatrical friends from
New York (he remained as contagiously stagestruck as ever) who included

Denver in their national tours. He was such a serious lover of Shakespeare that he has always been credited with imbuing his younger son, Douglas, with an equal enthusiasm for the theater and the spoken word. (Courtroom lawyers, politicians, clergymen, and actors have, I've always maintained, a shared talent.)

The young Douglas had an unusually retentive memory for verse and began to "ham it up" at about the age of five or six for all who would listen to his childish treble exercising the classics. No doubt his father, had he been present, would have been proud, but others, I'm sure, wanted to crown him with one of the empty bottles that H. Charles was apt to leave around. Whenever H. Charles made one of his sporadic returns to the family hearth, quite a few empty bottles gave evidence of his presence. He had always been a moderate drinker but now, as his fortunes fell, moderation was sliding into excess. The mining ventures, for which such high hopes were held, and for which security and reputation were sacrificed, had collapsed. Finally, in an attempt to recoup some status and influence, he accepted a position as paid professional Republican Party Campaign speaker for Benjamin Harrison in the Presidential election campaign of 1888. He had been in Colorado nearly eight years. His own sons were seven and six. He was fifty-five.

H. Charles Ulman left for New York that summer. Ella saw him only once more, half a dozen years later. And after that, never again. She had been completely, and nearly silently, abandoned. Her eldest son, John, steady and serious, returned home, started in a new job with a wholesale grocery firm, and shared his wages with his mother. As gracefully as she could in such needy circumstances she began taking in lodgers.

The little boys started going to the local public school. They both did well but Robert did better. Douglas was bright but he lacked concentration. The school's principal reported that he amused everyone by swinging easily through branches of trees and walking on his hands "around the entire perimeter of the school wall."

When Douglas was twelve he was surprised one day to find his father in Denver on business, and also looking for him. The boy enthusiastically urged him to come home with him "to see Mother" but the older man demurred. He took his son to the nearest bar and, although already noticeably unsteady, dismayed the boy by downing at least two more shots of Scotch. This did, however, give H. Charles the Dutch courage to go home to Ella with Douglas holding his hand. "All hell broke loose" behind closed doors, ending with Ella furiously ordering the stumbling wreck of the once eminent man out of the house.

That was the last Ella ever saw of him. Douglas did see him again in the years to come. H. Charles would quietly come around, "out of nowhere," to his son's dressing room in a theater where he was playing and, as subtly as he could, would ask for handouts. Money was always forthcoming, though my father grew increasingly bitter—not only because of H. Charles's weakness, but also because of his own devotion and loyalty to his mother. It was not hard for him to convey this feeling to the old man, who finally just stopped coming around. He died in New York, alone and unnoticed, in 1915, the year that his son Douglas first burst upon the world's motion picture screens.

The day that Ella ordered my grandfather out of her boardinghouse was a day that brought in its train a decision with a major effect on my father's life. Ella grabbed young Douglas by the hand and rushed him to the local office of the Woman's Christian Temperance Union. There she made him swear, literally on the Bible, never to take a drink! He kept that promise scrupulously, until the last year or two of his life when his young third wife, Sylvia, teased him into making an occasional ceremony of sipping a little white wine. That and a couple of infrequent beers were all he ever knew of alcohol. It was a good thing, because so many members of my family—on both sides, including stepparents and in-laws—looked for far too much of what they needed in life from alcohol.

With whatever profit she could clear from her lodgers' payments, and the small but continuing assistance from sister Belle, Ella managed, in the mid-1890s, to send the young boys to the reputable nearby Jarvis Military Academy for a couple of years. Although they enjoyed it, family fortunes, seldom healthy anymore, constricted once again and both young fellows came back home, where they attended the East Denver High School under the name of Robert and Douglas Fairbanks—not Ulman. No contemporary comment or document from family or friends has come down to me as to precisely when the change was made. Up to Douglas's and Robert's respective ages of seven and eight they carried the name Ulman and probably continued to do so until H. Charles's last brief and calamitous return home.

I own a typical illustrated Victorian eight-page Christmas card, the text of which is "While Shepherds Watched Their Flocks by Night." It is inscribed "To Douglas Ulman from Mrs. Tebles—Xmas, 1888." Inside the cover in my father's immature, but unmistakable handwriting is the signature "Douglas Ulman, Denver, 1890." It is the last record we have of the name being used by either of the boys. It was not a subject either of them talked about. Their utter devotion and uncritical loyalty to their mother was, and remained, legendary.

From then on, Ella revived, "for solace" she said, lovely memories of her first, beautiful but ill-fated marriage to John Fairbanks. It must have been about this time that she scratched around the roots of the Fairbanks tree and began to drop claims here and there that would establish that she was herself a second or third Fairbanks *cousin* to John—a connection that she was sure would give her and the boys a better foundation, however distant and uncomfortable, from which to return to the better world she once knew.

Thus from about 1895 on, Robert and Douglas joined John in the use of the family name of Fairbanks. Norris remained a Wilcox in the south. Douglas became more and more inexhaustibly and mischievously active in sports and acrobatic tricks, while remaining only a fair-to-middling student. Ella became almost obsessively devoted to him, leaving no doubt that he was her favorite, always the first to be forgiven and the first to win sympathy. She was my father's first and most devoted audience, and she encouraged her son's love of storytelling and theatergoing. Although his enthusiasm was hardly more than a boy's unsophisticated enjoyment of a show for its own sake, for Ella the theater was a temporary, vicarious refuge. The rapidly developing West of the 1890s encouraged an active theatrical participation. The biggest international stars—Sir Henry Irving, Eleanora Duse, Sarah Bernhardt, John Drew, Maurice Barrymore, Ellen Terry, and others —toured the country performing the classics and popular plays of the day.

In addition to regular schooling, young Douglas attended a surprisingly good (for Denver) drama school, grandiosely called the Broadway Theater Stock Company. The drama school was run by two retired, but once noted, New York actresses, Margaret Healey and her daughter, Maude.

To keep up appearances, Ella discreetly scrounged money for everything, including school fees. John continued to help and Robert and Douglas both did odd jobs after school and during summer vacations but could hardly bring in more than a few extra dollars a week. At one point, Douglas had a bellboy's job at a local hotel.

Douglas did well in drama school. In an 1897 program of one of the school's periodic public performances "Master Douglas Fairbanks" is prominently listed. Two years later, in early April 1899, just a month short of his sixteenth birthday, Douglas left the East Denver High School. He wasn't exactly expelled, but was "allowed" to leave well before the end of the term.

A fortnight later, Frederick Warde, a then well-known English classical actor, arrived in Denver with his company to play at the National Theater as part of a national tour.

The story persists in our family that Warde had a letter from his colleague Edwin Booth advising him of the existence of his friend H. Charles Ulman's son. Booth was said to have added that he would appreciate anything Warde could do for the boy. However, when young Douglas was brushed off by the Great Star's minions, he climbed into the theater via Warde's dressing room window. Warde was so bemused by the lad's nerve that he gave him a job—sweeping up and then, on tour with the company, carrying a spear on stage.

Douglas's nearly two years with Warde were all on tour, never in New York City. His first professional part was that of Florio (a lackey) in *The Duke's Jester,* performed at the Academy of Music in Richmond, Virginia, on September 10, 1900. My father was seventeen, going on eighteen. When the company got to Duluth, young Douglas was given a crack at Laertes in *Hamlet.* The local critic said, ". . . Mr. Warde's supporting company was bad, but worst of all was Douglas Fairbanks . . ." A similar assessment was made by the principal critics in Lafayette, Indiana. Nevertheless, Warde liked him and at the end of his engagement sent him off with a paternal pat on the shoulder and a recommendation that he gain more knowledge in the outside world if he "sincerely wished to bring more maturity" to the roles he wished to play.

How he went about following this advice is mysterious. My father was an incorrigible exaggerator and although some of his reminiscences were reliable, many were not. A famous example was his spirited account of having entered Harvard for a year. No evidence whatsoever exists to support his claim. His account of joining two adventurous contemporaries in working their way to Europe on a cattle boat is more trustworthy. They worked and cycled across England and France for three or four months.

When he got home, theater work was hard to find. Ella sold all her furniture, linen, and jewelry as well as the house in Denver and, leaving John and Robert to their respective jobs in the West, joined her future star in New York. Douglas held a job in a Wall Street brokerage house until, early in 1902, he made his Broadway debut in a small part in a short-lived play, *Her Lord and Master.* Soon came a year of touring in a stock company and then a number of slightly better parts in several plays over the next two years. He was a prominent member of the male chorus in a musical called *Fontana* and hated the job, but it turned out to be lucky because one of Broadway's best-known stars of the era, Grace George, saw him and thought his exuberant personality unique. Her husband was one of New York's most important manager-impresarios, William A. Brady, and he promptly signed the delighted young Fairbanks to a contract.

The first play in which he was assigned a star role, *Frenzied Finance,* was not very successful. The next three plays were not much better. But in late 1906, he had the second lead in *The Man of the Hour,* which became a really big hit. The name Douglas Fairbanks went up in lights on the marquee of a Broadway theater. He was established and in demand.

After the New York run, the play went on a brief tour that included Boston. One matinee was attended by Beth Sully, who, like many girls her age, was stagestruck and often sneaked off with friends to see as many plays as possible. She developed a real crush on Douglas Fairbanks and, with her father's cautious help, arranged to meet her hero. His response was almost immediate. Young Fairbanks thought the buxom Miss Sully absolutely entrancing. He invited her for a chaperoned tea (that he could ill afford) in a Boston hotel. One tea date led to another.

Beth Sully, aged nineteen, saw in Mr. Fairbanks, aged twenty-five, the handsome, virile hero of her dreams. She was very shy and called him Douglas, at his request, only after their fourth meeting. Douglas was flattered by Beth in every way. She was as blond as he was swarthy, as feminine as he was masculine, and she epitomized that upper-class world in which he felt very much at ease, and which his mother had always thought their due. It wasn't long—a month or so perhaps—before Beth and Douglas exchanged declarations of love everlasting.

Ella was delighted. This was the right choice for her son and his future career. It reminded her of her own lost romance. Dan and Emma Sully were less captivated. Although they couldn't help but like the irrepressible young Fairbanks, they did have misgivings about *their* daughter marrying an *actor*. But Beth was determined and Douglas was enthusiastically persuasive.

Dan Sully had a plan to lessen the social embarrassment his family might suffer if his daughter were to marry someone of the theater. He owned the Buchan Soap Company, with which he planned to make his big financial "comeback." Its offices were in New York's Flatiron Building. Dan agreed to approve the marriage if Douglas quit the stage and accepted a partnership in the soap company. After much consideration, my father accepted.

Daniel Sully was pleased, of course. The wedding was to be a grand affair, to be held at Kenneth Ridge in Watch Hill where, a year or so before, Beth had enjoyed her great coming-out ball. *"Toute la Rhode Island"* and New York were invited, and all was gushingly reported by contemporary social columnists. Thus in June 1907, my mother-and-father-to-be were, in the sight of God and the face of whoever comprised their congregation, married . . . for better *and* worse! They left immediately for a honeymoon in Europe, courtesy of the Sully family.

2

The honeymoon over, ex-actor Fairbanks plunged into his new job with his usual enthusiasm. His duties were those of a high-level salesman. If he failed to make any big deals or improve the shaky condition of the company (which advertised on a large electrical sign in Times Square), he did manage to amuse some potential customers by offering to take a bite out of a bar of Buchan's "Twelve-twenty-three brand" soap to prove its purity. All this time, Broadway and William Brady, to whom he was still nominally under contract, kept steady pressure on him to return to the theater. I particularly like one of Brady's early pleas—from one of the few letters of that period my father took the trouble to save:

". . . I cannot tell you how much I regret your decision to retire from the stage whether temporary or permanent. Whether I ever see you act again or not, I want to be on record as saying that I think you are making a great mistake abandoning a professional career which indicates so bright a future for you for any other occupation or career. What do you care for the vulgar money?—and even if you do, there will be as much money in the theatrical business in the future as in any other business, and easier to get. Better think it over some more for your own sake . . ."

He did think it over. Before the year was out he notified Brady he would return to the theater. So Douglas, in August 1908, opened as the star of a play called *All for a Girl* by Rupert Hughes. From then on he remained a "star"—that is, his name was always above the title. As his fame grew, his name just got bigger. In September 1909 he costarred in *The Gentleman from Mississippi* with the popular character actor, fat, jolly Tom Wise.

Sadly, Dan Sully's fortunes had slipped so far that his final "Waterloo," as he liked to call it, was surrendering control of the soap company and salvaging what he could. His spirits rallied at the news of an impending Fairbanks grandchild—Beth was expecting in December. This cheered him so that he advanced enough of his remaining credit to his extravagant daughter and her equally extravagant actor-husband to enable them to rent a luxurious apartment in the Apthorp, at a then snob address between Seventy-eighth and Seventy-ninth streets, on Broadway. The grateful Fairbankses moved out of their friend Frank Case's theatrical but very proper Algonquin Hotel on Forty-fourth Street and into the Apthorp, way uptown.

At four-fifteen on the ninth morning of December, I weighed in at nine pounds. From the start I was a singularly happy baby, rarely crying and rapidly bouncing back from early illnesses. Some friends, less carried away by my rosy nature, infuriated Mother by saying my smile was obviously just wind!

I have no reason to question my family's assessment of me as the most adorable of infants, but such perfection just doesn't exist. During my father's infancy, the worry had been about his solemn mien and dark skin shade. My appeal was tempered by the fact that I had no hair! Although Mother would hold my head up to the light to persuade doubters that that fuzz would eventually become real hair, I remained billiard-ball bald for nearly two years.

As soon as it was convenient, my grandfather Dan Sully arranged for me to be baptized by the Reverend Percy Grant, the Episcopal rector of New York's oldest parish—Trinity. I was christened after my father, Douglas Elton Fairbanks, with the addition of the uniquely American tag "Jr."

My first summer was spent with my parents and, presumably, a nanny in a small village on the Upper Thames called Bourne End. My parents had rented a good-sized mock-Tudor Victorian house with a very large garden, extensive lawn, and a tennis court on the banks of the narrower reaches of the river. They seemed to have no particular reason to summer in England, but it must have been idyllic. Despite Edward VII's recent death, the summer schedule of fixed social events proceeded as planned and my mother and father took in as many as they could get invited to. They had a fully equipped coach-and-four to drive them, dressed to the nines, to their first Derby at Epsom Downs. Then there was Ascot, tennis at Wimbledon, and the boat races at nearby Henley.

I was not a reliably healthy child. Long, robust periods would often be interrupted by fairly severe illnesses. For example, sometime during my first year I contracted scarlet fever. This led to paralyzed intestines. I had one or two mild pneumonias, my share of pleurisy, bronchitis, too many colds, and a steady collection of such conventional illnesses as measles, whooping cough, and everything else except—thank God!—mumps! Nevertheless, my genes must have been fairly rugged and as I've now passed my biblically accorded life span, I don't even knock on wood anymore.

Back in New York, we left the Apthorp and lived for the next several years at the old Algonquin Hotel. (I have often thought that I was conceived there, but I never dared to ask.) My mother enjoyed having her picture taken, over and over, with her baby son. My father was very busy—first, starring in a new play called *The Cub* (a newspaper story), then in an all-star revival of *Lights O'London,* followed by *A Gentleman of Leisure,* written by the young and not yet world-famous English writer P. G. Wodehouse. Like many big stars of the day, my father then went on a short but immensely profitable national vaudeville tour with a one-act play called *A Regular Business Man.* On his return to New York, having left Brady, he joined in partnership with his friend and theatrical hero George M. Cohan, and his partner, Sam Harris.

Douglas (or "Senior" as many of his friends began to call him—no more to his pleasure than mine, since I was, for two-score years more, called "Junior"), began this new arrangement with a long run in Chicago in the play *Officer 666.* I was about three by then and a dumpling of a boy—fat but not sassy enough, immensely spoiled by an overindulgent mother and mildly ignored by a kindly but preoccupied father. One matinee I was taken to see my father act. We were in a box at the Blackstone Theater, next to the Blackstone Hotel where we were staying. (I remember the hotel best for the large wicker chairs in the bathrooms which discreetly concealed the toilets beneath them.) For a long time I had been paying more attention to the audience than to what was happening on stage, but during the play's second scene, when my father and his leading lady were playing a romantic love scene, my attention was suddenly galvanized and I realized that that was my father in a sort of moonlit garden. In my three-year-old treble, I cried, "Oh, Mummy! Look what Daddy's doing with that lady!" It took some time for the audience—and the players—to settle down.

The team of Cohan and Harris plus Fairbanks proved very successful. My father acted in four plays under this management over the next year and a half. Today, four plays in eighteen months would not suggest successes, but they were at the time. Occasionally a play would run a year or two, but three to six months often proved excellent and profitable runs for a Broadway or a London West End play. One of my father's hits was a play imported from England titled *Hawthorne of the U.S.A.*

In early 1914, we made another trip abroad—to both England and France. Our ship stopped first in Ireland, at Queenstown (now Cobh), and then went on to Liverpool. This time my mother engaged someone who became from that moment on an undischargeable family constant, a nanny who evolved into a governess and then a housekeeper (actually an honorary title as by then we had no house). She was very Irish and very Catholic and her name was Delia O'Dowd, which was, in the course of time, shortened by me to Dedie Dowd.

In August of that year, World War I exploded and shamed the civilization that bred it. But I was four years old and didn't know or care much about it. What I did know, and learned to enjoy, was, like Christopher Robin (though he was older than I; he was six), watching the Changing the Guard ceremony at Buckingham Palace.

We first stayed at London's Rubens Hotel, and later at the Rembrandt Hotel (an artistic accident, I'm almost sure). From the balcony above the street I'd watch with great joy as the scarlet-jacketed, bearskin-hatted Guardsmen marched smartly off to their daily palatial ceremony. Some days I'd trot along beside them, far out of step, behind the fifes and drums. How I loved the twirling sticks of the bass drummers! (I still do.) One day, as Dedie held my hand during the ceremony, the King, George V, drove out through the palace gates in his great maroon Daimler. There were not too many people watching the Guard change that day and those few were taken by surprise. Dedie and I were right by the gate through which the royal car passed and as it did I bawled out, "Hello, King!" Dedie, though Irish as could be, was nonetheless thrilled that "her" boy received a special royal smile, wave, and nod *"just* for him."

At length we returned to New York and Watch Hill, leaving behind my parents' friends in the British Isles and France to face the outbreak in August of what one of them called a "nuisance of a war."

My godmother, Aunt Madge (Murray), wrote my mother from London: ". . . that frightfully silly Kaiser has gone too far this time in expecting us to ignore our promise to protect the Belgians just to avoid a conflict with him. He even called our treaty with Belgium 'merely a scrap of paper.' My dear, *can* you imagine? The cheek of the brute! Well, everyone says it's all just a great lark and our boys are joining up by the thousands daily. They say it will be over in a few months (or less)—just long enough for the Frenchies and ourselves to give that moustachiod [sic] bully a bang on the nose . . ."

In the meantime I continued to enjoy four-year-old games and paddles in the sea at Watch Hill. I remember the day at Kenneth Ridge when my playing was disturbed by a yell and I found my mother's much younger brother, Grenville, on the ground, my father bending over him. They had just been competing in archery and Grenville narrowly escaped being blinded when a misaimed arrow embedded itself just beside his left eye. A few years later, during the making of a film, my father was himself temporarily blinded when an actor accidentally fired a blank cartridge too near his face and he had to wear a black patch over his eye for weeks. It was said he rather fancied the dashing look it gave him.

I see another time when, after sliding down a huge rock on the back slope of Kenneth Ridge's vast lawns, my black-and-white setter, Junior, joined the game, barked happily, and bit me playfully in the neck as I landed . . . I screeched with terror. Although Mother promptly banished the poor dog, I remained terrified of dogs for several years afterward.

And I remember the large bathhouses on the Watch Hill private beach, and the time I accidentally got a peep through a crack in the bathhouse door of Dedie undressed and getting into her bathing suit, hoping for another chance to confirm my astonishing discovery of the differences between the sexes.

I've been told that I *must* recall, and I suppose I do vaguely, my old great-grandfather Thompson stomping slowly around the grounds of Kenneth Ridge. Just when I wanted to run off and play, he settled me down to listen again to his Civil War experiences. I couldn't know until forty years on, when I was doing the same thing myself, that old war veterans love marking their survival with embroidered yarns.

And I remember waking up in the middle of the night, getting up out of my small bed, and peeking through a door to watch my parents trying out a new dance called the fox-trot as they hummed the music . . .

I recall that somewhere my father introduced me to a conspicuously stout jolly foreigner, saying, "Yes, this is my boy!" Then to me, "Junior! This is the great Mr. Caruso you've heard me speak about so often. You know! Mr. *Caruso!* Say 'How d'ya do.' " (I'd never heard of Mr. Caruso—or of opera, for that matter—but I never forgot the incident.)

And, oh, those days in Watch Hill when Mother called for the family's large, blue Pierce-Arrow "touring car" model, with the headlights on the fenders. I loved its shiny looks but hated the drives that Mother insisted were good for me. She also insisted that I wear one of her veils over my face to protect my fair peaches-and-cream complexion. Even at the age of four I was embarrassed by this sissy treatment and dreaded being seen. I resisted as best I could but Mother and Dedie prevailed. Mother was determined to raise a pudgy little hothouse flower.

I still have fleeting recollections of the delicate smell of summer lavender, faintly dampened by the sea-salt air that breezed in over the grasses, through the trees, and up to grandmother Munnie's window as she sat in a small oval morning room adjoining her large bedroom. It was like a tower in a castle. She would sit, darning egg in hand, on soft afternoons when my parents were away, mending, reciting poems and telling stories. When it was Munnie's day to bathe me, she dried me off afterward and then powdered me all over, with a huge, soft, fluffy puff that rested in a large bowl of scented powder. I can shamefacedly recall asking her to "powder me again" all over because it felt so curiously pleasant. It must have been my first innocent experience of sensuality.

The decline of the Sully fortunes continued inexorably until there was neither a New York house nor a Providence house, and just hotels when they went to any city. There was no business left and only a skeleton staff at Kenneth Ridge. The diminished income was occasionally augmented by my father or by the sale of an heirloom. My Fairbanks grandmother, Tu-Tu, lived in New York at the Seymour Hotel. She was not really very welcome at Watch Hill, nor at the Algonquin. She and Mother, both inclined to dominate, kept each other at polite arm's length as much as they dared without upsetting the husband-son objective they shared. During this summer of 1914, however, my father didn't stay in Watch Hill very long, as he was obliged to go quickly into rehearsals for a new play, *He Comes Up Smiling,* which, when it opened, ran successfully for about three months.

The coupling of my parents was only slightly unconventional. To their friends, they seemed ideally matched opposites. Beth was blond and pretty, nicely plump, charming and modest. She was frequently torn between being in Watch Hill with me and in New York with my father—between her concentration on her child and her unstated but justifiable anxiety that my father might be out of her sight for too long.

He was handsome, contagiously cheerful, and had come out of the West with such a persuasive gift of projecting his ideal self-portrait that he came to believe in it himself. He designed the living of his life, almost from the start, coloring it as he went along. He did it so successfully that his best friends and biographers were seldom able to see him accurately. He had been indulged from childhood and when he grew up he expected life to continue the custom. And life acquiesced. Except in his romantic and do-

mestic adventures, he rarely had a setback. Most of his dreams came true—
with a minimum of struggle.

In public, my parents behaved as the ideal couple their world expected,
but in the inner family circle they could and often did become violently hot-
tempered. Although my mother's heart and eyes were obviously only for her
husband and idol, my father was ridiculously jealous. If, when introduced to
any man, she failed to keep her eyes modestly downcast, he would accuse
her of flirting or being brazen. Sometimes his scolding made her cry. My
father could never easily accept the possibility that a friend or relation could
be fonder of or closer to anyone than they were to him.

Although Douglas expected absolute, undeviating loyalty from his intimates, he blithely disregarded such expectations of him in return. He did
sincerely love and depend upon Beth, but only his mother, Ella, could demand and receive the almost total devotion from him that he insisted on
from others. Some have theorized that his smiling, heroic, physical persona
was the reverse side of a wish to remain always a "mother's boy"—dependent on his real or substitute lover-cum-mother to whom he could turn for
protection from his fears and insecurities. The more I have come to learn
about him, the more I'm inclined to believe these theories. It was a source of
wry amusement to his close friends that his possessiveness extended even to
his extracurricular fancies, whose numbers, it turned out, were surprisingly
large. What my mother never realized was that she most emphatically
shared all my father's breath-constricting suspicions and passionate possessiveness. She longed for—but seldom got—the kind of smothering devotion
that she lavished on her own loved ones.

My parents' moods, ranging from exuberant highs to ominously seething
lows, were interspersed with impulsive blowups. Although my father was
the only practicing artist in the family, all the members of my mother's clan
had one characteristic in common: a disarming charm that in a flash could
be transformed into a demoniacal rage. So common were these explosions,
particularly with the Sullys, who reveled in "scenes," that they undoubtedly
influenced my evolving personality. Of all these conspicuous tempers, I was
most frightened by Mother's. Consequently, moral cowardice was fine-
tuned in me by my real terror of Mother's sound and fury. Servants would
be fired out of hand for what seemed to me trivial reasons. Faithful, difficult
Dedie was frequently told to "Get out! *NOW!*" but never did she really go.

All of this is not to suggest that my father did not on occasion let fly with
a pretty good show of his own anger. He did. But it was always a summer-
like thunderstorm followed quickly by grumpiness and then his personal
rainbow. Although I doubt he ever knew it, I was frightened of him too—

not in the same way I was of Mother, but frightened nonetheless. I kept my own introverted character protectively to myself.

Whenever I sensed early rumblings of a family row, my pulse leaped. I bolted down my own words and thoughts, my own angers and feelings, hiding them all behind a bland expression. I instinctively developed a fine talent for getting out of the line of fire or going along with all the moods, unprotestingly. Although it was one of an assortment of cowardices that never altogether left me, I wasn't always able to get away with my pusillanimous instincts. When imminent personal or domestic discord threatened, I sometimes failed to find an escape hatch. I still face up to personal and private issues with shameful reluctance. I'm always convinced before *anything* is said that I *did* steal the jam, even if there was no jam to steal. I stall to the limit whenever I must convey bad news or discharge someone from a job—and yet at all times I try to *appear* poised, a bit detached perhaps but not *too* unfeeling. I have at times had to seem intrepid without when actually shaking within. At other times I have pretended to a temper I have little of, merely as a tactic.

One day, in the autumn of 1914, as my parents were dutifully giving me a stroll through Central Park, my father was unexpectedly photographed and then interviewed by a motion picture cameraman. This was an unlikely event in those days. However, several weeks later, the film, showing my father walking with wife and toddler, and even vaulting a park bench, was seen by two motion picture executives, Harry and Roy Aitken, the founders and directors of the newly formed Triangle Film Company. This was a partnership between the great master of masters D. W. Griffith, the famous slapstick comedy producer Mack Sennett, and the gifted producer Thomas Ince. As a result of the filmed charisma of this Broadway favorite, the Aitkens made Douglas a handsome offer to appear in one motion picture with an option for a subsequent series of films.

Douglas did not make up his mind for some time. He was in the middle of the run of *He Comes Up Smiling*. Although he was impatient with his prospects and his development as a popular star in the theater, like most of his prominent contemporaries he looked on movies as a cheap, undeveloped medium in which only a few unemployed players would deign to work. Of course, several very big names had effortlessly increased their bank balances by strutting through a few silly scenes in front of a hand-ground box camera. His outrageous friend Jack Barrymore was one and the "Immortal Sarah" Bernhardt was another.

Still Douglas stalled—though tempted by the money offered just for bouncing around in this new kind of dumb show or miming in flickering pictures. He confessed his dilemma to one of his most trusted confidants, Frank Case, the suave, witty proprietor of the Algonquin. Case urged him to accept. His procrastination had succeeded in raising the Aitkens' handsome ante to two thousand dollars a week for the few weeks necessary for the first picture. Case reminded him that it was much more than he could expect from the stage and, besides, he could make the trial picture next year during the usual summer slump on Broadway. If he didn't like it he could return to New York and only a few people would ever know or, for that matter, care.

Douglas continued to ask the opinion of almost everyone he could find. Beth, still seeming for all the world the shy, retiring, nonprofessional, was not enthusiastic at first, largely because she feared it would mean a slip in prestige. Mother Ella, however, advised him to accept. When he finally agreed some months later, Beth, smiling sweetly, took as much credit as she dared and, as usual, proposed most of the financial conditions involved in the deal. Beth was intensely protective of those she loved and she had a good business instinct. She was more interested in details than Douglas. Because he realized this, he usually agreed to her recommendations.

Further delay was necessary because he had a commitment to do another play first—*The Show Shop*. But 1914 was the year my father finally formally accepted the offer to try his luck in the movies—"sometime next summer—in 1915." It was the last day of that year of 1914—New Year's Eve—when he opened in *The Show Shop*. It proved to be the very last play of his career.

During the play's run a down-at-heel backstage visitor turned out to be his nearly forgotten father—Douglas gave H. Charles a small roll of money and made it clear that another such visit would be unwelcome. H. Charles slipped away into the night. Douglas was still feeling the hurt inflicted on his mother, but he must have been deeply disturbed.

Sometime in May 1915 a small obituary appeared in a few New York papers. It drew little attention. The item reported the death of ". . . the well-known lawyer and former President of the American Law Society, H. Charles Ulman, aged 72 . . . from unknown causes . . ." No surviving member of his family was mentioned.

On a fine autumnal Sunday before that last play opened Beth and Douglas Fairbanks left their "adorable curly-headed son" with Dedie and drove to Tarrytown, outside New York City. They had accepted an invitation to spend the day with their friend, the immensely gifted musical star Elsie

Janis. Elsie often had Sunday parties at her large, rambling manor house in the country. Her guests could expect to meet a fascinating variety of the currently famous—many, of course, from the theater. It proved to be more than just another pleasant Sunday with "darling Elsie"; Elsie, the super-mimic, the witty-bitchy entertainer; Elsie, the "professional virgin" (and hence above the suspicion of such jealous wives as my mother soon learned to be).

On that Sunday my father stopped flitting from one discreet indiscretion to another and fell in love again. This time it was an event that would completely change all our lives. It began as a mild flirtation and grew into the most public romance of the next two decades. For it transpired that among the several guests at Elsie's house that day were the well-known Irish film actor, Owen Moore, and his incredibly rich and famous twenty-one-year-old Canadian wife, Mary Pickford—already known as "America's Sweetheart."

Mary and Douglas met and their mutual attraction became evident during an uneventful stroll along a nearby river. By their own subsequent admissions, he was by far the most smitten at the time. Mary was intrigued, amused, and attracted. But not very much more—then. They would not meet again for nearly a year, but neither forgot the other, and neither could really be deeply in love with anyone else ever again.

The Show Shop ran until mid-May 1915. By then D. W. Griffith's film *The Birth of a Nation* had become a celebrated event. For the first time audiences reserved high-priced seats to see a movie as they would for the theater. This did much to assuage Douglas's concern about the inferiority of what sophisticated aficionados called "photoplays." He went out West ahead of his family, taking the 20th Century Limited to Chicago and then the Santa Fe's Sunset Limited to Los Angeles, to discuss the proposed scenario, director, cast, and other plans for his first picture.

Griffith had reluctantly accepted Douglas as a temporary star of the Triangle Company. Griffith, the first of the truly great film directors, did not believe that my father had motion picture potential. In fact, he admitted he hadn't the slightest idea of what to do with "that jumping-jack, that grinning monkey" Douglas Fairbanks. "Perhaps," said Griffith later on, "I could arrange to place him with Mack Sennett and all his roustabouts instead."

After days of conferences it was decided that one of Douglas's former plays, *The New Henrietta,* would be adapted for the screen. His character in the play was Bertie, the Lamb, and the picture would be titled *The Lamb.*

Griffith took credit for the story's adaptation. Christy Cabanne, an experienced director in the Griffith stable, would direct and Seena Owen was cast as the leading lady.

When all had been settled, Mother, Dedie, and I were summoned. We were to travel by train from New York. This adventure to the far West was anticipated with a joyous nonstop five-year-old tingle. I was going to the *Wild West!*—where real cowboys came "a-hootin' and a-hollerin' " into dusty little towns all the time, and real Indians were everywhere.

After Chicago, the trip really did begin to get as exciting as my imagination had anticipated. The powerful hulks of the steam engines went *shwuhff* . . . *shuff-shuff-shuffing* along; the clanging bells and sad whistles punctuated the night, through corn, wheat, and prairie country; and the coal soot from the engines came through the windows, open against the increasing heat, dirtying our clothes and hair. The best stop was Albuquerque, New Mexico. The train stayed there for nearly an hour and there were many real Indians squatting around the edge of the walk to the station selling blankets and rugs and trinkets. There were more, too, inside the station, weaving and fashioning metal objects. I didn't know or care if they were friendly or hostile. They were real *Indians!* They were also uncommunicative and inscrutable. I hated getting back on the train but enjoyed the onward promise echoing in the conductor's shout of "Awrah-baw'rd! . . . Bow-ard!"

My excitement at arriving in Los Angeles was seriously mitigated by the fact that it was after dark. I was glad to see my father again, waiting there at the station, but there were no cowboys or Indians anywhere. Furthermore, it was not the balmy starlit night that Mother, Dedie, and I had expected. It was raining hard. As our chauffeur drove us splashing through the streets of Los Angeles, I could see that they were indistinguishable from most other city streets. There was the familiar jumble of traffic, hooting horns, and noisy trolley cars. At last we reached the Alexandria Hotel and I was quickly tucked into bed, bewildered, sleepy, and disappointed.

My spirits perked up a bit next day. The rain had turned to bright morning haze. My father was bubbling with excitement about his new venture. He bounced around the suite provided by the Triangle Company calling, "Boy! *Boy! C'mon,* Boy! *Hurry!*" (My father, whom I conventionally called "Daddy" at the time, called me either "Junior" or "Boy." The latter led to confusion because he sometimes called my mother "Boy" as well, although she was utterly feminine. His reason for this was that she seemed to him to have quite narrow hips—for a girl.) As soon as possible after breakfast, we were to be taken out to the studio. The previous night's disappointment dissolved in new and exciting anticipation.

Mother, anxious that the round pink apple of her eye should look the proper little gentleman in the eyes of the roughnecks out here and because, despite the sun, the day was not really very warm, dressed me in a short dark suit with short dark knee breeches, leather leggings over high-buttoned shoes, a dark blue overcoat with fancy frog fastenings, a round blue sailor hat, and leather gloves. I looked a real Eastern big city little twerp.

The Triangle—or Griffith—studios were not in what was then geographically thought of as Hollywood. Hollywood, as such, is today hardly more than the generic description of the film industry in general, specifically an area within a suburb of Los Angeles. These studios were in what was known as Edendale—a true suburb of Los Angeles and not too far from the associated Mack Sennett studio (now unrecognizably rebuilt as a TV studio).

The first thing that morning, we were shown the sets Griffith had had constructed for his film *Intolerance*—the largest and most elaborate sets ever built for a motion picture until my father's *The Thief of Bagdad* in 1923 —which holds to this day. The sheer immensity of the *Intolerance* sets astonished all who saw them. One can imagine how they would appear to a child from the East.

But the best was yet to come. The studio publicity department, with my father's encouragement, had a surprise for me. We were taken behind the *Intolerance* sets where there were some real cowboys and Indians and a keen press photographer. My father explained they would all be in *The Lamb* and they were all to be photographed with me for the movie magazines. This boosted my father to a higher niche in my estimation. Up to then both mother and I were kept strictly away from the press and their cameras. It was a healthy idea which I remembered to apply to my own children a quarter of a century later.

But this great day was an exception. I met and got to shake hands with my new heroes. In later years, I even got to know some of them. In one of the pictures, I am seen standing with three real cowboys squatting in their chaps, with spurred, high-heeled boots, big broad hats, colorful neckerchiefs, and leather slip-on cuffs. On my other side in the picture is another cowboy, and a real Indian, with feathered hat, blanket, and long braided hair. His name was Charlie Eagle-Eye. I was popping with glee at this dream come more than true—especially when, at the last minute, a Colt .45 six-shooter was put in my hand. Mother damned near had a conniption. "Take that gun away from the boy! *Douglas!* Don't let him *point* it!" Mother screamed, much to my embarrassment. But she was overruled. My father put on my sailor hat and placed a huge cowboy hat on me. That moment was my idea of heaven. My father was at least pretending to be proud of me.

Later, Mother, horrified at the thought of all the bugs that might have crawled from that "dirty Indian" and those "filthy cowboys," had Dedie give me a thorough scrubbing. I was mortified.

Many years later, looking at the picture taken that day, I see an overindulged, overfed, soft, but nice little boy. Alas, I was soon destined to grow quickly—as much around as up. I was shy and, although not exactly frightened, at the very least apprehensive if I were so much as present when someone else did something or inspired a forceful reprimand. Even Dedie's Irish-Catholic discipline was far too strict for me to indulge in normal childish rebellions or tantrums.

I was never spanked. Mother disapproved of corporal punishment. But there were other forms of discipline. If punishment was in order, I might be forbidden to play, be shut in my room all day, be forbidden to speak to anyone or to leave the table until I had swallowed every bite, or have my mouth washed out with soap.

What Mother never did know—and would not have believed had she been told—was that whenever she was away and my behavior was judged to warrant stronger action than usual, Dedie would get a wet washcloth, hold both my hands in one of hers, and give me a few strong, sharp slaps across the face. This was usually followed by the admonishment that if I ever told Mother I would be "very, *very* sorry!" I never knew what would happen that would cause me to be sorrier than I already was but I was sufficiently impressed to take good care that Mother never knew—ever. Otherwise, I was normally but guardedly mischievous, and so successful was my boyish duplicity that I often accepted, without so much as a twinge of conscience, undeserved praise for my model, docile behavior.

I certainly enjoyed the jolly and vigorous but infrequent presence of my father. Whenever he did turn up somewhere, from work perhaps, anticipation naturally exceeded realization, even though for me his home appearances were rarely anything but pleasant. He would come, to my secret delight, and go, to my secret regret, and rarely seemed to be more than vaguely aware of my presence.

I'm glad I didn't notice at the time that my pudgy mama's boy image influenced him to keep a benign distance from me. My hero worship for him made me even shyer. Just a glance at early photographs taken of that same chubby boy helps me to understand, at least a bit, what he meant when he often said that he was born with "no more paternal feeling than a lion has for his cubs." Although I failed to win any real affection from him, it never occurred to me to feel sorry for myself. I minded, of course, but in silence.

Not for a score of years was I to feel I "knew" my father well. Occasionally the words slipped out—unguarded—but usually just to myself—"I know *him!* That's my dad!" He was never unkind or unjustly stern with me. He loved children in general and with his considerable repertoire of stunts and magic tricks he got along with them famously. But alas, I was too shy, too plump and awkward, and he was such an evanescent sprite. Could we really be connected? The difference between us seemed too great.

The Fairbanks family soon rented a two-story frame bungalow—California-Japanese style—toward the Hollywood foothills, on North Highland Avenue. And there we all stayed for the summer—my father sleeping more or less outside on the screened-in sleeping porch and the rest of us in the two bedrooms. I have no doubt my father enjoyed living once again in a Western environment, and in a smallish town at that. It reminded him of his youth, and even though he probably liked being thought well traveled and sophisticated, he loved the sense of space, of clear, warm days and cool nights with innumerable stars in an infinite sky. He transmitted his enthusiasm for southern California, "room to expand, to be free," and most things Western to me.

I remember how I looked forward to being with my father early each morning while he exercised and before his quick tub, lathered his heavy beard and shaved—with an awesome straight razor. I would stand beside him grinning as he delighted me with endless repetitions of a "Wild West cowboy song." I've forgotten all the verses but I do recall that, with his razor strokes marking the tempo, he would end up singing:

> "I'm so—goll-darned tough,
> I'm so—goll-darned rough,
> That I—shoot—
> My goll-darned
> Whiskers *off!*"

In those days Hollywood Boulevard was not built up and there were many vacant lots between the one- and two-story buildings, interspersed by two or three small suburban movie theaters that lined the way for a few miles. Mother often told how she and my father would sometimes go to one or the other of the movie theaters along the not very brightly lit boulevard. They would frequently be accompanied by a friend, such as the tall, gangling former actress and now literary agent Ruth Allen and one or another of my father's many, newly acquired men friends. Walking home after the show, my father, who loved playing practical jokes, would stride along well ahead of the rest. Then he would hide behind a bush or in the high grass in one of the vacant lots and, as the others passed by, suddenly jump out to frighten them.

His family and friends encouraged him in this immaturity. When he was still in the theater, visitors to his dressing room were sometimes seated in a special chair that was wired for a weak but effective electrical shock whenever he pressed a hidden button. Once an ex-schoolmate brought his daughter to meet his friend the famous actor. She was seated in the chair, my father pressed the button . . . and the young lady didn't budge. He "buzzed" again, but there was still no sign of surprise or shock whatsoever. She continued to look merely wide-eyed and star-struck. My father buzzed and buzzed but no reaction from the young lady was forthcoming. Finally, her father asked her if she hadn't felt anything. "No," she answered, simply and happily breathless.

"Nothing like an electric shock?"

"Oh, yes," she replied.

"Well," said her father, "why didn't you jump?"

"Because," came the answer, "I thought that was just the thrill you got when meeting a great star."

The electric chair was revived when he went into films.

These tricks characterized his attitude toward people, places, the day, or the moment and were the harmless games and whimsicalities he played at all his life. I took after him and was inclined to play some rather silly, mildly amusing practical jokes myself—including, dammit, the electric chair.

When *The Lamb* had been completed, it was thought so poor and Fairbanks "such a waste of time and money," with all his "ridiculous shenanigans," according to one review, that the Triangle Company was on the verge of letting its option on his services lapse. However, they decided some cutting and rearranging of scenes might save the picture from total loss. After the editing was completed, Griffith and his colleagues thought the picture a little better but still felt it best to eliminate it from their important distribution outlets as they feared it might harm Triangle's reputation.

Just at that time "Roxy" Rothafel, the New York theater impresario, was planning a gala opening of his new, gaudy Knickerbocker Theater showing the latest Griffith picture. But it turned out that the only picture available was *The Lamb* starring Douglas Fairbanks. Roxy knew his business and splashed New York City with posters of one of its favorite stars in his first movie. A first-night audience, which included the great Paderewski; Howard Chandler Christie, the artist; Otto Kahn, the international banker; William Randolph Hearst, the newspaper giant; Irvin S. Cobb, the author; and other literary, financial, and cultural figures, attended in full evening dress. The opening took place on September 23, 1915, and tickets were an unprecedented three dollars apiece. Next day the press was ecstatic in its unanimous high praise for this bright new "movie star" and his picture. From that moment on, the public stormed the theater in droves.

Soon after we arrived home in New York, the Triangle Company, having been provided by press and public with second thoughts, quickly approached their new star with an offer of a bigger and better deal. Douglas again went first to his mother to hear her ideas. Beth was extremely irritated that Tu-Tu's opinion was sought before her own, but when at last her turn came she quite emphatically took the decision-making process into her own hands. Formal legal advice and representation was assigned to the most famous theatrical lawyer of the day, Dennis F. (Cap) O'Brien (whose firm also represented Mary Pickford). My father, from that time on, made more motion pictures and fewer business decisions.

I don't know why it was that on our return to New York we went not to our old home at the Algonquin, but to the old Netherland Hotel (now the Sherry Netherland) on Fifth Avenue and Fifty-ninth Street. It may be that the Triangle Company thought the Algonquin no longer suitable for their spectacular new "property." I remember enjoying the grander appointments of our suite and particularly going down to the hotel dining room with Dedie every evening just before the string quartet began to play. Whenever I hear an orchestra sound the "A" and begin to tune up, I have a dim memory of the Netherland Hotel dining room string quartet.

A large formal dance was given soon after our return to which my parents were invited. It became a happy evening for my father particularly, when he spied the famous Miss Pickford, chatting with friends in a corner. The two were conspicuously inseparable that evening. Their spark of mutual attraction had been rekindled.

The dance was crowded with friends and friends of friends, drawn from a cross section of New York life and dominated by celebrities from the arts. Beth may have noticed that Douglas and "dear Mary" (as she innocently called her celebrated new acquaintance) danced together several times, but she failed to give it any importance. However, only a few days later Douglas paid his mother a secret visit. Although he brought along a few extravagant gifts, Ella's delight did not diminish her shrewdness. Sensing that he was bursting with a secret, she urged him to confide in her. Douglas blurted out that he was in love with Mary Pickford. Moreover, he said he wanted to bring Mary, and *her* mother, Mrs. Pickford, over—very quietly—to meet Ella. Ella agreed.

There is no doubt that Douglas's domestic and social life had been as easy and agreeable as his professional life was successful and stimulating. Although their hopes for another child (whom they would like to have named Gwen) were not realized, my parents were, at that time, quite congenial. Beth was very much in love with Douglas and he was certainly devoted. He was increasingly dependent on her. Her star-struck view of this alien but glamorous world of the theater was keen. She certainly did not disguise her enjoyment at being the gently born heiress, married to the handsome, dashing star to whose business and career decisions she was a vital contributor. But despite this, Douglas's deeply romantic heart was never so full as when he fell in love with Mary. It wasn't long before his love became openly and fully requited.

Mary's mother, Charlotte Pickford (née Smith), was a prototype of the breed of ambitious, pushy stage mothers. Though a Canadian national, she still spoke in her pleasant native, Irish brogue. She had been deserted by a heavily drinking husband, whose handsome looks and memory were, nevertheless, forever after revered by his children. Charlotte was hard put to bring up her two daughters, Mary and Lottie, and her son, Jack. Believing they were all gifted, she successfully maneuvered them into very minor, young children's roles on the stage. Only little Mary showed immediate and unique talent, but she needed training. The others just got by. Nevertheless, Mrs. Pickford pushed on—supervising, promoting, and managing her progeny with uncanny shrewdness—albeit creating some resentment along the way.

Mary at twenty-two—ten years younger than my father—was already a world star. Shrewd, intelligent, and enormously gifted, she had a salary to match her talents, but she lived mostly on perquisites provided by Adolph Zukor's Artcraft Company. Among these were allowances for sister Lottie and brother Jack. Her intimates knew she was desperately unhappy with her attractive and charming but alcoholic husband, Owen Moore. They managed to keep up appearances while discreetly living separate lives in separate apartments. One reason that they both remained nominally married was their shared Roman Catholicism.

As agreed, accompanied by Charlotte, Mary paid a discreet call on Ella. The meeting apparently went very well. Ella warned Douglas afterward that although one "couldn't help falling in love, nor be blamed for it, still"—no doubt thinking, for a change, of Beth and the never-healed wound of her own desertion by H. Charles years before—"everyone must be held responsible for his actions . . . Only you and Mary can decide . . . but be careful! Sometimes we pay dearly for the unhappiness of others."

Douglas, characteristically, deferred making any emotional decisions. Beth truly liked Mary and seemed to enjoy the shadow of her celebrity. Thus she was invited to the Netherland Hotel for tea one day to "meet the family," as Douglas put it. Although I was surely unaware of the significance of this incident, I do recall it fairly well.

When Mary at last arrived—"apprehensively," she said later—she was cheerfully welcomed by my parents at the door to our apartment. I remember very clearly sitting on the living room floor playing with a modest set of toy trains. I got to my feet, as commanded, bowed, as taught, and shook the hand that was offered. My father said, "This is Mary Pickford." My mother, with a tactful smile, added, "She's 'America's Sweetheart'!"

Of course, none of this meant anything to me, but I remember thinking to myself, how did such a little girl, only a *little* bit taller than I, get to be so important and go places all alone? Apparently Mary understood my thoughts immediately and, pointing to the floor, asked, "Are those your trains?" I nodded. Mary smiled. "May I play with them too?" To my delight, she knelt down to the floor and joined me. Mary had made another conquest.

A few months before Mary died, about sixty-five years later, I was sitting by her bedside, holding her tiny, frail, skin-and-bones hand. Her voice quavered, weakly, in pleasurable reminiscence, and with one of her last smiles she retold this story exactly as I remembered it.

Nothing concrete in the way of domestic decisions happened for some time—only confusion and frustration in the lives of the two new lovers. The imminence of Douglas's next film, to be made in California, helped transfer some pressure from his heart to his head. At the same time he yielded to Beth's insistence on being acknowledged the ultimate arbiter of his career and business affairs. Ella was very angry at this and the schism between mother and wife grew wider than ever. Douglas, typically, refused to intervene, but for the sake of domestic tranquility he sided with Beth. Ella then determined to break off relations, which expedited his and Beth's plans to get away to California as soon as possible.

Double Trouble was at once the title of his next film and a hint of things to come. Our intention was to make California our more or less permanent residence and we settled in a rented house on La Brea Avenue. As filming began on *Double Trouble,* Mother issued extravagant orders for the running of the new house, my father, Dedie, and me.

At my father's insistence, my uncle Jack Fairbanks reluctantly quit his good job with the Muray Mercantile Company in Denver and moved with his wife, my aunt Margaret, to southern California. They brought with them their two daughters, my first cousins, Florence Belle, two years older than I —forever after known as Flobelle—and Mary Margaret—called "Sissy"— who was two years younger. We soon became like brother and sisters and remained that way all our lives—or at least until I unfairly outlived them.

A highly recommended "exclusive" school was selected for me to begin what was to become a very dicey education. The school already had other children of "noted" parents, such as Cecilia, the adopted daughter of the famous producer-director Cecil B. De Mille, and the two daughters of his brilliant playwright-director brother, William C. De Mille—Margaret and her elder sister, Agnes, who was destined to become the renowned choreographer. A few years later, two daughters of "proper" (i.e., nontheatrical) families were also enrolled. One was later known as Jean Harlow and the other, a Pasadena society girl called Jane Peters, eventually changed her name to Carole Lombard. When I first attended, one of my first grade classmates was Joel McCrea, who grew to be a successful actor and the husband of a lovely leading lady of mine, Frances Dee.

Another pair of schoolmate sisters were the daughters of the not yet so widely known movie mogul Louis B. Mayer. His girls, Edith and Irene, were possessors of as many loyal friends as their father had devout enemies. And *that* is saying a great deal!

The presence of so few boys in this school (they were accepted only for kindergarten and the first two or three grades) was a source of embarrassment to me for years. The school was called the Hollywood School for Girls! I'm sure that my hatred of this situation was only a little less than my distracted father's. Alas, "they" said, there was no other school of comparable "quality" nearby. It was also arranged that I should begin learning French, and be guided by a ma'amselle, a special teacher who, with skinned-back hair and pince-nez spectacles, seemed a casting director's ideal French teacher. At that age, I found learning languages a bore, but easy.

As winter and the New Year of 1916 began I didn't take much notice of the fact that the European war was going badly for the Allies and that stern-looking, long-chinned President Wilson was reelected. I do remember hearing that a big ship (the *Lusitania)* had been sunk without warning by the Germans and that many people had drowned. I also remember hearing of people who urged everyone to get rid of all dachshunds because they were German. This was the period when my father began acting in movies and only a very few of his and Mary's closest friends even suspected that they had fallen in love. My mother, completely in the dark, continued to devote her high-strung self to her own particular world.

My father finished *Double Trouble,* and those who saw it were very nearly unanimous in thinking it horrible. A worried Griffith proposed that, since his company was committed to make several more Fairbanks pictures, the very young and very bright writer Anita Loos and her fiancé, John Emerson, be assigned to "keep that crazy Fairbanks within bounds!" The collaboration worked successfully for the next few years, except for the fact that "that crazy Fairbanks" almost completely dominated his colleagues (as, indeed, he continued to do for nearly all of his career). At this time he discovered that not only were his own off-the-cuff ideas good but also that he could completely create his own pictures.

During the next twelve to fourteen months, my father churned out ten pictures (one account credits him with making eleven). Indeed, in his first five years of movie-making—from 1915 through 1920—my father made twenty-eight pictures—more than two thirds of his entire output for the eighteen years of his film career. These films were five to seven reels, each film about an hour in length. However entertaining, most of them are largely forgettable; his so-called "classic" period did not start until several years later.

Meanwhile, these modest features followed an enormously popular pattern. Regardless of their plots or settings, the Fairbanks character—which he designed for himself—remained virtually the same. Alistair Cooke has written that "At a difficult time in American history, Douglas Fairbanks appeared to give all the answers . . ." Richard Schickel, who has studied and written extensively and objectively about both my father and me, describes the early "Fairbanks (senior) type" as "essentially urban," one who could ingeniously cope not only with big city problems "and the inventions that made them functional," but also "master them with the skills of the frontiersman . . ."

With few exceptions the young and vigorous hero started from a background of superior circumstance but soon found himself, either accidentally or on adventurous purpose, in an unfamiliar place. Predictably, he would be challenged by a number of devious and ruthless villains. Somewhere along the way an obviously chaste and utterly defenseless pretty girl would be in desperate need of saving from a fate which of course was worse than death. Then, with bubbling and quick wit, a mischievous grin, and near-balletic grace, he would swing, leap, and/or dive from one place to another, joyously outfighting and outfoxing the oafish villains at every turn, until, in his own good time, they offered unconditional surrender. His outrageous but brilliantly funny offstage chum John Barrymore described the Fairbanks hero as "the only man who can convincingly fight off a determined company of heavily armed sons-of-bitches with no more than a bloody nail!" Once the evil lechers had been disposed of, the dare-anything young man would suddenly turn girl-shy as his one and only, now daintily swooning with relief, indicated modestly that she returned his feelings. And there the films ended.

My father's talents were to my mind best assessed by Booth Tarkington, who wrote:

Fairbanks is a faun who has been to Sunday school. He has a pagan body which yields instantly to any heathen or gypsy impulse—such as an impulse to balance a chair on its nose while hanging from the club chandelier by one of its knees—but he has a mind reliably furnished with a full set of morals and proprieties: he would be a sympathetic companion for anybody's aunt. I don't know his age; I think he hasn't any. Certainly he will never be older—unless quicksilver can get old . . .

Few of us would care to do the things that Fairbanks likes to do. For my part, if I were fairly certain that I could sit on a fleck of soot 381 feet above the street, on the façade of a skyscraper, I wouldn't do it. In fact, most people wouldn't do it, and their judgment in the matter is praiseworthy, but the world's gayety is considerably increased because there's one man who would do it, and does do it, and *likes* to do it!

Fairbanks would do that sort of thing if he had to pay for the privilege. If the movie people had really understood him they'd never have given him a salary; they'd have charged him a fixed sum every time he risked his neck on their property. Their films would have been just as popular—and think what they might have saved! But everybody's glad they didn't think of it, because everybody likes this national bit of property, called Fairbanks, so much.

It might be surprising to all but the most cynical to learn that the basic tenets of my father's make-believe heroes (usually ghostwritten by his lifelong friend and quasi-secretary, Kenneth Davenport) and of his own real-life philosophy were: "Live cleanly and honestly" and "Keep physically and mentally fit and agile." As he was splendidly human, he wasn't always able to abide by his precepts. The first real slippage was when he fell out of love with my mother and in love with Mary.

By 1916 Mary succeeded in having a special distribution company formed for her—Artcraft—which also provided notional jobs for her mother, her sister Lottie, and her brother Jack. Provisions were also made for cars, chauffeurs, and all other expenses. To cap it all, she accepted a virtually tax-free offer of $10,000 per week and shared with Adolph Zukor (head of Famous Players–Lasky and of Artcraft) the right of first refusal on every film she was to make. In those days income tax, when paid, was 1 percent after $4,000!

Mary created a distinct and world-famous image: the sweet, mischievous, warmhearted little girl, usually with long golden ringlets. Completely feminine, her character in nearly every plot would nonetheless outdo the challenges of naughty boys and big, brutish men. Sometimes the stories were comedic, sometimes rueful, and invariably sentimental. Mary was, by any standards, an accomplished technician and a fine artist.

Probably an even greater favorite and contemporary was the former English music-hall comic and Mack Sennett graduate, Charlie Chaplin. He became a close friend, companion, and later partner of both my father and Mary. It was the beginning of a triumvirate friendship that was to develop many ramifications over the years.

Charlie, who was every bit as keen a student of the dollar as Mary, had also branched out into independent production, but he was more intent than she on having complete control of his work. My father too was more concerned with absolute say-so over his own pictures than he was with money. However, anyone as carelessly spendthrift as he could never despise it. It took the combined efforts of my then business-wise mother, my shrewd and cautious uncles Jack and Bob and their lawyer, Cap O'Brien, to make him insist on and get gigantic guarantees against percentages of the profits. Within the next year, these gains were justified. My father became practically even with the other two in worldwide popularity. By the end of 1916, thirteen Fairbanks films had been completed for Triangle and a declaration of complete artistic independence brought forth a new producing company: the Douglas Fairbanks Pictures Corporation.

Meanwhile, I was growing up . . . a little.

3

My first full year in that "sissy school" included such mortifying experiences as participation in a school pageant. I resisted to the point of giving way to a very rare temper because I knew I was asked only because of my father. I shared my self-consciousness with my eldest cousin and closest friend Flobelle. She was also fat and awkward and we were both called Fatty by other children. Otherwise, my nickname was Junior, but Flops was a private nickname we gave each other. We had no other really close friends and were equally shy, withdrawn, clammy-handed, and ungainly. We clung to each other. Flobe's sister, Sissy, four years younger, was very small and pretty. Sissy was everyone's favorite; she had the sweet and attractive personality that Flobe and I lacked.

At that time our two families lived together much of the time and we three children slept on cots on a screened-in porch. Flobe and I found revenge against being left out of so much on Sundays when we shared the funny papers exclusively. We surrendered them to Sissy only when her goddamned pathetic weeping obliged our parents to order us to share them.

Sissy was one of the pretty fairies—naturally—in the school's outdoor winter pageant. The De Mille girls were something less than baby ballerinas, and Flobe was a backstage assistant. My own part in the performance was memorable. I was a roly-poly butterfly dressed in wrinkled, drooping tights, a puffy brown and yellow jumpsuit with large cardboard wings strapped to my shoulders, and a brown skullcap with two great wires as antennae sticking out in front.

During my school days Mother remained frightened and overprotective. I was not allowed to ride a bicycle and had to sneak rides on the bikes of others. My opportunities for harmless adventure were limited. One of the few risks permitted was a kid's pedal racing car on which I painted a big number to correspond to the one belonging to my racing hero of the day, Ralph de Palma. My own brand of daring consisted of coasting down the nearest hill. This I did with my cousins until the day a tree got in the way of my car and me and we were both hurt. Henceforth, I was forbidden further downhill coasting.

On Saturdays, Flobie, Sissy, and I were packed into a car with Dedie in charge and driven out toward the sea at Santa Monica, past open bean fields and citrus orchards, over the long, dusty road that was even then known as Wilshire Boulevard. If the weather was warm and there was not too much undertow I would, as the more experienced show-off, precede my cousins in splashing and windmilling about in the surf. On the way home we would stop in the village of Sawtelle, at the Old Soldier's Home where at 5 P.M. a surviving two dozen Civil War Veterans shuffled in a semblance of marching order to the middle of a great greensward. There a huge flagpole was guarded by an ancient cannon. These old boys followed a small fife, drum, and one-bugle corps that was clearly younger, presumably of Spanish-American War vintage. As this splendid squad reached the flagpole, the cannon fired a loud salute and emitted a cloud of exciting black smoke. The lone bugler blew taps—at least one note of which was off-key. A wobbly old sergeant slowly hauled down the Stars and Stripes, reverently taking care that it did not touch the ground. When the flag had been tenderly folded, the tottering commanding officer yapped out an order to the bent survivors in their special blues and grays, who shouldered their arms and wandered off in somewhat varying tempi. The Fairbanks cousins returned home, each time as thrilled as when we had seen the ceremony the week before.

My father was obliged to move back and forth across the continent according to the settings of his movies. When he was in California, he spent almost every day, except Sunday, at the studios or on some wild and woolly location. Consequently our Hollywood social life was much less busy than it had been in New York. Mother's only early intimates were my Aunt Margaret (Mrs. John Fairbanks) and literary agent Ruth Allen. With a well-trained, live-in Japanese couple as domestic help, she concerned herself mostly with firmly managing everything and everybody.

Dad was absent so often I hardly noticed, although everything, including me, brightened and bustled when he returned. His marvelous assortment of friends and hangers-on served him variously as companions, game competitors, or the good-natured butts of his practical, often bawdy jokes. All but he drank and caroused—though only a few did so to excess. Some of these pals were: his closest confidant Charlie Chaplin, one of his favorite directors, Allan Dwan, his cameraman (and later director) Victor Fleming, the wonderful rogue Jack Barrymore (whenever he could be found), his close writer-companion Tom Geraghty, and his press agent and co-conspirator ("beard") Benny Ziedman. On a quieter, almost intellectual roster were sometime secretary and ghostwriter Kenneth Davenport and his "assistant," Earl Brown. His brother Jack was stout and serious, all business and protective—hence, not so close. Brother Bob, the brainiest member of the family, was more tolerant and therefore his principal "confessor."

Also among this group of disciples were those who became so attracted to my father and his work that they became his lucky pieces. In one way or another, they were included, in unconvincing disguises, in almost every one of his pictures. The half-Cherokee Indian Charlie Stevens became such a necessity to every picture that short roles were sometimes written into stories just for him. Years later, I carried on that tradition and engaged Charlie, who had named *his* son Douglas, to work in my own self-produced pictures.

For me, the most exciting of these studio regulars was a near legendary figure from the real Old West, Al Jennings. Al boasted of being the last of the famous stagecoach robbers, but of course what he really had been was the last of the old train robbers. Once, to Mother's horror, Dad brought Al home and he regaled me with wondrous accounts of his adventures and even showed me his old "six-gun" with notches in the butt to prove the judge and jury were right in sending him to prison for a spell. Whenever Al couldn't get a job as an extra he would go on a lecture tour to tell Americans that crime doesn't pay!

In one of the pictures my father made in or near New York at the end of 1916, there were some exterior scenes requiring fairly sizable crowds of extras. One of the extras, in fact, was Leon Trotsky. It is riveting to realize that less than a year later, in October 1917, he was back in Russia, helping his beloved comrade Lenin conduct the Bolshevik revolution.

It may correctly be supposed that however hard my father was working on the preparation of picture after picture, he still managed to pursue his ardent romance with Mary. With the devoted connivance of his brothers, his press agent Benny Ziedman, and a few trusted friends, he and Mary took extreme precautions in the practicing of such guile as was undoubtedly necessary to protect their privacy and preserve the saintly image held by their devoted fans.

Many stories grew around the flowering of their romance. Anita Loos, for instance, wrote that Douglas's habit in California of sleeping on a sleeping porch was not just for his health, but also because it made it easier for him to slip silently out of the house late at night. She said he let his car roll noiselessly downhill until out of earshot, then started the engine and drove to Mary's. She did not explain how he managed to get the car silently back up the hill on his return and himself into the house without being discovered. Nor did Anita ever divulge how she happened to know about Douglas's risky style of illicit courtship. (Mary certainly never admitted it.) Thus the story arouses my suspicions because both lovers were intensely wary—at that time anyway—of any breath of scandal that might endanger their quite fantastic careers. Douglas, of course, being headstrong, was less likely to follow his star than to lead it, but he had his own pre-Raphaelite sense of romantic values. He very much feared a scandal—not just for his own sake, or Beth's and mine, but for Mary's sake as well. Mary was, after all, still formally married to Owen Moore and still a practicing Catholic (unlike Douglas, the Mother Church's misplaced sheep!).

Our 1916 summer was again spent at Kenneth Ridge. I think it was fun. It should have been. There was my never-ending fascination with the ocean and the lively calliope music of the merry-go-round that punctuated the air of the main street of the village. Mother rarely allowed me to ride unattended on this exciting whirligig, though it didn't whirl very fast and though the children were strapped to the up-and-down wooden nags. But I somehow managed it and other forbidden adventures without permission. At each turn, riders on the outside circle would reach out like daredevil cowboys and try hooking a finger into one of the many iron rings that slid down to our outstretched fingers. At the end of the line of rings was a gold (brass) one, and if you were lucky and caught it you got a free ride. After the ride there was, up the street across from the movie theater and drugstore, Mr. Beebe's popcorn establishment. He had an early type of popcorn machine that had a little dancing clown inside the protective glass, twirling around and stirring up the newly popped fresh corn. It turned and bowed and whistled a brisk tune as the popcorn popped. It was the most fascinating place in Watch Hill to spoil an appetite for anyone below a certain age.

Dad's next picture was *The American Aristocracy* and Watch Hill was considered a fine natural location for all the exterior shots. This was another fluff-weight fable concocted by Anita Loos and Dad. The movie centered around the by-now-familiar Fairbanks hero who began as a pseudo cream puff but proved his red-bloodedness when put to the test. The ultra-proper Watch Hill summer regulars jumped at invitations to be extras in an honest-to-goodness movie. When the director, Lloyd Ingraham, proposed to my father that I be allowed to have the bit part of the newsboy on the corner from whom he would buy a newspaper, both my parents, surprisingly, agreed.

I was made up like a pasty-faced apprentice performer and Mother insisted that I wear my best white sailor suit and high-buttoned shoes. No real newsboy ever looked like that. Nevertheless, they shot some publicity stills of my father and me. I got nervous giggles and my father did his best to look enthusiastic.

I don't know whether the brief scene remained in the finished film, but I do know that my father was sport enough afterward to authorize his cameraman to photograph a one-reel "kid's movie" in a story that I devised and starred in with my playmates as the supporting cast and a pretty, freckle-faced girl called Sally Thatcher as my leading lady. She was about my own age of six. I chased her until I accidentally tripped and fell into a rosebush. Manfully ignoring the painful thorns, I began, right then and there, a life-long habit of trying to cast myself as the hero.

In our mini-movie, I engaged in what I hoped would look like a struggle with my "villain," a pal called Teedy (i.e., T.D.) Ley. After a few gently rehearsed pushes back and forth, Ley fell on cue and rolled over and over down a sand dune. Following our first try, I feared injury, as did Teedy, so we cut the fight scene very short. I won both the fight and Sally in the end. This 1916 silent still exists.

Back on the coast we rented a huge white house with a red-tile roof on the westward residential end of Hollywood Boulevard. The house sat high on a property of about three acres with a long lawn rolling down to the street. It also had a fine tennis court and a swimming pool.

We had another dog by that time. Dad said it was a half-wolf Alaskan malamute, which sounded exciting enough to suit me. He was called Rex. When the coyotes came down at night from the Hollywood hills behind us and howled their presence to the moon or some lost partner, Rex answered with a wolf-like bay of his own.

Since my unfortunate early Watch Hill experience, I had slowly made headway in conquering my fear of dogs. I had even gotten to the point of actually playing with Rex. One day, during a romp, I chased him across and down the lawn and tripped and fell on a lawn sprinkler hidden in the grass. This caused a very deep cut just above my right kneecap. Mother nearly fainted when she saw me bleeding profusely and although I was quite able to walk I was carried into the house where towels were spread on a couch and they tried to check the flow of blood. Dad came in and watched and I immediately determined to be brave.

Apparently no one in our family had heard of first aid, so we had hardly any supplies to cope with accidents. Mother and Dedie decided that possible infection would be nullified by pouring from a bottle of iodine into the bloody gaping hole above my knee. The pain of that angry disinfectant was considerable. Somehow I managed to grit my few brand-new permanent teeth and the remainder of any old ones and let out not a peep.

At last the blood stopped and enough bandages were wrapped around my leg to satisfy the women. Dad started a shy, proud smile and came over to pat my shoulder, saying, "Good boy! Good boy! Proud of you!" From that moment, the pain diminished and the day that had seemed sharply painful (I also got grass stains all over my white shirt and short pants) became one of personal victory. I'd been manly in my father's eyes and was rewarded by his verbal approval in front of everyone.

Shortly after, a temporary but nonetheless rueful setback took much of the flush off my victory. Dad had seemed to enjoy my being around more than before. Whether he really did or not is no matter. I thought he did, and that was enough. As my knee healed, I even started batting tennis balls with him, and as I had been swimming off Watch Hill's beaches since age four, I was by now a strong swimmer and aspiring trick diver (somersaults, back-flips, and the like, interspersed with accidental belly flops). These signs of physical prowess encouraged more playtimes together than ever before. One day he was due to have one of his frequent business meetings at the house. Mother was away from the house and, as I was curious and anxious to be in on everything, I asked Dad if I might sit in the room during his conference. Dad agreed but said I had to sit in the far corner of the room and be very, very quiet. If I moved or distracted him, I would not again be allowed such an experience.

Obediently, I sat myself down silently and listened, uncomprehendingly, to whatever it was that was being discussed. I decided to shift my position ever so slightly and inconspicuously. As I did so, to my own great surprise and Dad's horror, a high-pitched squeak of small boy's wind broke out. Once it started, I couldn't stop. I was mortified. Dad, of course, was furious. I was ordered, sternly, from the room. I obeyed, crushed and speechless with embarrassment. I stole out in a shame so intense no further punishment was necessary. It was many years before I again sat in on a conference of my father's.

In 1917 the United States at last entered the Great War against Germany and the world was shaken by the Russian Revolution. And 1917 was also the year when my father's first five pictures for his new company were made; when the first of his several ghostwritten books on the virtues of physical fitness and clean living were gobbled up by an adoring public; when he was ever more insatiably and secretly in love with Mary. She certainly requited his passion in a discreet hideout in Hollywood's Franklin Canyon, acquired via the surreptitious good offices of Uncle Bob. That same year, after months of increasingly well-justified suspicions, strains, and stresses, he and Mother came close to the end of their marital high road together.

Dad wanted all of Mary—herself and her talent and her fame and her exclusive devotion. And he longed to be able to display their union to the world like a double trophy.

Mother had at first heard only whispered bits and pieces of what was going on, but that was enough. She sensed, however, that he hadn't yet quite brought himself to give her up altogether and that he still loved her, after his fashion. His intimates were aware that his real concern was to maintain the public image to which Mother's presence as the traditional wife contributed. To be truly convincing, they advised him, he must at least appear reluctant to lose me as well. Though admittedly not in the least paternal, or even particularly fond of me, I was, after all, his and Mother's only child, the one and only son and heir and all that having a son symbolized.

Presumably, because of all this, Dad did make sporadic efforts to steady his rocking domestic boat. An example was a telegram sent to Mother during a blistering summer when his train, en route east, stopped in Salt Lake City: TERRIBLY HOT TRIP. SORRY I DID NOT TELL YOU MORE THAT I LOVE YOU BEFORE I LEFT. CHEER UP AND GIVE MY BEST TO THE BOY— DOUGLAS.

Two months later, in early autumn, Dad was finishing another picture in California and Mother, Dedie, and I had gone back to settle in New York. By then the situation between them had worsened. One more telegram from Dad clearly indicates that a previous message, pleading for more faith in him, had failed in its intent: WIRED YOU AFFAIR WAS OFF BECAUSE YOU THOUGHT IT WAS ON. YOU HAVE MISJUDGED ME TERRIBLY. THERE NEVER WAS ANYTHING WRONG. WILL FINISH PICTURE AND LEAVE FRI- DAY FOR EAST. CAN YOU JOIN ME IN CHICAGO? WANT TO SEE YOU ALONE. AM WORRIED ABOUT YOUR CONDITION. WIRE ME HOW YOU ARE. LOVE— DOUGLAS.

Mother remained stubbornly and deeply hurt. Her replies were negative. Yet not even then did any but their closest friends and the Fairbanks brothers do more than whisper into one another's cupped ear. The public still knew nothing. Neither did the Sullys.

In the meantime, I was most concerned with the constant packing and moving between the East and West coasts. There was Hollywood and Southern California, and then New York and environs—such as Southampton on Long Island, or Larchmont (where my Aunt Gladys and her lawyer-husband, Uncle Henry Mahlstedt, lived), and, of course, the fresh salty air of Watch Hill.

I was as ignorant of my family's imminent disintegration as ever. There was no particular shock about the news of "the end" for me when it came because I so often heard of events only after they happened. When I did finally realize that Dad wasn't coming home again at all, I must have been sorry, but I was promised I'd see him often.

It may appear insensitive of me today, but I believe I was more aware of and excited by the war we had just entered than by the news that Dad was going to live elsewhere permanently. War fervor affected everyone. Wherever one looked, there were pictures of fluttering flags and bands and soldiers and sailors. I remember joining other kids playing at marching and war games that were all extensions of our well-practiced cowboys-and-Indians. Since it was, to us, a bit *less* real than the movies we were allowed to see, we therefore decided war must be fun. Serious concerns were the hoarding and rolling of all the tinfoil we could collect into great balls. They said they were to be used for making bullets. The girls helped make bandages. The connection between the two activities never occurred to us.

For as long as she lived, and in spite of two subsequent marriages, Mother never got over the pain of the loss of my father and his love. When admonishing me always "to love and respect your fine, great father," she sometimes slipped in a qualifying or critical phrase. Almost as an aside, she would remind me that, although a "wonderful artist and a great man," he would probably continue to forget my birthdays and even Christmases, because "though wonderfully generous . . . with everyone else" he was not with her. Or me. Such little digs were, in the end, usually rounded out with words of honest admiration and more than a hint of her own kind of undying affection.

On the whole, I think I was more fortunate than most children of divided parents—particularly of parents who were so conspicuous. Long after their divorce, whenever either one of them had reason to refer to the other when talking to me, it was usually done with warmth and admiration. To this day

I remain deeply grateful for that sweet conspiracy, and commend it to other separating families.

Dad's efforts to enlist in one of the nation's armed services were discouraged on the presidential level. He and Mary (who was Canadian) and Charlie (who was British) were advised by Woodrow Wilson that they would be of "far more service to the nation" if they helped with filmed and personal propaganda and in cross-country drives, selling Liberty Bonds.

My schooling, meanwhile, went into one of the first of many slumps. I had loved being in California and outdoors so much with my beloved cousins Flobe and Sissy. New York had different, although equally pleasant distractions. It was big, busy, noisy, and exciting. In those days there were nice chatty cops on all the main intersections (Dedie's favorite was *not*, curiously enough, an Irishman, but a kindly, smiling German called Emil). In New York I could play and skate in Central Park with Frank Case's son, Carol, and have fun avoiding his pretty older sister, Margaret, who liked to boss us about.

Across from the Algonquin on Forty-fourth Street stood the old Hippodrome—a colossal theater that fronted on Sixth Avenue and stretched a full block down to Forty-third. This super-showplace presented performances that were somewhere between spectacular vaudeville and a circus—but all on a stage, not in a ring. How everyone loved that show! We could never see it too often—and Dedie didn't seem to mind taking us. The show changed from year to year, but some things seemed to be there every year. Among the "regulars" were the perfectly drilled chorus, the precursors of the Rockettes, who, after some initial high kicking and stepping in row upon row facing the audience, descended stairs that led to a huge stage-wide pool. They then completely disappeared under water, not to reappear until the end of the show. We delighted in our own bafflement about how they could hold their breaths so long and rather resented having the secret revealed to us. They just ducked under the stage behind the stairs, and came up on the other side of a board, wet but safe and not even puffing.

There were other wonders that never seemed to cease, such as the man who piled ever smaller-sized tables one on top of the other and, climbing carefully to the top, sat in a chair and rocked the whole tower back and forth until finally it toppled and he tumbled into a somersault. There were clowns, too, of course. But best of all was the great Houdini—breaking out of chained straitjackets and locked-up crates that had been dropped into a fully visible tank of water. It was an incomparable thrill when once I met him backstage. Both Carol and I were speechless with excitement and awe.

New York summers are famously hot and sticky, and in those days there was little relief to be found anywhere in Manhattan. The slums were hardly more miserable during the heavy, airless nights than uptown or midtown. At the Algonquin, we were further plagued by the irritant of the Sixth Avenue El which loudly clattered by every few moments ensuring sleepless nights. Electric fans blowing on blocks of ice helped some. My favorite activity was planning mischief. It was during one of those heavy summers that I was caught early in the evening, hiding behind a rug draped over the railings of the Algonquin's sixth-floor fire escape landing, blowing "BB's"— small shot—through a blowpipe at the Hippodrome's clowns cooling off on their fire escapes across the street.

However, for a too-closely watched and strictly raised boy of seven or eight, big cities have limited possibilities for mischief. Sometimes misbehavior—as it was sternly described—was unavoidable, as when I came zooming into the Algonquin Hotel's lobby on my roller skates. The floors were then tile—nowadays they are carpeted—and I rolled out of control the whole length of the lobby until I plopped into the lap of the great John Drew, aging doyen of the American theater (and uncle of Lionel, Ethel, and John Barrymore). Everyone in the lobby froze in horror; everyone, that is, except Mr. Drew himself. He thought it great fun and commended my high spirits to my mother and saved me from any excessive punishment for my misdemeanor.

Our 1917 Christmas was out West again. Mother finally relented and allowed me to have a bicycle. It was the best present I've ever received. She still panicked each time I rode and restricted my biking areas. Naturally, the moment I got out of sight I disobeyed with gusto—took many falls, suffered many scratches and bruises, for which I invented convincing causes, and had a marvelous time disobeying and lying as often as I could.

For most of my childhood at least one facet of my education was not neglected: religion! My father, though not in the least religious in a formal sense, sometimes found it useful to recall, even boast about, his Roman Catholic baptism and upbringing. He was embarrassed by whatever amount of Jewish blood he had. Both my mother and stepmother Mary told me (on separate occasions years apart) that there were days of spiritual agony before he could bring himself to "confess" to his mixed-up ethnic origins. Both Mother and Mary tried, but failed, to persuade him either to be proud of his roots or, alternatively, not to be so ridiculously self-conscious about them.

Nevertheless, Mother's outward behavior was strictly in accordance with her own standards of upbringing: very high Episcopalian, very WASP-ish, as, indeed, were all the Sullys and Thompsons—Anglicans every one. Thus

I was taken almost every Sunday to either Sunday school or church, and sometimes both. The regular private day schools I attended were Protestant and there one ear would receive further religious instruction, much of which soon drifted out the other. Dad didn't seem to mind where any of us went on a Sunday, and he only put in personal ecclesiastical appearances at weddings or funerals.

Moreover, no one ever seemed to consider Dedie's subtle plans for her precious charge. Dedie was as Irish as it was possible to be and as devoutly Roman Catholic. She was convinced that even if my being a church-going Protestant didn't necessarily condemn me to everlasting hell (after all, I was too young to resist my mother's orders), *she* was better suited to save me from the worst and, by taking me to a Catholic church as often as possible during the week, to limit the first part of my afterlife to a spell of purgatory.

Flobe and Sissy Fairbanks were extra-devout Catholics who spent much time trying to save my immortal soul. My Catholic-born but unpracticing Uncle Bob had married my aunt Lorie, who was a Mormon from Utah. It therefore follows that my two younger Fairbanks cousins—the beautiful and gifted Letitia and Lucile—were also Mormons (at least until they got older and strayed from the fold). Neither of these baby cousins tried to convert me, but I nevertheless encouraged discussion. Our exchanges informed me at least superficially about this other remarkable sect of Protestant Christianity.

What really put the cat among the pigeons was Gladys Barnett in New York. She was Mother's manicurist, who came two or three times a week, not only to do her nails but also to tell her fortune from tea leaves or playing cards. She was also Dedie's gossipy best companion. Gladys was very small and I was tall even for my seven or eight years, so I always considered her at least a near contemporary. She was the best fun of any grown-up of the time. She looked a bit like a jolly witch, or Judy's Punch, with her long hooked nose and pointed upturned chin. I thought her lovely.

Gladys Barnett made little attempt to be surreptitious about anything. She was Jewish and proud of it, and, knowing all about the Ulmans in the Fairbanks blazonry, thought it only fit and proper to instruct me in the history of Judaism, to read passages from the Talmud and describe the forms of Hebrew worship.

All these disparate religious influences allowed me to mature with such an open mind that no one religion could claim my exclusive and unquestioning allegiance. By the same token, my natural curiosity about the whys and wherefores of everything—a characteristic that was to lead me to lie down in many strange green pastures later in life—helped me to learn a great deal about the histories, philosophies, and ceremonies of a number of religions. The abiding faith, enjoyed by most of my family, and most of all the Catholic Fairbanks females, was something I have always envied but could never bring myself to share.

Mother, energetic as usual, and trying to put a brave face on her private misery of separation from Dad, had me entered in New York's Bovée School, an exclusive boys' grammar school. Escorted by Dedie, I roller-skated ahead each morning from Forty-fourth Street up Fifth Avenue to the Sixties and back again at the end of the day. I welcomed the chance to attend a real, honest-to-goodness school for boys only. I was delighted to escape the hothouse of family protection. Once, however, on the way to school, Mother walked partway up Fifth Avenue with Dedie and me, and when she had to branch off somewhere, she stopped to kiss me good-bye—in front of everyone on the street! I was so mortified that I burst into bitter tears right then and there, quickly skated ahead, and hid behind a corner. Mother never forgot it. Neither did I.

To become the model little gentleman that Mother had in mind, I attended a children's dancing school. Our dark blue suits, with "knickerbocker" breeches, black socks and tie, and patent leather pumps would make any boy of today retch. One day I was doing my assigned steps with some horrid little girl. I bowed, as prescribed, but mistimed it. My mouth hit the top of her skull, knocking out two of my very loose teeth. I was too embarrassed to spit them out and so remained tight-lipped for the rest of that session. Shortly after, Mother was told I was "hopeless" and could leave. I did.

Bovée was administered by a Miss Kate (none of us knew her full name), whom we all looked on as a witch incarnate. When we were caught, *flagrante delicto,* in some contravention of the rules, she whacked us good and proper wherever she could. Or she'd pull us up the school stairs by the hair, twist our ears, and otherwise make her disapproval unmistakably clear. Apart from that, we had a pretty good time. Bovée was where I had my first real fight with another boy—in the school basement. The issue between us was quickly forgotten, but since I won the fight, my physical self-confidence began to grow from that day. It helped me to feel I now really belonged at the school. I was delighted to be counted among the better belligerents to deal with our bitter rivals, such equally snob schools as Cutler, Buckley, and St. Bernard's. Our surplus coltish energy was used to confront each other on the Central Park Mall either at supervised games or, more likely, in unsupervised fights. In winter we continued to vent our developing masculine pugnacity by contending for top-dog status in terrific snowfights. In one of these skirmishes a nail hidden in a snowball punctured my finger, causing me to lose a certain enthusiasm for a few weeks.

By the time 1918 was well into its stride, my parents decided, at last, to end their clashes and to separate—formally, painfully, and for good. That spring, just before the break was officially announced, I was taken to San Francisco—presumably as part of a publicity showpiece. Dad was the Parade Marshal of a big Rodeo for the benefit of the Red Cross. I reveled artlessly in all the excitement and vowed that one day I too would ride a bucking horse. Dad agreed to have me photographed with him on the back platform of a train just before he went off on another Liberty Bond drive. I was still fat and awkward and the silly sailor suit I was put in made me look even more repellent. I wouldn't have felt fondly paternal about me either!

When the story of my parents' separation first broke in the press, Dad made an impromptu asinine denial saying it was "all pro-German propaganda, designed to interfere with the Liberty Loan drive"!

That turbulent summer included the closing down of everything Californian, including our great white house on Hollywood Boulevard. We went back to Watch Hill, to Kenneth Ridge, which was slowly getting down-at-heel. Of course, it was still the Sullys' house and the whole tribe naturally showed up: beautiful white-haired Munnie, my dignified grandfather Ganka, my Uncle Bubber (a baby-talk name for brother—really Uncle Grenville—or Bill). He was only a few years older than I and was usually out at local garages learning poker and drinking with the family chauffeur. Aunt Gladys and Uncle Henry were also part of the family cast of characters.

Although I loved the mid-Victorian space and comfort of Kenneth Ridge and the dreamy views from its hilltop overlooking the Atlantic, the house itself was too constricted by my growling, argumentative family for me to fully enjoy staying indoors. One of the few sedentary things I welcomed was hearing Munnie recite the same enchanting children's poems she had recited to all her own children when they were my age. I never tired of hearing them, over and over again.

The only other grown-up I felt really close to was the still splendid, militarily grand old Daniel J—my beloved Ganka. He was as benignly, unthinkingly racist as fitted his time and class; he was as chauvinist as they came, a hater of progress and women's babble, and I adored him. His former business colleagues, however, thought him a tyrannical villain. I am certain we wouldn't have much to agree about today, but I still remember my grandfather as my favorite. In spite of our undisguised mutual affection,

I always got hard-to-smother giggles as a result of that dear man's unexpected and undisciplined belching. The old buccaneer would hold forth at the head of the table on whatever subject he chose, commanding attention in his bellowing baritone. Then he would periodically interrupt his own monologues, seemingly unaware, with short burps, followed by loud exhalations, sounding all together something like *"BRRP-zzz-zzz-Bzz-Bz!"*

My next favorite fun was a locally formed Boys' Club. This was a splendid device to keep the very young boys of this summer colony resort out of trouble and their family's hair. We swam, raced, sailed, biked, played team games, and ended up the summer days too pooped to be obstreperous bores to our elders. It was to continue each summer for several years.

The general public paid little attention to the initial news of the division of the Fairbanks family. This indifference would change surprisingly within a year, but meanwhile, when Mary and Doug and Charlie—a literally unequaled constellation of stars—toured the country on behalf of the government's Liberty Bonds, people turned out in multitudes to see them from Wall Street to the Golden Gate. They raised a forgotten-how-many millions of dollars in the days when dollars were real solid gold-backed respectable currency.

In late October of 1918, a month before the War's end, the Great Trio were invited to Washington as part of their tour, and to the White House by President Wilson. There Dad met and became friends with the then Assistant Secretary of the Navy, Franklin D. Roosevelt. (Thus I later got to know and went roller-skating with the Roosevelt sons in New York's parks, especially with F.D.R., Jr.) While inside our American Presidential Palace, my father snatched one of the President's private note cards, with a picture of the White House on it, from a writing table and, in his usual hurried scrawl, wrote a brief message to me saying: "Dear Boy, this is written from the executive office of the White House while all around us they are settling some of the greatest questions in the history of the world—Daddy." He never signed himself Daddy before or since. Had it been typed, I would have thought someone else had signed it, but the card was in longhand. It is one of fewer than half a dozen handwritten notes or letters I received from him in his lifetime.

The Great War ended with an Armistice on November 11. Strangely, I can still remember the false alarm Armistice two days earlier and the spontaneous outburst of excitement in the streets all day and night. When the real Armistice was confirmed, contemporary reports were that it was almost an anticlimax, that it lacked the spontaneity of the premature celebration. I whooped it up on both days, without really knowing why.

The more intimate war between my parents ended legally in divorce on the last day of the same month. The New York *Times* headlined: WIFE DIVORCES FAIRBANKS OF SCREEN FAME. Then there was a sub-headline: *Interlocutory Decree Granted on Evidence of Beautiful Girl Party Given by Movie Star.* And, lower down: *Actor Denies Charges, but Fails to Defend Case in Court, and Wife Gets Custody of Only Son.*

No mention was made in court of money because Mother's lawyer, my uncle Henry, and Dad's (and Mary's) genial and brilliant lawyer, Cap O'Brien, came to two private arrangements. First, Mother was to be given $400,000 in the form of securities and, second, I was to be given $100,000 in the form of a trust. Somehow my trust was greatly depleted over the years— I never understood how or why (except that I know Mother's family bene-fited somehow). In the mid-1930s, when I asked for my trust to be broken so as to save my economic skin, I think there was only something like $25,000 to be set free for me. I was grateful for even that.

Mother was rather bitter at what she always maintained had been a poor settlement. She had never been brought up to think much about money and, in fact, never really came to grips with it up to her last breath. She always maintained that Dad had a net worth of more than a million dollars at the time and, since he earned well over half a million a year, could easily have afforded to double his alimony grant. But Dad, and Cap O'Brien, and my cousins (particularly Letitia—who became the principal and most reliable family biographer) maintained that he was so extravagant and so generous to so many people that, even as it was, the settlement practically broke him. All I did know then for certain was that the Sully fortunes were virtually nonexistent, except, of course, for what my parents had given them from time to time, and what they could make from the occasional sale of a still considerable assortment of pictures, furniture, china, odd heirlooms, and other reasonably marketable bibelots.

The divorce action itself, when it came to court, was based on the only legal grounds available in New York State at that time: adultery. One of my godfathers, Clifton Crawford (a Scottish musical comedy actor), was the first "perjuring witness" and Dad's early director (Anita Loos's husband), John Emerson, was the second. "Uncle" Clifton testified they had been present when my father was at a party with a group of "beautiful girls" (intimating a jolly orgy of sorts) and to the fact that Dad sat with a young woman who was "smoking cigarettes in a negligee." Emerson said that Dad reported to him that he'd "had the best time in his life." Not a soul—not even Mother—believed these stories, as they simply didn't sound at all like Dad's taste in irregular enjoyments. But they satisfied the judge.

The press, aware of Dad's liaison with Mary but inhibited by the then-effective libel laws against printing the story, tried to pry an indiscreet word or two from Mother. She was marvelously protective. The reporters found her so "different," so "unprofessional," that they were sympathetic to her. They wrote about how pretty and happy she looked and how charmingly dressed ("saucy little hat covered with pink roses, not near so prettily pink as her cheeks"). When they tried to pump her for intimate quotable disclosures, she tried to protect Mary by becoming "indignant" about such rumors. However, she added she was tired of defending my father in public, even though he was "the most considerate of men," but that for "the sake of our son" (whom the court had awarded, without challenge, to her), separation and then divorce had been decided upon.

4

Shortly after everything was signed and sealed, Beth Sully Fairbanks disguised her pain by gratefully accepting the never-say-die devotion of James Evans, Jr., her old beau from Pittsburgh, the one who attended her coming-out party, and who was now a stockbroker. At this later juncture, when Beth felt that her image was that of the wife rejected in favor of a rich, younger, beautiful, and fabulously famous actress, the reappearance of Jim Evans, with the romantic story of having waited patiently all these years for her, was a welcome tonic. As soon as all the old legal dust was swept away and the decree became final in mid-1919, fresh dust began to form as Mother solemnly swore to a judge in New York City that she was prepared to be Mrs. James Evans, Jr., thereby providing me with a stepfather.

Jim was really a very nice, gentle man, with a wry and necessary sense of humor. His patience in the face of Mother's interchangeable sweet-and-torrid temperament (which she always blamed on her Gemini birth sign) inspired an unexpressed admiration and sympathy in me. Jim (like his identical twin Jack) was a pleasant-looking man, quite bald, stocky, and of medium height. He dressed neatly and conservatively. He tried hard to be a good stand-in father. I liked him very much.

A problem arose about what I was to call him. Just "Jim" was thought disrespectful. What was I to do? The decision was made for me. I was told, with some forced levity, to call him Pop. When Dad first heard of this he was angry and hurt—and though I didn't know it for some time, I couldn't blame him. Even if he had almost too frequently admitted he was an indifferent parent, he still didn't want me to address anyone else with even a slangy name for father. And to make matters even more confusing—especially to me—it wasn't more than a very few years before I had become for my age so overgrown and so advanced in manner and looks that Dad came to be less than enthusiastic about my calling *him* Dad.

But even out of sight, my father continued to be a strong presence in my life, one to which I was somehow attached even though he was not attached to me. It was difficult to alter this state of affairs because I had no real chance to know him—*really* know him, that is, either as a friend or a close relative—until the last ten years of his life. Even so, I fear it would be beyond my capabilities to fully explain him.

With a new husband and name, Mother wasted no time in turning over as many other new leaves as she could. Ever reluctant to adjust her standards downward, she uprooted us from the Algonquin and took a huge, comfortable, high-ceilinged apartment on Central Park West. Convinced that Dad's half million to her, which was somehow administratively blended with my Trust, had left us in what she called "disguisable straitened circumstances," she proceeded to repose full trust and confidence in the financial wisdom of Jim Evans. He took hold of the new family finances straightaway—hers, mine, all the Sullys' (old Dan was occasionally consulted, but only out of courtesy)—and joined them with what Mother wishfully thought were his own comfortable and solid interests.

To say that Mother's assignment of our family finances to Jim Evans was ill-advised would be inaccurate. Mother rarely accepted advice of any kind. She, who in many ways was the pink-and-white epitome of WASP femininity, was, beneath it all, as willful as an army tank. So now Jim, who actually had had an unpretentious insurance business, calmly and charmingly went about trying to rebuild a fortune for his life's love and her son.

The first effect of our new setup was my transfer from Bovée to another school that was closer to our new, grand West Side apartment. This particular grammar school, Collegiate School, was at the time semimilitary. It still prides itself on being the oldest boys' school in America. It was founded in pre-British Colonial New York when the town was called New Amsterdam.

In my day, Collegiate student-cadets were obliged to wear not uniforms, but only American Civil War army hats as a sort of school identification when outdoors or in the drill hall. We drilled a bit each morning and some afternoons with real but old lightweight rifles and wore fancy belts with blunted (also Civil War) bayonets attached, around our middles. My entrance application had comments written on it stating that I had had good average marks at my previous school, that I spoke French, was large for my age, and "was especially fond of drawing." (I had, it is true, a gift for drawing and music which lack of time and self-discipline failed to fully exploit.)

Mother was also set on my being entered in another institution called the Knickerbocker Greys. They were—and indeed still are—a sort of after-school drill academy where, twice a week, boys from about eight to twelve dress up in miniature adaptations of West Point uniforms and, having shouldered their arms or, as the case or rank may be, drawn their swords, march around and around inside New York's 7th Regiment Armory at Sixty-sixth and Park—going, and getting, nowhere.

The "Greys" were then very hard to get into. Most boys' families were expected to be included in the New York Social Register, a publication said to be a sort of local Almanack de Gotha, with entries based on a combination of wealth, social position (a certain genealogy, real or tampered with, was considered helpful), and absence of scandal (the published kind only, of course). The intended function of the Greys was to keep that half-pint age group occupied for at least two afternoons a week. And the same bluff, sour-smelling retired regular army major who drilled us at Collegiate School was in command of the Knickerbocker Greys as well.

But when the no-longer well-known, socially unregistered Mrs. James Evans, Jr., submitted the name of her son by her previous marriage, Douglas Fairbanks, Jr., for acceptance as a cadet, she, or rather I, was turned down by the all-female Entrance Committee. They explained to one of my proposers that the son of a divorced actor would not do. They hinted that were such a boy admitted, he might lower the tone of such a distinguished corps of future defenders of our nation.

Mother was not one to stand by and be defeated so easily. She enlisted the aid of the only very rich and socially influential doctor I've ever known, who, incidentally, brought me into the world. This good friend, Dr. Samuel Brown, went to bat for us, impressing the Entrance Committee with my mother's *(not* my father's!) "impeccable" social credentials. In the end I was properly admitted, fitted for my uniforms, and sent to begin more drilling.

The chairman of the Entrance Committee was Mrs. William Burden. By an amusing irony of life, her youngest son, Shirl, was not only one of my Bovée schoolmates but also, years later, the husband of my beloved cousin Flobelle. They had two marvelous children, Carter Burden and "Muffie" Childs (her married name), who grew up with my own daughters. Old Mrs. Burden and I became the most affectionate of relatives-by-marriage and she died without ever having been reminded of the incident at all. Mother, on the other hand, never forgot it!

As I was fairly adept (say, enthusiastic) on the drums, I was assigned to the Drum Corps and soon learned how to rap out smartly the traditional assortment of regulation drumbeats to back up and complement the bugles and fifes ahead. I soon rose to the rank of lance corporal and a large gold V was sewn on the sleeve of my uniform, but I didn't retain that exalted status for long. I was busted to buck private! I still don't remember, and can't imagine, what I had been caught at. I don't believe a slander spread by one or two friends that I giggled so much on parade that I became incontinent, but *something* must have gone seriously amiss. What it was has become a still unexplained black mark. In any case, we were told that "veterans" of the Greys would be listed, after our twenty-first birthdays, as "honorary second lieutenants of the New York 7th Regiment." As such, we could tramp down to Brooks Brothers where, after giving proof of our connection, we could purchase the New York Regimental tie. (Very pretty, but as I went into the Navy during the war it wasn't as appropriate as it might have been.)

I attended the "Greys" but one year, because after that we were on the move again.

In February 1920, nine months after the divorce, a major milestone in the motion picture industry was reached. My father, together with Mary, Charlie, and one of the greatest film directors of all movie time, D. W. Griffith (the enthusiastic "creator" of Mary Pickford, and the disapproving but tolerant first film boss of "that legit fellow, Fairbanks"), formed a partnership. They called it the United Artists Corporation, Inc. Despite their very considerable earnings, these four had long believed that the big companies for whom they made their films were charging them, the *real* "makers of movies," far too much for distribution and advertising.

There is hardly any way in which a modern public can imagine the sheer immensity of the worldwide following these four enjoyed in those first postwar years. The currently overused term "superstar" should have applied only to them and to no one since, for the simple reason that no film star or director, in any part of the world, has ever so much as approached their fame and popularity. One may categorically state that no woman ever lived who was so widely known and loved in her time as Mary Pickford. Neither could any face and figure ever again be as globally recognizable and adored as the tiny-mustached, splayfooted, baggy-trousered clown, Charlie Chaplin. And the name "Douglas Fairbanks" alone promised everyone everywhere a chance to relive improbable dreams of high romance and to believe in the invincibility of right over wrong and the achievement of the impossible. Griffith's name as producer-director meant the highest degree of quality and intelligence; it also meant spectacle *(The Birth of a Nation)* and drama *(Way Down East* and *Broken Blossoms).* He was the first widely known great director, the inventor of the closeup, the moving-camera shot, fade-outs, and dissolves. He was the discoverer of such actors as Lillian and Dorothy Gish, Richard Barthelmess, and Lionel Barrymore.

These, then, were the *real* giants of the movies. Not only in the developed Western world but in many of the remotest villages of Africa and Asia, where few could even read, these four names were spoken. For very little money, uncountable millions found refuge from their particular worlds in the wonderland of black-and-white silent movies. No modern sound or color film, viewed at high prices with the help of costly electronic machines, no TV performance via satellite, however well translated, could ever hope to overcome the language barriers—even with the best dubbers.

When these four, under the legal guidance of Cap O'Brien, joined forces to create their United Artists company, Adolph Zukor (still the King-Emperor of the Famous Players–Lasky Corporation and of Paramount Pictures, Inc.) was at first very annoyed that his own beloved pet, "Little Mary," and the "grinning bouncer—Doug," had left him and joined with Chaplin and Griffith in a big, well-financed partnership. It was then that he coined the oft-quoted phrase "The inmates have taken over the asylum!"

It was a funny crack, but way off course. The new partners found out, for one thing, that instead of paying out 35 percent or more of the gross takings for distribution, they now only needed to pay something like 18 percent. Many other surprises were in store as they gradually discovered how efficiently the big companies could get away with everything short of murder. Nor, as *I* was to learn—the hard way—have they changed since—except that they have become even more efficient at their shenanigans, and on a grander scale.

The industry was staggered by the nerve of these four, and, fearing an end to their monopolies, the majors (as the big companies were called) tyrannically tried (often successfully) to persuade other, lesser stars from becoming independent. United Artists grew very successful—for its partners, the Big Four. Later, when they began to slow down a bit, other new partners, mostly independent producers rather than artists, were allowed to buy in, and little by little the company's personality changed—in time almost beyond recognition. But over the next score of years, the company's and the partners' mutual aging process would show what equally dramatic effects each one had upon the other.

On March 2, 1920, wearing a black dress and with her blond curls hidden under a hat, Mary Pickford (i.e., Gladys Smith Moore) was granted a di-

vorce from Owen Moore in Genoa, Nevada. Mary was a Catholic only
when it suited her. The grounds were desertion and, because collusion was
suspected, a cloud of legal technicalities hung over the divorce for two
years.

Nevertheless, my father, a faithful follower of astrological predictions,
had been told that the thirteenth day after the Ides of March—the twenty-
eighth to be precise—of the year 1920 was the most propitious day for him
to embark on "a new life." Thus it was that he and Mary—the brightest of
the earthbound stars—chose that date to be married. It was a simple, solemn ceremony. It was also, as Richard Schickel has called it, "a symbiotic
joining." Alistair Cooke has commented that the worldwide attention and
excitement that the event inspired was "living proof of America's belief in
happy endings."

The marriage was performed in the house my father had bought and
rebuilt for Mary, which the world's press came to call Pickfair. The guest
list was small—just Charlie (of course); Uncle Bob and Aunt Lorie; Mary's
mother, Ma Pickford (née Charlotte Smith of Toronto); Mary's brother
Jack; British playwright Edward Knoblock and Marjorie Daw (Dad's once
or twice leading lady, rumored to have been, at an earlier time, "a great and
good friend"); and the inevitable press agent Benny Ziedman.

In the summer of 1920 the Sullys felt obligated to increase their income by
renting Kenneth Ridge, so there was, for me, one more something gone
from the family's tangible past. We took rooms in the best of the town's
hotels at Watch Hill, the Ocean House, a large, rambling clapboard place.
It's still there, but somehow it doesn't seem as spacious today. As an extravagant sop to our diminishing status I was given a small one-cylinder motor
wheel. This was attached to my bike. I had wanted something called a
"buckboard," a popular item of the time for kids whose families could
afford one. They were long and low to the ground—rather like a large sled
with four wheels and a fifth wheel with a putt-putt engine attached at the
back. However, this was thought too dangerous. Surprisingly less spoiled
than might be imagined, I had a grand time with my motored bike, which
whizzed along at a top speed of about 10 or 15 mph.

Still called Junior by all—except Mother, who called both Dad and me
Douglas, thus causing occasional confusion—I was enjoying my Watch Hill
summers more than ever. With the Boys' Club I learned to sail, to win cups
for swimming but not running, to go on daylong hikes to Westerly and back,
picking blackberries and raspberries by the roadsides along the way, and to

play six-a-side baseball games on the vast lawn of the Lehme family mansion.

Those were the summers when my real (as opposed to fictional) heroes were the great sports figures of the day: champion heavyweight fighters like Willard, Dempsey, and Carpentier; wrestlers (most wrestling then was on the level) like "Strangler" Lewis and Ed Koch; and baseball players like Babe Ruth. Ruth's record of over fifty home runs the year before so inspired me that one afternoon, with the help of Teedy Ley pitching softball to me and another guy catching, I slammed balls out of reach of yet another pal in the outfield. If the ball landed sufficiently far from him, I decided that these would have been home runs in a real game. One day, after I'd hit over fifty of them, I boasted to my family that I had at least equaled Babe Ruth's record. I think this must have been one of my earliest experiments in self-persuasive truth-stretching; to make myself an achiever in order to satisfy family expectations.

On another but not unrelated plane was the story Mother told of how I had been so anxious for Dad to know of my growing up and thinning down, and of my growing proficiency in sports, that I scrawled him a letter of several pages telling him all. Whether he ever really read the letter I don't know, but I do remember how impatient I was to get an encouraging reply. Finally, several weeks later, a telegram arrived saying *something,* such as "Got your letter. Good for you. Keep it up. Love, Dad." I carried it in my pocket for a long time. It was only when I was well into my twenties that I learned that, like many of Dad's thoughtful gestures, the wire was really my Uncle Bob's idea.

One summer's Watch Hill vacation marked my first experience of actually earning money. In fact, I developed two sources of income—neither known by Mother. The first was a part-time job helping in the village drugstore at the soda counter as a soda jerk. This, of course, meant developing a fine careless flourish with the drinks, thus impressing customers with my expertise. First, I would press one of the squirters beneath the counter to get Coke syrup in a special Coke glass with a couple of hunks of ice inside it. Then a pull on the soda lever—hoisting and lowering the glass in an easy manner—and then, as the soda gushed out, *"pshh—shh . . ."* followed by my glib "There y'are!" it was all done! Ice-cream sodas were impressively prepared with plops of scooped-out ice cream (three flavors), a bit of milk, and then a fine series of the same soda gushes, two straws and a spoon stuck in, and ending with another "There y'are!" Business was only fair, but I had a great time—until ordered to stop by Mother and Munnie. Still, for only a couple of hours on the couple of afternoons of the weeks I got away with it, I think I got about a dollar a week, maybe more.

I got about two dollars on another two afternoons a week for setting up pins in the village bowling alley. No machines then. Each one of the tenpins was set by hand, and then—there were two alleys—we would jump quickly up out of the way onto the "sideboard" so we wouldn't get hit by a hard ball rolling down and sending pins a-flying.

I felt proud and rather smug about having actively earned so much money. Now, when not spied upon, I would be able to treat myself to extra popcorn, or, on rainy days when our Boys' Club wasn't doing something, go with somebody's permission to the local movie house where every nine or ten minutes the picture would stop and a slide would be projected saying: *One minute please while we change reels.* As I had been given the twenty-five cents admission money by Mother, I was soon ahead of the game because of my earnings.

Other pictures float by. There was a girl at the Ocean House in 1920, the daughter of a big tycoon, who, according to the caddish rumor begun by one of the Boys' Club members, was willing to *kiss! Really* kiss, he said! When some of us, who had formed a secret gang, convened in a cave dug out of a huge sand dune on the other side of Napatree Point, we would confess "no progress" with the girl for any of us—except for the one who started the story in the first place.

The girl with whom we had planned to exchange this real kiss was not actually very attractive. Her face was a splotchy, pimply red, matched by her wiry red hair. But she *was* good-natured, sneaked puffs on cigarettes, and swore she had once tasted a cocktail. She *was* a tease! She let us conspire as much as we wanted, knowing all along she'd only allow some of us (me included) a quick, undetected peck while riding in the hotel's open-grill elevator from one floor to another. But even that much was enough to inspire our first confessed stirrings of animal desire! This consciousness had still a long way to go to be more expertly expressed, but the broad hints of what that particular kind of future held for us sometimes became so obviously disconcerting that the director of the Boys' Club was instructed by our families to provide us with even more strenuous sports in order to burn up our distracting energies.

As full of good things as those last two Watch Hill summers at the hotel were, I'm sure everyone felt sad at the final loss of Kenneth Ridge. My grandfather Ganka finally sold it. It slid from being our family's old house to being just someone else's summer boardinghouse. No one in the family wanted to go near the place anymore. I missed it too, of course, but managed to ride back every so often on my bike-with-the-extra-motor-wheel. I invariably stopped to enjoy the familiar romantic bronze statue of the kneeling Indian that stood on a plinth at one of the small crossroads.

Out in California, Mother's best friend, the tweedy agent Ruth Allen, had persuaded Dad to buy a short story about early California called "The Curse of Capistrano" by Johnston McCulley. At first he needed considerable urging to appear in period costume. Dad maintained it was risky to change from his established "ultra-modern" image, but he finally gave in. When the retitled picture was released, it turned out to be by far the most successful movie he had ever made (quite the opposite from his very disappointing, quickly turned out next film, *The Nut*). Indeed, it became a more than minor classic of its kind, widely imitated and remade (without distinction) several times since. It was called *The Mark of Zorro* and was to be his trademark for years to come.

The phenomenal success of *Zorro* convinced my father from then on to take more time and concentrate on producing a series of high-quality, expensive films that would be exhibited first for long runs in regular theaters (not movie houses) with reserved hard-ticket seats. It was then that he began a six-month hatching period for Dumas's *The Three Musketeers* in which he would take the part of his own favorite hero of heroes, D'Artagnan. He wrote the scenario himself but called on the British playwright Edward Knoblock to collaborate. He engaged the same director he had in *Zorro*, Fred Niblo, and chose the same leading lady, too, Marguerite de la Motte. Adolphe Menjou—a splendid newcomer discovered by Chaplin for his own film *A Woman of Paris*—was perfectly cast as King Louis XIII of France. When the picture finally opened, with two showings a day in a legitimate Broadway theater with a full orchestra in the pit playing a special score, another major film milestone had been reached, and Dad rushed on to think about the next one. *The Three Musketeers* (1920) enjoyed the same tremendous success everywhere it played, all over the world.

Mary and Charlie, too, had been making their own spectacular successes, and Griffith's contributions brought him more kudos than ever. The United Artists Corporation was now, after two years, a giant company hated and envied by the old, impotent majors.

While all this was going on, I was completely detached from Dad's life, continuing my perambulations under Jim Evans's symbolic fathership and Mother's actual guidance. Our Watch Hill summers were almost wound down, but in addition to my marked improvement in sports and games, there were still a few memorable days of picnics and sailings to Newport or Block Island or Narragansett, the marvelous End-of-Season Ball and the "Cake Walk" contests by the all-black staff at the Ocean House, the final Boys' Club contests, the small money-earning jobs, and all the rest of a New England seaside season.

My most treasured memory was the making of a new and eventually best friend, Genie Chester. Genie (for Eugenie) was one of three wonderful-looking children of Mr. and Mrs. C. M. Chester—all of us within a year or two of each other in age. One day Genie and her brother had been playing clock-golf on the lawn of the Ocean House when I asked to join. Although I was not yet really taken with the idea of girls, Genie and I hit it off immediately. She had a remarkably beautiful face with a permanently angelic expression and personality to go with it. Genie had been partly but badly paralyzed and, though she didn't know it then, was to remain handicapped for life.

Genie had contracted polio a couple of years earlier when it was called infantile paralysis and no one had found a real treatment, let alone a cure. Genie's family (her father was the chairman of the General Foods Corporation) had taken her to every specialist at home and abroad for years, both before and after our first meeting. Her muscles and bones were changed around, braces were attached to legs, back and/or neck, and all to no avail —except to make things more painful or uncomfortable for Genie. Most of the time she spent in wheelchairs, but with her leg braces locked in place she learned, with help, to walk a bit. Her body grew little in height from the age of twelve on but her mind blossomed gloriously, and she has always been beautiful. She became a brilliant student, enthusiastically interested in almost everything, extensively traveled, and an omnivorous reader of all she could lay her hands on. More important she was, and still is, my principal confidante. If there was such a thing as a special supercategory for close friendships, I suppose I must record that Genie and my cousin Flobe have been, in their different ways, and apart from my immediate family, the two closest and best-loved people in my life.

Although the Sully poke was by now virtually empty, Jim Evans struggled manfully to invest Mother's settlement money. As one investment plan replaced another with slowly diminishing success, we continued to give the appearance of living on only a slightly reduced scale. In New York, the Central Park apartment was given up and once again we went back to the Algonquin. I didn't mind a bit, as both George, the Greek headwaiter in the main dining room, and Miss Bush, the switchboard operator, would jolly me along whenever I was being disciplined for something. Also, the move downtown brought me much nearer all the theaters that I was just beginning to be allowed, at almost age eleven, to attend more often.

However much I liked being a little bit on the inside, my father's fame as an actor had not yet inspired me to follow in his steps. I had been kept as far as possible out of the public eye and away from the actual work of theater and films, and so was aware, only from afar, of that lovely land of story-telling. I kept very much to myself my own imaginary world of vivid dangers safely risked, of stirring fanfares for gallant knights and their ladies, and of the kind of quiet, modest wit that triumphs in spite of odds.

There were reasons besides my father's shadowy existence for my slowly growing attachment to the theater. Up until the time I was about twelve or so, when some actual danger or drama was imminent I'd somehow ease my inner fright and calm down by persuading myself that, whatever its cause, it wasn't really happening at all, that it was just another make-believe game from which, if I obeyed my own rules, I'd emerge safely. I'm certain that much of what influenced my romantic attitude toward work, life, and adventure, and imparted an ultimate confidence in my own survival, were other people's yarns, books and stories by Robert Louis Stevenson, and the Arthurian legends, greatly aided by the illustrations of N. C. Wyeth, Charles Russell, and Frederick Remington. These, more than movies or theater, formed my inner preteen character.

In those first years after the Great War, I was lucky enough to see Eleanora Duse on her last American tour. I saw Jeanne Eagels in *Rain* and the Lunts in *The Guardsman.* In London, I became a lifelong fan of Sir Gerald du Maurier after seeing him in *Bulldog Drummond.* In Paris, I was taken to see the great Sarah Bernhardt on the last night of her last play (which I *think* was called *La Gloire).* Mother instructed me never to forget the experience. That was easy to obey. The Divine Sarah's golden voice by then sounded more like an aged croak, but her personality was still impressive— or could it be that Mother and others *told* me to be impressed—and so, again, I obeyed? I can't really tell!

It was John Barrymore of the classic profile and the fabulous voice and presence who became my first real stage hero. Jack, in the play *The Jest,* was costumed in a fifteenth-century short dark-green jacket with long sleeves. As his legs were well proportioned, they were exploited by long bright-green tights in which he deliberately exaggerated the kind of male falsies used by some ballet dancers. It was said that this costume, by which some professed to be shocked, was very helpful in increasing the box-office take. Jack, however, described himself as looking like "a decadent string bean"!

Offstage Jack was bawdy, heavy-drinking, witty, vulgar, and well read.

Often, when drunk, he was offensive and belligerent. After attending London University and working for a while as a professional cartoonist, he drifted into acting largely because his tribe expected it of him and because he was so undeniably talented. All that generation of Barrymores had, in fact, intended other careers for themselves. Ethel had wished to be a concert pianist; Lionel, a composer and painter; and Jack would have preferred art. Jack had acquired a set of widely mocked "ham" mannerisms, both onstage and off, which he once told me he had subconsciously acquired from watching his own hero, Sir Henry Irving. Throughout his life he won and kept a small mob of admirers and friends—an odd bunch composed of an even assortment of intellectuals, aristocrats, con artists, and bums. In spite of his aesthetic stage looks (he was as nearly beautiful as a he-man can be), he was almost affectedly sloppy—often plain dirty—in his personal life. He knew I had developed a boyish theatrical hero-worship for him and he always remained particularly kind and well behaved with me. As I grew up, our lives ran curiously parallel for a period and in those days he behaved as a sober and responsible friend. It was a facet of Jack Barrymore's character that few saw or would even believe existed.

My boyhood admiration for him—equal in intensity to that for my favorite ball-players and fighters—began when I saw him in the film of *Dr. Jekyll and Mr. Hyde.* (I was later told that my father was jealous that I favored his friend over him.) This movie, and his scary performance, haunted me for days, but I still managed to see it, *and* my father's *The Three Musketeers* (my favorite inspirational adventure movie up to that time), at least half a dozen times each. Only shortly after that, Jack staggered Broadway with his performance of *Richard III.* I was so taken with the play, and Jack's acting in it, that by the time I was twelve I had learned the entire play, everyone's part, by heart.

Jack also lived at the Algonquin, and when I found that out I was so excited that I thought I would burst. I remember how irked he was when he descended from his room, at about midday, sauntered into the lobby, and, it was said, too often found the beautiful but very pesky, aspiring young actress from Alabama, Tallulah Bankhead, waiting for him. She told her friends that she had pleaded with him to seduce her but he was so afraid of her youth and the trouble such an act might bring in its wake that he brusquely refused. That is to say, he refused until a few years later, when he asked, "Do you think if I screwed you, you'd leave me alone?" and, she reported, "Such shreds of decency and conscience as he had had were no longer obstacles."

I, on the other hand, was just interested in having him make the fearful grimace he had affected as "Mr. Hyde." It was the *most* terrifyingly evil expression, evolving from a face as nearly perfect as a Greek god's, that one could imagine. When this chum of my father's, soon to be recognized as one of America's finest actors, re-performed his "Mr. Hyde" face for me, personally, in the Algonquin Hotel lobby, I screeched in delighted terror and backed off.

Only a couple of years later I saw Jack in what many said was the finest *Hamlet* in memory. (Later, in London, when he surprised even himself by duplicating his triumph there, Bernard Shaw wrote a letter congratulating him on his wonderful performance as Hamlet, adding that one day he would like to see him in "Shakespeare's version"!)

By autumn 1920 we were back in California and I was glad. I don't remember exactly why we left New York, but the reason was probably financial. Jim Evans was away a good deal—back East on business trips and still working unsuccessfully to increase the family resources. Mother rented a small dark house on Hawthorne Avenue, a quiet pepper-tree-lined back street in residential Hollywood. It was a bit crowded because the Sullys— Munnie, Ganka, and Bill—moved in with us as well. They had moved West from Rhode Island for good and settled at first in an apartment house. But now the whole tribe was back in one house—and not a big one, by any means. Yet, I don't remember our being unduly squashed in it. Perhaps being young, adaptable, and in a good climate made it easier not to notice our very gradual downward shifts of fortune. After all, I had a bike, the Pacific a few miles away, and friends. All was fine enough for me.

I had heard and read of Dad and Mary's summer honeymoon trip to Europe and about the masses of hysterical fans who blocked their various hotels and their movements wherever they went, for at least a quarter mile in all directions—in London, Paris, Amsterdam, Madrid, and Rome. I recall that the news had only moderately interested me. I was naturally pleased it was about my own father—and now I had a half-understood claim to Mary, too, but I really hadn't seen much of them for a long time. I knew, of course, about their marriage, but I was not disturbed or confused. I thought about it a great deal but never talked about it. I was pleased they were so famous and popular and that I was related to them. I was distantly proud, and even distantly "possessive."

I had entered yet another military school, a very strict Episcopal one, called the Harvard Military School. We wore ordinary high-collar, khaki military uniforms with leather belts to hold our bayonets and, at what seemed every out-of-class, nonsports moment, we drilled and marched with heavy rifles and bayonets fixed, all about the huge school parade ground. Sports were intramural, but I was not yet old enough or big enough to get a better position on our football team than that of substitute left guard for the Blues, one of the four school divisions.

On the last big day of the football season, all my available Western-based family—except Dad, of course—came expecting to see me, a sad-sack substitute, play. When the last five minutes of the last quarter found me on the sidelines, on the bench, and still not once called in to help when our team was behind by two goals, I begged the coach to let me in the game. I *had* to show the family my mettle. He gave disgruntled approval and I dashed on the field to relieve the regular left guard of his defensive post. The Greens— our main rivals—had the ball. In less than a flash, I believed my chance for glory had come at last. But before the thought was even fully formed, my opposite number lunged forward, dumped me hard and heavy on my backside, creating most effective interference for his halfback teammate following hard on his cleated heels, and, through me, he proceeded on a clear unobstructed run for another touchdown. By the time I'd picked myself up, angry, frustrated, and red-faced, the coach had already sent in someone to relieve me. I'd been in only one play in only one game that whole season. Later, the family discreetly sympathized and then talked of other things.

That episode was just one more item to add to the growing list of things I didn't enjoy about Harvard Military. Among these items was the fact that any infraction of school rules, however small, was punishable by forced marching around and around a huge cellar, in single file, behind other cadet miscreants, with shouldered arms and full packs on our backs, for however many hours our individual punishments called for. When I at last left— again, a month or so earlier than the end of the term—I had only fair to poor scholarship marks and something like twenty-three hours of extra duty to perform.

About twenty-five years later, when I returned from World War II, the school had changed its location, and its character. It had become rather grand in its new buildings. One auspicious day I was invited over and ceremoniously presented with a splendid and impressively signed and red-sealed diploma making me an "honorary graduate" and one of the model boys of whom the school would forever feel proud.

Uncle Bill Sully was very much a part of my life in those days. He was only about five years older than the rest of my pals and a little more sophisticated. Bill couldn't make up his mind what he wanted to do. I think he'd finished high school, but because he was the last Sully male, he had been spoiled since he was born. Most of the time he was very good-natured, with the exception of an occasional familiar Sully burst of red-haired temper. Although he tried hard to emulate his father, old Dan J., a lack of education, self-discipline, and luck kept him from ever rising above modest mediocrity. When I was eleven and twelve he couldn't decide whether to join us younger ones in our conventional sports or get deeper into the tougher village garage-gambling fraternity. He once took me out back to our own small, dark garage and tried to explain to me, in graphic detail, certain basic sexual activities about which I had not previously heard very much. He augmented this by making some tentative homosexual advances that so scared me that I ran away and couldn't speak to him for days from embarrassment. Mother and Dedie sensed something amiss and tried to pump me but I couldn't, and wouldn't, tell. In fact, the subject was never mentioned by anyone ever again.

He was often in different kinds of trouble from which various members of the family had to extricate him. Yet he was basically kind and he tried as best he knew how to succeed. He married twice. His first wife was Cathleen Huntington, a lovely ballet dancer. They had a daughter, Patricia. Patsy was fragile, talented, and beautiful, but plagued with asthma and other illnesses for most of her life, so her promising career as an actress was a series of heartbreaking stops and starts. Uncle Bill later married again and had four more girls. I never got to know them very well or for very long.

Out of school, out of California and out of New York we were en route to Europe in 1921. It didn't really matter that I was at this time neither old enough nor wise enough to recognize the signs of change that were subtly taking place around my life. They were inexorable and I would not have been able to redirect them had I wanted to.

Mother won new friends wherever she went, but her favorites were mostly people of the theater rather than society. She had always been stage-struck and had often exaggerated to ridiculous lengths her role as chief adviser in my father's business affairs. Because she was not really one of them, they clung to her, flattered her, and enjoyed their easy exchanges of confidences with her.

Some of those with whom she mixed in Paris that year were the Gish sisters (Dorothy in particular), the Talmadge sisters (Constance in particular), John Charles Thomas (the great singer), and Elsie Janis (despite her part in introducing my father to Mary). Mother fancied herself not only a guider-of-careers but also a discoverer of as yet undiscovered talent.

Mother developed a new, special friend through "dear Elsie." It so happened that Elsie had organized a sort of precursor of a USO show consisting of talented American service veterans whom she had encountered during her tours entertaining troops during World War I. She billed the show as "Elsie Janis and Her Gang." This particular fellow had been Elsie's leading man. He was an absolute charmer, good-looking and intelligent, with a beautiful baritone voice. He had come to France in 1914 to study singing, and when the war broke out he joined the French Ambulance Corps. His name was Jerome (Jerry) Thayer (changed, wisely, from Hoekstra) and he hailed from Kalamazoo, Michigan. Jerry Thayer soon became a family familiar, going out often with Mother and Jim, and sometimes helping to "cover up" for Connie Talmadge (who was having a discreet "walkout" with John Charles Thomas).

Faded snapshots remain to recall that spring and summer when, with Dedie maddeningly in tow, Mother, Jim, Jerry, and I toured the vast, treeless Belgian and northern French battlefields, still terribly scarred by war. I thought it all very exciting and couldn't wait to have my picture snapped standing with a small Belgian boy next to Big Bertha, the world's largest cannon, with which the Germans had bombarded the English coast across the Channel. Still unable to relate this panorama of postwar horror to any reality I had ever known, I went on, impressed but unfeeling, to the Netherlands.

There I was delighted to see at least a few places still clinging to such traditions as windmills, canals, wooden shoes, lace caps, and wide trousers. I didn't care if they were there only for tourists. Such gentle, unaffected, timeless places as Volendam and the Isle of Marken (no longer an "Isle" now since the Zuider Zee is virtually no more) enchanted me. We stopped at the town of Edam and ate cheese. We visited big cities like Amsterdam and The Hague, where, as in London, there were fine-looking, full-dress foot and cavalry sentries at the Palace. It was a trip of pleasure for me and I learned a lot, though I hardly knew it at the time.

On this same tour we passed through the Dutch town of Doorn. On a rambling walk to nowhere with Dedie, I remember passing a big place which was surrounded by high iron railings and great bushes that more or less obscured the house and garden behind them. Still, being eleven and curious, I peeked through the bushes and the railings and saw two old gentlemen walking slowly along a path together. The more striking of the two was, as I remember, genial-looking with a white mustache and a goatee. He kept one hand in his pocket while the other hand gesticulated to his deferential walking companion. Somehow the old man caught me peering and smiled and waved at me. I smiled and waved back, and called out a cheery American "Hello!"

The old man called back in English but with a faintly foreign British-influenced accent, "Are you an American or British boy?"

I called back, "American! What are you?"

He didn't answer my question but merely smiled, said, "Enjoy your visit!" and continued his stroll.

Later I learned I had exchanged greetings with Wilhelm II, the recent German King-Emperor! I found it difficult to reconcile the white-haired, gentle-looking, cheerful old man with the viciously spiky upturned black mustachioed, helmeted Kaiser I'd seen caricatured as a villain for so long.

Europe had our custom for a shorter time than usual in 1921 and we slipped into Watch Hill early in June. Again we stayed at the Ocean House, where, to my joy, the Chester family and, best of all, Genie were also in residence. I spent most of my time outdoors again. At last most of my puppy fat had gone. I was bronzed, active, and would have been, I think, quite a bit less of an embarrassment to Dad had he seen me.

The only activity of the Boys' Club that I thoroughly disliked was hiking from Watch Hill to Westerly, about nine miles altogether, there and back. The one enjoyable part of this long haul was picking wild blackberries beside the tarred road. I'm sure that those hikes became the subconscious reason why, more than twenty years later, I determined *not* to join the Army if I could help it. I always preferred the water, ships, and the romance of the open sea.

The most exciting event of the summer was the Dempsey-Carpentier fight for the Heavyweight Championship of the World, to be fought on July 2. Many of us had been influenced by an unfair press that had made Jack Dempsey out to be a slacker during the war. At the same time the young, handsome, lighter, gentlemanly Frenchman Georges Carpentier had had a splendid battle record in the French Army. When he finally lost to Dempsey, my friends and I were very downcast. A few years later, I got to know and like both of them and regretted ever having taken sides at all.

September and school, and California, again. From birth, I had never seen the calendar around a full year from any one place (and haven't to this day), nor did I attend any school for more than one year (sometimes less). Thus I took each new migration in stride.

Stepfather Pop had, at Mother's direction, rented still another nice but smaller house—happily, near Flobe and Sissy—in Hollywood. Mother had heard that the only suitable private school was in Pasadena, a self-consciously sedate community that looked down its civic nose at Los Angeles, its sprawling, formless near-neighbor to the southeast. Once again family

friends were called on to help, this time to get me into the Pasadena Poly-
technic School, its rambling one-story wooden buildings surrounded on
three sides by an orange grove.

It was silly to live in one community and go to school nearly an hour's
drive away along winding, pre-freeway roads. There was no satisfactory
public transportation and we could no longer afford a full-time chauffeur. So
it was that most mornings poor Pop, whose own work was in downtown Los
Angeles, drove me in our new Buick the whole damned way to Pasadena in
the morning and the whole damned way home in the afternoon. Still, he
kept in wonderfully good humor most of the time.

Mother decided to put a feather in her social bonnet by getting us into the
expensive, Pasadena-oriented Flintridge Country Club. It was a fine place,
nestled almost triangularly equidistant in the hills above Los Angeles and
Pasadena. But I had no friends there and I preferred the Santa Monica
Beach Club, to which we also belonged, with its salt-water surf. Of course
whenever Dad and Mary were away (which was quite often), I'd go with my
cousins and friends to Pickfair and swim out the fine idle weekend days in
the large, kidney-shaped pool, high in the still fairly empty Beverly Hills.
Today I wonder how on earth Mother managed to pay for the Beach Club,
the Country Club, the new car, my school, the house rental, our Japanese
couple, and occasional entertaining. I can only surmise that she had been
slyly off-loading a few minor *objets d'art* and that Pop must have had an
occasional lucky investment or deal. I grew up to believe that although
Mother's extravagance was born and bred in her in Rhode Island, many of
her affectations were due to the fact that my father's desertion of us still
hurt. She wanted to show that she was now completely out from under what
she called "Senior's stifling influence."

Once I got into the Pasadena Poly's eighth-grade routine, I rather enjoyed
myself. I continued sprouting and thinning and became ever more active in
sports and school plays. I played a smashing Richard III—really a juvenile
imitation of John Barrymore. Poly was a coed school and this seemed
strange to me for a few weeks, although that didn't last long. What did
inhibit me was that here I was more conscious of being a curiosity. On one
of the first days, the principal of the school addressed the students after
opening prayers: "We want you all to treat Douglas just as if he were like
every one of you." It was the first time I'd ever thought of my own celebrity
(a word I wouldn't have known then) as being freakish. My name was ever
more conspicuously the same as my widely hero-worshipped father's. It was
then that I first began consciously to shrivel with shyness at one moment,
only to swing over to expansiveness the next. Did I want to hide or did I

want to be even more conspicuous? I don't believe I have ever consistently decided on one or the other.

By this time, Dad had finished filming *Robin Hood,* the third in his series of classic films (which I was allowed to watch being made a few exciting times). Dad's old friend Allan Dwan returned to collaborate and direct. Wilfred Buckland, the great art director, imported from New York, had designed the largest sets yet built. They were every boy's dream of a Norman-English castle with a huge drawbridge, portcullis, battlements, and towers. Oh, it was wonderful! On a Sunday afternoon, when I could escape the family's many eyes, I would persuade some girl that I was fourteen or thereabouts and, with a bit of Blarney, take her to Dad's studio and climb up the back of one of the huge castle sets. The studio's weekend gatekeepers never questioned my right to come in (if Dad was on tour, my Uncle Bob authorized my entrance) and so I managed to swank about a few times with no one around to say me nay. The word among the boys from Hollywood and Beverly Hills was that the girls from nearby Fairfax High School were the best. They had the raciest reputation and were said to be quite willing to kiss a guy *the first time out!* Imagine!

One girl whose easy reputation was widespread admitted she would like to visit the Pickford-Fairbanks studio and climb to the top of the *Robin Hood* castle. When we finally got there my hope of appearing poised and experienced went unrealized as I lost my nerve, stuttered, and blushed. But the girl was more poised and worldly than I. She suddenly, and absolutely unexpectedly, proposed that we cooperate in a mutual anatomical inspection. As such an advanced idea of romance had not so far come my way, I couldn't think of how to respond. I was dumb and paralyzed. It so happened that at that very most unnerving moment one of the studio cops on his rounds caught sight of us and bellowed, "Get the hell down outta there!" I don't remember now whether I was sorry or relieved. But we obeyed in a hurry.

Shortly after that, my sudden sprouting from childhood to preteen found me dizzily enchanted with a special girl in my class. She was pretty, had a Dutch-bob haircut, and my every thought—sacred and almost-but-not-quite-yet-profane—was of her. Her name was Agnes Hawkins. Although she was always friendly and sweet, I was clearly not inspiring the same mooning devotion in her as she managed to inspire in me. In fact, it was no secret that she and the school's big-shot Eagle Scout, his arms laden with merit badges, was her "steady." Agnes was about a half year older and he was two and a half years older than I. Since I was still a few weeks short of twelve (though I looked fifteen), I was just that much too young to be a Scout at all.

A day came when I somehow mustered the courage to invite her out to the school's adjacent orange grove. I muttered that I liked her a lot and begged her to let me kiss her. I also promised that she would be my very first real girl and it would be my very first real kiss. This was possibly the first and last time I told the whole truth to a girl. But Agnes was not at all impressed. She politely gave me to understand that she couldn't even consider such a thing until I had joined the Boy Scouts!

Naturally, this none-too-subtle recruiting gambit worked with smitten me. From that moment on, I was determined to become a Boy Scout as soon as possible. I began studying all the entrance examinations required for Tenderfoot, the first and lowest rung (then) in a Boy Scout career. I set to work, learning to tie a variety of knots and how to make fires outdoors by rubbing two sticks together, cooking over a campfire, learning the compass and a lot of mottos and rules. It all went along well enough and after my twelfth birthday on the ninth of December I was qualified to take the tests. If I passed, I could be a full-fledged Boy Scout! But to my fierce annoyance, the one thing I couldn't complete was the test on signal flags.

Agnes was gently tolerant but unmoved. My rival, the Head Scout of the school, was patronizing. Our Scoutmaster had been very strict with me until the day I discovered that his weakness was movies. In a friendly mood, he let slip that he would "love to visit a studio sometime."

I said that I couldn't promise, as I didn't see my father very often these days because my parents were divorced, but I'd see what I could do "sometime." I didn't consciously "bribe" such an unquestionably honest man but it worked out as though I had. I didn't find it difficult to get him into the studio on a Saturday (they worked six days a week then) and very shortly after that I barely passed the signal flag tests. Subsequently I was officially enrolled as a full-fledged Tenderfoot (Third Class) Member of the Boy Scouts of America.

I couldn't wait to get into my Scout uniform (which Mother had bought in advance, having had no doubt of her son's eventual triumph) and present myself to Agnes. She was as good as her word and one day soon after she slipped me a note saying she'd meet me after school, way in the back of the orange grove—out of sight!

Well ahead of the appointed time I went out to the grove—as far as possible from any snoopers. I thought Agnes would never show up and my heart was pounding away with the first great romantic excitement I had known. Finally, she appeared—her white school jumper looking something like a sailor's jacket hanging loose over her slim figure. Her bright smile and bobbed blond hair were so pretty that I was unable to speak coherently. Or if I did, I haven't the slightest idea what I said or what she said. All I remember is that we put our arms shyly and loosely around each other. She daintily turned her cheek and I pecked at it with all the first tremors of lust.

Somewhat shakily I reached forward to repeat the performance, but this time *she* kissed *my* cheek! The orange grove seemed to whirl like a pinwheel in my dizzy head. Oh, the ecstasy of that instant, of that gesture! And with that, Agnes giggled and ran off. I was too weak to give chase but stood rooted to the spot like a damned fool. I supposed that Agnes had now put me on a par with her Eagle Scout! I knew I hadn't supplanted him yet—she made that quite clear—but I thought I did now at least have a chance. She did admit that she liked me enough and hinted that one day I might be the one.

I remember, too, the day she gave me a slightly enlarged snapshot of herself, which I kept hidden in my room for some time. This was the era when young girls' likenesses were best caricatured by John Held, Jr.: cloche hats, flattened chests, boyish figures in sweaters and/or short-skirted dresses with belts worn very low, just above the hips. Many girls wore white, flat-heeled shoes with a brown leather band across the instep. That was how Agnes was dressed in the picture she gave me.

I must have been far more lecherous than my innocent face or manner betrayed. I was very conscious that Agnes had not developed the bumps on her chest that I had long since learned were her due. I was beginning to note with interest that some of the other girls had them, but some also followed the new fashion of strapping themselves in much too tightly in order to seem more boylike. It looked to me as though that was what Agnes had done. Whatever it was, it was the only thing I regretted about the lovely picture of the lovely Agnes. And so, very privately, I took a pencil and shaded in a vague but convincing semblance of a discreet pair of budding bosoms.

I kept the photo well hidden under school books in a drawer in my small bedroom. One day when I was away, Mother was snooping around and found the retouched photograph. When I returned home, I was confronted with it and sternly lectured on the "dirty mind" I had no doubt picked up from some unknown "rowdy" companions. With that, she tore up my precious photograph and threw it away. I was furious and sad to have been caught in this shameful episode. I never dared ask Agnes for a replacement for fear she'd ask why.

I saw Agnes once or twice a few years later when she came to visit me in the studio where I was making an early film. But the romance had faded when I left the school. I suppose almost fifty years then passed before Agnes and I nearly met again. I was about to open in a play in Los Angeles and I thought it would be the greatest fun if I could find Agnes and invite her to come to the first night. It took long and exhausting detective work, aided and abetted by many friends. Finally I located her, still living in Pasadena and married to an eminent doctor called Buckingham. I wrote and telephoned and though she was shy about meeting after so long, she finally agreed to come to the opening night with her husband. She never showed up. I gather she was overwhelmed with timidity, but she wrote a most kind note of apology. I was very sad about it all, as she had become such a charming memory.

5

Mother and Jim were not making much of a success of their marriage. Mother was clearly touched by his patience and loyalty, but his continuing business disappointments and frustrations and the subsequent depletion of their bank accounts suggested that she was not quite touched enough. Poor Jim had been henpecked for more than two or three years across oceans and continents. Although they were undeniably fond of each other, they must have decided to separate at about this time. This may have been the reason I was pulled out of "Poly" in the early spring of 1922 and taken back to New York and then over to England. As usual, Dedie came with us, but not Jim. I was told he had business to attend to in Los Angeles.

It was on this trip to London that I first escaped the watchful eyes of my keepers and made my way to the Serpentine, that lake-like body of water in London's Hyde Park. There I got myself into a boat, rowed out to the center, happily lit up and smoked my first-ever cigarette (it was a Gold-flake), began to choke, must have turned murky green, got sick, threw up, and rowed back—proud as Punch. There were no other aftereffects, good or bad—just great satisfaction at the latest step toward getting older.

A month or so later, we went to France. Waiting for us in Paris was Jerry Thayer, who was still a resident, studying singing. He soon became Mother's constant and increasingly close companion. It took a while before it occurred to me that this friendship could be something more than it seemed.

Jerry must have had at least a little family money and some saved from his stage tours with Elsie Janis. He shared an apartment with a tall, bearded, gently grave and aesthetic soul named Noël Sullivan, another student of voice and music, who seemed indefinitely older—but perhaps it was only his manner. Jerry and Noël had met when they served with the French Ambulance Service during the Great War. They were the most contrasting of friends. Jerry was strongly masculine and handsome, with a thick head of well-trimmed wavy hair, and cheeks so rosy and lips so red he was teased about them. But these did not "feminize" him in the least. Rather, they seemed to confirm certain Anglo-Dutch ancestral characteristics. He spoke and sang in a fine rich baritone.

On the other hand, Noël spoke almost in a stammer, with a soft, deep, and hesitant voice that suited both his looks and mannerisms. He sang poorly. He was tall, very lean, and wore a neatly pointed beard. His high forehead was partly divided by a deep widow's peak. His bushy eyebrows turned upward as they nearly met above his classic nose and sad, droopy eyes, giving him an expression of constant pain or sympathy. He was a devout Roman Catholic and might easily have become a priest. Noël had inherited a reasonable fortune from an uncle and spent it not just on his large studio apartment in Paris but also on a charming house on Hyde Street in San Francisco (once lived in by Robert Louis Stevenson). His only real interests were music, the Church, and entertaining.

Noël's salons attracted a marvelously mixed bag to which I would, in the course of the next year or so, sometimes be brought with Mother and Jerry. It was at Noël's that, as an eager, overgrown (now in long trousers) new teenager, I first met Gertrude Stein, Ernest Hemingway, and Louis Bromfield. Since I could chatter fluently, *sans* accent, in French I came to know the famous Alexandre, the reigning star of the Comédie Française, the affected, fascinating Sasha Guitry, and the birdlike Jean Cocteau. I think it was also the place where I first met the friendly Cole Porter and Elsa Maxwell, who was bowling her jolly way through the Europe of the whirling early twenties.

In unaccustomed simplicity, Mother, Dedie, and I had begun living in a small, very inexpensive suite in a small, very inexpensive but respectable *demi-pension* called the Hôtel des Champs Élysées, situated quite near that boulevard on the Rue Balzac, just a few blocks from the Étoile.

Mother was more concerned than I about our new quarters and with rueful sighs would explain periodically that we were in Paris only because life there was infinitely cheaper than in New York, London, or Los Angeles. Even so, she was quietly selling or pawning a few odd bits and pieces that she no longer had need of. She said this sacrifice would help us all to live reasonably well—provided we were careful.

Of course Mother had been born extravagant. Although she made no real effort to compete with the ultra-chic, she was always well dressed and probably even more tastefully groomed than most. Just a bit smartly out of date, she clung to her best furs, dresses, coats, and jewelry for quite some time. Indeed, she kept some to her very last days. This was the earliest I can remember that Mother made martyr-like asides that our declining state was largely due to Dad's niggardly settlement—of about *half a million*—squeezed out by the family lawyer, Cap O'Brien, who had represented my father against her. She called him a "turncoat."

Mother had many fancy friends in Paris, of various nationalities and with various interests. She met most of them away from the hotel in the evening, at restaurants, in private homes, or at the theater. Because she was far from Jim, business, the Sullys, and California, Mother blossomed. She looked prettier than she had in some time and her moods were calmer and brighter.

As for me, I relaxed in direct proportion to the quality of the atmosphere around me. My own needs were few. By certain standards I suppose I ought to have been far more spoiled than in fact I was. I was overindulged by my mother and oversupervised by Dedie. I had hardly noticed the subtle downgrading of our style of living. I lacked only one important thing: the normal life of an American schoolboy, and its corollary, a wide assortment of companions. Paris was fine, broadening, good to look at and listen to, but my clothes gave me away as a foreigner even if my speech didn't. Even worse—to the French—I was seen to be an American, and a very young American at that, which meant I had no money to spend and was therefore hardly worth cultivating.

Then, suddenly, by absolute accident, I came across a familiar minnow in my tub of Parisian bouillabaisse. It was one of my pals from Watch Hill, Teedy Ley, now going to a school in Paris. Through him, in both the Bois de Boulogne and some smaller parks, I met a few other fellow-expatriate American and British boys with whom I could chatter and play more naturally. In time, even a few French boys joined us.

Teedy and I created great fun for ourselves by telling our mothers that we were being well supervised by the *other's* family. Having got away with that, and having heard that older ladies went to tea dances in the Casino near the Rond Point and paid young men to dance with them, Teedy and I, carrying empty pipes and hoping we looked at least seventeen or eighteen, went and sat outside on banquettes waiting for an offer. None came, but we did have fun thinking what we'd do if a lady came along. Then, as the weather improved with the season, we purchased very surreptitiously, copies of *risqué* books like *Lady Chatterley's Lover*. Sitting on a bench under a tree in

the Tuileries, we read aloud to each other, our giggles disguising an unfamiliar tingling sensation that we both enjoyed immensely.

My Paris schooling was haphazard and took no notice of seasons, vacations, or holidays. In fact, it was virtually nonexistent. Mother was dissatis-
fied with the schools the other American and British boys attended, and she
had heard that the standard curriculum for French schools was so difficult
that it often led to juvenile alcoholism and emotional breakdowns. The end
result of all this was a series of individual tutors. On certain mornings, I
would go to a place near the Church de la Madeleine, where a dear old boy
perfected my French grammar, accent, and written composition. Another
time of day was set aside for history, algebra, and the dawning of geometry.
I kept on a plateau with these subjects, but didn't advance during my two or
three hours a week with a helpful Jerry Thayer.

Styles Dickinson, a fashionable American miniaturist, taught me drawing
and painting. He was a strange, fussy, pixie-ish little man, bald except for a
great shock of red hair that fringed his skull. Mother confided to him that
although she wanted me to go to the Sorbonne eventually, we were actually
too broke for a real art school of any kind now. However, she insisted that
my ability to draw and paint was a "naturally advanced talent." Dickinson,
not unimpressed by Mother's connections and my name, took me as a student on a "semi-friendship" (i.e., cut-rate) basis, and a promise from
Mother to find him some more prominent commissions. There was the
added condition, quickly agreed to, that I would arrive at his studio early
before each lesson and help arrange and mix paints and clean his brushes
and palettes. He would then give me various assignments, criticize, correct,
guide, and advise me.

When I indicated an interest in sculpture as well, Dickinson said he had a
Russian émigré friend who was a talented sculptor, though he made a modest living as a caricaturist for various publications. He was professionally
known by the piquant name of Spat (his real name was both unpronounce-
able and unmemorable). Mother found him to be so poor, grubby, and
pitiful that she felt she had to scrape up enough to pay him for three lessons
in sculpture *and* caricaturing a week.

Both artists lived in studios quite near each other on the Île St. Louis,
Quai de Bourbon, an island in the middle of the Seine, not far from Notre
Dame Cathedral. Dickinson's studio reflected relative prosperity, but poor
wretched Spat, with his hawk nose, kinky hair, and cadaverous body, lived
in a small, messy, damp room-and-a-half that looked like a stage set for
Svengali's studio.

Almost every morning for the first month or two, Dedie escorted me on a bus to my various lessons. Finally, after much nagging, this humiliation was dispensed with and I was allowed to hop aboard the back platform of the bus all alone and make my way from one lesson to another. I can still remember one of my favorite bus ads, which read: *Le Sherry de mon chéri est mon Sherry—Mistinguett.* Mistinguett was not only the most popular musical star of the Folies Bergère, with celebrated legs, but she was also known as the lady friend of my tennis friend, Maurice Chevalier. Actually, it was the other way around: Maurice had been helped to stardom by Mistinguette, and so it was more correct to say *he* was *her* "friend." I had been sorry to hear at first that the popular and charming Maurice Chevalier was, in private, nothing of the kind, but rather a stuffy, humorless grouch. Though he was never exactly amusing, peeking out behind his offstage correctness was a shy and very nice man. I didn't mind at all that his special niceness to me was very probably due to his hero-worship of my father (whom he had not met at that time).

I continued my art and other studies for the next few years, except when we left France for England or the States. With Spat's encouragement I eventually managed to enter a small plaster head of a child and a bas-relief of Napoleon in a minor local exhibition. I startled no one, but I did get an honorable mention. Dickinson was complimentary, though he rarely went beyond saying I was "quite promising." At one time, for about two weeks, I was allowed to draw nothing but ears, from every conceivable angle, outside and in. It was all part of a general study of anatomy. Unfortunately, I never did learn to draw ears well at all—or hands or feet, either.

On one memorable day I was thought sufficiently advanced to draw a half-nude female model in the company of two other students. The wretched girl was all goose bumps and shivering with the damp cold that permeated the studio walls. The other students were more experienced and paid no attention, but I was in such a tizzy trying not to show my true excitement that my hand shook worse than the poor model's whole body. When her shivers were noticed, I said I too suffered from the cold. Dickinson was so absorbed in his own work he was impervious to temperature of any kind. But when he ordered the girl to dress and told us to sketch her in her clothes, my own thoughts were very mixed.

A more conventional form of exercise came when Jerry took me along for an occasional doubles tennis match on two or three mornings a week. One day when I'd played better than usual, Maurice Chevalier invited me to see his popular new musical play, *Dédé.* I went back to see it so many times that I was finally able to amuse him by imitating his singing in the "Montmartre" accent that is most nearly the equivalent of a mild Brooklyn or Cockney accent in English.

Another of my tennis-playing thrills was the occasional game with a friend of Maurice's, the great Georges Carpentier, my then boxing idol. He was easy and sophisticated with a warm, friendly manner—quite different from the world's idea of a professional prize-fighter. I had been hearing a lot about Carpentier's forthcoming championship fight with a French-African colonial, Battling Siki, according to the papers a virtually unknown, ignorant, and inexperienced "setup" who had only recently come out of the jungle. Carpentier seemed to be sensitive about such comments, telling us that, on the contrary, he heard that Siki made up in toughness what he lacked in experience, but even so he did very little serious training. My delight can be imagined when the "Charming Champ" gave Jerry and me ringside seats for the fight.

When the great day came the handsome, smiling, jaunty Georges came trotting down the aisle and bounced lightly into the ring, acknowledging the public's ear-cracking acclaim with happy waves. But by the sixth round, Carpentier had become a battered, bleeding, almost unrecognizable pulp of a human. The crowd shockingly turned against him with whistles, boos, and cries for Siki to finish him off for good. This sudden switch of loyalty made a lifelong impression on me. I was never again able to fully enjoy watching two athletes pummel away at each other, competing in an effort to batter the other into senselessness. After the fight, Carpentier disappeared. It was years before I saw him again.

We welcomed the *nouvelle année* of 1923 in the South of France, in Nice. I remember only the fine Southern California-like weather, and the thrill of taking tennis lessons from the great French champion Suzanne Lenglen, who paired me off as a doubles partner with an agile, kindly foreign gent— Count Bernadotte, she said. Long after, I learned he really was King Gustav V of Sweden, on his annual incognito holiday. Our undisguised vacation ended a fortnight later when we took the overnight train back to cold, damp, drizzly Paris.

The Great War had been over for nearly five years and yet almost everyone, except in the chic restaurants, still uncomplainingly ate horsemeat. And dogmeat as well, it was whispered. But I was never fussy about food and have always eaten almost anything. I suppose this was due to Dedie's refusal ever to let me leave the table until I'd eaten everything put in front of me. Mother once boasted I was so strictly trained I would probably eat stewed knitting.

The year that I was thirteen proved to be eventful. Mother had become convinced that in addition to my several teachers of this and that, I should have one regular tutor—preferably American or British. But who? And how to pay for him? Jerry Thayer had the answer. His younger brother, Carlton, had graduated from a college in Michigan the year before with an excellent scholastic and athletic record. He had no job yet and would make an excellent tutor, said Jerry, who guessed that if his living expenses were paid, he wouldn't worry about salary. Carlton was a quiet young fellow of about twenty-two, not quite so good-looking as his brother Jerry. He had not yet changed his name from Hoekstra to Thayer, as Jerry had, so I quickly nicknamed him "Hookie." We hit it off right away. He didn't patronize me or even treat me as a boy of thirteen. My lessons, unpressured and patiently taught, were in mathematics, English, history, and geography. Only math eluded me—and has continued to do so ever since. Hookie was a good companion and joined my friends and me in our ball games in one of the parks. He contributed to my growing up more than might have been predicted.

Hookie had not been in Paris more than a month before he fell for an extraordinarily pretty French girl. I never knew where or how he found her, nor can I for the life of me remember her name. Since neither of them could speak the other's language, Hookie would ask me to walk with them on the afternoons they met so that I could start things off as their interpreter. I enjoyed chattering away with her, and she, in turn, was amused by my glib use of rough Parisian *argot*. Once they had settled on where to go and when, what to eat, and so on, they released me to join my pals and went off by themselves. When it was time for me to be escorted home, they returned. This was much less humiliating than what I used to have to endure with Mother or Dedie. But it was still bad enough. All my friends seemed to come and go more or less as they pleased, whereas I was still on a leash, however loose.

Hookie's girl was about twenty-two or three. As I was within two or three inches of my adult height, I made Hookie promise to tell his girl that I was nearly seventeen. For several weeks I had been unable to dismiss from my most private fantasies the idea that it would be a tremendous thing for me to really kiss, not just a girl like Agnes, but a grown-up very pretty French girl. The thought often disturbed my days and nights. A Machiavellian scheme hatched when Hookie asked me if I would very tactfully ask his girl if she would ever consider accompanying him on a weekend sight-seeing tour of the *Châteaux* on the Loire. I agreed, but told him that it would be easier and less embarrassing for her if I broached the subject when he was not present. Hookie, more naïve than I suspected, went along with this idea.

On an unusually fine, warm day in late March we were deep in the lovely Bois de Boulogne. With heart pounding and hands clamming, I told Hookie to take a stroll in one direction while I walked with the girl in another to present his invitation as discreetly as I could in my best French. She and I strolled deeper and deeper into the thickest part of the woods—the premature spring having brought out some lovely concealing leaves. At last I determined the moment I'd planned had now come for me to speak for myself. How I actually phrased it, or how long it took, I can't remember. All I know is that I did make myself clear enough! The girl had surely sensed that I was unpracticed in kissing—or necking. She giggled sweetly and led me behind a great clump of bushes quite away from the eyes of other wanderers.

And there and then, to my numbed but ecstatic delight, she kissed me! I was in no way prepared for the vigor and enthusiasm with which she went about it. I had never thought of kissing as being such a devouring process. The movies of the day were heavily censored and I didn't remember that either *Lady Chatterley's Lover* or the other books I had studied so keenly had gone into the details I was suddenly learning. Nevertheless, mildly shocked though I was, I enjoyed it thoroughly and tried hard to be an apt and attentive pupil.

The next thing I knew she suggested that I stretch out on the grass beside her—a proposal that needed no urging. And then all sorts of previously unknown sensations whizzed about in what was left of my consciousness. I had, of course, a pretty good idea by then of the conventionally recommended method by which the species is perpetuated. But I was too bewildered to be aggressive and was quite content to, as it were, take lessons. Very strange—and strangely agreeable—things were happening to me about which I had never heard before. What on earth was she doing? It wouldn't have occurred to me to protest, but I never in my life so much as suspected that variety could also be the spice of carnal gamesmanship.

And then I became delightfully dizzy and just plain passed out! When I opened my eyes, I realized the girl was trying to revive me, fanning me with her hanky, gently slapping my face, and asking, *"Est-ce-que cq va, mon chou? Tout va bien? Oh, mon pauvre, joli chou!"*

Suddenly I shakily suggested that we go and find Hookie. The girl was gently understanding and, of course, amused by what was clearly the technical end of my innocence. She even laughed as she wiped her lipstick off my clown face and reapplied her own.

As soon as Hookie and I were alone, I couldn't help but confess my premeditated duplicity. I was enormously relieved when he proved not in the least angry. He actually thought it all a great joke and took it so well that, with his permission, I arranged several more meetings with the girl, alone. Why she liked me, or seemed so keen on her extra-tutorial activities, she never said. All I remember was her dark, straight, and short "Louise Brooks" bobbed hair, and the bright scarlet dresses that she always wore.

Eventually, this part of my education had to be deferred. Mother complained to Hookie that I was obviously studying much too hard, that I was looking tired and pale and there were dark circles under my eyes. She ordered a brief respite from all my studies, to rest, take things easy, and spend more time with my friends. Or go to museums. I don't know if Hookie ever saw the girl again. I know *I* didn't!

One day at a party Mother encountered an old friend of the family, a once popular but now retired New York actor and a former son-in-law of the great impresario David Belasco. His name was William Elliott, he was newly remarried, to a pretty Frenchwoman, and had gone into theatrical management in Europe. Billy Elliott persuaded Mother that he could promote a fine deal for me as an actor with a big movie company in Hollywood. Such a deal would help replace the worrisome burden of having very little money with the happier weight of having quite a lot. He assured us all that my education, such as it was, could be continued by California tutors, in accordance with state law. I think Mother saw at once a way that she could again supervise a career and involve herself in business. And she could oversee the reunion of our spread-out family.

Billy Elliott began negotiations with Jesse Lasky, the partner of Adolph Zukor, director of the Famous Players—Lasky Corporation and Paramount Pictures. They were still angry at the departure of their great stars Mary Pickford and Douglas Fairbanks and their colossal success as independent producer-stars of their own United Artists company. Lasky later admitted that Billy Elliott's proposal appealed to him as a "sort of minor revenge on the senior Fairbanks." As he saw it, Fairbanks senior was a world hero of unequaled popularity who represented young, clean-cut, virtuous American vitality and good humor. He would be bound to be embarrassed to have his overgrown thirteen-year-old son around as an All-American boy with similar athletic agility.

At the time, neither Mother nor I had the least suspicion of an ulterior motive behind Lasky's acceptance of Billy Elliott's proffered deal. Mother jumped at the deal. I ambled unsteadily toward it.

After a couple of trips across the Atlantic and back, the exchange of a number of cables, and some conferences, Elliott made a deal for one trial picture, with options for four more years. The terms were ridiculous, particularly for an untried boy whose only known talents at the time were minor artistic ones and fairly good manners.

My contract called for me to receive a thousand dollars a week for the estimated six weeks' filming, with round-trip tickets to Los Angeles and back and travel and living expenses for me, Mother, Dedie, and the Elliotts.

The announcement of the deal to the press did not set the entertainment world afire. Within certain movie circles there was a fair amount of criticism of Paramount, which, at this distance, I feel was deserved. In fact, the obvious exploitation of a gangling, pimply-faced lad was apparently a boomerang that inspired support for Dad and pity for me: I ventured to tell a journalist that I wanted to change my name to avoid accusations that I was trading on a greater name. But that wish died in its tracks when other reporters elaborated on the idea, saying that if I became, say, Sam Snooks, the public would be bound to comment on what my real name had been, thereby defeating the whole purpose.

Mother was very cross indeed. "With a fine name like that, how *could* you be so disrespectful? You should be proud! After all, it *was* the name you were baptized with . . ." Most important of all, Lasky told Elliott that if I did change my name the deal would be canceled. That did it. The Big Idea died a-borning. However, I made a solemn pledge to myself that somehow I would grow up to be "my own man," that I would make the full name, *plus* the "Junior," as individual and independently recognizable as my father's name was for him. I hadn't an idea how to do this, but that determination remained one of the basic influences on my life from then to now.

While we were still in Paris the high-powered, worldwide resources of the Paramount publicity department, overlooking my own pretensions, went to work on their own. For a couple of days they had me pose for press cameras in a wide assortment of ridiculous shots. Their intention was to suggest to a gullible movie-going public that I had inherited my father's athletic prowess and bursting vigor. I had grown so quickly that even the necessary enlarging and lengthening—by one of Mother's private dressmakers—of my De Pinna and Brooks Brothers suits barely helped. I affected the then collegiate fashion of a flat round porkpie hat, which made me feel even more an elderly teenager. In one silly snap I had to pose on one foot atop a post with my arms flailing out in fearless abandon. The cameras shot from a low angle, helping to make my balancing act look perilous. My efforts to obey the photographers' orders to smile usually resulted in self-conscious mouth-stretching. In another pose, at a local gymnasium, also aimed at suggesting a young apprentice daredevil, I hung like a chimp from a ring with one hand. Again the cameras shrewdly avoided disclosing that, if my hand slipped, the resultant drop would be about two feet.

There were several rounds of interviews which must have inspired as much boredom among the reporters as they caused monosyllabic embarrassment to me. However, in response to a question, I did let slip that I hoped there would not be any girls in my movie, since I was against "all that silly old hugging and kissing stuff—and if you hardly knew them, it was worse!" (I spent many subsequent years disproving those views.) After seeing a picture of the U.S. President looking idiotic in an Indian warbonnet, I realized that even politicians and statesmen were frequently obliged to make asses of themselves in public, merely to attract some attention.

We began packing up, saying good-bye, and preparing to stop en route in London to see friends, plays, and get more publicity. Then, yippee, six days at sea aboard a great, lovely Cunard liner. However, a week or two before leaving there was one great, unexpected (and most sharply remembered) hurdle I had to face: a meeting with my father.

Shortly after their marriage, Dad and Mary had begun to make annual pilgrimages abroad between pictures, combining business with private fun and games. At this particular time, Mary had just made *Rosita.* Dad had the famous London Pavilion theater converted from the production of lavish musicals to a movie theater, shocking many by so doing. He reopened it with appropriate hoopla for his classic film *Robin Hood.* His next project was to be an Arabian Nights fantasy, *The Thief of Bagdad,* destined to be the biggest and most expensive production of his career.

The news of the trips taken by "Mary and Doug," the great mobs that continued to greet them everywhere, their receptions by heads of state and prominent figures in many countries, more than smothered the relatively chintzy news of my upcoming debut as an actor. Just the same, it was inevitable that Dad would be asked what he thought of my entry into motion pictures. "The boy," he said, "would be better off going ahead with school . . . I don't know why he's doing it . . . Yes, I hope to see him and we'll have a talk . . ." Had it been left up to me at that moment, I would gladly have scuttled the whole project. I had had enough "scenes" in my first dozen-plus-one years and wanted no more.

Dad and Mary arrived in Paris from London almost too shortly after Paramount's petty noisemakers had done their job on me. Dad's secretary-companion, Kenneth Davenport, as well as the Fairbanks company's press agent, Benny Ziedman, informed Mother that Dad wished to see me at his hotel. I had not seen him in over a year—and before then for only a few brief self-conscious times at his and Mary's studio (rarely at Pickfair) when we were still in California. In fact, it had been years since I expected to hear from him at all, except for the occasional Christmas or birthday cable. Mother minded his lack of interest in me dreadfully, but although I was sorry, I didn't brood about it. He remained my distantly related hero and I tended to forget dates and such things too. I still do.

I was thus "asked" to meet him at the Crillon and Mother needed no special instinct to predict that I would be given a very strong lecture and be ordered to get out of the contract and proceed with my studies. She was right. But I had been forearmed with respectful rebuttals—and particularly strict side instructions not to so much as hint that our depleted finances were in any way an influential element.

I arrived at the palatial Hôtel Crillon and announced myself to the concierge. I was very nervous and all my poise was threatening to desert me. When the concierge haughtily declined to believe who I was or even announce me, thinking I was some young fan trying to crash the great star's apartments, I almost welcomed the excuse to slink away and blame the gold-braided functionary for not keeping my appointment. But just then one of the Pickford-Fairbanks entourage (invariably quite a sizable one) came by, recognized me, and brought me upstairs to the large "Royal Suite" and the well-guarded "presence."

As I slinkily entered, clutching my porkpie hat, Dad was in the middle of the large living room of the elaborate suite, surrounded by company representatives, some personal staff, and two or three friends. It was what one might have imagined the anterooms of a royal court would look like. When he saw me, he called out, "Hullo, young fella! Come in!"

I mumbled a reply and smiled a twitchy smile.

"This is my son," he announced to the room full of suddenly turned heads. He whacked me good-naturedly on the back and said, "Come on back here! Great view!"

Since it was an unseasonably warm day in spring, we went outside without our coats. I was led through other rooms out onto one of the Crillon balconies overlooking the Place de la Concorde. We stood quite alone together. I remember how enraptured I was by the vast proportion and grace of that historic square and the hundreds of honking cars whirling around the tall Egyptian obelisk centerpiece that marked the site where the guillotine had lopped off so many heads during the excesses of the French Revolution. My own fate was not destined to be quite that catastrophic, but it was momentous enough. The balcony on which my father and I stood was the very same one on which, in another three years, Charles Lindbergh would stand acknowledging the cheers of the world, represented by the crowd below. When that great event did happen, I told everyone, *"That's* the balcony where my father and I had the worst row in my life!"

After a long silence (we were always embarrassed, self-conscious, and undemonstrative in each other's company), he began to say exactly what Mother had said he would say. He added that he had particularly hoped I would go to Harvard, just as he had (quite untrue, as I've noted, but I didn't know it at the time), and after that on to Cambridge in England. For the next several years, I often thought back on that idea and had reason to wish it had worked out. I think I would have liked it. Mother's advance prompting had been so intense that I was shaking inside—invisibly I hoped. It took a bit of time for me to gather the wandering words with which I was to answer his argument. I did remember not to mention our need of money. Mother always maintained that the money Dad had given her (and me) as a settlement was niggardly. It was by now almost gone.

I managed to say that I had not been coerced into a movie job, that I was old for my years (but not that much, I now see!) and knew what I was doing. I added that I would indeed continue my studies, as in fact I would have to under California state law.

As we argued back and forth, I remember he became quite angry and I replied, I'm ashamed to say, more stubbornly—even perhaps rudely—than I ever had before. The reason I behaved badly (for me) was that I was more afraid of Mother's reaction if I lost the day than I was of my father's. I must have felt I was unlikely to see Dad again for some time, but I still had to go on living with Mother.

Most of what we said I no longer remember, except that for many years afterward I had ample and continuing reasons to regret my impertinence. I left under a cloud of solemn, frustrated disapproval—still shaking. I never did see Mary, who remained discreetly out of the way.

I am glad that after a period of some years I was able to express to him, privately and publicly, my regret for having said my piece so bluntly. I was praised for being courageous, but it was less courage than fright and a knowledge that in any case my die had been cast.

Dad apparently didn't want to see me again on that trip. Under the circumstances, that suited me very well. Mother was, of course, livid with him.

6

On arrival in New York, I was told that my first film was to be one of Richard Harding Davis's adventure stories called *The Grand Cross of the Crescent*. It was a yarn about an American high-school boy who somehow gets into and out of a multitude of dangers in Turkey, where he hopes to persuade the sultan that his old schoolmaster deserves a decoration for his definitive history of Turkey.

The director was to be one of my father's former directors, now under contract to Paramount, Joseph Henabery. A surprisingly fine cast from Paramount's "stock company" was assembled, headed by the cigar-chomping, scene-stealing character actor Theodore Roberts (who, the following year, would play Moses in De Mille's first version of *The Ten Commandments)*. Another well-known player, Harry Myers, who had only recently made a personal hit in *A Connecticut Yankee in King Arthur's Court*, joined the cast. And the deep, dark villain of the piece was to be played by Noah Beery, famous half brother of the even more famous Wallace Beery. It must be admitted that Paramount was preparing to do all they could to launch their untrained new star. They planned to give me every advantage of production, cast, story, and director. The rest, they said, would be up to me.

Dad and Mary had returned to America weeks before. They whizzed through New York and on to California where he immediately dived into intensive preparations for his most ambitious film, *The Thief of Bagdad*. I was carefully kept out of his way, and stayed quietly with Mother at the

Algonquin in New York. A few weeks later I went back to giving barely noted bits of interviews and jumping through more publicity hoops.

Eventually we repacked and were taken in style to Grand Central Station. Mother and I boarded the 20th Century Limited for Chicago, where we changed to the Santa Fe Super Chief and the nearly three-day run to Los Angeles. I was welcomed by a troop of Boy Scouts and a Scoutmaster. For all I knew, they could have been movie extras dressed up. The welcome— including a sign or two—was so obviously posed that one of the papers accurately described it as "so much brouhah-ho-hum."

We settled into a house on Franklin Avenue and I was given a really nice welcome to Paramount Studios, a long set of dark green wooden buildings that stretched down Vine Street from Hollywood Boulevard to Sunset. It had expanded on the same site from the barn that Lasky, C. B. De Mille, Bill Farnum, and others had rented and it sat in the midst of what had been called Hollywood Ranch. Hence, the origin of the name "Hollywood," which was then, as now, not even an "official" suburb, but rather a section of one in Greater Los Angeles.

People were extraordinarily kind and friendly. I was as bug-eyed as any movie fan from a small town when one of my favorite actors, a courtly, handsome Virginia gent came up and, as if I hadn't known him from a hundred yards away, said, "Hello! Welcome! I'm Jack Holt!" Then Richard Dix did much the same. Lois Wilson, whom I had put on a pedestal after seeing her in *The Covered Wagon,* walked by and smiled. And the grizzly old Western character star Ernest Torrence, from the same picture, sur- prised me by speaking in a most cultivated Scottish accent—completely at variance with his professionally scrubby looks.

I was surprised as could be when Dad invited me over to his studio and asked if I wanted to join his exercise group, play his game of DOUG, a form of badminton, and, at his publicity man's suggestion, pose for some pictures with him. I don't know to this day how or why he decided to at least look as if he approved, but I suspect he was advised to put the best face he could on the awkward situation. As it turned out, he was in wonderful form, and until my own work started I returned as often as I could, trying to be as agile and expert at the games as I assumed he wanted me to be. (I later learned that he really wanted me to be far, far away, but I didn't know it then.) The pictures of us together are genial and jolly—and very self-con- scious.

My picture had been retitled *Stephen Steps Out.* Shooting began after several bewildering makeup and clothes tests, and I frankly had to admit I hadn't the foggiest notion of what was going on. I know I tried to appear poised and reasonably grown-up and unspoiled, but I went on being very embarrassed by Mother's constant presence. She insisted that because I was a minor, California law made her presence obligatory. Hookie was there too, though that was all right. But he, poor fellow, was obliged to have a California-approved tutor alongside him. *I* had to have a certain number of lessons each day, until, in a few weeks, the summer vacation would be legally in force.

There was quite a lot of action in the silly picture and I was often scared I would be hurt. But everyone was most protective, except for Noah Beery who, as the villain, had carefully rehearsed a fake blow that was supposed to rock me back. When the scene was shot, either he or I misstepped, threw off the timing, and his blow landed solidly. I went down for a count of certainly five or six. Although I put on an "Oh, it's nothing" act, everyone, including Beery, was in a dither. Happily Mother was away on one of her many-dozen trips to "the Ladies' " and missed seeing her darling hit the deck.

Since I had no real need to do much acting apart from looking serious, then happy, then defiant and brave, and then the same all over again in a different sequence, and to look or move in a variety of directions, everyone around me acted and grimaced for all they were worth. (Movies were still silent, of course.) My relative inactivity made me look far more expert than I could possibly have been. The much-beloved character Theodore Roberts (whom I suspected of being livid at having to "support" a young, inexperienced pawn of the producers) kept up his famous barrage of cigar smoke in every scene, which made paying attention to anyone else an effort. Harry Myers, a friendly and gifted "old hand" advised me to counter such tricks by taking out my handkerchief and refolding it and looking straight out at the camera. The director, Joe Henabery, was so busy keeping his eye on other things that he missed my sly counter-trick until the next day when he ran the rushes (or dailies) in the projection room. By then it was too late and too expensive to go back and do the scene again. After that, he kept a closer watch on me—*and* "Daddy" Roberts. I was learning—slowly but surely. Then they were only tricks, but in the course of time and circumstance, such techniques would prove handy.

The picture finished shooting and was launched on an undeserving public. It really wasn't all that bad, but it was light-years away from what the publicity suggested. Still, I was hardly aware of its mediocrity, and through much of the autumn I was sent about making appearances at one place or another. The critics were surprisingly tolerant of me but blamed Paramount for their disproportionate exploitation. Finally the tour was over, and we were allowed to stay put in New York where we caught up with friends and the latest plays.

Then, in December 1923, indeed, on the ninth, my birthday, we boarded the 20th Century once more for Chicago, the first leg of another trip to Los Angeles. The 20th Century Limited was certainly the best, fastest, and most luxurious train in the America of that era. It whizzed nightly from New York to Chicago and its three sections were usually packed with affluent folk from all over the world. Every departure, going west or east, always carried at least one smiling, flower-clutching celebrity, surrounded by clumps of reporters and photographers with their early explosive flashbulbs. It was very exciting to be the object of all that exaggerated attention.

Before leaving the East Coast my Aunt Gladys and Uncle Henry gave me a snazzy raccoon overcoat, the older boys' fashion of the day. I thought I looked pretty hot stuff. A godparent gave me a Chow dog which I promptly named Stevie, after my film.

Loaded down with too much luggage (Mother's habit), plus Stevie in a box in the baggage car forward, we settled into a Pullman drawing room on the second of the three sections. There was no way I could take all the attention seriously. Too many people felt it their duty to warn me, with a sympathetic slap on the back, that I could never equal either my father's or my grandfather Sully's eminence.

After dinner in the dining car, I climbed, fairly tired but with spirits still on a medium-high cloud, into my upper bunk, and, with Mother below, and the agreeable monotony of the train's wheels clickety-clacking outside, I was as out as the lights by ten o'clock.

About two in the morning there was a tremendous bump, a crash of steel, and a screeching stop that awakened everyone. Mother made a frightened cry. I hopped down from my bunk, threw my jacket on over my pajamas and just managed to open the jammed door, while Mother yelled at me to come back. I ignored her and groped my way out into the dark corridor and then to the ground outside. Most but not all of the train's lights appeared to have gone out and I heard women screaming and men yelling into the dark at varying distances from where I stood, not even noticing the chill drizzle that was coming down. Here and there flashlights began to search the wet night and orders were barked out above the growing cacophony of panic.

I began to see more lights here and there, and finally someone answered my repeated question "What happened?"

"Third section crashed into us . . ." "Lots of people hurt down there . . ." I had no idea where "down there" was, but I stumbled over rocks and railroad ties, past rushing, stumbling, yelling, or just wandering people, back past our own Pullman car, which was still standing upright on the tracks and, as far as could be seen, luckily intact. However, the very next car behind us was severely damaged, half on its side and off the tracks. It was now clear that it, plus the last two cars of the train, had been partly telescoped and badly twisted. We had been in the fourth car from the end.

I began to see a bit better. Several people were staggering about, with blood streaming, looking for help or missing friends. I tripped over some who were badly hurt and one shockingly dead body. It was my first sight of death, twisted, bloody, and awful. I scrambled around for handkerchiefs, towels, torn sheets, anything that could serve to bind up bad cuts, and tried, as did others, to tie up the most badly hurt people I could find. I fear I didn't remember much of my Scouts' First Aid training but I did remember how to make a couple of rough tourniquets and some elementary bandages. It was all too frantic, wet, cold, and scrambled for emotions to surface. Ambulances arrived from somewhere, and those of us from the train went on doing what we could to help carry the worst cases to them. It was still drizzling a bit when dawn came, but by that time the wrecked cars had been detached and those of us still outside were ordered back aboard the rest of the train. It then proceeded to limp slowly on to Chicago, where we arrived in the very late afternoon. Mother had been frantic, calling out for "her baby" until someone assured her that I was well, warm, and inside another car. Fortunately, she then quieted down.

There were hordes of reporters at the Chicago station to meet us, asking questions of the passengers and crew, and noting statistics. Of course no one knew or cared who I was or what I was doing on board. I remember the first reports were that over a dozen people had been killed or seriously injured, but later papers said perhaps less than half a dozen were killed but about twenty seriously injured.

When the Big Story of the wreck was followed by further details, the Paramount flacks decided to capitalize on it and gave out early revolting stories that their new star's first thought was of his mother and dog! I denied this vigorously, although I suspect Mother rather liked the story and hinted it was true. A day later, however, one of the more seriously injured passengers, who turned out to be a prominent member of the Wrigley family of Chicago, gave an interview from his hospital bed about the wreck. He said that "among the unsung lifesavers" was a young teenager who had been the busiest and most helpful of anyone—"a real young hero," he added. It turned out, to his surprise (and mine as well), that it was "young Doug Fairbanks." Although I was embarrassed by the wildly overstated credit of finding a large handkerchief bandage for him, we exchanged letters and cards for some years.

Stephen Steps Out deserves no more space here. Not long after we'd un-packed in Hollywood, Billy Elliott grimly told Mother that Jesse Lasky had decided not to exercise the option for my further "services." In short, I was fired. Mother was indignant and bewildered. I don't know what I was. I had been a friend of young Jesse Lasky, Jr., for some time and had hardly bothered to think of our companionship as being in any way involved with his father's letting me go.

Whenever we were in Hollywood, I hinted discreetly to my Uncle Bob that I would like to unobtrusively visit Dad's studio now and then to watch the spectacular filming of *The Thief of Bagdad.* Once in a while it worked. I would go, outwardly shy but inwardly eager, increasingly absorbed in the magic of movie making, particularly on such a large, serious scale. I wanted to watch my father's dedication to every phase of his job as writer, pro-ducer, and star. I also loved being asked to join the group that went to his gym. Over the entrance hung a sign signifying that this was the "Basilica Linea Abdominalis" (Temple Dedicated to the Waistline). Inside there were rings and bars and mats and a badminton (DOUG) court for games and exercise. The game of DOUG that my father invented was based on bad-minton but used heavier shuttlecocks and racquets and a larger court. It enjoyed a wide but brief popularity in the twenties.

After the general workout everyone repaired to the large Turkish bath complex at the end of the day. The routine was steam, dry heat room, ice-cold plunge, masseur, and then tomato sandwiches and glasses of Château d'Yquem for everyone except Dad, who never drank, and me, who didn't dare. Occasionally, his trainer Chuck Lewis, an ex-Olympic Decathlon com-petitor, would slip me a glass on the sly. Conversation of great variety filled the next hour—some serious but most witty and amusing. If Chaplin or Barrymore was present, it would be hilariously bawdy. Dad, who rarely told dirty jokes himself—and strictly forbade them in front of the ladies—was nevertheless a wonderful, coughing, weeping, guffawing audience for other people's raunchy stories.

Though I watched the filming of *Bagdad* as often as I could, most of my time was spent in studies. I progressed without much trouble in those that would have corresponded to a freshman high-school year, particularly since my professional life had seemingly died in its infancy. Mother and grand-parents undoubtedly worried, but I was still too young to share their con-cern. Then suddenly one day Billy Elliott announced with pride that he had a deal for me. Jesse Lasky had finally given in to Elliott's pleading and agreed to give me another chance. Mother told friends, "Of course it was only a matter of time. *Now* they'll see . . ."

There were, though, some minor catches to the deal that were to be expected. No kind of advertising, star or feature billing would be guaranteed, and I was to play any part in whatever picture I was assigned. Another stipulation was quite disappointing to my family: my former salary of a thousand dollars a week was to be reduced to something like two hundred a week, payable for only forty weeks a year. Paramount (Lasky) would have options to renew my contract each year for the next four after that. Furthermore, like all other contract players, I was forbidden to work for anyone else during the twelve-week lay-off period unless "farmed out," i.e., ordered to work by the company. This was, and remained for many years, common practice in Hollywood. There were to be no more expense accounts, except when on location. California law, of course, obliged the company to pay for my tutor—*not* Hookie (he was private and didn't count) but a state-appointed one, and then only when I was in a picture and actually shooting. The worst catch was that my new contract was not to begin until the late midsummer of 1924. As usual, Mother, Bill Elliott, Uncle Henry, and some good friends (plus, I later heard, a couple of pawnbrokers) helped see us through.

Mother had by now divorced Jim Evans (he had slipped out of my life almost unnoticed). It was decided we should return once again to Europe, where failure could be more cheaply disguised.

This transatlantic trip was particularly memorable for me because the 1924 American Olympic team was also on board our ship on its way to the Olympic Games in Paris. As soon as possible I ingratiated myself with my favorite athletes: Charlie Paddock from USC, "the World's Fastest Human" and world record holder of the 100-yard and 100-meter dash, and his pal and rival, Loren Murchison, co-holder of the 220-yard record.

Dad and Mary had also returned to Paris for the Games and were at the Crillon, as usual. He was very surprised when I rang up and asked if I could see him. One reason for my boldness was that my new friends on the team had made me the unofficial U.S. team mascot and had given me one of the navy blue jackets with the U.S. Olympic shield over the breast pocket as well as a straw boater—the recognizable team uniform. I couldn't wait to show it off to my father and perhaps win a hint of approval. (Mother took my honorary position for granted. It never occurred to her that these gestures were actually ploys for an introduction to my father.) I must say he did seem pleased, and impressed. So much so, in fact, that when his own representatives failed to acquire extra tickets for the big day of the finals he asked me for help. I modestly murmured my willingness, knowing damned well that I could get them from a member of the team—but for a price. I succeeded all right, and when he laughingly boasted that it was I who arranged this *("some* way—I don't know how!"), I puffed up with pride.

During the training period, some of the athletes mingled with others from different countries, particularly the British and the Americans because there was no language barrier. Tagging along, I was therefore able to meet the British sprint champion from Cambridge, Harold Abrahams, as well as the popular world champion hurdler, Lord Burghley (later to succeed to the Earldom of Essex—and become hopelessly crippled with arthritis).

Before the sprint finals, the bets were heavily in favor of Charlie Paddock to win the 100-meter dash easily, with Murchison second and perhaps Abrahams third. As it turned out, Abrahams created a fantastic upset by beating both the great Paddock *and* Murchison to set a new world and Olympic record. Nearly sixty years later the story of that race became the marvelous award-winning movie *Chariots of Fire*. Having seen the real race, I got a special thrill from the movie that so faithfully reproduced the looks and spirit of those times and that day. Of course, no one not closely involved had an inkling of the drama behind the race. All we knew was that "our" Charlie Paddock, the unbeatable, *was* beaten. He also lost the 200 meters to Murchison (Abrahams didn't run in that race). Although Charlie seemed a good loser, in private he was deeply bewildered by his defeat.

Before the studio assigned me anything when we returned to California, I enjoyed visiting other picture units' sets, trying unsuccessfully to persuade various Paramount directors to give me a chance. The most important of them was C. B. De Mille. He had just released a huge production of *The Ten Commandments* (which he would remake many years later). Now he was planning to make another biblical picture, *The Prodigal Son*. The title role was the most sought-after by all the very young actors of the day. I shamelessly capitalized on my kindergarten and early school friendship with Cecilia De Mille, the "old man's" daughter, and his nieces, Agnes and Margaret De Mille, daughters of C.B.'s more serious but less famous brother, William C. De Mille. Mother was a good friend of both the De Mille wives. My new pushiness did get me a screen test. However, it was very poor—my extreme youth and lack of technique were pitiably obvious. William "Buster" Collier, Jr., an older and more experienced actor, quite rightly got the part.

Another important picture had just started. It was *Peter Pan,* directed by a clever caricature of a wildly temperamental movie director, Herbert Brennon. After exhaustive tests, Betty Bronson, a pretty and gifted girl in her middle teens, was given this famous role. The part of Wendy went to Mary Brian, a sweet, equally pretty younger girl from Texas. I fell for Betty! It was my first intensely juvenile, deep-sighs-and-bad-sonnets love. It was not fully requited. She only flirted with me. My rival was a fellow in his twenties, a newspaperman who was to become one of New York's most respected theater critics, Richard Watts, Jr. (His architect father designed the George Washington Bridge.) In any event, I was so smitten with Betty, I could think of little else, except when I could call on her, even though her protective mother was always just in the next room.

My reduced salary had at last begun, but it was only after some tedious weeks of walk-on assignments that I was given a movie role in some melodramatic nonsense called *The Air Mail.* In those days the U.S. air mail was a very new sign of progress. In 1924–25 the mail was flown in two-seater biplanes and, although they never flew at night, letters sent from one coast to the other took only an amazing three days to deliver instead of six. (Planes today can make the trip in about five hours, yet actual delivery often takes the same six days!)

The stars of my picture were Warner Baxter and Billie Dove. The director was Miss Dove's handsome but very tough husband, Irvin Willat. In the mercifully forgotten plot, the young people were to be Mary (Wendy) Brian and me. Sweet, pretty Mary was made up with a plethora of phony freckles, long braids down her back, and one front tooth blacked out. I just had long grubby hair and wore old clothes. Our location was the outskirts of the then small desert town of Reno, Nevada. The actual shooting took place either in or around a local excuse for an airfield or in Ryolite, a Nevada ghost town. It was one of many small communities that had flourished during the great gold rush but was now totally deserted—and well looted by tourists.

Mother and Hookie were obliged by law—and Mother's insistence—to be with me. I chafed under this unnecessary reminder of my fourteen-year-old minority. I certainly thought I looked, felt, and behaved older. Mary, another minor, was also accompanied by her mother. But she was a girl, so that was different.

There was one bit of the script that I kept from Mother. It called for me to make a parachute jump from the type of plane then used to fly the mail while I clutched a precious sack of letters in my arms. I was determined to do the jump myself and was secretly reassured and emboldened by both the pilot and the director. All I had to do, they said, was to jump when told, count to ten, and pull a ring on my straps—the ripcord—at which point my chute "would open up real wide and safe-like," allowing me to float grace-fully down to the desert some four thousand feet below where the film crew would pick me up.

All started well—very matter-of-factly. Since no one seemed at all im-pressed by my volunteering to jump myself, I decided the backslapping would come later. So off I went, while Mother and Hookie, ignorant of my duties for the day, remained in our Reno hotel (it was cold and windy and there were not enough cars for everyone to join the crew at work). The plane was made ready. A camera was secured to the side of the pilot's cockpit. The aim, focus, and aperture were adjusted and, since there was no room for a real cameraman, the pilot was instructed to keep the plane on an even flight by clamping the joystick tightly between his knees while he simultaneously hand-cranked the camera at the correct speed. I was given more last-minute advice, and off we went. The higher we climbed, the more frightened I became, but it was too late to turn back. When we reached what I assumed was the right altitude, I looked back at the pilot, well protected from the wind by his helmet and goggles. He signaled me to go ahead and jump. I had no helmet or anything around my head and wore only the old dirty suit that was my costume. I was, however, allowed to wear blackened tennis shoes so I wouldn't slip on the wing. Gulping down my fear for the moment, I crawled out, clinging to the struts on the port-side wing. I began to wonder why on earth—an apt phrase—I had ever been so determined to show my mettle. After an age of inch-by-inch creeping and strut-by-strut grasping, I finally got to the tip of the wing from which I was to jump. The pilot began to crank the camera and waved at me to go ahead.

I looked down—*far* down—*way* down. I knew he wouldn't flip me off as that would spoil the shot. But I stalled and stalled. And reconsidered. And got more and more frightened. Both my arms clung to that last strut and to the stuffed old mailbag. In my mind's eye my hand was ready to grasp and pull my parachute ring. I reviewed my instructions: "Jump! Count ten! Pull!" That was it. But I just couldn't let go. Then, suddenly, the fourteen-and-a-half-year-old boy inside me rose to the surface and, damn it, I began to cry. Ashamed of my fear but incapable of conquering it, I crawled back along the wing and into my seat. We turned around, descended, and landed. Willat, the director, met me in silence, except for a terse word to an assistant about all that time having been wasted. The "double," who had originally been engaged for the jump got into my suit; the cameraman put a different, longer range lens on the camera, and again the plane took off. In a few minutes, the chute with the double attached came safely down. Then the plane landed and all was well.

I was so ashamed and angry with myself I wanted simultaneously to hide and to smash something. I was also embarrassed because, except for Warner Baxter and Mary, who were kind, no one gave me an understanding word or gesture and I felt worse about my cowardice every moment. When Mother heard about the event, she exploded with rage: "How *dare* the director, the production manager, the producer—*anyone*—have the *stupidity* to send a fourteen-year-old up in a plane and *order* him to jump when . . ." and on, and on. The bosses said that I had insisted on trying it, that there was really no risk, and that a double had been standing by. I then intervened and said that I had at first deceived the director, who thought it was the double in the plane, but when he learned it was me he signaled the plane to return. Then *I* got hell.

So much for *The Air Mail.*

Although no contractual clauses allowed for it and there were no strong unions to stop it, to keep busy and to learn, I would sometimes volunteer or be asked to help electricians in handling the Cooper-Hewitt or Klieg lights or changing the carbons on the big arc lights. I also occasionally lent an eager hand to a propman. I rarely told Mother or anyone about these side-line jobs as I feared I would be told to stop, and I was not only learning but really enjoying it.

With the lack of any truly memorable assignments, I turned briefly to music. As my cousin Flobe was progressing well on her piano, I hoped to catch up by practicing on the old one left by the owner of our house. At my request Mother rented a banjo, a saxophone, and a xylophone, all for no better reason than I said I wanted to learn each one of them. On my fif-teenth birthday I was also given a fine secondhand set of drums on which I reprised all the military banging I'd learned in the Knickerbocker Greys. Unfortunately, within a short time I found I could play almost any instru-ment I tried reasonably well. My overconfidence resulted in my conclusion that I needn't take lessons any longer. Thus I was unable to play anything more than halfway through on the piano. This absence of an ability to apply the seat of my trousers to the seat of a chair (or piano stool) is now a source of much personal regret.

When eventually I was assigned a small but "decent" (the studio's word) juvenile part, I welcomed it for more than professional reasons. It was a Western, to be made on location in Arizona, called *Wild Horse Mesa,* adapted from a book by Zane Grey. Once again I supported the leading lady, Billie Dove. One of my favorites, "Gentleman Jack" Holt, was to play opposite her. My part was Miss Dove's kid brother, whom the author arranged to involve in a "sweet young romance" with Mary Brian again, this time looking her own pretty self. As before, Mother had to accompany me.

I've quite forgotten the plot (undoubtedly a blessing), but I recall almost every detail of the adventure itself. It was, for me, all very exciting. And romantic. I had done quite a bit of riding of all kinds over the past years. Just the year before, I'd organized a Boy's Rodeo, with myself as the star, of course! One of Dad's studio cowboy-wranglers gave me the "permanent loan" of a fine white pony and I asked all my cousins and friends to come and watch. We did some tame calf-roping and "bull-dogging" (how we did that with no horns to grab, I don't know—but that's what our program said). Then with the help of a couple of wranglers I got on a comparatively mild, tired old bucking horse. Within a couple of mortifying seconds I was up, up, and way *down!* I staggered to my feet and—bang!—the damned old horse kicked me, high up in the right inner thigh. Had the kick been about two inches higher, I would have had cause for a lifetime of self-pity. The mark of the hoof remained for years afterward. Luckily, once I got out of the cast and away from crutches, there was no real damage at all. In short, I had been tested in my cowboy skills and was ready for *Wild Horse Mesa.*

I soon learned that many of the Old West's working cowboys, as opposed to decorative or tourist-trap cowboys, were actually just illiterate, knavish roughnecks of limited ability, and that too many of the Indians had become flabby, drunken, and diseased as a result of the abuse and the exploitation by their white conquerors. Since my fifteenth year, I have felt strongly about the American Indians, the only people whose ancient roots *are* American, and our delayed acceptance of them as equal Americans. In a sort of inverse romanticism I have taken every opportunity to champion them against our more bigoted fellow citizens.

These ideas didn't occur to me on the late afternoon that I experienced, for the first time, the thrill of seeing, a few miles from Arizona's Painted Desert, about five young Navajo braves prepare to race just for their own fun. They stripped down to their breechclouts and unwrapped the bindings of their long black hair so that it fell down their backs nearly to their waists. That done, they jumped on the bare backs of their newly "broke" wild horses, guiding them only by their knees, shifting their weight and pulling and tugging on their manes. With the lowering sun, the Arizona desert and mesas exchanged their colorings of tan and red for shades of lavender and purple. Well away from the rest of us, the young bucks began their race. They streaked across their desert like windstorms, their trim brown bodies glistening and their long hair trailing high behind. Now *that* was a romantic sight I'll never forget. Perhaps I invested it with something special of my own. Perhaps not. But soon after that I became a collector of books about the Old West and of prints of pictures by Remington, Russell, and others.

These Indians were shrewd and had learned well the white man's canny lessons in bargaining and cheating. The Zane Grey script called for thousands of wild horses, but though the cowboys knew we were in the area where there were great herds of them, descendants of those brought over by the Spanish conquistadors, they searched for days in canyons, mesas, gulches, open desert, and plains and could locate only a few hundred. Most of those small, swift, shaggy horses had never seen a human being—but vast herds of them were known to wander all over the area. *Where* were they?

After days of production inactivity the studio production manager weakened and agreed to meet the price the Indians wanted. Then, only two or three days later, literally thousands of wild horses were driven from somewhere into the canyons and the other protected areas where we were working. It was a wild and beautiful sight. The wranglers and Indians controlled the herd day and night by softly singing and whistling and otherwise keeping them quiet, preventing a stampede, yet allowing them just enough grass or scrub to eat and a trickle of river to drink.

Zane Grey himself visited our location. He was then probably the most widely read author of books about an old West that never existed, at least never as nobly or as honestly as his books suggested. I felt pretty hot stuff when Mr. Grey and I had our picture taken together.

My part in this Western was innocuous, but it did add a bit to my enlarging trove of movie experience. When I wasn't making faces, riding, or doing something inane before the camera (in daytime temperatures of over 100° F. and night readings of 50°), I willingly doubled up as an assistant to the second cameraman.

Every silent movie had two cameramen. The first negative film was shot for the United States only, and the second "neg" was for Europe and the rest of the world. I also sometimes assisted the second unit cameraman—a chap charged with photographing long-range action shots of running horses, runaways, and battles. I carried the heavy camera cases over the soft sand, up the rocks, and over the hills, emptied and reloaded the heavy boxes of film, set the focus and aperture as instructed, and learned the tricky technique necessary to turn a silent movie camera crank steadily at all the different speeds that might be required.

Dad's next film, *Don Q, Son of Zorro,* was to be a sequel to his first great costume classic, *The Mark of Zorro.* As usual, the story was largely his own invention, augmented by contributions from friends and associates. The splendid Scottish actor Donald Crisp not only played the villain but also directed the picture. The leading lady was the fabulous Mary Astor. (I was destined to work with her myself about thirteen years later in *The Prisoner of Zenda.*)

One of the principal gimmicks of this Zorro sequel was the expert cracking of a giant Australian bullwhip. In order to learn how to do tricks with the monster lash, Dad sent for the famous Australian athlete and bullwhip expert Snowy Baker. It didn't take long before Dad was able to whirl the long blacksnake, make it crack like a pistol shot, and then snap a cigarette out of a brave and steady mouth fifteen or more feet away.

At the first opportunity, I decided to take a lesson myself. With my usual penchant for wanting to move things along too quickly, I began by cracking the great whip pretty well right away. A few days later I was much too cocky. I mistimed the pullback after the crack and damned near put my right eye out. I was rushed to a hospital, bleeding and in pain. But after being bandaged, I felt temporarily heroic. Later, Dad gave me *and* Snowy Baker hell for trying the trick so soon. Mother, as might be guessed, went puce with anger at Dad's lack of protection. I had to wear a black patch over my eye for two weeks—one week on doctor's orders and another because it made me feel dashing.

Toward the end of my contractual year, in September 1925, I was informed that my option was again being dropped. Bill Elliott gave up, sadly but kindly, and moved back to Paris with his wife. Mother got me an agent and I soon got a few jobs making "quickies" at a small increase in salary. The trouble was that these were always with second-rate companies—making B pictures in small studios, mostly situated quite near each other. These studios and their product had such an inferior status in the motion picture industry that their general location was known as Poverty Row. It was considered professionally ill-advised and unfortunate for anyone with serious ambitions to admit to having worked there. Very few directors, writers, or actors counted these films among their recorded credits for fear that such professional slumming would prevent their getting a really good job at one of the majors. During the middle twenties the majors were Paramount, Metro-Goldwyn-Mayer, Samuel Goldwyn, and First National. But at this time I had no choice. I went as directed.

The major companies' silent features took from four to eight weeks to shoot. The specials, in particular those for United Artists, might take anywhere from ten weeks to a year. But along Poverty Row, pictures were shot in about two weeks at most; sometimes we worked ten to twelve hours a day, and six days—occasionally seven—a week.

I still jumped at the few chances I had to visit Dad's studio. A cross
section of Dad's guests continued to be fascinating. My own favorite was
Chaplin. Charlie frequently let me visit his studio and I was always intrigued by the time he took over every scene. Since there was no tape then,
he took days and days over one small scene and waited a day after each to
see the results—considering them rehearsals. His method of directing others, male and female, was to play their parts for them first and hope they
could imitate his performance. He was infinitely patient, and even though he
paid his staff and crew less than almost anyone else would have, he kept
them on salary practically all year round and they didn't dream of working
for anyone else.

Charlie came around to Dad's office for the ritual steam bath at about
half past five or six almost daily, along with the others. He rarely failed to
keep everyone convulsed with his imitations and brilliant, often vulgar
mime stories. Jack Barrymore, still my personal hero, came less frequently.
When he did, he was his usual bawdy and hilarious self. He rarely
"steamed" or, indeed, bathed; he said he was practicing a form of self-denial
that had become a lifelong habit—like drinking! The rest of the company
was mixed and included captains of industry, eminent statesmen, artists,
society dandies, and the nobility of many nations.

Once when Dad's old friend Frank Case arrived in Los Angeles he went
straight from the railroad station to the studio. "Boss is in the steam, sir!"
said Chuck Lewis.

Frank disrobed and groped his way into the large steam room but
couldn't find my father in the thick, hot fog. "Doug!" he called. "It's me!
Frank Case! Just got in from New York!"

My father felt his way with a bit more assurance toward Frank's voice
and said, "Frank, come over here!" He led Frank over to where he could
barely discern a small, dark figure leaning back in a canvas chair. "Sir," said
my father, "may I present my old friend Frank Case? Frank, this is the King
of Thailand."

Even Frank's famous poise deserted him. The man in the chair *was* King
Prajadhipok of Thailand. Frank's confusion defied description. For years, he
admitted that he could not think how one was expected to acknowledge a
reigning monarch, stark naked. The steam and Dad's giggles hid Frank's
embarrassment.

The gap between my father and me was slowly closing. Stepmother Mary
had always been my friend and intermediary. She and my uncle Bob worked
patiently on Dad's various complexes, one of which was me. Most children

of broken families are torn between the parents. I was enormously fortunate in that each of my parents, whenever I was present, spoke of the other in warm and admiring terms. Mother was very occasionally critical of my father, but usually she reminded me that he was a fine man. She said, "Your father has faults like everyone but he was never unkind. I should have been his sister, not his wife." Or, "Mary is a great and tender woman and neither could help falling in love. She has always loved and been kind to you, so you must always be sweet and love her as well."

7

My sixteenth birthday brought a great surprise. At Uncle Bob's suggestion, Dad gave me my first car. It was a Chrysler roadster, with a convertible top and a rumble seat. It might not have been brand-new, but I loved it anyway. Mother, quite rightly I suppose, forbade my driving alone in it for many months. I disobeyed whenever I could get away with it.

There was a small piece of beach property that Dad and Mary owned near Laguna, a two-hour drive south of Beverly Hills. It was an isolated quarter-mile crescent of sand lying at the foot of a small bluff, with rocky promontories guarding each end against intruders. In the middle, as far back from the high tide mark as possible, at the foot of the rise to the meadow above, a line of eight or ten large, square tents had been erected. They were fairly luxurious. Each had finely carpentered wooden floors, two reasonably comfortable small cots, a chair, a chest of drawers, a tiny bed table, a rack for clothes, and one reading light. One was a large kitchen tent, complete with a resident cook borrowed from the studio, Mrs. Bock. Connected to the kitchen was the dining tent. The whole lot was impeccably served by two or three of the Pickfair staff who lived in the village a few miles away. It was a marvelous setup. Dad and Mary used it as a place for long weekends with a constant parade of distinguished guests. The grander the guests, the more they enjoyed a weekend of what they imagined was roughing it. I could hardly have been comfortable in this company, so I never expected to be invited. Still, I longed at least to see the place, but preferably when everyone was away.

My chance came when Dad finished *Don Q. Son of Zorro* and he and Mary took off for the Orient. Uncle Bob continued as my constant ally. In Dad's absence he approved my going to the Laguna camp for a couple of weeks. Furthermore, I could take four or five chums along with me— Freddy Anderson, Bob Gillette, Phil Holmes, Cable Miles, and Hookie. Because none except Cabe Miles had much money, we agreed we'd all chip in equally for Mrs. Bock and for our food. It was my first taste of real freedom from a sweet but suffocating family, unrewarding work and studies. I had never been on a fishing or camping trip before, not even with the Boy Scouts. I reveled in every moment.

We were up at the crack each morning, competing in jumping, running, and swimming races and, thanks to Phil's advance planning, shot-putting and throwing the discus and javelin. We were in and out of the water all day, soon brown as nuts and more fit than ever. At night, we piled into one of two old jalopies and drove into the then little village of Laguna. Before each evening's fun could begin, our group had to wait while I went through the mortifying apron-string business of phoning home to assure Mother of my continued well-being. (Actually, it was good training for other situations later in life when I managed to keep family boats from rocking by such glib reassurance.) After the nightly ceremony on the only town telephone (with an operator always present), we'd all go to a movie or a local dance hall, and . . . well, that's all *I* did anyway. Others drank bootleg booze or hair tonic (it was still Prohibition). Others, like me, just had soft drinks. Freddy, who was working hard at becoming an alcoholic, could and did drink shoe polish, sterno liquid, or shaving lotion, yet never appeared drunk.

We managed two separate trips to Laguna that year (Dad was abroad for months.) On the second one, Freddy brought his girlfriend, Polly. Having no girls at all at camp was the only rule on which Uncle Bob had insisted. But I was so excited by the idea of such forbidden fruit that even though she was Freddy's girl we decided not to tell anyone. In any case, Polly could only stay with us for two or three days and would then take a bus back to Los Angeles. It would be easy to hide her from Mrs. Bock at mealtimes.

As luck and connivance would have it, Polly sat in the back seat of Cabe's car, between Hookie and me, on one of our evening trips to Laguna. Freddy was in front, feeling quite swizzily happy with life and offering his bottle of gin around. Everyone took turns. I pretended to gulp, but really took only a few sips. I was not being prudish or following my father's teetotaling example. I really didn't like the stuff. The others were soon tight as hoot owls and very jolly. Freddy called over his shoulder to Polly in the back, "Go on, Pol! Give Doug and Hookie a kiss! Go *on!* Be a sport!"

No one, I daresay, ever seriously called Polly a poor sport and meant it. However tightly squashed the three of us were in the back seat, she nevertheless applied herself to carrying out Freddy's suggestion with surprising (to me at least) enthusiasm. Apparently she considered conversation redundant and, determined to play no favorites, shared her aggressive attentions equally, shifting from me to Hookie and back again. I couldn't help but recall my most recent erotic experience a couple of years before in Paris. Only now I was less likely to pass out. In any case, if Freddy didn't mind, neither did we!

I felt wild, wicked, and sophisticated. And in the unthinking way of most young male animals, I was relieved to learn that she could, after all, stay only one whole day and one more night! She was a good, happy, amoral sort of roughneck—nothing delicate or ladylike about her—but she *was* a good sport and loved her visit. Freddy acted as if he'd contributed a great gift to the camp. I suppose he had.

I was squeezed into one more program picture at Parmount called *Padlocked.* And that was it. After my "release from my contract"—the euphemism for being sacked—I did two or three minor, poorly paid jobs. One was a juvenile lead at the then small, cheap Warner Brothers studio in a shamefully corny sob story, *Broken Hearts of Hollywood.*

Then, out of the blue, I had a call for an interview with Samuel Goldwyn. Even then, his heavily Polish-accented English and inability to speak as rapidly as his brain worked made him the subject of many jokes—some true, some apocryphal. Professionally, Sam was a hard but good taskmaster. At this time he was planning to make a film of a then best-selling novel by Olive Higgins Prouty called *Stella Dallas.* He had already assembled a fine all-star cast headed by the popular matinee idol Ronald Colman. Also in the cast were lovely Alice Joyce, Jean Hersholt, and Belle Bennett as Stella. The ingenue (Stella's daughter) was Lois Moran, a young wisp of a girl. Goldwyn said I was in the running and would be tested for the young society fellow the girl finally marries.

After considerable nervousness on my part (and Mother's—she was anxious to get her better jewelry out of hock) we learned with great relief that I had the role! I was then at the end of my sixteenth year—the right age for most of the film—except for the very last scene when Stella stands outside a window in the rain, forlorn and forgotten, watching her little girl marry the rich, high-society boy. When we got to the point of shooting it, Goldwyn and the director, the very special Henry King, decided that tall and athletic though I was, I looked far too young to marry. For that last scene only, I was ordered to grow a mustache. After a few days I had to confess the obvious: I couldn't! The only solution was, clearly, to have a fake mustache stuck on with special makeup glue.

I withstood the teasing well enough. Of more importance, under King's often impatient direction, I turned out to be surprisingly good at adapting to what little I had to do in the picture. When *Stella Dallas* was released, it became a huge success, and though Belle Bennett was *the* success, all the others in the cast were very well received too. For the first time I got splendid (though small) notices. Even though I was usually mentioned only at the end of a review, I was very much heartened. Mother walked on air for weeks. Dad, however, was away again and didn't see it for some time. When he did he was very kind about it—and me (although I was told he didn't like the mustache).

Mother decided—and I agreed—that I should add drama lessons to my curriculum. We had taken a lease on a nicer, larger house in Beverly Hills, on Beverly Drive. My income had at last begun to increase by the end of 1926 and at last I was in a quality picture that was a hit. Mother talked with lawyers and agents and took just enough of a gamble on my future to negotiate a mortgage for the purchase of the house. The Sullys, for some time wholly dependent on me, were all established Californians by now. My young uncle Bill, who did not yet have a steady job, announced that his bride, Kathleen, was expecting a child in not too many months. Between the ages of thirteen and twenty, my list of almost total dependents (family and others, like Dedie and Hookie) varied from a minimum of six to a maximum of thirteen. At this point, the list consisted of only about seven. After Uncle Henry, another victim of alcohol, tragically hung himself, my beautiful aunt Gladys married again, divorced, and became, little by sad little, another of my responsibilities. But I rarely thought much about it. We were all reasonably well off. Many others were far worse off and I never took my fortunes quite for granted. The cracks behind the family façade hardly ever showed. Nor did my father yet have an inkling of the true situation. How could he? Who would tell him?

My drama coach was Cyril Delevanti, a fine English actor who had once played opposite Ethel Barrymore. He had been a student of classical drama at, I believe, the Royal Academy of Dramatic Art in London. I applied myself to the control of breathing, voice projection, elocution, mime, the classics. After several months it was arranged for me to appear in some semiprofessional performances of *Romeo and Juliet* (sometimes as Romeo and sometimes as Mercutio), *Richard III* (the lead), and some excerpts from *Hamlet* and *Henry V* (in which I fancied myself a budding genius). Also, I began to take up fencing. My mentor was Nickolas Muray, a well-known

Hungarian photographer and friend of Mother's, who had been on the U.S. Olympic fencing team, after being naturalized.

After the release of *Stella Dallas,* for a brief period there was a considerable improvement in the quality of jobs I was offered. Of course I grabbed them greedily. *Women Love Diamonds* was for MGM, which was an important step in the right professional direction for me. It was directed by Edmund Goulding, an immensely talented and amusing young Englishman who was to become famous for directing *Grand Hotel.* In *Women Love Diamonds,* Pauline Starke and Owen Moore (my stepmother Mary's first husband) had the leads, but for me the main excitement was that Lionel Barrymore had a major part. I suppose most young people are inclined to imitate those whom they most admire. For example, when I was about twelve, I copied Rudolph Valentino by slicking my hair down with Vaseline, hoping it would then shine with his same smooth, patent-leather look. I thought it fitting now to adopt all the Barrymore tribe into my personal fan club. It was a very youthful hero worship that acknowledged no flaws in their images. I had seen some of Jack Barrymore's best stage performances and I saw him in *The Sea Beast,* a film adaptation of Melville's *Moby Dick,* twelve times. His only rival was John Gilbert in *The Big Parade,* which I also saw a dozen times. Gilbert was totally different, but in every way I believed him deserving of my unquestioning admiration.

In the case of Jack Barrymore, I tried, with a widely noted lack of success, to look like him, dress like him (loose, wide collars), keep my hair long, use my hands like him, and wiggle my eyebrows at appropriate moments. The net effect was an acceptably comic mimicry—I was just an inch short of making an ass of myself. I didn't do this when I was actually with Jack. When he was making *Don Juan* and, later, *The Beloved Rogue,* he invited me to visit the set a number of times. I often brought along another manic Barrymore fan, Genie Chester, who had now moved to California to live. I always pushed Genie in her wheelchair to the shooting stages and onto the set. Whenever Jack saw us, he dropped all his bawdy manners and talk, his offstage sloppiness, and even his deliberate "image-spoiling" habit of deeply and leisurely picking his classical nose. With Genie and me he was gentle charm itself—amusing, warm, considerate. Indeed, in all the years to come, this gloriously talented, temperamental dipsomaniac never once allowed Genie—and seldom me—to see him truly drunk. He wanted us to preserve our illusions about him even though he knew that we knew that was all they were.

Now, in my new job, I was actually going to do scenes with his brother Lionel, a wonderful artist himself. I was delighted with my continuing flood of good fortune. I still remember, with great shivers of embarrassment, actually going too far by asking Lionel if he thought I looked like his brother. His gruff answer acknowledged the question without answering it.

The finished picture, despite all its assets, was rotten. And the public recognized it as such. Still, my role was so small (opposite Constance Howard) that no harm was done.

Next came the juvenile lead in an adaptation of a Broadway hit by and with Jimmy Gleason, called *Is Zat So?* Edmund Lowe and George O'Brien were in it. It was done for the old Fox Film Corporation, the status of which was "big big second-rate," much like the old Universal Pictures Corporation.

I kept on having romantic crushes and getting over them every few days. Lots of girls seemed as attractive as the devil, but once I got to know them beyond the first exciting stolen moments in dark corners, gardens, or the rumble seats of runabouts, I found none whose brains or charm could come near those of my cousin Flobe's. She and Genie, whom I wheeled to dances now and then, carried into theaters on my shoulder and set down in her aisle seat, were my two feminine ideals of character, charm, and beauty. I vainly sought their counterparts in early girlfriends. However, such romantic idealism was from time to time put aside by my more immediate young animal instincts. It was still a year or more before I was even remotely serious about any one girl.

At about this time I found myself in a picture with that frighteningly honest cowboy philosopher Will Rogers. It was called *A Texas Steer.* It had a good cast, but one that—except for the delicious comedienne Louise Fazenda—even modern film buffs would be unlikely to know. I was half of the very incidental "young love interest." The other half was Ann Rork, the pretty, round-faced daughter of producer Sam Rork.

We went to Washington, D.C., and environs, on location. We always had to delay shooting while Will cogitated on the short comic comments that he wrote for the newspapers every day. Watching the sometimes grumpy but serious and disciplined "funny man" at work was a fine experience. In a way, he was like the sober and conscientious Chaplin. As has been said, comedy is very serious business indeed.

While we were in Washington, Mother decided I was in safe enough hands, with the company's manager close by, for her to venture to New York on business for a few days. What she didn't know was that the whole film unit was going on another location, well outside Washington, to shoot sequences I wasn't in. The company manager thought I'd gone to New York with Mother and gave up our hotel accommodations. The city was full to overflowing for some reason and I couldn't get in anywhere. I didn't know anyone to ring up and I had six dollars—a five and a one—plus fifty cents in my pocket. Luckily, it was a balmy night so I strolled and strolled until I was so tired I lay down on a bench in Lafayette Park and fell asleep. Just as dawn pushed the night away, a sharp rap on the soles of my feet brought me to my senses. A remarkably nice cop, clearly satisfied I was no drunk or potential disturber of the peace, just told me to get up and move on. Which I did—right away.

I thought as I ambled back into the awakening capital of the United States that I could now add another adventure to my list. However, certain realities remained to be coped with. I still hadn't solved the question of what to do that day for food—after I'd spent my few dollars. And when night fell again, where would I spend it? Then, a bit after noon and more wandering, by sheer inexplicable luck I bumped into the company "gagman" (writer of on-the-spot jokes) walking down Pennsylvania Avenue. He was a tough, heart-of-gold, show-biz intellectual by the name of Rob Wagner.

"Wotcha doin', kiddo?" said he.

"Nothing," said I. Then I added proudly, "I'm out of our hotel and alone. Could you lend me—?" I never finished.

"Come along, kid!" he said in a voice hoarse from years of dissipation. "Let's tie on a bag of bekfiss."

And that's how I had someone pay for my breakfast. First problem solved.

We spent the day together. I followed him incredulously through the National Gallery, the Smithsonian, the Capitol, the Supreme Court, and then, late in the afternoon, back to his small hotel where he plopped into a bed and I into a straight-backed chair, and we both dropped off.

That night he took me to a honky-tonk show and then to a smoky dive where he drank glass after glass of bootleg hooch. I, from choice rather than character, stayed with root beer and Dr. Pepper. I was truly fascinated, experiencing at first hand a world I'd previously known only from books, or copies of the *Police Gazette* in barbershops. Later he took me to a house where, he assured me, friends of his lived. It turned out to be a brothel. And the ladies who entertained there were all black. It was not a very attractive place—rather messy, I thought. At first, being inexperienced, I could only guess at what was going on. But the prostitutes were terribly sweet and concerned about me. I remember them welcoming their old friend Rob, but berating him for bringing an innocent kid like me to a place like that. Rob laughingly replied that it was time I "got around a bit and saw the woild."

The end of the episode restores one's faith in warmhearted whores—if, indeed, one ever was so ungenerous as to lose it. They refused to let me mingle or drink with them or their visiting "friends." Instead, having heard of my previous night on a park bench, three of them piled sheets, pillows, and blankets into a large bathtub—making as comfortable a bed for me as possible. Then, with the nicest, most impersonal pats on the head, they shut me in for the night. I slept as soundly and well as I ever would again.

Back in California, I was offered two plays by the Pasadena Playhouse, which had a reputation for putting on fine productions. Many experienced players worked there for the satisfaction of doing something "worthwhile." Many young inexperienced players begged to work there, hoping to be "discovered." But I decided to make my own actual stage debut in a series of one-act plays at a small theater in Hollywood, administered by the members of the Writers' Club—those frustrated scribblers who sought to regain their literary self-respect there after selling their talented souls to the Mephistophelian movies. My first play was by the well-known author Rupert Hughes; it had an American Civil War setting. My part was that of a presumably deaf-mute Yankee spy who in the last scene points to the villain and for the first time speaks two words: *"That's him!"* Curtain. Applause. Bows. It is one of my all-time favorite parts.

Such little-noted plays seemed to increase my prestige (if not the family bank account) as a promising juvenile, a "totally different type" (thank God) "from his father."

I had not been able to be around Dad much during his making of *The Black Pirate* in 1925 because I myself had been, *grâce à dieu,* working and traveling a good deal. However, I did manage to see some of the planning for this first-ever full-length Technicolor feature. It proved to be another helpful lesson in the importance of careful preparation. Dad engaged scientists who took months experimenting with relative color values, which shades were most soothing to the eyes, and so on. As usual, he spent an equal amount of time devising and practicing the stunts he would do—including the memorable (actually impossible) feat of slicing and sliding down a ship's sail (a mechanical trick invented by Uncle Bob) and the quick easy climb up the high stern of a seventeenth-century Spanish galleon (done by adjusting the speed of the camera).

I had outgrown Hookie as a tutor by now and Dedie was on a half pension and about to retire to Ireland for good. Mother heard from her friend Veda Buckland about Thomas S. Patten, an extraordinarily wise old gent, a steamship heir, confidant of Woodrow Wilson, and former postmaster general of New York whose overdependency on drink cost him his for-

My paternal grandfather, H. Charles Ulman.

My paternal grandmother, Ella Marsh Weeks Fairbanks, whom I called Tu-Tu.

Daniel J. Sully, the Cotton King, my maternal grandfather, whom I called Ganka.

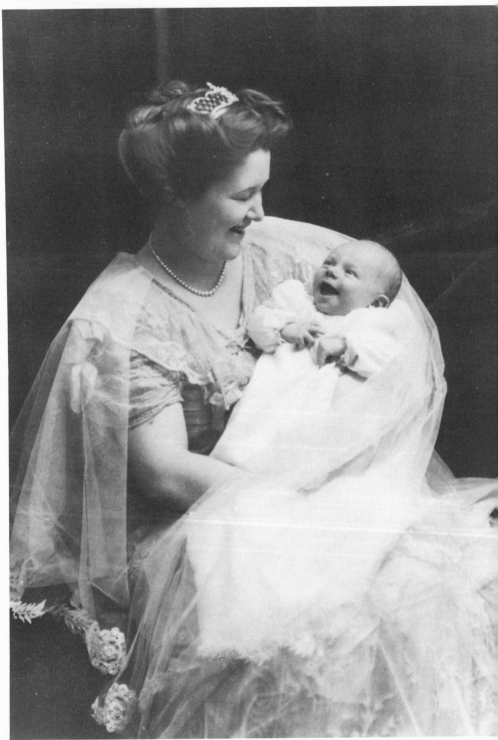

My first recorded smile. With my mother, Beth Sully Fairbanks, 1910.

Kenneth Ridge at Watch Hill, Rhode Island. The scene of Beth Sully's debutante ball, her marriage to Douglas Fairbanks, and my early childhood summers.

At the age of five with my parents.

In California with my pony, 1920.

With cousins Flobelle and Sissy.

Charlie Chaplin, Mary Pickford, and Douglas Fairbanks in Hollywood, 1917. (FOTOFOLIO)

In the uniform of the Knickerbocker Greys, New York City, age ten.

Playing the saxophone in California at age thirteen with Carlton (Hookie) Hoekstra at left.

With Warner Baxter and Billie Dove in *The Air Mail,* 1925.

Jack Pickford, myself, Mary Pickford, and my father, 1926. (THE MUSEUM OF MODERN ART/FILM STILLS ARCHIVE)

As Greta Garbo's degenerate younger brother in *A Woman of Affairs*, 1928. (MGM)

tune and high connections. When cured, he and his wife (coincidentally related to the Barrymores by marriage) retired to Hollywood, California, where he gave informal lectures drawing on his intimate knowledge of European and American literature, philosophy, history, and art. Veda and Mother asked if he would consider being my "graduate tutor" for a nominal fee. Patten agreed to take me on *and* Genie Chester too. She arrived with her nurse and a chauffeur who helped her from the car into a special chair in the Patten living room. Every morning for the better part of three years we both sat and listened, enthralled by our "personal Socrates," as we called him. He suggested books and studies for us to read, absorb, and later discuss with him.

I had had only the beginnings of a formal education and for the past four or five years my studies had been inadequate. Therefore, I now tried to catch up rapidly in more than the rudiments of history, government, foreign affairs, art, literature, and philosophy. I am bound to ascribe the most important part of my education to my three years as a disciple of Tom Patten. He didn't just teach, but instilled in me a passion to learn as much as I could that has never been satisfied.

One of his very occasional but devoted students was a tall, lanky fellow who slip-slopped his way up and down Hollywood Boulevard, acting as noticeably eccentric as he could. He wore only dirty white pants and dirty white shirts. His brown hair was long and dirty. He was even more fanatic a fan of Jack Barrymore than I and tried even more comically to imitate his manner and speech. In time this fellow settled down, became more conventional, and proceeded to make a fine name for himself as a character actor: John Carradine.

I did not aim to supplant or rival my father nor to outdo my grandfather as a business tycoon. I did believe, quite as a matter of fact, that I would be better at whatever I put my hand and heart to than most people and that any shortfall would be due as much to my own lack of interest as to anyone else's superiority. I wanted very much to be my own self, well clear of anyone's shadow, but I had no very specific goals in mind.

I have never lacked awareness of the diversity and potential of my talents. By the same token, I have never been burdened with the conceit that I was another Noël Coward or Chaplin or even a carbon copy of my father. I have, since maturity, known full well the limits of my capabilities (which I've never quite reached), the perversities of my personality, and precisely how much self-discipline I should, could, and would apply to get whatever I had to do done well. I may have exaggerated myself to other people, but I have rarely deceived myself. That is probably my only real virtue.

At this time of my life I often sat up late at night alone in the attic of our house on Beverly Drive and, with a bottle of sherry at my elbow and a portable Victrola on a table playing Grieg's *Peer Gynt Suite,* I composed the most awful, grim, Poe-like poetry imaginable. Then, under the influence of Gustave Doré, I tried to illustrate this morbid verse with my own pen-and-ink drawings. I fancied myself a species of poetic genius just waiting to pop out in full flower to enthrall the world. After enough sherry, I was certain I would be another Shelley. Then come 2 A.M. I reminded myself that I had better work quickly as I would probably die in my early twenties. Quite early on, I cultivated a pale, consumptive look that was effective enough for me to almost believe my own story.

I was periodically saved from this sophomoric behavior by work and companions. I made friends with Charles Farrell and Janet Gaynor, who had just made spectacular successes in the film *Seventh Heaven.* That palship helped. We three were so chummy that I became their "beard," the coverup for their secret romance. I would drive them out to a little run-down, wooden house well south of Los Angeles, near the sea. I'd leave them there and go sailing or swimming until time to collect them and then we'd all have a bit of dinner. (I first telephoned my habitually worried Mother with a list of innocent lies as to my whereabouts.) I began to drop some of my aesthetic affectations and return more or less to normal.

I was not without a new romance, myself—a serious one at that. I had met Jack Barrymore's leading lady and wife-to-be, blond, beautiful Dolores Costello. I also met her older, darker sister, Helene. Although Helene was about five years older than I, I made her believe there was a difference of only two years. As far as I was concerned, our romance was as intense as anything I'd ever felt before. We even joked about what fun it would be if Jack and I were brothers-in-law. For several months we were inseparable.

When she took a business trip to New York, I discovered how painful the separation of young lovers could be. In a few weeks, however, she returned. My father was away and Pickfair was empty so we went up for some surreptitious swimming. After a long, moody silence, she announced that she had a confession to make. My heart began to pound so loud I was sure she could hear it. I suspected she was about to confess that she had had an affair with someone during her New York trip. I kept my first surge of jealous anger neatly controlled because I'd decided to act the grown, tolerant sophisticate. Calmly, though I imagine my voice quivered slightly, I said I would understand—whatever it was.

"Well," she said, after a tearful but encouraging embrace, "I got married!"

I can still feel today the shock of that moment. Not only had she married secretly (for a reason I've forgotten), but she had married a much older man, the renowned stage star and director Lowell Sherman. I didn't get over this first romantic blow for months. But I do remember that I had no wish or opportunity to confide in either of my parents. I *did* go to her sister's fiancé, Jack Barrymore. For the brief period following this drama, he became a surrogate father and brother. I called on Jack, and his pet monkey, Clementine, in his bungalow on the grounds of the Ambassador Hotel. He calmed and counseled me and when with youthful intensity I proposed to drown my depression in drink, he adamantly refused to let me make a tragedy of my crashed romance: "No drinks for you, you poor son-of-a-bitch!"

With hindsight I see that I got over the pain of my lost love rather too quickly. In a few weeks my heart had healed. For the special "inside" group of Los Angeles *jeunesse d'or,* the thing to do on a Friday night was to compete in the dancing contests at the Cocoanut Grove. The orchestras were world famous—Fred Waring, Paul Whiteman, and others—the best and biggest. I usually took Cousin Flobe and we did marvelously well together—actually winning two or three times, and we almost always got a second or third prize. Our chief competitors were Tommy Lee, the smooth, elegant son of the owner of the local Cadillac franchise, Sally (Young) Blane, Mike Cudahy, the heavy-drinking, meat-packing heir and one of my backlot ball-playing pals. There was also his striking girlfriend, the young MGM dancer "find," Joan Crawford, of whom the press predicted we would hear more in time. It proved to be one of their accurate prophecies.

The Whiteman band in those days had a uniquely popular trio. Their lead singer was a husky baritone named Bing Crosby who periodically crashed a cymbal for emphasis. We became friends and occasionally played golf together on the Lakeside Golf Club course near Burbank. My uncle Bob designed most of this course and arranged for Crosby and me to have guest cards. One day Bing confided that he'd had an offer to make a film test for Mack Sennett but that Whiteman threatened to fire him if he dared try such a thing. What to do?

My advice was emphatically to the point: "Stay where you are! How can you *ever* hope to have a better break than to be on a record label as one of the Rhythm Boys with the Whiteman band! Don't get Paul mad at you. You'll never get another break nearly so good!"

In the Orient, Dad and Mary made the informal acquaintance of the then Crown Prince (later Emperor) Hirohito and played golf with his Cambridge-educated cousin, Prince Konoye. On their return home they tried to think of a gift for the Crown Prince that would serve as a suitable gesture of gratitude for his hospitality. It was a sorry day for me when Dad decided that the white pony from his stable that I had been allowed to call mine was just the thing for His Imperial Highness. I consequently had an anti-Japanese chip on my shoulder years before World War II. (After the war, visits to Japan and the kindness of Japanese friends succeeded in blowing the chip away.)

However, there was a brighter side to this particular coin. Luckily it turned up not long after my broken romance with Helene. One of the aristocratic Japanese families whom Mary and Dad had visited on their trip asked if their beautiful young daughter could visit them in the United States while she was learning to speak English. Naturally, they welcomed her warmly.

After her arrival in California she moved into a large guest room at Pickfair. She charmed everyone. She remains crystal-clear in my memory. Not only was she as pretty as a Japanese doll, but her manner was as classically shy and delicate as everyone's ideal Madam Butterfly. I should say *Mademoiselle*—I think she was about sixteen. She always wore Japanese dress and seemed as fragile as fine porcelain. I soon relegated my broken romance to memory's junkyard and, oh, how I fell for her. Whenever I could arrange to see her, I did. For weeks I paid ever-so-respectful court to her. Since I rarely saw her at Pickfair, I could only offer to drive her to the beach in my new car. (The Chrysler had been traded in for a gray Packard roadster with red wheels and red lining! *Hot dog!)* Occasionally I was allowed to take her to a Saturday or Sunday afternoon movie and then bring her back promptly—my head in a greater whirl each time. After about a month, I ventured to hold her hand. Another month, and she shyly let me kiss her cheek. When she returned the compliment, I was overjoyed. Then came a Sunday when I was permitted to take her off for the whole afternoon. Deceitfully I planned to take her to the empty studio, where I'd promised to show her—secretly of course—Dad's "Holy of Holies," the "For Men Only" office–living room–dressing room–Turkish bath complex. The guard at the studio gate let me in without question. I nervously began my guided tour knowing very well that if I were *so* romantic, *so* charming, she wouldn't be able to resist something more than a kiss on the cheek.

My face twitched with nerves. With clammy hands I led her to a sofa. She sat down beside me with exquisite reticence and the sweet dawn of a smile. Although I was still impulsive I kissed her with matching reticence on the lips. She returned my kiss with more than a hint of appreciation and interest. I next dared the unheard-of: I loosened the pins in her carefully done-

up, soft blue-black hair so that it fell below her waist. I was not very practiced in this kind of courtship, but I felt sure I was more sophisticated than
she. After all, I was *nearly* a man. And she was younger than I. But I soon
became astonished at the suddenly all-knowing and enthusiastic way in
which she not only responded to my advances but took a delicious initiative
all her own.

My innate masculine conceit rose to the boiling point. I must, thought I,
be absolutely irresistible. Then suddenly the swirling mists in my head
cleared and I was horrified with myself. I had been too aggressive, too
impulsive, too young and inexperienced to restrain my ardor. I had been a
brute—a young, impetuous savage, intent on despoiling this frail, trusting,
innocent creature. After a moment of silence, I began to search for words
with which to apologize, weakly, for my animal attack. But she began to pat
my hand, sweetly, affectionately, and understandingly. For the first time she
spoke in soft but unhesitating and very clear English. "Don't worry, please!
You are very, *very* sweet." Then, after a pause, she added, "You are *so* like
your father!"

I had a very difficult time over the next days speaking normally to Dad. I
couldn't erase my Oriental dream. I now persuaded myself with all the
melodrama at my teenage command that I was bitter against *all* women! I
decided "virtue" was nonexistent and henceforth I would believe in absolutely no one! I masochistically recalled the circumstances that ended my
love affair with Helene Costello. And now, *this!* Oh, the reams of dreadful
poetry that followed hard on this new episode!

In 1927 Dad was preparing another large-scale costume film, *The Gaucho*.
The story had a semireligious theme with an action background, but it did
not have the grand sweep of his earlier classics, and he was uneasy about it.
His team continued to flatter and encourage him, but his imagination
seemed to be slipping just a bit. One might say his earlier films were cinematic murals. Now, they were just very big and entertaining Fairbanks
features.

Dad's eldest brother, Jack, had recently died after a long illness. Uncle
Jack had been like a father to all the Fairbanks brothers since their early
Denver days. Even though he had been paralyzed and speechless from a
stroke for several years, his actual death was a serious and depressing blow
that was subtly reflected in my father's work. Dad was only forty-four at the
time, but he jokingly complained of already feeling old. Nevertheless, the
genial barriers that still existed between us were now and then showing little
cracks.

Since I had been out of work for a couple of months, I asked Uncle Bob, once again, if I might try my hand at directing some of the many screen tests of those aspiring to play parts in *The Gaucho.* There were already two overworked test directors and they needed another, so I got the job—for $150 a test. I directed two—quite well, as a matter of fact, despite my inexperience. (I had lots of help from a wise old cameraman.) Both ladies I tested got the roles they sought. One of them was Lupe Velez, who later became quite popular (on screen and off) as "the Mexican Spitfire." When the film finished shooting I picked up another $200 by writing a few of the subtitles, a very specialized job in those silent movie days (they kept three of mine). That led to Sam Goldwyn's hiring me to write some subtitles for two pictures, starring Ronald Colman and Vilma Banky. For these I earned $250 a picture—a welcome sum, even if he only used six of my subtitles per picture.

Romantically, I was keeping my too impressionable heart quite aloof. I determined that from now on I would pursue only older, more sophisticated women, not girls. The more inaccessible and remote they were, the more desirable they became and the more intensely I pursued them. If I made an impression on one, I celebrated discreetly and altered course for the next one. It may have been outrageous, but I continued this procedure for some time. It diverted me from more serious entanglements and provided me with, as Chaplin said, "the most fun you can have without laughing."

I won a junior membership in the Hollywood Athletic Club where twice a week I took some boxing and wrestling lessons from the pro. There I made a long-lasting friendship with the tubby little Mexican masseur Fernando (Fred) Miron. Over the decades he was also a gentle counselor and a devoted supporter. His later employer, Bob Hope, took him everywhere, until he died full of years.

For some time I had felt I could tour the plays that Glenn Hunter had so successfully done in New York. I tried my best to promote a tour playing his part in *Merton of the Movies* but was turned down. I had better luck with his other hit, *Young Woodley* by John Van Druten, and enviously wondered why it hadn't first been offered to me. This was a hit play that I had seen in London, and I made up my mind then that somehow I would play that part. After all, thought I, Hunter was "too old" (in his late twenties!) and I was a bit young but *about* right. Furthermore, Hunter, very successful at playing a lad in a top-notch English public school, nevertheless failed, I thought, to get quite the right accent required for the part. I considered myself pretty good at accents and was thus emboldened to talk Barton Hepburn, a rich young entrepreneurial friend, into setting up the play around me in Los Angeles. And he did, forthwith.

Even if it proved successful, we agreed to limit the run to a certain number of weeks. We would decide whether or not to tour with it later. A disproportionate amount of local publicity had been generated in advance of the opening, presumably because I was just beginning to show promise. Also, there was a leak to the press that my father and Mary, now ridiculously called "the Royal Family of Hollywood," would attend the first night. The news that Charlie Chaplin would accompany them made it a "social must." Thus, on a night in the autumn of 1927, the Belasco Theater in downtown Los Angeles was the place to be. And, further, word got around that "Fairbanks senior's ex-wife—now the ex-Mrs. James Evans—would also be attending *Young Woodley,* starring Douglas Fairbanks, Jr. . . ."

Consequently the atmosphere was only slightly less carnival-like than a Grauman's Chinese Theater premiere. The Belasco was sold out and the first dozen rows of orchestra seats were crammed with Pasadena high society, plus squads of motion picture executives, directors, and *real* stars.

All went far better than I, or anyone, could have predicted. At the final curtain, the audience roared its approval. The cast made several curtain calls, I made a few on my own, and I was even obliged to make a very brief curtain speech. I was honestly unprepared for such a reception. Luckily I did not take all the huzzahs to heart. I was pleased, of course, but by no means fooled. Most enjoyable was the crowd that came backstage afterward —including my mother and father, who jockeyed their way in and out of the big loud group to avoid coming face to face with each other. Mother sneaked home to avoid embarrassment; Dad and Mary stayed and were hearty and complimentary. Then my cousins, friends, and just gushers departed and I, weary but gratified, spoke my thanks to my colleagues. I left the theater with Charlie Chaplin, the only one to wait behind after everyone else had gone.

This was a never-to-be-forgotten gesture of a great artist to a timid youngster having his first whopping success. Charlie was my only serious supporter that evening. The streets were deserted, the autumn night was mild, and we sat on the curbstone outside the theater and talked. His praise was thoughtful. He took enormous pains to give minor but helpful criticisms. Most important, he gave me a long and encouraging lecture about my future, about what I should do and how. I've forgotten the details now, but I do remember they were very constructive and enormously helpful. No other friend or relative took so much time or trouble as did Charlie that late night.

The next day, the local press was unanimously favorable. I received congratulatory telegrams and notes from friends, acquaintances, and people I had never heard of. One special message came in the form of a small note of congratulations, hand-written and hand-delivered, asking for a signed photograph and, if I had time and was so inclined, a telephone call. It was signed "Joan Crawford."

She had attended the first night with Paul Bern, a gentle, cultivated MGM producer, one of the few who could merit such a description, and a man whom I knew and respected. Most of the nicer glamour girls usually chose him as an escort because he had exquisite manners, a soft Austrian accent, great charm, and a reputation for never making a pass. The girls felt safe with gallant Paul.

I was twitching with excitement at this note from Miss Crawford. Imagine! Me! A note from *Joan Crawford!* For a year or so she had been the object of a big MGM publicity buildup, had won a big Charleston dance contest, played in a few pictures, and was now doing leads. She had her picture in every fan magazine and was sure to be a star. I'd seen her, of course, when she had been the girlfriend of my pal Mike Cudahy, but they were no longer "an item," as his family had disapproved. She was a few years older than I, but that was fine with me—quite in accordance with my continuing preference for older women. Anyway, she evidently thought I was her contemporary.

So, of course, I did ring her up, and she did ask me to her small house on Roxbury Drive in Beverly Hills for tea or a drink before the theater some afternoon. I went gladly and giddily. I also brought along, as requested, a small signed photograph. It was a nervous stilted first meeting for us both. I hammed it up, trying to appear an intellectual artist, and she played the part of an overwhelmingly impressed country girl who saw glamour in her future. After an awkward but pleasant hour, I got up to leave. I asked if I might have a photograph of her in exchange. She produced a large 11 × 14 portrait, taken at the studio. On it, she inscribed: "To Douglas, May this be the start of a beautiful friendship. Joan."

And for a time, it was.

Plays never ran for long in Los Angeles. It was not a theater town. *Young Woodley* ran for something over a month, but short of six weeks. Then we moved north to San Francisco.

During those weeks, a budding mutual interest began to develop between the vivacious Miss Crawford and me. My initial impression of her was of a vital, energetic, very pretty girl, quite unlike anyone I had known before. Her looks were not classic, but despite an irregularity of detail her features projected an overall illusion of considerable beauty. For example, although she barely avoided being pop-eyed, she shrewdly made her eyes up in a manner designed to make them appear even larger. Her mouth was wide and generous. It was once described as resembling a torn pocket. She put lipstick on with broad, brave strokes. Her cheekbones were wonderful but her jawline was so square and severe that she could sometimes look hard.

She had remarkable mastery over her ever-changing expressions. Even then, in her prestar days, the total effect was magnetic. Hers was less a talent than a distinctive gift that inclined her to "perform" her passing thoughts as if she were going through a repertoire of characters at an audition. She had two voice sounds—one resonant and professional and one more blatantly flat. Her speech shifted between a natural and agreeable Texas-Midwest mixture with New York icing and another affected for those times when she tried too hard to be what Noël Coward called "piss-elegant."

Her figure was beautiful! It was fine-trained by years of dancing and a continuing devotion to keeping fit. Her gracefully muscled legs were just a little too short, but few noticed it. However, her looks were not really her strongest attraction. Joan's true magnetism was something superimposed over her striking appearance.

Even in the early stages of our acquaintance, her quiet dynamism seemed almost deliberately turned on. I started off quite undisguisedly entranced by her. She, I'm relieved to say, made no bones about her crush on me as an *actor,* and, according to my principal informant, Paul Bern, she also concluded from my successful "show-off" chatter that I was well read, very sophisticated for my age, and "a gent." In fact, she built up a press-clipping-influenced fairy-tale prince in her imagination. I, sensing how she felt, played up to it for all I was worth. I postured too much, made outlandish statements, and read classical poetry aloud. If she had been even a little bit more sophisticated, she would have seen right through to the affected, infatuated young ass that I was.

We could meet on certain afternoons and Sundays but rarely in the evening, since I was still in the play and not free until after eleven. Joan was usually working on a film. Like most film actresses, she went to bed at ten P.M. at the latest and rose at six A.M. in order to be at the studio by seven or seven-thirty.

When finally I left for San Francisco, I knew I was once again "involved," although, as I told myself, not seriously nor exclusively. I still thought it all a great lark to go after and be with the most attractive older women, while not allowing my sentiments to run away with me. And Joan was really only a bit older.

This new situation ran afoul of a purely imaginary romance I had developed for Gertrude Lawrence. I had seen her in the great imported English musical *Charlot's Revue,* first in New York and much later in Los Angeles. The distant, unattainable Miss Lawrence was about ten years older than I, but of course that was no deterrent for the moment. Beatrice Lillie and Jack Buchanan were also stars of the show, but Lawrence was the toast of both Britain and America, offstage as well as on. And I dreamed hopeless dreams of her.

Joan, however, was a tangible, honest-to-God girl whom I just might fall for. Her approaches to me were so flattering I practically melted. She was my more realistic crush. I began to wear her like a flower in my young buttonhole. We exchanged notes and telephone calls. Neither of us was making much money at the time, and, although she was supporting her mother (according to Joan, her father had died), her "problem" brother, and a few others back in her hometown of Kansas City, it was still a lesser load than mine.

Mother came on tour with me, of course, and we settled down in San Francisco in Noël Sullivan's beautiful old house at the top of Hyde Street that had once been the residence of Robert Louis Stevenson. I rang Joan to tell her that it appeared we would enjoy the same success there as in Los Angeles.

Right next door, at the Geary Theater, an excellent repertory group was presenting Sem Binelli's *The Jest* during our run. They had different matinee days and, unlike us, played two performances on Sunday, so I was able to see this fine, lecherous Italian Renaissance verse-melodrama a few times. Then I had to brag by saying, in my best offhand manner, that "of course" I'd seen Jack and Lionel Barrymore in the play in New York some years earlier. My prestige expanded instantly, and I went on to say wistfully that I wished I could have played a small part in it. "By the ghost of the young Roscius," they said, "why not?" I could have "a smallish bit," understudy a bigger one, and still be free to play *Woodley.* I accepted on my producer's condition that no publicity or program record be made, as that would be a contravention of my contract. Before I knew it I was in two plays at once, though very few really knew and, of course, I was only being paid for *Woodley.*

During the last days of the *Woodley* run the audience petered out most discouragingly, but we were booked into the theater until the night before New Year's Eve and had to go on. We were all depressed—not only did none of us have other jobs waiting, but we loved the play. Our rich, young impresario agreed that we should play just *one* more performance and put an advertisement in the papers announcing that, "by public demand," there would be one last performance on New Year's Eve.

The company was invited to a New Year's Eve afternoon party before the performance. I did join the others this time in multiple toasts. This no doubt contributed to my arriving last at the theater. It also meant I had no time to makeup and hardly time to put on my proper costume for the first act. My head was woozy, and though I knew I was tight as a tick, the very knowledge of it scared the devil out of me. I took great pains to enunciate my words, ever so meticulously. Several times I drew absolute blanks of memory. Others on stage or in the wings whispered cues. I was miserable! But the theater, a fairly large one, held hardly more than fifty couldn't-care-less customers that night. We came to a heavily melodramatic incident in the second act, when I was supposed to be in a jealous rage and threaten a jeering schoolmate with a knife, but instead of being furious, I got hopeless giggles! Onstage the rest of the company were so horrified that they stayed straight-faced.

At length, I pulled myself together, cut the scene short, and the curtain came down in a rush. I was far tighter at that moment than when I began— I can't imagine why. In the wings I loudly expressed my shame and shock to all within earshot. I was, I announced, going out to make a curtain speech and apologize to what remained of the audience, most of whom were dozing out front. "I have disgraced you all," I told my fellow players, "I've disgraced our profession—my and my father's name! I *must* apologize!"

I was forcibly restrained by members of the cast and a couple of stagehands. The next scene was delayed a few minutes while cold water was applied to my head and I changed into a fresh shirt. I pulled myself somewhat together and finished the play to no applause at all. By that time there were no more than ten or fifteen people left.

I did not enjoy my first real reaction to too much alcohol. But it did serve to make me especially appreciative of my father's first-night gift to me when we had opened in Los Angeles. It was a beautifully bound, signed first edition of Sir Henry Irving's learned lectures, *The Art of Acting*. On the flyleaf, Dad had written:

To Junior,
  Let your own discretion be your tutor—(Hamlet).
The occasion being your first appearance on the dramatic stage.

Dad—1927

8

Young Woodley's success did not immediately translate itself into other good jobs, thus confirming that most theatrical bouquets or brickbats are short-lived and unreliable. This first important lesson is one none of us ever completely learns.

The issue that would soon demand resolution was my life at home and my relations with Mother. I was not what today would be called a dropout. After years of indifferent scholarship, I was at last beginning to love my learning sessions with old Tom Patten, who had generated in me an absolute hunger for knowledge for its own sake. I continued with my drama classes as often as I could—sometimes in the evening—and I also continued my swimming, boxing, and wrestling at the Hollywood Athletic Club under Miron's and old Swedish Carl's guidance. All in all, it would appear there was enough activity for a secretly slothful, sporadically employed young "juvenile" movie actor to keep as fit as he ought and as he imagined his father wanted.

My interest in other girlfriends had begun to diminish in direct proportion to my increasing absorption with the glowing Miss C. Though jobs were intermittent and indifferent and income just barely sufficient, life nevertheless began to seem decked in brighter, more stimulating colors, and I was growing more and more impatient with family apron strings. To my continuing mortification, Mother insisted on coming to the studio when I was working. It not only distracted me but invited much well-deserved leg-pulling. When I tried to persuade her not to come, she either flew into a temper or began to cry, saying no one "wanted or needed" her any longer. Of course, it was easier to give in, and I did.

I had not yet come to any firm ideas about how to live a really independent life. But my new freewheeling, dashing girlfriend deliberately watered the seeds of my discontent and nurtured my impatience with Mother's possessiveness. I began to speak out with a frankness that clearly distressed Mother a great deal. The more self-confident I became, the more desperately she tried to keep me tied to home. There was no doubt that Mother had considerable charm. Serving sherry and tea, she filled the house with her friends and friends of friends whom she judged to be somehow artistic, musical, or merely aesthetic. They were for the most part agreeable and inoffensive lightweights and they comprised a kind of nonstop *salon*. Unfortunately, these friends of hers did not mix well with my own friends, who were more sports-loving.

I was still the sole support of seven or eight people. Yet despite the fact that I was eighteen and had a better head for business than my other relatives, I had absolutely no say about the disposition of anything I earned. I made about four hundred dollars a week when I worked, and I worked about seven months a year, earning, roughly ten or twelve thousand a year. I was given twenty-five dollars weekly pocket money. My job was to make the money and turn it over to Mother.

I was so determined not to be a "mother's boy," that I finally went to Veda Buckland, Mother's best and wisest friend, for advice. I also wrote a long letter to our old family friend, Noël Sullivan in San Francisco. And I confided in Tom Patten. And Genie. And the cousins, and my darling old giant of a grandather, Dan'l. I also told them how strongly Joan felt about my restraints. They all agreed that I should stand up to Mother, but, they all pointed out, Mother had herself suffered so much from Dad's desertion she could never in her life envisage a replacement for him or for me. If I left home now, they said, it would stir up a desperate storm. So I must be patient and considerate. I did try. In succeeding weeks I often stayed home instead of going out to a dance or a movie or the beach. Instead, I continued to work late, in the attic, on punk poetry and pen-and-ink sketches.

As the year wound onward, the strain of my struggle increased and the situation worsened. Just to make things more upsetting, 1928–29 marked the beginning of the downward economic slide of many nations. The great "crash" had begun. On a personal scale, Dad was then said to be worth between fifteen and twenty million dollars. Mary had amassed considerably more. (Dad paid for all personal and domestic expenses, while Mary, according to my understanding, rarely spent anything—clever girl!)

Dad's one great apprehension, even before the Lindbergh baby horror, was the threat of kidnapping and he carried two guns in his cars at all times. Nearly everyone else everywhere worried about their jobs, savings, and futures. Dad and Mary didn't. Over the next five years Dad lost about three quarters of his fortune, but since he was as carefree as his screen characters —and as extravagant—he hardly paid any attention. He allowed his brother Bob and his production manager, Clarence Erickson, to worry about it. (How much Mary might have lost is not definitely known.) However, none of this concerned me much at all. I had been told many times by Mother— with corroboration from others in the family—that my father had paid Mother and me all we were ever going to get (except for my small trust when I became thirty-two years old). I was also given to understand that he had cut me completely out of his will on my entrance into the movies. I took that bit of information with a minimum of interest. As I expected nothing, none of these matters gave me a moment's pause. I enjoyed being a "non-heir." It helped a bit to cancel suspicions of advantage inherent in our identical names.

The professional year of 1928 began with an absolute stinker of a quickie. It was a racing-car movie called *Dead Man's Curve,* with my old Hollywood School for Girls–mate Joel McCrea playing a villain. We worked a twelve-hour day and at the end of one seven-day week this celluloid rubbish was finished. There followed two or three other Poverty Row pictures that are best forgotten. But then, in mid-autumn, there was suddenly another break.

I did not have much confidence in this picture at first. It was to be made by Columbia, then a scrawny Poverty Row company, whose pictures were produced by a man known to be coarse, vulgar, egocentric, and brutal— Harry Cohn.

Therefore, I looked forward to this new job with trepidation. But it was, after all, the first straight movie "lead" I had ever had—that of a young cub reporter on a big city newspaper. The leading lady was the popular Jobyna Ralston. The director was a young man—actually only a few years older than I—named Frank Capra. The picture, *The Power of the Press,* was a success and Capra amply sustained predictions by becoming one of the very best—he was certainly one of the very nicest—directors in the world of cinema.

Soon after I finished that job, I received an offer from MGM, then the most prestigious of American motion picture companies. The company was Joan's contractual employer, so that was nice, and, best of all, the movie for which I was hired was an adaptation of Michael Arlen's best-selling novel and successful stage play *The Green Hat.* It was to be directed by one of

MGM's finest directors, Clarence Brown, and its stars were to be (I held on to my seat) Greta Garbo and John Gilbert! They were supported by the wonderful old character star Lewis Stone. Of course, "Miss G." (one of Garbo's nicknames) always had Bill Daniels as her cameraman. My part, a supporting but fine dramatic one, was that of Garbo's wastrel younger brother who, besotted with debauchery, dies young and helps trigger much of the subsequent action. The industry's self-censoring board, known as the Hays Office, banned *The Green Hat* as immoral. The United States still had prohibition and so even though my character was supposed to die of drink, no bottle label was ever allowed to show. The book's hero commits suicide on his wedding night when he finds he has syphilis. In the film, he does himself in because he's been caught out as an embezzler. They also had to change the title to *A Woman of Affairs,* but MGM took great pains to see that the public knew that the movie by one name smelled as naughtily sweet as the book by another.

What luck! Two good ones in a row! And it all went surprisingly well. The work was hard and serious but it did not lack amusing sidelights, one of which was that G.G. (her other nickname) was having intermittent disputes with her dear, ardently devoted *amour,* the wonderfully attractive Jack Gilbert. The great Jack, bless his foolish heart, extended the hand of comradeship and trust to me, about ten years his junior. One day when a scene was over and "setups" were being selected for the next one, Jack, in a pet over something with G.G., asked me (as he had once or twice before) to be a go-between, carrying his scribbled note to her and, he hoped, returning with her loving reply. I resisted the temptation to peek, but I doubt if Jack's notes won many Brownie points. The offstage atmosphere seemed quite chilly for days. Then all would be well again—until the next time.

While we were filming, Joan had not yet begun her own next film and sometimes managed to visit our set. She doted on Garbo, admired Jack, and, I conceitedly supposed, wanted to see me as well. When no one was looking, I was still just uncommitted enough to try to ingratiate myself with G.G. so that she might take a shine to me. I remember how my deceitful heart bubbled when for a few days I thought I was well on the way to an underhanded conquest.

During one of many long waits between scenes, I inveigled G.G. into following me to a dark, remote corner of the shooting stage with the excuse of passing another of Jack's private messages to her—this one, I told her, was verbal and quite detailed. She was always warm and friendly to me—quite different from the public image she so successfully presented—and she obviously did not suspect my dire motive in luring her away from the set.

She came along quite unsuspiciously. When we got to my dark corner of the giant stage, behind the flat walls of an unused set, I just stammered, blustered, and said something silly about Jack's message that I don't remember. She, clearly confused by the unnecessary secrecy, volunteered a non sequitur having to do with stories she had heard about "a romance" between "that nice Joan Crawford" and me. And that, I fear, was that. The very question threw me and I nodded sheepishly and, I suspect, guiltily. A muffed opportunity.

On two or three other occasions, when G.G. and Jack were even more on the outs, she asked me to escort her to some party or other. I was by now too openly involved with Joan for Jack to dream of being jealous. Therefore these invitations must have been for evenings when Jack and Joan were otherwise separately occupied and I was at loose ends. Usually we went to parties given by what the columnists called the "German-Scandinavian Colony" (if such a thing existed). These parties were small and usually held in the rented Hollywood Boulevard house of the great German actor Emil Jannings. Among the guests were sometimes Conrad Veidt or such famous directors as Ernst Lubitsch, F. W. Murnau, or Miss G.'s discoverer, the Russian-Swedish Mauritz Stiller. Almost everyone spoke only German, of which I understood not a word.

Once, when G.G. felt tired and decided she had downed enough wine (and I had had none), she asked me to drive her home to her cottage on the sea, north of Santa Monica. Here, thought still-lecherous-minded I, was my chance again! But, damn it, though she slumped half-asleep in my old car, I was disgracefully "proper." She was just so very nice and trusting that I, pretending to be far nobler than I really wanted to be, did absolutely nothing except see her safely into her house, where I whispered, "Good night," and drove home to Mother's "Where-have-you-been?-I-was-worried!"

I sighed.

A memorable moment from *A Woman of Affairs* was a death scene I was scheduled to play wherein Lewis Stone was to talk to me as I sat in my chair, eyes staring ahead. As he spoke, I was supposed to die. Sadly, at that time, poor Mr. Stone was suffering from Parkinson's disease and his head was always nodding, ever so slightly. In 1928 most movies were still silent, but we nevertheless learned and spoke lines, because it was believed we would play our scenes with more conviction if we did. In this instance, Mr. Stone had a long speech that ended with something to the effect of, "Now, you'll never do such a thing again, will you?" But even though the words were phrased in negative form, his head contradicted him by nodding in the affirmative. The result was that each time we started the scene, I began to giggle. I couldn't—and wouldn't—for the world have offended the very eminent man by admitting that his affliction made him appear to oppose his own plea. I therefore "confessed" that I couldn't, in feigning death, keep my eyes open without blinking for as long as the scene demanded. I said it was beyond me and made me giggle. Director Brown, normally the soul of quiet, gum-chewing patience, became justifiably angry, especially by the time we came to "Take 20!" Somehow, a few takes later, I managed to steady myself and "died" properly. Mr. Stone, thank God, never knew why I was behaving so stupidly.

The slow-burning infatuation between Joan and me had now blossomed into a full-fledged romance that began to intrude joyously on both our daily lives. Each week, as we got away from our mutual self-consciousness and showing-off, we also got to understand more about each other. Joan used movie magazines for her research on me. I did mine on her more directly. I asked her straight—and then checked however I could. She had begun her career as Lucille Le Sueur, the name she was born with. After leaving her native Texas for Missouri, and growing up a bit, she got a job in Columbia waiting on table at St. Stephens College in order to earn her tuition. Sometime earlier, I gather, her mother's name was changed to Cassin, by marriage. Lucille then became known as "Billie" Cassin. And then, in her middle-late teens, when she left school for Chicago, a job in a chorus, and finally another job in another chorus in New York, it was changed back to Lucille Le Sueur.

As our involvement with each other became more intense, she asked me not to call her Joan anymore. After all, it was only a name that MGM had invented, claiming it was suggested by the winner of a fan magazine contest. So, she said, she preferred to be called Billie by old or close friends. And so I did for the rest of her high-pitched life.

Ever since *Woodley* my father had become markedly more at ease with me and I reacted, happily, in kind. Mary, Uncle Bob, and Dad's old cronies Tom Geraghty and Kenneth Davenport (still doubling as a special secretary) had evidently been working successfully on his paternal side. He listened to my poetry, praising or criticizing, showed off my sketches and caricatures, and very occasionally praised me in front of others. I was invited more often (about once a week, when not working) to workout-and-steam at the studio and about twice a month to Pickfair, usually after dinner, to see a privately projected new movie. I had not ever been invited to a single one of the infrequent big Pickfair dances or dinner parties (usually

Dad and Mary were in bed by 10:30 P.M.). I was not even asked to the one given for the British Empire's young Prince George (later the Duke of Kent and the youngest son of King George V and, of course, brother of the Duke of Windsor and King George VI). I thought I was old enough and I did, after all, own a dinner jacket (for film purposes). But despite every hint, I was not asked. I was very put out and it continued to annoy me for years. I seemed to know hardly anyone who *wasn't* going.

But I had my private revenge. Once when they had a good-sized dinner party, I rang up saying I was the Beverly Hills Water & Power Company; there was something broken and all houses in the area had to turn on their taps, faucets, and keep all toilets flushed until further notice—otherwise there was serious danger. The party broke up while hosts, guests, and servants turned on every source of water, inside and out, until about 2 A.M. when my father rang the city fire department and learned it was a hoax. He suspected everyone but me, and I never had the nerve to confess.

Billie and I were so strenuously preoccupied with each other that I was delighted when Mary thoughtfully suggested that I show her off at Pickfair one evening. After all, Billie was by now getting a big publicity buildup from MGM and they were as curious to see Joan Crawford as Billie Cassin was to see them.

Billie later told of her nervousness when she first went to what the columnists of the day foolishly called "Hollywood's Royal Palace." She was nervous; so was I, but for different reasons. We arrived early. I went off somewhere with my father, thoughtlessly leaving Billie alone in the study. In order to quiet her nerves, she took her ever-present knitting from its bag and began to knit. Then she heard Mary's heels coming down the winding stairway and clicking on the parquet floor in the hall. She said she jumped to her feet as Mary entered the room and extended her hand. Years after, when recounting the episode, she said that Mary greeted her coldly and condescendingly—thereby increasing her existing discomfiture.

However, with much residual respect and affection for the lady, and a reluctance to contradict her, I must say that I returned only a few moments later and so recall the real story clearly. Billie was absolutely thrilled by what she then said was Mary's warm reception. And so, as an anxious and frightened swain, was I. Mary is, in my memories, always the essence of gentle, hospitable charm. Whenever we were asked to the house she did all she could to make the clearly shaky young girl feel at home—just as she had with me. Dad, on the other hand, let it be known through others (his aversion to direct showdowns was undoubtedly one of his principal legacies to me) that he was not at all enthusiastic about this "overexploited affair."

But he was gentleman enough not to show it—not to knowingly hurt a nice young girl with whom his incomprehensible son was involved. I knew of his swallowed opposition but swore to Billie that he thought her "great."

When Mother met "that Crawford girl," she was not nearly so nice to her as Dad and Mary had been. She was correctly polite but also condescending, as with a soft smile she described Billie to a friend as "my son's current chorus-girl fling."

Many "inside stories" were printed, some invented by studio press agents, some by gossipy friends, and some by dear self-dramatizing Billie. With wide-eyed awe and near reverence in her voice, she said I had taught her how to read and understand classic poetry and other literature. If I did, I don't remember it. God knows I didn't know much about either, but it is more than possible that I showed off if I thought I could get away with it.

Billie was also quoted a score of years later as saying that were it not for me, she would not have known proper table manners, nor the correct use of knives and forks. This was laughable, patent nonsense, as all her friends knew. She was a very experienced lady. After all, she had never made a secret of how she had, in her first chorus job in New York, caught the discriminating eye of "Jake" Shubert, the famous Broadway producer. Then, a few beaux later, she was very taken with her new boss, the immensely popular nightclub singer Harry Richman. And a year or so after that, she followed the sun and her destiny westward, at the behest of Harry Rapf, an MGM executive who was credited with discovering her. His outsized nose made him a caricaturist's delight. He was nicknamed "the Anteater." After that, there were rumors of another executive in her life, not counting her honestly platonic friendship with Paul Bern, the most civilized of men. Then, a year or so before I came into her life—actually about the time I first saw her—she was virtually engaged to my rich friend Mike Cudahy. In fact, when Flobe and I entered the Friday night dance contests at the Cocoanut Grove, it was often Joan and Mike, both superb dancers, who won first prize.

By the time Billie and I were a Winchell item, one would be safe in assuming that the now well-known Joan Crawford had read many a fine book and dined in many an elegant setting. Billie always harbored an inferiority complex which she used as a whip to spur herself onward and upward. It seemed to bolster her self-confidence to enlist as confidantes and beneficiaries of her largesse those who worked in humbler backstage studio jobs than she. She retained the loyal friendship of an old school beau in Kansas City, but otherwise her closest friends were those to whom she could appear as Lady Bountiful and Fairy Godmother. I always suspected she exaggerated her pre-career life history, even to me. But who am I to talk or throw stones?

To be honest, in her own way she taught *me* a great deal and pushed me to a fuller height as my own self and away from the person hiding his shyness behind such affectations as imitating Barrymore and pretending to an unreal aestheticism. It is probably fair to say that at that particular brief juncture of our lives, we were constructive and happy influences on each other.

That a strain of sorts developed between my parents and me was, to a large extent, my own fault. Billie was more symbol than cause. In their different ways, my family would have disapproved of my being too romantically serious about anyone just then. That Billie was spectacular and came on strong certainly didn't help to ingratiate her with those whose preferred manner of living was more restrained. But she was fascinating, and I was wildly in love with her.

The first big family crisis began during one of the evenings when we were invited to Pickfair to see whatever movie they were showing that night. They ran a new film at least four nights a week. Dad, Mary, their guests, and often Charlie Chaplin from next door, sat on rearranged sofas or large overstuffed chairs. Billie and I shared a well-cushioned *chaise* for two, pushed far over to the side of the long living room in which the films were projected. Two large professional projection machines were installed behind a wall in the hall. They were covered with tapestries when no films were being shown.

We thought we were being very discreet in the way we expressed our mutual ardor over there in our shadowy corner. After all, we only "embraced" when the lights were out and the others were watching the silent movie. But that was my mistake. Apparently we had not been as inconspicuous as our youthful fervor allowed us to think—if indeed we did much thinking at all. After two or three such undisciplined and distracting indulgences, Dad, in an angry but controlled voice, let me (not Billie) have it! To this day I can feel the deep scarlet flush on my face. There can be few occasions more mortifying than one in which from the start you know you're wrong and you have absolutely no excuse whatsoever.

"Don't you blame Joan, now! It was all *your* fault!" Dad was as angry as he had been at any time since I let slip some wind among company as a small boy. In any case, it was some time before we were asked to see a movie at Pickfair again—and when at last we were, we took good care to sit well apart from each other. However much we restrained our public behavior, though, there was no disguising our head-over-heels look. On separate occasions both Dad and Mother worried aloud that we might indeed marry. Dad protested to Kenneth and Uncle Bob that we were not "well suited" and, besides, "Junior is far too young."

Excessive publicity can be very destructive. But as a natural chauvinist, I loved it—especially when Billie clung to me in crowds like a frightened little animal. We also annoyed or amused others with the frequent use of our own special "Pig Latin," employed so no one could understand us. On being overheard, our most trivial comment was expanded and repeated, thus encouraging us to believe our private lingo might be one of the few good ways really to be private.

She and I had come a good way toward creating our own images of each other, some of it no doubt influenced by what the columnists and fan magazine hacks wrote about us. Although it is hard to recapture one's intimate thoughts over half a century later, I think it is entirely possible that the idea of our getting married was first propounded by the press, gossipers, and the generally fierce light of publicity. However the idea did come about, we thought well of it. But I've often thought since that had we been ordinary citizens, we might well have enjoyed no more than an intense sowing of wild oats.

I have read many yarns about those days and have learned to suspect their veracity. For instance, I know that I was more attracted to Billie than anyone I'd known before, but I certainly don't recall, as was printed, slyly giving her a secret engagement ring. Perhaps I did—I did a lot of foolish things—but I can't remember for certain. I was frankly far from being the artistic, intellectual, completely altruistic young knight in armor she thought I was.

For my part, I suspected that she had had a greater variety of seamy experiences than I, but that actually intrigued me. My own past romantic attachments had usually been swathed in soft-focus idealism and sentimentality. Billie did not fit my previously known pattern. But we certainly shared a strong physical attraction. And as we both liked the idea of being "in love," and we sincerely thought we were, that was enough.

We worried only slightly about the disparity in our ages, although Billie successfully kept her true age a secret from press, public, and me. She was, I think, about four years older than I. My own age had been public knowledge, but as I began a campaign to make myself a little older, she arranged to slip quietly backward.

The most important contribution that Billie made to my evolving character was her insistence that I break away from home and Mother. The greatest gift Billie gave me (far better than anything I ever did for her) was a ramrod up my backside—the encouragement to be courageous. It paid many dividends in after-years. She made no bones about telling me that I'd "never be a real, responsible, grown-up man" as long as I let myself be controlled by Mother. I couldn't deny that I had become pathologically frightened of family scenes. In brutal short, the question was: Had I the gumption to tell my "blood-sucking family where to get off"?

Each time I hinted to Mother that I intended to leave home, she became hysterical and threatened all sorts of dire actions. Once, I came back fairly late from Billie's house and found a cryptic note from Mother asking me to look in and say good night. I squeaked her door open a bit. Her bed light was on, and there she was, sprawled across the bed as if in a deep, deep sleep, or a dead faint, or perhaps even a coma. A three-quarters empty bottle of gin was on her bedside table with a nearly empty glass and a spilled bottle of sleeping pills. A rough shake of her shoulders produced no reaction. I was horrified and about to ring for the police or an ambulance. I picked up the phone and, almost without thinking, took a quick sip from her glass. There was neither gin nor vodka in it—just plain water. I slammed the glass down in sudden anger at this childish, badly executed trick. At that, Mother opened her eyes blearily, and, seeing me, mumbled semicoherently, "Oh, don't call the doctor! I'll be all right! I'll be all right! But look, *look* what you, my beloved son—you and that dreadful girl—have done to me!" And she sobbed hysterically into her pillow.

Unintentionally, I managed to shock Mother into another white fury when, for the first time on another night, I didn't return home from Billie's until morning. Billie's small Moorish house on Roxbury Drive was a ponderously "decorated" house—as if for a deeply religious, Latin American *femme fatale,* a vintage Theda Bara perhaps, who had been left to her memories of old triumphs. Billie's bosses and friends at MGM had arranged for the purchase of the house for her a year or so earlier. I must say I felt pretty sophisticated and daring when I awoke that morning, for the first time, in the house of a girl I was serious about.

I still had one major problem. As a minor, I had no money I could legally claim as my own, except my weekly allowance. Mother still controlled the family purse strings and she was hanging on to me and them with all her loving and acquisitive guile.

Eventually, sweet but not rich Veda Buckland conspired with dear and very rich Noël Sullivan in San Francisco to lend me a healthy sum of money and also to put a small but adequate additional amount in a special secret account. With that kind of adult encouragement, I surreptitiously packed essentials and checked myself into the most modest room a junior member could get at the Hollywood Athletic Club.

I braced myself in anticipation of the hell that would break loose when Mother discovered my move. Instead, her reaction was an eerie, melodramatic silence. I guessed that Mother was up to another of her "performances." I received a concerned phone call from my grandfather Dan'l that confirmed this. His encouragement, all the old ex-King of Cotton could by now afford, was enormously helpful. And then, best of all, came an accolade of praise from Billie. Having faced up to what I had feared, I felt I'd at last jumped into the icy waters of maturity.

My new residence thus established, I bit the bullet and returned home to face Mother, who, to my immense surprise, received me with docility and charm. Her naturally beautiful skin was now powdered a sickly white. Her soft wavy hair, only a bit whiter than her face, was now pulled back straight with a bun at the back. But her smile was as gentle as her voice. It was like that forced tone of hollow congeniality one hears outside a church after a funeral service. Nevertheless, her manner, whatever she felt inside, was charming. She was solicitous about my comforts at my new address, though she couldn't resist saying, "Oh, do give me the Club's telephone number, dear. You know, just in case I should need you suddenly . . ." I knew that this kind of "hanging on" was unnatural. Veda had deliberately taken her to a theater in downtown Los Angeles to see a play called *The Silver Cord* about the unhappiness caused by a woman who clings too long and too hard to her son. But Mother liked it very much, and never for a moment recognized herself in the story.

While I gradually and, I hoped, discreetly made myself Billie's practically permanent houseguest, there was little more heard directly from either of my parents. Professionally, Billie and I had now acquired a very able agent, Mike Levee, who, with the help of family friends, was able to persuade Mother that his office would be the most efficient administrator of the family finances. He took over the payment of bills, gave her and the family what was needed, and added an allowance for me to pay for my newly acquired expenses. Of course, without Noël Sullivan's substantial help I still couldn't have made it. It was many years before I managed to repay him, in installments, despite his resistance. Mother must have been more mystified as to how I managed than she would admit.

Billie's career was developing more spectacularly than mine. Earlier on, she had had a marvelous daily escape from our public and private pressures by playing her first real leading part in a Roaring Twenties film called *Our Dancing Daughters.* Although it was one of the last of the completely silent pictures, she was called upon to dance a wild Art Deco interpretation of the Charleston—at which, of course, she was unsurpassed. She made a spectacular impression. It was an exciting performance, so much so that from that time on, Billie—as Joan Crawford—became and remained, in success or failure, in good times or bad, an honest-to-God big star—until her restless retirement.

Quite properly on the strength of her achievement, she was awarded a new contract at something like $1,250 a week for forty weeks a year, with $250 a week annual raises (provided her options were exercised) over the following four years. Thus her career had a wonderful first bounce into the top rank of box-office stars.

Then my own professional luck peaked again—luckily for my own ego. My performances in *A Woman of Affairs* and *The Power of the Press* were now being talked about in the front offices that counted. One day, away from "Neurosis Corner" (what I privately called my family's home) my new agent, Mike, told me that the big First National Company had offered me the juvenile lead in a movie adaptation of the Broadway and London hit play *The Barker.* Milton Sills, a popular "he-man" star, was to play the title role, and the two leading ladies were to be the equally popular Betty Compson and Dorothy Mackaill. Furthermore, *The Barker* was to have six or eight talking sequences. All the publicity, and the ads, made a big point of this and, from my point of view, it was to be a bright new feather in my cap. Billie had yet to be in a talkie—and was terribly frightened of them. But I was getting a fine new chance with a big producing company, in a well-known play, an all-star cast, and with a top director, George Fitzmaurice.

My talking scenes were very well received by the company's producers and executives. My limited stage experience and drama courses were now paying off. Thus, before I'd even finished the film, I too was offered a new "five-year contract." In reality it was for only a year of only forty paid weeks in that year, with the company retaining yearly options after that. In addition, I had no right to work elsewhere during the twelve-week "layoff," unless my company ordered me to do so.

Most of the better actors' agents with big and important clients scrupulously kept on the best of terms with the studio heads lest they be barred from the studio, as they sometimes were. This also meant they were obliged to take sides (very secretly of course) with the companies against their own clients. We always assumed that even the best of them couldn't afford to have a real set-to with a Mayer, a Warner, a Schulberg, a Schenck, a Goldwyn, or a Zanuck. But Mike Levee, a shrewd man, rode the wave of my latest "high" as best he could. He conned my new bosses into giving me an advance on my new contract. He was only able to do this after arduous buttonholing in which he successfully disabused them of the widely held belief that I, as my father's spoiled son, had scads of money.

While all these routine pictures were being churned out like sausages, Billie and I made a big decision. Actually, she made the decision and I, after quite a bit of foot-dragging, went along with it. She saw a house and set her heart on acquiring it as our prospective dream home. My hesitation about such a transaction was readily traceable to male chauvinism: I couldn't yet afford to buy it myself or even to pay an equal share. I argued that though my contribution might at first have to be less than hers, because of the difference in our incomings and outgoings, I would catch up as soon as I damn well could. She remained unimpressed with my financial frustrations ("What's wrong? It's only money!"), and so the business of her buying the house became the first snag in our relationship. It symbolized an unwished-for rivalry and a contradiction of her public manner of "wifeliness" or even of "equal partnership."

Indeed, in her impatience to be mistress of a bigger house than her old one, and in anticipation of a wedding and of subsequent entertaining in a manner befitting her status as star and my (future) wife, she wheedled Mr. Mayer and other friends at his MGM Court into advancing her enough to start payments. The house was several miles west of Beverly Hills in Brentwood, a new development halfway to Santa Monica and the sea. I agreed that it was charming—medium-sized and unfinished. It was capable of expansion since there were vacant lots for sale beside and behind it. In fact, the house underwent many changes as Billie continued to live there for a great many years. Eventually she sold it, but it still stands, virtually unrecognizable—at least to me.

She got her old friend, occasional costar, and eventually famous decorator William Haines, to decorate it. Billy Haines was, in most ways, her most intimate confidant, but since he was not interested in girls I welcomed his good, earthy advice to her. Billy was a vastly amusing fellow with a great gift for decorating. He was one of the few close friends who called her Joan. He did the job "for cost." He took more than a hint from the famous Syrie (Mrs. Somerset) Maugham's decorating tricks—such as all-white rooms. Billie became so enamored of this style and so fanatic about cleanliness that when the house was finished, she insisted that everyone, even her closest friends, take their shoes off when they entered. Aside from Muslim mosques, the only other place where I've seen this order enforced was Merle Oberon's house in Mexico (I really think she just wanted to copy Billie).

While I still argued against buying—at least until we were married—

Billie presented me with a *fait accompli.* The house was bought in her name and I began to figure how and when I could contribute my share and continue to be the man she had pushed me into becoming the year before. I still carried out the fiction of living at the Athletic Club. Actually, I was there when I was working, which was a bit more than half the time. We agreed to give our new house a name. Despite the fact that it turned my stomach, Billie had nicknamed me "Dodo," so she thought it would be cute to combine shortened versions of our names and call the house El Jodo.

On reflection, this seemed too silly, so we invented another name, this one sugary: Cielito Lindo (Beautiful Little Heaven), after the popular Mexican song. If it was possible to be cornier we hadn't yet heard how.

I was angry at allowing myself to be overridden by the purchase of the house. It was my first major experience of winning skirmishes but losing battles; of being so keen on possession that, like certain insects, I was myself possessed.

As long as I knew her, Billie had a different set of values than I. Hers were based on the belief that success was the alpha and omega of life—a condition of mind adjudged typically American by some but in her case more pronounced and visible than in most. Her horizons, her standards, her interests, and enthusiasms were limited to her own professional world. At work, her powers of concentration were immense. Once, when a role required her to sing a couple of songs, she stubbornly refused to have her voice dubbed. She knew her own singing was unmusical, so, with typical determination, she drove miles at least twice a week for lessons with a renowned singing teacher. As I sometimes accompanied her, I can vouch for the boredom. The results were not overwhelmingly successful, but they were just barely good enough for her to demand to be allowed to do her own singing.

All this effort was directed at leaving nothing to chance in her campaign to win the public's adulation. This was reflected in the vast amount of fan mail that she answered, in her financial rewards, and in her advertised and legal status of star. And she won the approval of all her peers hands down. She could dance very well, swim, and hit a tennis ball, but she had few diversions away from work—unless one counted her favorite tranquilizers: knitting and learning how more sophisticated folk decorated their houses and bodies. A favorite time-killer at home was competing to see who could flip the most cards into a wastebasket from six feet. Her one *real* game was Backgammon, and I was talked into playing it so excessively, that I doubt if I have played the damned game more than three times since those years.

Billie insisted that everything had to be spotless all the time. She was also understandably concerned with maintaining her famous figure. She watched her diet and her scales daily, gloried in doing her "daily dozen" push-ups and having my little old Mexican, Fred Miron, give her a massage. After any strenuous exercise she would rub her skin down with hunks of ice, believing this would keep muscles and skin tight. Although she would later deny it, she did worry about ever having a child lest it somehow ruin her figure and she saw to it that she had none. She was an excessive smoker but even though, later in life, stories of her drinking problems abounded, when I knew her she didn't drink at all. Nor do I recall her having any domestic temper. She might get fiercely angry at something or someone connected with her work, but her reaction was to argue vehemently and, if defeated, sulk, or affect a quiet, tight-lipped retreat. But temper? I never saw one.

In retrospect, I am sure our marriage was psychologically hastened by the quiet, unpublicized but vehement opposition of my parents. Billie's mother, on the other hand, thought the idea "very nice," even "swell." The embarrassing picture the world saw and gobbled up was the once poor and humble, now bright and beautiful, hard-working, talented little girl from the Middle West and the gifted, worldly "Crown Prince of Hollywood." It was irresistibly romantic. Only the far more famous romance of my father and Mary exceeded ours in gossipy press coverage and letter writing (MGM and First National Studios reported that literally thousands of letters a week, addressed either to Billie or me, or both, were received and handled by their respective mail departments).

In June of 1929 we did marry. By that time, Mother had long since sold the big house on Beverly Drive, leaving the Sullys in a Hollywood apartment, Dedie on a pension from me in Ireland, and replanted herself in New York. Dad had grown ever more strongly opposed to our marriage, but refused even to discuss the situation—for which I was just as glad since *I* was reluctant to discuss it, too. Mary, as always, was helpful and sweet and tried to persuade him to ease his opposition; to accept the fact that I was now older, wiser, and more responsible. At the same time she tried to persuade Billie and me to wait just a bit longer. Six months, or a year maybe.

And as I say, the public pushed us on. The opposition of my family actually had much less to do with the unsuitability of glamorous movie-star Joan Crawford as my future wife than it had to do with my youth (I was nineteen).

One day in May we decided to get away from it all and take a train to New York. We gratefully allowed Frank Case to put us up at the Algonquin. Mother was staying there too.

Although she had moved back to New York with some anxiety, Mother's life there had not been as uneventful as she feared. The Cases and other friends helped her adjust very well. To keep the seas calm, I had to promise that she would hear from me several times a week. It was an expensive promise—in time and effort rather than money. That I felt it was well worth it, if only to be relieved of the emotional pressure of her opposition, should not be construed as any diminution of my deep affection and admiration for her. But in addition to Mother's prides and prejudices and the charm that she could turn on like a tap, she never let one forget her various ailments: the nearly numb left side of her chin resulting from a dental mishap, the stone-deafness in one ear from the same cause, her close call with death from an appendectomy, and her panicky conviction that the slightest bump to her oversized bosom was bound to bring on cancer. With all that, I loved her. She had been utterly devoted to me and I was the focal point of her life. She had done all she knew how to encourage my wide-ranging if unconventional education. In some respects she failed, but she did try and I remained deeply grateful.

Ever a theatrical outsider, but always trying to get inside, Mother found herself involved in a discreet but nevertheless nerve-racking (because his wife was her close friend) attachment to stage star Taylor Holmes. Eventually, after prolonged tension and occasional hysterics, they broke it off, convinced that no one had ever been aware of their secret. But they were quite wrong, as I, for one, suspected something but kept well out of the way.

In any event, once she had dug herself back into life in New York as a young fortyish, white-haired lady, Mother was flattered to find a number of beaux paying flirtatious attention to her. One very brief (and, I believe, uneventful) "walkout" was with Gene Markey, a talented, witty author and man-about-Europe from Chicago. For years he was the principal love in the life of Broadway's superb comedienne Ina Claire. He was one of the few who did not marry Gloria Swanson, but they lived very happily together for quite a while. He did, however, marry such glamour girls as Joan Bennett, Hedy Lamarr, and Myrna Loy. Finally, after innumerable fabulous mistresses in between, he wed the very rich widow from Chicago, Lucille Wright, whose late husband willed her Calumet Farms, one of the nation's greatest stud farms and racing stables.

One evening, shortly after her return to New York, Mother attended a performance of the hit musical *Hold Everything* with Aunt Gladys. The leading man was Jack Whiting. Jack was a handsome redhead, about twenty-seven or -eight years old, with a virile baritone that helped make "You're the Cream in My Coffee" a successful song. He had a talent for dancing that was equal—some said—to Fred Astaire's or Gene Kelly's. Mother apparently developed an immediate crush on him.

Despite the difference of over twelve years in their ages, Jack, to everyone's surprise, was also very taken with the still pretty Beth. By the time Billie and I arrived in New York there was more than a hint of romance between them. Jack was warm and friendly to us both and we hit it off handsomely. Privately, however, I thought it damned odd that a conventional fellow like Jack would fall for a woman like my mother.

Mother's new situation no doubt contributed to her marked change of attitude toward Billie and me. For a year or more she had told all who would listen that the first time she had met Billie was when we had picked Mother up in my car to take her to the theater with us. Billie, she said, sat well back in her seat reading a book, both going and coming, and never spoke a word all evening. "*Very* rude!" said Mother, and then added, "But what can you expect?" Billie, poor girl, was terrified and, with her rough treatment by the Cudahys so fresh in her memory, still unable to cope with frosty families. Now, however, Mother suddenly became warmer toward Billie. She even seemed enthusiastic about our marriage.

She and Jack accompanied us to New York's City Hall where, ducking in by back and side doors to avoid the press and the curious, we applied for our license. Billie swore her San Antonio birth certificate was lost but that her mother's letter ("Here it is . . . !") confirmed she was born March 23, in 1908—and not, as we suspected, in 1904 or '05. Mother likewise amended the statistics by vouchsafing my birthday as December 9, 1908. Of course, had anyone taken the trouble, they could have popped upstairs to find my birth certificate where it still is filed, showing the true date of 1909. In later years it was only natural for Billie to be pleased with this juggling of dates, whereas I had many reasons to regret it.

Although in later life she briefly became a Christian Scientist, at that time Billie professed to be Roman Catholic and therefore wanted to marry in the Church. From no real conviction except to declare myself stolidly for something, I acknowledged I was raised an Episcopalian. I could not swear, as required, to bring up any children we might have as Catholics. This good-natured impasse meant we were not allowed to marry in the church itself. As a compromise, we were married in the chapel of St. Malachy's Catholic Church, known in New York as "the Actors' Church" because it is close to the theater district and most favored by theater folk. Mother and Jack were witnesses, as were the Frank Cases, Jack's best friend and colleague John Hundley, and an amusing, unemployed actor friend of mine who happened to be there at the time, Allen Vincent.

Never mind that it wasn't the full "bridal dress, maid-of-honor, flower girls, groom and ushers in morning coats" kind of wedding Billie would have preferred. It was, nevertheless, in its simplicity, sobering and very moving. We couldn't have had anything more elaborate anyway since we had neither the time, concerted family blessings, nor financial support. Thus we also avoided most of the publicity we dreaded.

Not long after the ceremony, when we got back to the Algonquin, the news came out and messages from Billie's mother and her brother, Hal, arrived. Then, to our immense surprise, came a long telegram from Dad. I don't know the fate of the original but I can remember quite well that it was absolutely charming and full of hearty blessings. It was in fact so very warm that Billie cried with relief on the spot. For two youngsters already over their heads in the choppy waters of life in a huge goldfish bowl, it was a never-to-be-forgotten (regretted, perhaps, but not forgotten) day. We were relieved and happy. We were truly married. And we lived happily . . . for a while.

9

MGM's "history" of the wedding insists that the New York trip was L. B. Mayer's idea. It was nothing of the sort. He didn't even know about it until Billie wired him. Taking a honeymoon was out of the question since we both had jobs to return to. But for a very few days in New York, and to the delight of the crowds wherever we went, we managed to see a few of the latest plays and enjoy ourselves.

A few weeks later in California we were astonished by a telegram from Mother and Jack, announcing that they had married. We were dumbfounded. And I was relieved. A great deal of Mother's pressure on me would now be lifted. I had a new stepfather—charming, gifted, and only about eight or nine years older than I. A devoted mother's boy himself, Jack, I imagined, might become both a proxy for me and for my never-forgotten father in Mother's life.

The bright Crawford skyrocket notwithstanding, her next few pictures were quite indifferent. However, they did further confirm her ever-growing personal popularity. They were designed to trade on the success of *Our Dancing Daughters* and with that paucity of imagination for which Hollywood in the thirties was famous, her next was called *Our Modern Maidens.* (MGM couldn't let well enough alone. Sometime later, poor Billie had to make a third one: *Our Blushing Brides.* Even I, long before, had had to appear in a bit of trash called *Modern Mothers*—but without the *Our.*) Billie's leading man in *Our Modern Maidens* was an old Malibu Beach camp friend, Rod La Rocque. And just to jolly up the potential box office, MGM "borrowed" me from First National to play the second lead.

It was a good exploitation stunt but we went ahead with mixed feelings. It was pleasant enough to work together, though we felt like commercialized puppets, and I was self-conscious. Mine was a silly, amicable part. In one sequence I had a specialty act—a sop, as it were, to my and First National's egos. I was expected to do my "party piece," which comprised a series of mimed imitations of well-known picture personalities. They included my father, John Barrymore, Jack Gilbert, and Maurice Chevalier. I'd started doing them for fun at parties. Once I'd performed in the luxurious beach house of Irving Thalberg, who, besides being creative boss of MGM, was the husband of one of its most beautiful stars, Norma Shearer. Because Billie was so jealous of her, she was Billie's *bête noire*. I'd been a nervous young bachelor at the time and flattered to be asked to that sophisticated party.

One of the supposed guerdons of film fame was planting one's hands, feet, and signature in wet cement in the forecourt of Grauman's Chinese Theater in Hollywood. The gimmick had originally been thought up by Sid Grauman himself, but only for Mary, Dad, Chaplin, and Barrymore. Later he was pressured by the studios to do the same thing for their Big Names. So when it was MGM's turn to plug its newest star, Joan Crawford, she and I were both sent downtown to a big, searchlight- and police-ridden event in front of the theater. The report that we both left our marks for posterity was only half true. The film and the star were MGM properties and I was a corporate foreigner from First National. Hence, no provision was made for my recorded hands or feet at all.

It must be said that my own new contract with First National fizzled down to another loan-out, this time for another quickie company, FBO, and a silly film that I choose to pass over quickly. It was only slightly better than a potboiler. It was called *Fast Life* and the villain was Chester Morris, a fine actor and pal who stuck to movies and did very well indeed. (We joked for years about the blurb on the posters for that picture: "They not only played their parts; they *lived* them!" The hell we did!) Another newcomer to movies who had a far lesser part and was a splendid guy to work with was Bill Holden. He possessed a mellifluous voice but we all privately agreed that his inexperience was still too evident—the competition too tough. In time he fooled us all.

My leading lady was a mere slip of a girl, hardly more than a child—Sally (Ann Young) Blane's and Polly Ann Young's baby sister, Gretchen. I recalled how annoying she had been a couple of years ago when I arrived to pick up one of her sisters before a dance. She always pranced around in pigtails, giggling, her big teeth in braces, trying to eavesdrop. She was a nuisance. Now, she was somewhere between sixteen and eighteen, had grown disturbingly pretty, and was given heroine leads demanding only that she be the object of the hero's devotion. Her name had been changed to Loretta. We hardly spoke on this, her first picture, but we became—against our wills—a popular "team" with the public. She worked and studied very hard until she became an excellent actress and, in time, an important star herself. After our next picture we began to warm up—purely platonically, let me promptly but sadly insist. We ended by making about six pictures together—three more that very year of 1929. Most of them were fairly successful, few were really good. The best result of our partnership was that we became the fondest of friends.

Whenever I was able to squeeze in a play between movies, even for a few weeks, I did. Most were of better quality than the movies I was making, and each was an advance in my efforts to master my craft as an actor. Among these plays were Maxwell Anderson's *Saturday's Children,* Philip Barry's *The Youngest,* and then, a few years later, *The Man in Possession,* in which Ray Massey had had a Broadway hit, as had Leslie Banks in London's West End. The latter was an amusing and well-written comedy with an excellent star part for me and a fine cast, headed by an Austrian actress named Nora Gregor. One night she confided she had been out "carouzing mit your freund, dat Bobbity Montygummarrry" and was feeling headachy and squeamish. I paid no attention until the second act, when I was obliged to kneel beside her—always a tricky business because I had once, in an action movie, torn a cartilage and chipped a bone in my knee. Every time I knelt it emitted a loud and painful *crack!* So I had to speak over the sound at the exact moment: "Oh, my dear one, you must give up your sordid life of play and [cue to kneel] come *AWAY*" (crack!) "with me to an island I know in Greece."

On this particular night, shortly after I'd knelt beside her as she lay stretched out on a couch, center stage, wearing a lovely white lace evening dress, she turned her head upstage, away from the audience, and, pushing me away from her at the same time, whispered, "Ach, I'm gonna be zick!" With that she rose suddenly from the couch, nearly knocking me off my bended knee, and dashed off stage.

I couldn't think what to do. I went over to the fake fireplace and pretended to stoke a nonexistent fire. I whispered through the opening, *"Bring the curtain down!* Bring it DOWN!" No luck!

The stage manager, who happened to be my ex-drama coach Delevanti, and who also played the small part of a London bailiff in the third act, whispered back at me from behind the prop logs, "You're doing fine! Just ad-lib! She won't be long! Keep going!"

I had no experience in how to follow such orders so, in desperation, I went to the stage telephone and dialed an invented number, reached an imaginary person at the other end, and began a series of quite unconnected, mildly rude stories and jokes that both amused and confused the audience.

Frau Gregor still had not reappeared, when I heard a knock on the set door, center stage. I went over and opened it. There, standing in the doorway, was Delevanti, costumed and made up as the bailiff. With a broad, easy smile, he said, "Good morning, sir. I wasn't expected until tomorrow but I decided to come today."

"Come in," said I for lack of a readier wit. And he did.

We sat down and exchanged totally unrelated pleasantries for several minutes, no doubt completely bewildering the audience, until we heard a hoarse stage whisper from the wings: "She's okay to come back now! All clear!"

With that Delevanti rose and announced, "Well, if madam can't see me now, I'll return tomorrow as originally planned." And he left as he entered. No sooner was he off stage than Frau Gregor came in through the wings, her somewhat soiled white dress covered with white handkerchiefs pinned to her bosom. She quickly returned to the couch and I to my noisy bended knee. The show went on.

Neither Billie nor I had much opportunity to settle down in the conventional sense; we both worked too hard and hectically. Never, before or since, have I known any other professional who expended more personal energy on self-improvement courses and on her relations with her fans and the press as did the girl known as Joan Crawford. With one or two really dear friends from Kansas City, she kept up a loyal handwritten correspondence. But if she decided that some particular fan was consistently ardent and devoted enough, or if someone in the studio made a voluntary slave of himself for her (as some certainly did), they were favored by her frequent thoughtfulness and extravagant generosity.

Inclined as she was to exaggerate in so many ways, Billie went about physical fitness in typical fashion. She went to dance classes (when not filming) once or twice a week, took swimming lessons and daily exercises and massage. The cubes of ice she rubbed over her body were always as handy as her face creams and cosmetics. She did not have a notable sense of humor, and was memorably indignant when anyone pulled one of her famous legs about this routine.

She had a chosen few favorites among the members of the press with whom she shared confidences, knowing just how far they would go in printing them. Sometimes her pet fan-magazine writers submitted their articles in advance so that she could amend them if she chose. She paid fake-friendly obeisance to Louella Parsons, the shrewd and vengeful syndicated movie columnist for the then-great Hearst chain of newspapers. But then so did most of Hollywood, including me.

"Lolly" Parsons had been a friend of Marion Davies in Chicago, long before Marion had gone to New York and found her most loyal and magnanimous patron, the press titan William Randolph Hearst himself. Everyone—and no contrary voices were ever raised—loved Marion personally, although her films never quite caught on. She was delicious, irreverent, and generous. There were some who liked Hearst and some who admired him, but almost everyone feared him. His power in those days can hardly be believed in these. I recall my father once asking him, "Tell me, W.R."—as he was called by those who knew him—"now that you've got your own film company for Marion, and your own newsreels are shown everywhere, why don't you concentrate your energies more on motion pictures? That way you can have a worldwide public, instead of just the city-to-city fame that comes from journalism."

Hearst thought a moment and then, in his high, piping voice (so strange coming from that towering giant of a man), answered, "Well, Doug, I *have* thought about it but I've decided against it. Movies aren't that powerful, really. Why, you know, you can crush a man with journalism but you can't with motion pictures."

When Orson Welles made *Citizen Kane,* the brilliant, fictional story of Hearst, he was virtually blackballed from the American film world his talent graced so well.

Warner Brothers, once a quickie company and now *nouveau-riche* because of their successful pioneering investment in sound movies, took over First National (and me with it, of course). My total credits for that work year of 1929 amounted to six pictures. As indifferent as the Crawford pictures had been, mine were several notches lower. MGM at least mounted their trash well. Warner Brothers didn't; most were just mediocre. I did make one picture that, though not very good, may be of some interest to movie buffs. It was called *The Forward Pass* and it was a football story, with myself as the quarterback hero and Loretta ("Gretch") Young as the heroine. It so happened that I was a fervent fan of the USC Varsity Football team and felt no honor could be greater than to be allowed to watch practice or visit a fraternity house. Many directors and producers who were also fans did what they could to help the USC athletes get summer jobs to help pay their tuition *(that* should indicate how long ago all this was). And that was how we happened to hire the whole USC football team to be the "school team" in *The Forward Pass.* Most of them were nice fellows who were unimpressed by movie people. When the cameraman began to shoot, the players thought it great fun to rush through my so-called protective linemen and, instead of letting me run with the ball or pass as rehearsed, to crash into me, set me down hard on my backside, pile up on top of me, and then apologize. The director, Eddie Cline, was in on their joke and thought it fun too. So did everyone, except me. It was summer, it was hot, and I was not prepared for such rough going. But I knew if I so much as cried, "Ouch!" I'd never hear —or feel—the end of it.

Two of the fellows on the team were friends of mine, one a quarterback, Marshall Duffield, and the other a huge guard, named Marion Michael "Duke" Morrison. Three years later, I got Morrison a job in another picture of mine called *The Life of Jimmy Dolan* in which he was to have one spoken line, perhaps his first. As one of my fight trainers, he came in while my gloves were being tied on, slapped me on the back, and said, "You okay, boss?" I nodded and he exited. Morrison decided to stay in films, but under the name of John Wayne.

It is impossible for me to recapture the degree of happiness or compatibility that existed between Billie and me that first year or so. I should say we were both sufficiently imaginative so that, inasmuch as we firmly decided we would "damn well be happy . . ." we were. This is not to suggest, however, that we were content—which is, of course, a more important state of mind and more impervious to passing influences.

There are accounts that after our marriage the atmosphere at Pickfair reverted to the marked chill Billie had caught the year before. It was said she was tense and unhappy whenever we went up there and that I had been neglectful of her when my father asked me to join him and his friends for a game of "DOUG" or a steaming first, meeting her at the house later.

Dad and Mary had been away again (he was beginning to make occasional trips alone) but had now returned. He was deep into the production of *The Iron Mask,* a sequel to *The Three Musketeers,* with another chance to play D'Artagnan.

I admit there was a discernible coolness emanating from "the Big House on the Hill" and invitations were few. Indeed, I myself was rarely relaxed there. I often felt I was "on sufferance" and I do remember Billie being occasionally uncomfortable about it. But as the outside world was not aware of this, she did not seem to take it with any real seriousness. There was certainly no outright unpleasantness between my father and me, but there was no great warmth either. Some said that Dad's fetish of youth made the reality of my marriage to a spectacular young star a disturbing factor. He and I hardly ever discussed personal or family matters. Nor did he seem to know or care much about my professional progress. Usually our conversation was limited to sports and the news.

It may well be that I have up to now been a shade too "understanding" of my father's variable feelings toward me. Perhaps, in balance, I have been too impatient with my mother's overdemonstrative devotion. Probably, because Dad had been my "hero of heroes," I overlooked many slights and rebuffs noted by others just because I didn't want to think they had happened.

Putting myself in Dad's shoes, I could see that, despite Mary's poise as wife and hostess and her shrewd business acumen, he preferred her public image of a little girl. Dad had created a child-bride for himself. He was always a very jealous man, and Mary and her world were the principal targets of that jealousy. He never let her sit next to anyone else but him at any dinner table. Nor could she dance with anyone else. He had built his career on a vision of himself as the ever-young champion. I belonged to him reluctantly—biologically, if not financially or emotionally. But I was by now physically bigger than he and becoming fairly well known to a new generation, so he couldn't exactly shake me off, or hide me.

Dad was never overtly unkind or unfair. Only rarely did he openly show anger or irritation—and then, with cause. He tried hard to be a conventional father but just couldn't quite bring it off.

He could not have enjoyed hearing Billie's frequent talk about having children. In fact, I never quite believed her. She often claimed she had had two miscarriages, but I had done some medical snooping that indicated nothing of the sort had happened. As she frequently voiced her fears that child-bearing might affect her figure, I suspect that was the real reason she never had children of her own. I was still too young to give it much thought. There was plenty of time for fatherhood and I was certainly not averse to it.

Nevertheless, the hint of a grandchild in the offing would not have been warmly welcomed by my father at that time—nor, I suspect, by Mary either. They enjoyed a status in the world's imagination that is totally inconceivable and incomparable by today's standards, and it was their serious business to keep it that way. I may have been uncomfortable in the private role of an unwitting threat to all that, but I never realized the full extent of my influence on their lives until I heard family talk of it many years later.

In 1929 Billie made four pictures and none quite measured up to the best of the six she had made the year before. *Our Modern Maidens* (the one I was in too) was the most successful, though *Untamed,* late in the year, brought a splendid young actor, fresh from the New York theater, as her leading man. Robert Montgomery and I became great companions and would share many agreeable adventures over the next dozen years. In order to get better stories and better parts, Billie carried on as hard a battle with the front office as she could without getting into trouble. She was too much in awe of Garbo to be jealous of her, but she made no bones of her jealousy of Norma Shearer, who was unquestionably given most of the plums. Since Norma was the wife of Irving Thalberg, boss of production, there was little Billie could do except grouse and protest, discreetly, to the press.

I have read that Billie tried to work single-mindedly at her career but found it difficult because of my insistence on a more "social life." Though reluctant to dispute the views of a revered person who no longer can rebut my rebuttal, I must say that that is so much rubbish. Billie let nothing stop her admirable though humorless dedication to professional advancement. It was useless to remind her that such other star actresses as Mary, Garbo, Gish, Hayes, Fontanne, or those younger ones who came later, like Hepburn, Leigh, and Davis, hardly ever bothered to curry favor with producers, directors, critics, columnists, or groups of fans. They learned their trade thoroughly, allowed their personalities full professional exposure, exploited their best qualities, and generally stayed away from all the circusing. Billie Cassin lacked some of the natural magic of some of her peers. Yet by dint of bloody-minded determination, intelligence, and guts, she invented Joan Crawford—and in that guise she stood proudly as an accepted equal to the best of all the others.

Although I doubt if she had ever heard of Stanislavsky's Moscow Art Theater or "the Method," she was one of a group of motion picture actors who really believed that to play a happy scene one must first get into a truly happy mood. For instance, she could not believe that Lynn Fontanne might feel physically dreadful yet be able to perform high comedy with supreme and subtle wit. Nor could she believe that a great actress like Helen Hayes could consciously reduce audiences to uncontrollable tears while she thought about having a juicy steak sandwich after the performance. Joan relied more than most silent movie actresses on the "mood music" created by a small two- or three-man combo that was, in those days, a regular part of a company's production crew. Her great saucer eyes could spill over with tears at the first chord of "Humoresque" or whatever sad incident she chose to think of at that moment. She was so very canny about the great size of her eyes that not only did her makeup carefully exploit them but in a picture she almost always tried to hold her head down and look up so that they looked even larger.

She respected my stepmother Mary very much, but she could not think of her as a real actress-artist (though she unquestionably was—and a great one), but rather as the cleverest, prettiest of "world personalities." She thought my father was a charming, magnificent accident of personality-plus-athleticism. He mystified her (and, I suppose, others) by his incessant doodling of the word "success." She was unsparing of herself in clawing after success. All her life Billie was driven by her own great "fire-in-the-belly" ambition—an ambition to succeed in spite of a less-than-great talent.

There was another impediment to our full contentment. Less than fully dedicated to my career, I was interested in a wider variety of other people and things. And I was encouraged in this by my old tutor Tom Patten and Mother's friend Veda Buckland as well as Flobe and Sissy. My cousins and I were so close we supported each other blindly. At this stage, Uncle Bob and Aunt Lorie's two daughters, the really beautiful Letitia and Lucile, were getting older and themselves becoming two more "sisters." Of course, Genie was always one of us as well. They never saw me in any but a sympathetic light. It is curious that Genie was the only one of my female intimates, and actor Allen Vincent among my male friends, whom Billie ever really took to and remained friends with through the years.

Money continued to be an unspoken anxiety. I wanted at best to be the main provider of our small household and at least an equal partner in dealing with all our expenses. But we had, over a period of weeks, exchanged much too extravagant gifts and I was in a poorer-than-usual financial state. By 1930, Billie was earning a bit more than $140,000 on her big new forty-weeks-a-year contract. My old First National (by now merged with Warner Brothers) contract was slightly more than half that. Yet out of that I was still giving Mother a rather liberal allowance, despite her recent remarriage. More "grants" went to my grandparents, and to my Uncle Bill and his new family. A youthful effort to put up an impressive "front" resulted in my getting further into debt—partly to the bank, partly to the Warner Brothers, and even more to Noël Sullivan.

Yielding to my instinct to show off, I traded in my old car for another secondhand one. The "new" old one was a freak—no longer in production —a sixteen-cylinder Cadillac. It was a very snazzy-looking vehicle but in this case the catch was that there were really only six, not sixteen, rather old cylinders under the hood. But few knew that. In a community where appearances were everything, I looked more prosperous than in fact I was.

When he first heard about my unweeded versatility in the arts, Noël Coward warned me to "beware of facility." He wagged his know-it-all finger, saying, "Don't ever, *ever*, take your own talent, developed or otherwise, for granted. Never relax and just sit on it." I never forgot his warning, though I doubt I ever applied it as rigorously as I should have. My interpretative talents had developed, but slowly, and my mind's ear heard only the same old words of feeble encouragement I got in my Paris student days: "Promising! Very promising!" For some time I lacked originality. I consciously fell back on imitations. Sometimes I assumed a vague set of Barrymore mannerisms. At other times it would be Gilbert, at others, Colman. I didn't want to adapt myself to "the Method" that encourages an actor to come as close as possible to living and actually feeling his part. I have come to believe that the best acting is a form of mimicry. One envisages how a character talks and behaves in prescribed circumstances and then rummages around in one's memory to locate a suitable model to mimic. "Natural acting" does not exist—it is a contradiction in terms. It is the illusion of the natural garnished with experience that is the actor's objective.

I had not yet fully understood the need for an actor to "become" the character he was portraying. Being young and impressionable, I was far too often tempted to affect mannerisms rather than wrap myself in the role I was to play. I found it more practical to follow Helen Hayes's advice. She once said to me, on the subject of whether actors should really weep in crying scenes, that in her view it was far more important for an actor to make an audience cry than to cry at will. The only man I knew who could weep at will, automatically, without emotion, and even control which eye (or both) produced tears and how many, was Jack Barrymore.

I could never cry to order. I invariably giggled, and that, clearly, was not helpful. But I could be chameleonlike in speech and manner. I always found mimicking people's mannerisms and accents fun and easy. Even in real life, I will sometimes quite unconsciously adjust my speech rhythms and intonations to those in whose company I spend some time. If I'm in the American South, for instance, I can be "you-alling" about the "Civ'l Waw-eh" almost as inarticulately as some of the natives, or if I'm in the "dese, dems, and doze" districts on "de Easide of toity-toid street of my own N'Yawk" no Damon Runyon character will sound more authentic. In the British Isles I catch myself slipping into either a very slight "Mayfair" or a very mild, suburban brand of Cockney, a moderate Lowland Scottish, or a softly lilting American-Boston Irish. Except in the conscious acting of an exaggerated character part, this off-stage adjustment of myself to others, this instinct to "belong" rather than be an outsider, has stayed with me always.

I continued to be plagued by comparisons with my father, both favorable and unfavorable. Often it was challenging, like: "I'll bet you'll never be as . . ." There is no denying that Dad and I were alike in many ways. If I did not deliberately alter my natural manners of walking and standing, they were very similar to his. However, my three and a bit inches more of loose-moving height, compared to his nervous and compact muscularity, meant that my athletic ability could never be as neatly abridged and executed as his. Also very different were some of our other mannerisms. My manner of speaking was not so explosive as his, nor my humor always so mischievous, fantastical, or extravagant. We shared blue eyes, but otherwise our coloring differed. His hair was brown and his skin dark and easily tanned; mine is fair, like Mother's. His face was a bit roundish; mine long and pointed, more like my uncle Bill Sully's.

Elinor Glyn once told me that, as my ears stuck out too much, I could never have the magic "IT," a vital requirement for success, and I was there-fore destined to fail as any kind of public figure. When I was younger, Mother strapped them back at night, or sometimes glued them, but since neither made any difference, I decided to bow to an "IT-less" destiny and get on with my handicap as best I could.

Despite all our dissimilarities, my father and I nevertheless gave many people an impression of being alike. The sharing of the same name was a great ambivalence to us both. How often Dad regretted his decision to pass his name on to his son can only be guessed.

Now that I was nearly twenty and married, it embarrassed him to call me Junior. So he used initials instead and I became "Jayar." Correspondingly, he didn't want to be called Dad or Father and I certainly couldn't call him Senior. I was uncomfortable with Doug, a name he never really liked any-way. "What would you like to be called if you weren't called Doug?" I asked.

"Oh, I don't know . . . Pete, I guess."

So from then on I called him Pete.

I certainly tried as hard as I could not only to avoid looking like my father but also not to be the same kind of actor. For many years I declined big offers to act in any swashbuckler film, regardless of its excellence, sub-ject matter, opportunity for advancement, or monetary temptation. I was determined to be a serious straight actor in either comedies, tragedies, or melodramas—as different in every way from my father as possible.

In an effort to further dissociate my still limited public image from his outsized one, there was a period during which I tried more assiduously than ever to appear at once healthy yet with the "lean and hungry look" of an aesthete. During my first married years I began to have short stories and poems printed—nothing sensational, but still good enough to be published by such reputable magazines as *Liberty* and *Esquire*. I had high hopes that as a writer I would be thought as slick as Arlen, as witty as Coward, as meaty as Hemingway. I was ever so wrong!

In 1930, without warning, my breaks returned, this time on a par with Billie's. The first sign of a change in my professional weather came when Jack Barrymore, himself under contract to Warner Brothers, was scheduled to remake *The Sea Beast*—this time using Herman Melville's original title *Moby Dick*. He requested that I be assigned the moderately good part of his brother. For me, the idea of working with and learning from my old hero thrilled me more than the picture itself. After all, despite Jack's seemingly infinite capacity for tankards of booze, resulting in frequent times off to dry out, he was nevertheless recognized as America's greatest actor (Warners billed him as "the World's Greatest . . ."). However, Howard Hawks, then a very good but not yet really famous director, had conspired with one of the most popular and powerful stars of Warners, Richard Barthelmess, to request that a picture of the British Royal Flying Corps be assigned as the company's next "Special." It was the original *The Dawn Patrol* and Hawks wanted to cast me in it.

Barrymore kept insisting—which was wonderfully flattering—that I appear with him. But he was finally overruled by my old friend from Poverty Row days, Darryl Zanuck, now executive boss of all Warner Brothers–First National pictures. Darryl was the brilliant driving force behind his company's series of tough and virile pictures. Actually, the nominal "Big Chief" was the youngest of the four Warner Brothers, J. L. Warner. The other three had less visible but more important jobs. "J.L.," as he was called, was often referred to (behind his back) as the "Clown Prince" because of his predilection for telling hoary old vaudeville jokes while chewing on or flipping ashes from an extravagantly long cigar. He was undoubtedly shrewder and probably brighter than he seemed, else he wouldn't have gone on being successful after Zanuck and, later, Zanuck's gifted successor Hal Wallis left him. But "J.L." did strain almost everyone's patience and loyalty with his show-off antics. Zanuck was quite young for his responsibilities—only twenty-eight or so—younger even than Thalberg at MGM but older than "Junior" Laemmle at Universal, the third and least-noted "Boy Wonder" of Hollywood. Although a sympathetic personal friend, Darryl agreed that I was better cast in *The Dawn Patrol* and predicted the result would be better for me. As I had no power of choice, that was, legally and in every other way, that!

Dick Barthelmess, a gentle, bright, and shrewd actor, made his first big success in the silents under Griffith and opposite Lillian Gish. He always correctly reckoned that a successful film was better for his career than a great part in an indifferent one. And so, with grace and the extension of a warm companionship that lasted for many years, he encouraged me in every phase of what turned out to be one of the best roles anyone had that year. The part, "Scotty," also provided me with an opportunity to push my mimicry button for a modified upper-middle-class English accent. It sounded reasonably authentic to those who didn't know any better, and even at its phoniest it was better than the accents of the other Yanks in the picture. Following *The Dawn Patrol,* producers thought I could speak good "English-English" and too frequently cast me in British parts. The British public knew better, of course, but tolerated me politely.

Set in wartime France in 1915, *The Dawn Patrol* is the story of a squadron of British fliers with only a handful of rattletrap planes to combat the powerful German Air Corps of the day. Rarely do all the British planes return from their forays behind enemy lines, and the squadron commander begins to crack under the strain of sending young men to their death.

The picture was very strenuous to make. Director Hawks was understandably anxious to bring this Epic of the Air War in at a cost not excessively over budget. This meant many weeks of long, late days and nights in the studio or locked into the airless special effects stages. After that came even longer days and later nights for weeks on end, shooting the exteriors on nearby locations intended to resemble wartime France. The effect, as in many Hollywood pictures, was not too bad if you didn't look too closely. Even allowing for a sit-down between scenes while cameramen and technicians prepared the next setup and the actors "ran" lines, we once or twice slogged on for periods of up to thirty-six hours without going home. We snatched half-hour naps on canvas chairs or in the backs of cars, wrapped up against the cold California nights in Indian blankets, with only paper-box meals.

Up to then there had been no effective trade unions organized or rules agreed upon that might have limited our working hours or provided us with better Gents facilities than prop trees, shrubs, small dried-up bushes, or the far side of the fuselage of some single-engine, single-seater De Havilland veteran. Sometimes there was nowhere to go and we just uninhibitedly did what we had to wherever we could. There were no women in the cast and the only female in the company was the script girl. Whenever she whimpered that she was approaching the limit of her endurance, an impatient assistant director (one of about five) commandeered a studio car to drive her to the nearest filling station and back. It was exhausting. Yet no one quit. Grumbled, sure. But quit? Not on your life! We knew we had something good and big and difficult, and everyone was well disciplined and part of a thoroughly professional team.

When *The Dawn Patrol* was finally released in mid-1930, I was delighted that my original hopes for *Moby Dick* had been overruled. Barrymore's new version turned out to be not nearly so good as his original silent one. But *The Dawn Patrol* became a spectacular, worldwide success. Neil Hamilton as the third member of our trio (that is, the first squadron commander, who cedes his post to Barthelmess, who in turn finds himself "executing" young fliers) was very good, though the part itself was unspectacular. Barthelmess, the star, was highly praised, as was Hawks's direction. My part was, glory be, acclaimed to the skies. It was, I admit, actor-proof, very sympathetic, and I made the best of it. At last, instead of aping others, I'd given an honest performance, using much of what I'd learned of my craft over the years.

In 1938 the same company remade the picture with Errol Flynn in the Barthelmess part, Basil Rathbone in Neil Hamilton's part, and dear David Niven in my part. Niv was, of course, great but always agreed with me that it was a fail-safe role—whoever played it.

The result of these kudos was that negotiations were soon begun between agent Mike Levee and Warners for a newer and better contract. The details were not to be agreed upon until I'd been "loaned out" to Universal to play the lead in a deliciously farcical (in its day) adaptation of a play about a bachelor father called *The Little Accident.*

It was followed by a surreal romantic melodrama from a successful English play, *Outward Bound,* about eight or ten passengers on a ship "somewhere they knew not where . . ." None of them are aware that they are all really dead. On the New York stage Alfred Lunt had played the lead most successfully and Leslie Howard made a hit as the young man who, with his sweetheart, feels unable any longer to face the vicissitudes of life and attempts suicide. In the film version, I was cast in the Leslie Howard part and Leslie was assigned the Lunt part. It was directed by Robert Milton, who had put on the New York stage production but was best known for having once angrily insisted that some poor actor speak "in pear-shaped tones." The picture was excellently done and praised by the critics but proved a disaster at the box office. However, Warners was happy with the film's prestige. And Leslie and I were pleased because all the principals in the cast came out with banners flying. Even better, Leslie and I established a hilarious and adventurous friendship off screen.

Leslie professed to hate acting and prefer writing, but his talent and technique were so uniquely subtle and appealing and his concentration on the job so admirable that he shortly became as popular on screen as he had been on the West End and Broadway. He was usually cast as the epitome of an aesthetic, sensitive, upper-class Englishman, when, in fact, he wasn't English at all. He was Hungarian, born of Jewish parents whose name was Stainer. Still, he thought of himself as 100 percent English—and he therefore became so—so much, in fact, that he gave his life for his adopted country. In 1943, he was shot down by the Nazis while flying from Gibraltar to England.

Leslie's wife Ruth, of whom he was absolutely terrified, was a large, buxom lady with a pretty face and a loud voice. Leslie persuaded her that he was a dreamer and so helpless that she should be responsible for the payment of all his bills and the management of his private life. This was a glorious, whimsical plan that provided him with time to have lots of private fun, though it sometimes got him into serious trouble. His easy charm plus his insatiable appetite for boudoir romance was responsible for a situation in which I was cautiously pleased to be the kind of friend-in-need we all hope to find in a pinch, except that it finally got me in trouble as well.

Leslie had always taken great risks in his casual-appearing but relentless philandering. He had masses of fascinating women everywhere, wanting at first to be either mother or sister to him—so helpless, vague, and dependent did he seem. But before the poor gullible wretches, of all social and economic levels, knew what was going on, they were supine in his arms.

Once when a studio girl became his eager victim, she also became pregnant. Such precautions as were then known and available were not in this case employed. The poor girl did not have enough money to pay for an operation and so, naturally, turned to Leslie. But Leslie, popular, generous, and well paid though he was, could not, because of his domestic arrangements, cash even a traveler's check for five dollars. Ruth handled everything. So he asked me to be his savior. Somehow I managed to scrape together enough out of my own usually near-empty till to pay for the "special" surgery. We all drew a deep sigh of relief and all seemed well again until Leslie sheepishly confessed he had no idea how he would repay *me!* Now *that* was *serious!* It was finally decided that we'd make up a story about how he had lost two big bets (on horses, perhaps—I don't recall) totaling five hundred dollars and Ruth would pay me from their account.

When Ruth heard this she raised the bloody roof and scolded him like a

Billingsgate fishwife for doing such a damnfool thing as betting with me—on *anything!* She even told him he should not consort with me any longer if I was such a foolish and extravagant gambler—who, she added, "is in any case backed by his rich father." In time, she learned that was not true, but she never heard the real story. Instead, she was destined for many another crisis resulting from Leslie's ardent lovemaking.

Billie and I hardly noticed when we began to take some of the publicity about ourselves seriously. I was still so delighted with having won the prize Miss Crawford that I lacked sufficient gumption to stand up against our exploitation by the studios and press. What little I did protest got me nothing except a revived reputation for being snooty and "uppity." Even Billie suspected that my reticence was an inherent snobbishness that was apt to handicap my career. The energy Billie invested in fighting for a good part with a good director and cast was no less than that she put into her publicity campaigns and her journalistic "friendships" and "confidants."

That she and I continued to fail to see eye to eye on this particular road to success was no secret. I couldn't persuade her that there were better paths to professional eminence than those she chose. I thought she should look beyond Los Angeles and at least take some cues from the stage. I tried to convince her that if she only wanted to appeal to what Thalberg once called "the lower-middle fairly common denominator of the American people," her hard-sell technique was all right. But since she protested that she had higher and more serious plans, I thought more subtle publicity would be best for her—and, very likely, for us both . . . in the long run.

10

The sudden and colossal success of sound motion pictures soon inspired the big companies to ask such great electronic corporations as Vitaphone and Western Electric to develop new and separately patentable systems for each of them. The race to capture and keep the public's newest taste was on. Inside of two years, from the time the first sound movie was shown, all major companies were distributing films with sound effects. Pen scratchings, door slams, thunder, engines, horses' hooves, and fully orchestrated background musical scores abounded. Actors' voices were still not widely heard. Then, gradually, spoken scenes began to be used and, finally, complete "all talking–all music" movies were shown.

The size of this investment can scarcely be imagined. In the first place, all the theater chains at home and abroad that were owned and controlled by the major studios had to be equipped with their "exclusive" system only. Next, all the old wooden, plaster, or stucco studio shooting stages had to be rebuilt and made soundproof. In addition, vast sound and electrical system cables and remote control centers for the recording of sound and turning film in cameras had to be installed and made practical by engineers who were still only a step beyond experimentation. Some studios recorded on wax records; some on separate, crackly film. All the cameras had to have large, clumsy, hard-to-move booths especially made for them. Each one contained extra-large cameras, one cameraman, and his assistant. They might nearly suffocate during the shooting of scenes—air conditioning was years away. And since only one recording of the voices could be made at a time, all photographically synchronized angles of a scene had to be shot at once. There were often as many as four or five—sometimes more—cameras shooting the same scene at the same time; one on a general long shot, one on a medium shot, and then special close-up cameras for each principal player in the scene.

At the same time the actual celluloid film changed with the introduction of increasingly sensitive negatives. This meant we could dispose of the old Klieg and Cooper-Hewitt lights, both of which often caused temporary blindness or pain for those who looked into them too long. The new lights had to be absolutely quiet, without the slight hum of the old lights that, with sound recording, could not be tolerated. New talking picture scenes took hours longer than usual to rehearse and for the cameraman (or "cinematographer" or "lighting cameraman" as he is now called) to light sets, groups, and/or each individual in each shot. Now the new subtle expertise has made such strides that the cinematographer is often not only the most technically knowledgeable person on a production, but maybe the chief—or only—true artist.

With the advent of color film, new kinds of makeup had to be invented that would photograph naturally. In the silent days, different types of black-and-white negative film stock reproduced colors differently—red lips went either coal black or just white. So some variations of brown began to be used on the girls with no more red at all. Many different concoctions of skin shades were created *ad hoc* for every complexion. Technicolor, the most advanced color system then in use, had been around for a while, but even after the success of my father's *The Black Pirate* (the first Technicolor feature) it was seldom used. The reason for this was that it added between one third and one half to the already soaring production costs and generally brought not one extra penny into the box office. I recall hating working in color because my "sailor's blue" eyes couldn't tolerate the necessary extra bright lights. Even in exteriors, the natural sunlight was augmented by reflectors and arc lights. I had a terrible time keeping my eyes open for more than a few seconds at a time. The big change from all black-and-white to all color was still nearly thirty years away. Today, of course, very little light is used and, except in character parts, men use virtually no makeup at all.

Today on an average feature film one hopes to shoot from two to five minutes of "story" from the script daily. To do this may require as many as five, ten, or more camera setups. In the early sound days, however, we might wait, sweat, and grow limp with rehearsing and getting into the exact chalk marks drawn for each individual's correct lighting—and *then* shoot the scene from beginning to end. But we tried to end up with a total of about ten minutes or more of plot a day.

At that time, really vast sums of money were expended on every phase of production. New budgets at least quadrupled the old ones—and all this was taking place just before and then during the first five years of the Great Depression. The world's economic and social organizations may have been on a terrifying and tragic slide downhill, but the Hollywood proconsuls found their profligate investments at least temporarily worthwhile. The movies remained, more than ever, almost the only place where a worried, jobless, and often hungry family could go for a couple of hours and live in a cheerful world of happy endings.

The twenties were a giddy hangover after the dreadful debaucheries of the Great War. Now that era had ended too. The surviving world rightly feared that even the few standards and faiths it had salvaged might soon disappear. No New Deal was yet in sight and people were still fearful of fear itself. For years, the favorite bolt-hole of the masses had been the movies in whose mass-produced prefabricated dreams they wrapped and reassured them- selves for a few lovely hours. No better opiate had been found, and there was a plentiful supply. Aggressive and resourceful publicity departments churned out delicious appetizers on their own assembly lines. Truth was not demanded. Its illusion was enough.

Of the seven pictures I made that were released in 1930, the last two were far below the standards of the others. The last one, a dreary show called *One Night at Susie's,* starred Billie Dove. Time had galloped in the six years since I had been her gangling kid brother in *The Air Mail.* Now, not only was I a married man, but I was chosen to be her leading man (though I still could actually have been her little brother). It was a "nothing" part in a "nothing" story. In fact, its main interest for me was Miss Dove, who was more beautiful than talented and who *appeared* to have the most beautiful bosom in pictures. (Toplessness was still many decades away, so only a very select few could report authoritatively on *any* lady's bosom.) Newly married or not, I was no pure Sir Galahad—and I was, frankly, hoping to see for myself. Caddish friends such as Leslie Howard kept teasing me about my salacious curiosity. Unfortunately, like *The Air Mail,* this picture was also directed by Miss Dove's tough, sadistic husband, Irvin Willat. Conse- quently, I was never able to find out a damn thing. But the illusion, if that's what it was, was excellent.

When the picture was "in the can," I heard the good news that one of my favorite studio companions, a stoop-shouldered but nice-looking young fel- low named Mervyn LeRoy had made a success of directing his first picture,

I Am a Fugitive from a Chain Gang, starring Paul Muni. I'd known and worked with Merv on several pictures over the past couple of years, when he was thought one of the best gagmen around. The gagman's job doesn't exist anymore—to my knowledge. His responsibility on a shooting set was to stand in the back or to the side and think of some bits to cause laughter or, in a melodrama, to heighten the excitement. Then he was to come forward and propose his idea to the director and the principal players. Sometimes it was accepted, sometimes not. Mervyn was one of the best, and an expert in the subtle application of "Old Hollywood's" most childish sport: the goose stick.

The goose stick was just any stick, a bit shorter than a walking stick or cane. The idea was to sneak up behind someone known to be ticklish and touch their bottom with the stick. They would either jump in the air, scream, run up the nearest ladder or slap the nearest person they saw. Of course, almost all the "victims" played up to the goose stick because if they made a sufficiently hilarious scene out of their reaction, it was a near guarantee of a steady job with that director on whatever picture he made next. The Warner–First National lot had more of these sensitive fellows than most other studios. I would fail in my duty were I not to mention that one of the worst offenders in this silly distraction was my father. He kept several carpenters, electricians, and handymen on the permanent studio salary list because they were "goosey" and for no other reason. He even gave bit parts to people just for the purpose of goosing them.

Merv's claim to more private admiration was that he was Ginger Roger's first serious beau. Certainly that had nothing to do with his promotion to director, nor the great success of *Chain Gang.* His next assignment was another hard-boiled picture, Zanuck's new "trademark" for Warner Brothers. It was more or less about Al Capone and titled *Little Caesar.* It would star another young actor, Edward G. Robinson—a serious, classic actor at that—in the title role. This seemed strange casting at the time, but the world knows how successful it was. Poor Eddie Robinson was type-cast for so long as "the tough guy." No gentler man ever walked. He hated being villainous, but it paid so well that he was able in time to acquire one of the finest private collections of modern art.

There was a very good supporting role in *Little Caesar:* a tough young Italian, Ricky, the hit man for the Boss, and his protégé. To my surprise, Merv asked if I'd mind taking such a small part after a year of leads and the big personal hit of *The Dawn Patrol.* Then Darryl said that of course they could make me do it by contract, though they preferred to persuade me. Little did they know I was dying to play Ricky! I hoped it would demonstrate my versatility. Indeed, it was a showy part that would be fun for me. I affected slick, shiny dark hair, with short, slanted sideburns, like Rudy Valentino's and Rod La Rocque's, and a light Chicago gangster accent. I enjoyed every minute of the film. I learned so much from the friendly Eddie Robinson and, surprisingly, from the young director and old gagman friend Merv. I was grateful to all of them because, although no one could have come close to challenging Eddie's classic performance, mine was still good enough to be my fourth personal hit in the past twelve months.

Jack Warner—at Zanuck's behest—called Mike Levee, asking him to come and talk about another contract, this time a starring one. I was to be paid quite a bit more. The raise meant a considerable boost to my pride and household morale, since I could enlarge my share of the contribution to married life so that it would nearly equal Billie's. I would still be able to carry my other family expenses. This was all very encouraging. I was to have my name above the title of the picture, which made me legally and literally a star. Furthermore, I asked Mike to ask Warner for the right to decline any story or script—not unreasonably, of course—and I asked to be able to refuse to work with any director I was not happy with—also not unreasonably. Lastly, I suggested that Mike request that I might decline the studio's choice of leading ladies and principal supporting actors—again adding that my approval "would not be unreasonably withheld."

This was the sheerest brashness imaginable. Except for the fact that I had my eye on the earliest possible opportunity to be my own producer, as my father was, and which Hollywood as a matter of course frowned on, there was no real reason why I, on the basis of only a few successes as an actor should be given what no one else in the studio (except Barthelmess, an older and long established star) was allowed. As a matter of fact, that is more or less what J.L. told Mike. But just for the fun of dickering I pressed the point. And so, obediently, did Mike. And lo and behold, to everyone's surprise, none more than mine, the Warner Brothers–First National Company agreed.

It was hard not to crow, but I didn't. I was barely twenty-one and I bounced for joy, though only for a while. An accumulation of incidents, plus the luck of the draw, got in the way of the new contract being of very long benefit to anyone. Most important, I learned that the best of contracts can be got around by the bosses if they choose.

Following *Little Caesar,* Zanuck produced *Public Enemy* with his new recruit from New York, James Cagney. The picture was an even bigger success than *Little Caesar* and Cagney became a big star just as quickly as Eddie Robinson. Both, unlike so many other overnight successes, fully deserved their triumphs. Cagney was quite a bit younger but had had masses of stage experience before coming to Hollywood. Again like Robinson, his off-stage personality was far from tough. He was gentle, humorous, and damned conscientious. He eventually won a new contract just like me. Whenever he and his "enemy" Jack Warner disagreed, which was often, Jimmy went on strike. His tactics and his assignments were, in the long run, much superior to mine. We were not in the least competitors, being quite different types. Besides, he was such a nice guy you had to be on his side, no matter what. We never had the chance to become close friends, which I regret.

As I began my third decade of life, my parents followed their own unrelated lives, now entirely apart. My father and Mary still managed to keep their growing tensions private, in spite of his few distant forays. All the Pickfords (Smiths) were as close-knit as any Irish family could be, and as they shared their important world-worshiped meal ticket between them, they were at pains to protect Mary from the public's and her husband's prying eyes whenever her desire to "have just one more" became overpowering. They understood her well, since they shared the same thirst, and to a far more conspicuous degree. Sweet Mary's weakness was hardly known at all outside the closest of family circles. Whether she then had any outside romantic adventures, as Pete was whispered to have, I do not know, but I doubt it.

Mary's last silent film, made in 1927, was *My Best Girl,* and her leading man was the much younger, charming new favorite of the fans, Charles "Buddy" Rogers. He was to become, in time, the closest and most devoted man in her life, but whether any spark had been lit at that time I never knew. Mary was always circumspect. As experienced as she was in taking care of herself in the tough spots, everyone always wanted to take care of and protect *her.* And even though she's gone now, everyone, including me, still does.

Pete had toned down his irritability and was reluctantly embarking on his second talkie *(The Taming of the Shrew* with Mary was the first). He and Chaplin never felt that talkies suited them. The silent screen, on which a story was told by pictures, mime, and action, was their medium and they thought sound pictures, which they certainly enjoyed watching, should be made by others. But their continuing responsibilities to their partners in United Artists required them to make at least one picture annually. For the past few years Mary had been making even fewer, but at least she had made two or three well-received talkies—good enough to satisfy her company and associates.

Eddie Goulding was chosen to direct Pete's picture, based on his own story. The very popular Bebe Daniels was to be his leading lady, with Edward Everett Horton supporting and Bing Crosby in a small part. Irving Berlin wrote the theme song, "Reaching for the Moon," which was also the picture's title.

Dad dragged his feet for some while, no longer seeming to care about the details of producing or, indeed, any part of the creative process. Clearly antipathetic toward the new development in the medium he so loved and enriched, he seemed to press on with what all his new associates thought was his usual high humor and energy. But his old friends, his brother Robert, and his company stalwarts knew—and cared deeply—that the spark was fizzling out, that he was uncaringly trading on past classics and forcing himself to continue.

Reports from Mother about her life with Jack indicated highly satisfactory conjugal happiness. Jack was in *America's Sweetheart,* a new and successful Broadway musical, with top billing. Of course, there were a number of familiar complaints, carefully spaced so as not to be too many at one time. First of all, of course, came money; Jack was earning a good deal "for the theater, that is . . ." but he was helping his father (a retired doctor) and mother (to whom he was almost excessively devoted). Mother was helping *her* sister Gladys and adding to my gifts to brother Bill "just a bit, here and there." And there was the familiar accumulation of physical complaints: pains here, pains there, "my old trouble"—whatever that was I either didn't know or have forgotten—"is back," and her hot flashes, going on for years now and blamed for anything untoward she said or did, were likewise giving her trouble. Her deafness was getting worse. The semiparalysis of a section of her cheek was, she feared, spreading. Her tendency toward flatulence and indigestion, constant but unsupported fears of breast cancer—all of these were dropped like little pebbles into three or four letters a week. "But," she would add, "please don't worry, darling, I'm really fine and Jack is so wonderfully sweet and attentive. I'm *so* lucky!" Actually, I had just about given up worrying a long time ago. Still, I didn't dare dream of challenging anything.

The only legitimate concern she had with which I did sympathize was her rising sensitivity to the very obvious difference in age between her and Jack. White-haired and, at about forty-three, getting plumper, she appeared less youthful because of her devotion to an ultra-conservative, not even remotely modish style of dress. Jack was a handsome and extroverted young man who, surprisingly enough, was absolutely devoted to her. He remained so all his life. Mother gloried in having another name now (having gone back to Fairbanks after her divorce from Evans), but she was not pleased when uninformed people pleasantly congratulated her on the performance of "your son Mr. Whiting."

There was little anyone could say except "Nonsense! How stupid of them! You look great!" We all said that. It didn't help much.

Billie made only about three pictures in 1930, so she had more time to study her role of housewife and continue her incessant knitting of sweaters, shawls, and blankets. She contrived with friends at the studio to get favored scripts. To her tactlessly open jealousy of Norma Shearer, she added a rivalry with Jean Harlow, for whom she developed a controlled detestation. It didn't help matters that I had known Jean in my even younger days when her name was Jean Carpenter. Billie was annoyed by both ladies, nursing her suspicions that they were in some way part of a conspiracy to hold her back.

Our domestic existence was unpredictable, largely because of the irregular hours our jobs demanded. When both of us were working (she, particularly, had very early morning calls at six or six-thirty A.M.), I would call the Hollywood Athletic Club and ask for Miron to come and massage us to sleep by nine-thirty P.M.

We both had our own idiosyncracies. Mine were harder for me to recognize, of course. Most of Billie's have already been noted, except for one amusingly inconsistent one: Despite her fundamental expertise with rough language, usually employed to tell jokes or curse someone suspected of retarding her career, she became quite demure and prudish in naming intimate things. She had her own personal glossary of euphemisms. If she was telling of a couple sharing a bed, she would never describe what they were doing in such vulgar terms as "making love"; she would, instead, invariably say, "They went to heaven." Any woman's breasts were her "ninny-pies." A kiss—even a *kiss*—was a "goober" (a long etymological trek from a word that young kids used for awful runny-nose jokes). Anything to do with the bathroom was given a baby-talk pseudonym. Not only I but many of her friends teased her for naming spades shovels, but to no avail. That is to say, not in *my* time. I'm told that she eventually created a set of descriptions more in line with accepted practice.

Although we disagreed about many things and thus were not above being quite cross with each other, I do not recall her anger ever boiling over into a temper tantrum. I nagged her about taking our first holiday in New York, to see plays and old friends. More gently and persistently, I talked about taking our deferred honeymoon in Europe. I got travel brochures, estimates, and ship diagrams from the British, French, and German companies that operated the huge, luxurious transatlantic liners. I succeeded only in getting smiling agreements, but no firm dates.

When possible I read or worked on my drawing or sculpture and also scribbled things that sometimes got into print. Some of my poems were given a page in the expensively chic and glossy *Vanity Fair.* Of course, it did no harm that the co-editor of the day was Frank Case's eldest daughter, Margaret, with whom I had been a fellow Algonquin child. Margaret proved a fine friend and champion—as did her coeditor, Clare Boothe Brokaw (later Luce)—when they convinced me to write a profile of a movie celebrity—beginning with my father—each month. I illustrated them with caricatures.

I had an upstairs study that was very cluttered with no sign of ever having been decorated (unlike Billie's pristine quarters, which looked rather like a small movie set, or as if they were on exhibition in a store, guarded by anxious French maids). On weekends I sought out tennis, golf, or beach companions (Billie wasn't really interested in outdoor sports, except for swimming).

I must admit that I emulated Billie in trying to win writer friends and influence directors to find me good properties. In such campaigning, I was not very successful. There were a few who had confidence in me, but they were not in positions of power. I suppose the proof of my contention is that in my more than five years and a score of pictures, not more than half a dozen could be called plums. There were very few stories, parts, or characters that Darryl Zanuck liked that fitted me. We were good friends away from work, but more macho types than I were better suited to his style of picture-producing. The fact that I ended up playing quite a few such characters was due more to my pestering him than to his confidence in me.

We even had a long, drawn-out argument about my first real "starring" picture. One story after another was discussed and discarded. Eventually, after being told there was a limit to my new powers of approval, I was advised the movie would be *Chances,* another Great War picture—this time with an English setting. A bittersweet romance about two brothers in love with the same woman, *Chances* recalled *The Dawn Patrol.* Again, there were French battlefield scenes and, again, my brother was killed in action.

The Powers in the Front Office decided I could speak with an acceptable English accent (London critics flatly disagreed). Luckily for me, the director assigned was the marvelous old boy Allan Dwan, who had directed so many of my father's early pictures. Rose Hobart, from the theater and unknown to movie-goers, was the excellent leading lady. We had a marvelous location sequence up near Pebble Beach, on the Monterey Peninsula. It was photographed to look like the beautiful rugged coast of Cornwall in England.

The picture, in spite of dear Allan's patient and paternal guidance and the expensive production given it, did not have a story of a power and sweep to match its background, nor a part that demanded anything unusual from me. It was good, but not good enough. Today it is still affecting, though a little dated. A memorable episode occurred at the end of the actual filming at the traditional company party at which presents are given. Allan Dwan gave me one of the few remaining "original" bronze copies of Napoleon's death mask. How he got it or from where, he would never tell, but I had been so drenched in Napoleona by my grandfather Dan'l that I prized it and the thought, beyond words.

At about this time a bizarre incident occurred involving Phillips Holmes, an old pal from my days at Harvard Military School in California. Phil grew up to become a most promising young actor, making a big hit as the hero in von Sternberg's version of Dreiser's *An American Tragedy*. While this film company was on location up at Big Bear Lake, they and millions of others heard a flash radio announcement that I had been killed in a motor accident in Santa Barbara. I heard it too while eating a studio box lunch on location for *Chances*. The announcement was weird enough for *me* to hear, but it meant that Phil's whole film unit stopped work. Though weeping, he read a prayer for my soul. All the studios in Hollywood came to a halt for two minutes of silent prayer only to feel damn fools when they learned it was all a mistake. My parents and Billie were not in the least disturbed, because they never heard the broadcast in the first place.

As Billie's social self-confidence grew, so did her enjoyment of entertaining. Old friends and acquaintances mixed with new visitors who phoned or brought letters of introduction. One of Billie's universally liked friends was Ramon Navarro—also a favorite of Mother's—who invariably delighted everyone with his charming, well-trained voice singing Spanish and Mexican songs. Another of Billie's favorites was Clifton Webb, whom I had first known at the Algonquin and who was now an elegantly tailored Broadway musical star. His unfailing shadow and constant companion—and the fairly good-natured butt of jokes—was his mother, Mabelle. His covert choice of companions was not as openly tolerated as it would be in, say, San Francisco today. He doted on "Our Blessed Joan," as he airily described her.

Other guests were Ria Gable and her recently wedded husband and protégé, Clark, who was seventeen years younger than she. I had seen him in a touring company production of *The Last Mile* and thought him very good indeed. Now he had been signed by MGM. Mayer or Thalberg instinctively sensed something special about the soft-spoken but rough, good-looking man with big ears. In fact, he was soon to replace Johnny Mack Brown as Billie's leading man in a remake of what was finally called (no joke!) *Laughing Sinners*. He was shortly to become an important factor in our lives.

Billie wanted to invite Howard Hughes to one of our parties, but I said a blunt no! My reason was that I had overheard him at my father's studio asking someone if he could "get a date with Joan Crawford." When he was reminded that she was married to me and was, furthermore, "not one of the girls," he boasted, in his quiet Texas drawl, that he could offer her "a *very* big present" if she went out with him. In the end he didn't ask her, but I so resented his "money will buy anything" attitude that I never allowed him in the house. I seemed a congenial acquaintance of Howard's for years but never liked him after that—and never told Billie why.

Life seemed to be puffing up. Our marital rocket was reaching its apex—and would hang there a bit before fizzling and sputtering out.

I grew tall believing that, in sexual morality, men were to be bound only by rules of discretion and gentle consideration. After all, that had always been the world's admittedly unfair double standard. How would it have occurred to me to think otherwise? I was demonstrably devoted to my bride, and she was at first equally attached to me. But if a singularly attractive female interposed herself between us and my eye followed—well, I was likely to prudently try to curry favor with its target. I was not flagrant about my blandishments and I took normal pains to be as circumspect as I knew how. It must not be supposed that I allowed myself an inordinate amount of time for prowling. Even after a year or so of normal domestic life, I was far too busy with work and far too concerned about avoiding the kind of philandering reputation that would distress or embarrass Billie. Nor was anyone in doubt that, all things considered, I was essentially faithful—"in my fashion."

Certainly Billie, whose own early explorations of life had been more varied than mine, turned over a completely new page of personal conduct during our courtship and early marriage. I have no idea when those enormous hungry eyes first locked onto someone else. The uncertain evidence suggests that it was roughly at the same time that I began rather aimlessly to wander. The dream went on for a while, but our eyelids were fluttering.

Darryl himself ordered my next company assignment—ignoring the terms of my new contract, which I did not insist upon, feeling too callow and unsure of myself. The film was *I Like Your Nerve,* a lightweight comedy with a bloodless Latin American revolution as a backdrop, shot in San Diego for atmosphere. It was another of the series that teamed Gretch Young and me. (By now we were getting on much better.) Our producer, Irving Asher, had been her intense beau for some time. The picture was a piece of indifferent froth by the witty British playwright Roland Pertwee. The film was memorable for only two reasons. It was the only time I grudgingly experimented with pasting my ears back on screen, and it was a first for a newly arrived Britisher who was part Indian, they said. He was a dark, husky, athletic fellow, very gentle and friendly with a fine voice but a bit of a lisp. His name was William Pratt, but it was decided that was unsuitable. He was renamed Boris Karloff.

This film was followed by *Union Depot,* a really good one. Darryl and I agreed I should try the tough guy approach again and I was cast as a rail-riding hobo. A large set, a near replica of the Union Station in, I believe, Omaha, served as the center for most of the action—made so much more attractive by Joan Blondell. Al Green, bless his jolly heart, directed and it was another hit. Not a big one, mind, but respectable and encouraging.

There followed a movie based on an excellent bestseller by Mary McCall (wife of the noted sculptor Dwight Franklin), a thinly disguised spin-off of the story of Charles Lindbergh and the drama attendant on his celebrity. It was at first aptly called *The Goldfish Bowl.* Despite the presence of delicious Mary Brian—so delectably grown up since her "Wendy" in *Peter Pan*—the picture was not good enough. Today it seems slow-moving and the on-again/off-again love story doesn't make much sense. Though it didn't lose money, it certainly didn't make much. The project wasn't helped by downgrading the title to the corny, mundane, Warner-style *It's Tough to Be Famous!*

My last movie for 1931 was *Love Is a Racket,* a brisk routine program picture directed by "Wild Bill" Wellman, a Great War air hero of the Lafayette Escadrille. It was a rapid-fire newspaper story that cashed in on the popularity of the classic *The Front Page,* with me playing a young Walter Winchell–type columnist. I was not very good in a part that was originally meant for the more important Warner star Jimmy Cagney, but a logjam of schedules pushed it my way—really too bad for all concerned. Still, it was joyous to make because of two wonderfully attractive and intelligent leading ladies, Frances Dee (later to become Mrs. Joel McCrea) and Ann Dvorak. My score since I became a star earlier in the year was one hit, three satisfactory break-evens, and one flop. Not good enough, I thought, for me or for the company.

Billie overcame the lack of important story properties by performing in each of her pictures a variation of what the average American working-class girl imagined herself to be: decent and hardworking but weighed down by responsibilities that she carried gallantly and uncomplainingly on her shoulders. She was sought after and often abused by unscrupulous men, but by sheer strength of character and native intelligence she knew Mr. Right when she saw him and, after much suffering, triumphed in the end. Her female public saw themselves reflected in the Crawford roles and came in droves. Depression or no, they found the money or the friend to take them to her films—often several times. Then men began to see her screen image as another kind of ideal: the smart girl who wasn't a pushover and could only be won by proven character. So she drew more crowds to the box office. Her films had no need to be really good, just well-dressed (by friend Adrian), with well-designed sets by Cedric Gibbons (the husband of Dolores del Rio), well directed and photographed, and cast by the best that MGM money could corrupt.

At home, her original baby-talk nickname for me, Dodo, disappeared (thank God!) and gave way to a more straightforward Douglas. The once extravagant exchanges of presents also stopped (again, thank God!). However, she had collected masses of clothes (some free or on loan from the studio) and some not very good but showy jewelry. I had acquired some treasured prints by the Australian artist Norman Lindsay, some fine books, and a few very expensive suits from Hollywood's most exclusive tailor, Eddie Schmidt. We were both sculpted by a Russian émigré, Prince Pierre Troubetzkoy—small individual bronze figurines of ourselves—and we had a couple of portraits done by reasonably good painters. Money went out as quickly as it came in, but I was rapidly catching up. There were no rows that I recall. If Billie was studying lines or otherwise preoccupied, I tried to write. A sort of doldrums or marital torpor seemed to be setting in.

On her next picture, with her idolized look-alike star Pauline Frederick in a supporting role, I began to notice that she went to the studio at least an hour earlier than usual and returned home equally late. She even went to work on her days off, explaining that she was so interested in what the others were doing and she "adored watching Miss Frederick." These explanations seemed quite in character for the girl who, I've always been certain, instinctively suspected she lacked the basic talent and technique of a first-class actress.

She still enjoyed—as have so many others who were once among the have-nots—being Lady Bountiful. She distributed largesse—often to her colleagues' embarrassment—to every member of her film crew, plus hair-dressers, maids, particularly ardent fans, and sympathetic fan magazine writers.

On a trip to New York we saw Noël Coward and my old long-distance teenage crush, Gertrude Lawrence, in *Private Lives*. We also met Laurence Olivier and his first wife, Jill Esmond, the other couple in the play. Noël was disarmingly star-struck by the current sensation, Joan Crawford, and charmingly helpful and encouraging to me after reading some of my writing. When the play finished its limited run, Noël and the Oliviers came out to California—Noël to visit and have a break, the Oliviers to work, they hoped.

Noël came to dinner quite a few times and was delighted when I took him to Pete's studio, where he met my father and Mary for the first time. After that, of course, he was asked to dine at Pickfair. Another time, Noël—always fascinated with all facets of the performing arts—came over to my studio to look around. There he ran into a well-known young English set designer, and a surprised old friend of Noël's to boot, who was just beginning a new career as a photographer. He was Cecil Beaton.

The Oliviers became our immediate friends. They both acquired RKO contracts, but Jill got more attention and assignments than Larry. Many of the local bigwigs dismissed him as a nice but stiff young Englishman who looked like a juvenile Ronald Colman. They said Jill was the one to watch and that Larry's future was limited! Away from work they provided us with a fine change of conversational pace. At last, I thought, Billie would begin to see that all the world's brains, talent, and wit were not a Hollywood monopoly.

Pete had taken off on a globe-circling trip with his faithful buffer Chuck Lewis and his former cameraman Victor Fleming. He took along a portable cinecamera to record the trip as a Fairbanks feature picture for United Artists called *Around the World in 80 Minutes*. It turned out to be a fairly amusing travelogue. But the public sensed a cheat, and it was not a success. In fact, he hadn't had a solid hit since *The Iron Mask*—precisely when he stopped caring about motion picture making.

Mary kept her private worries to herself and struggled to adapt the play *Secrets* into a movie, playing opposite Leslie Howard. Disappointed with its first cut, she went about completely remaking the whole picture. It took more than a year, but it was worth it. When Pete returned, they kept up a good front—so good, no one realized how deep their rift was becoming. And Mary began producing *Kiki,* her next picture.

Neither Billie nor I was the slightest bit aware of any trouble in "the big house." The cousins were closer to Pete and Mary and knew that something was going wrong, but since I didn't see them so often, no gossip reached me. Meanwhile, Billie made another picture with Clark Gable, this one called, with MGM's traditional subtlety, *Possessed.* And she was getting ready to start another with Bob Montgomery.

By 1931 Larry Olivier and I had become good friends and spent a lot of time together. If our ladies had to retire early because of work, and we didn't, we retreated to the Russian Club in Hollywood proper. It was run cooperatively by a flock of exiled White Russian admirals and generals who dreamed of restoring the czardom to Holy Russia. We became so enamored of the balalaika orchestra that, after a few vodkas (I was changing, if only for a while, my temperate habits), we'd borrow some Russian silk smocks and try to sing some of the gypsy songs. One night there we were introduced to a great, swarthy, pockmarked man whose profession was swallowing miscellaneous objects. Larry and I had watched him at Grauman's Chinese Theater, where he downed a small bowl of goldfish, a handful of almonds, and some sewing needles, which he regurgitated in whatever order the audience directed. No trick, he assured us. He had learned it as a boy in Egypt, swallowing small fish whole and coughing them up as he swam in the Nile. He settled in Russia later, developed his act, joined a circus, and . . . now here he was. We delighted in the old knave—for a while.

Another night he asked us if we had ever tried cocaine. Neither of us had so much as thought of it.

"Well," said he, "if not, you may try some of mine."

We were simultaneously excited, frightened, shy, and curious. "I will if you will!"

The decision was made. This gross Egyptian Cossack led us into the "gents," took out some little papers, poured white powder from them onto a nail file, and offered us a sniff. We hesitated, laughed self-consciously, and then took turns. All I felt was a head too clear and light to be natural and wide-open nasal passages that made me talk like a masculine version of Claudette Colbert. Larry, poor soul, never very robust, got sick to his stomach and asked us to leave quickly so he could throw up.

Larry later said that while he was bent over and miserable, who should come in but his friend from Canada, the tall and very solemn Raymond

Massey, who asked in his slow, rounded speech, "Are you all right, Larry?"
Under normal, straight-up, face-to-face conditions, Ray always had a hang-
dog, worried face, but "when viewed upside down, between one's legs, old
boy, the only answer I could give him was to retch again!" That was the first
and last time we ever tried the famous "Happy Dust."

Warners—like all film companies—was at last feeling a real financial
pinch and not only laid off many old-time employees in every department
but requested that everyone under contract—actors, executives, writers, and
cameramen—take a 50 percent cut. This was a pretty stiff reduction of
income. There was still no such thing as the dole or unemployment insurance and the film community suddenly found out what the rest of the country had painfully known for some time: depression plagued the world.
Zanuck had no contract at all but had been so well paid that he voluntarily
cut his own salary 50 percent. However, he openly disagreed with J.L.'s
request that everyone under contract do the same. From that moment Jack
Warner doffed his usual clownish behavior and overruled him.

I can't recall the extent to which other companies requested salary cuts.
All of them, however, fired employees, decreased production, and slashed
budgets. It would be foolish to claim that, with so much real deprivation
everywhere, my financial situation, however serious to me, could have
caused anyone else anxiety. Billie and I would not starve, or even suffer a
sudden descent into genteel poverty. She still made a very handsome (even
though reduced) stipend. We would have to live more moderately, that was
all. It wasn't difficult in the Hollywood of that day. We very seldom frequented popular restaurants or nightclubs. Los Angeles city ordinances required that on Saturday evening all music and dancing stop at midnight.
Even when Prohibition was repealed no one was allowed to drink after that
hour. In any case, there were still only three or four good restaurants or
nightclubs.

My other family expenses were, however, increasing. I was more and
more worried about what to do, yet determined not to admit it to Billie. The
only solution I could find was, of course, to borrow—from the bank, from
my agent Mike, or from Noël Sullivan. Then, finally, I took a very long,
deep breath and, breaking my proud career-long rule, asked Uncle Bob if he
would see if, by any chance, Pete would lend me, say, a thousand dollars.
That was quite a sum then.

I kept well out of sight for a few days until Uncle Bob rang to say "the
deal" was approved—albeit reluctantly. I was suitably grateful—though
miserable, after all those years, about having to ask for money. I rescued a

bit of pride and insisted on sending my father—via Uncle Bob—a warm letter of thanks plus a formally written and signed IOU. For weeks afterward I was too shy to see him. I did manage to repay the loan exactly three years later.

I was about to start a movie with a good original screenplay by my friend Mary McCall, Jr., titled *Scarlet Dawn.* It was a story of the plight of aristocratic Russian refugees escaping the Revolution by way of Turkey, with much violence and subtle mischief en route. Nancy Carroll was the sweet, trusting love of the aristocrat—me—and Lilyan Tashman played the sexy seductress who tried to lead me astray—both on and off screen. Lilyan was a fairly notorious lady in private life, despite her congenial marriage to the popular Edmund Lowe. Quite disarmingly, she admitted that she was really more interested in her close friend Tallulah Bankhead than in anyone else.

I enjoyed the picture as an exercise in narcissism—and escapism. My self-confidence, never very strong, had slumped. Finances and domesticity were taking their toll. But in this picture I deliberately costumed myself as nearly as I could like one of my old idols, Jack Gilbert, as he had appeared in *The Merry Widow.* I wore several varieties of tight and becoming Russian uniforms and I shaved all but the very top of my head—just as he had. A psychologist might have suggested I was hiding myself and my anxieties in the guise of a shadow-play character I admired. The picture was beautifully photographed but otherwise wasn't much good.

Of course there were a few people around who managed to ignore the Depression and keep their candles brightly lit. Chief among them was Marion Davies, supported by her powerful protector, William Randolph Hearst. When they gave a party, it was usually large. It seemed a fortuitous time for Marion to give a huge fancy-dress ball at Hearst's immense white Colonial-style beach house in Santa Monica. It was, as the Hearst papers (naturally) said, "star-studded." Every "name" one could think of, plus some one couldn't imagine, joined a list of producers, Hollywood literati, and Marion's relatives. Everyone either rented a costume or had it specially designed at their own studio, as did Billie and hostess Marion. Adrian, of course, designed Billie's. All I remember is that it was very becoming. Since most of my head was still shaved for *Scarlet Dawn,* I came in my "Jack Gilbert" white uniform. It was a fine, euphoric evening, especially for those as "detached" as Billie and I. We looked the picture of nuptial bliss and the evening went well for everyone except Gary Cooper. He brought the "Mexican Firecracker," Lupe Velez, who complained loudly and violently that "Coop" had tried to attack her. No one could believe this, but everyone suspected, not without reason, that Lupe would do or say almost anything to get attention. She was the Zsa Zsa Gabor of the thirties.

A day or so after the ball, Billie wondered aloud why, since we were on very good terms with Marion and polite terms with W.R., we had never been asked up to San Simeon, the vast Hearst ranch. So many friends and acquaintances had gone and returned with glowing reports of the oriental splendor of life there. For some reason best known to her, Billie would, in recounting her life in later years, say that I had gone up to the Ranch several times without her. That was not true. I went only once, several years later.

I next made two Hollywood films in the French language. The others in these casts were all non-English-speaking French actors, imported for the purpose of helping Warners mark up another first—a foreign language picture made in Hollywood. The pictures were not in the least good. They were too quickly and cheaply made. Nevertheless, they were the first of their kind, so none of our reputations was harmed. In fact, the records indicate that I made a third film that same season, but I don't remember it at all.

No sooner was Pete's *Around the World in 80 Minutes* completed, edited, and scored than he was off again. This time he chartered a large, luxurious two-masted schooner, dropping anchor in Tahitian waters, where he planned to film a modern adaptation of a classic, called *Mr. Robinson Crusoe.* As cohorts, he chose witty Tom Geraghty for ideas and companionship; Eddie Sutherland, a vigorous young director; Earle Brown, a writer; and Henry Sharpe, a top-notch cameraman who had photographed *The Black Pirate.* The picture turned out to be amusing enough, complete with good, ingenious gags and stunts, but it lacked the magic of the Master, the magic of silent film balletic action and the imagination with which audiences invested those movies. What's more, he knew it.

Billie's next professional challenge was as one of the all-star cast of *Grand Hotel.* The idea of being in the same picture with her idol "Miss G."—though sharing no scenes—was almost too exciting. There were also John and Lionel Barrymore, Wallace Beery, Lewis Stone, and Jean Hersholt to be frightened of; not to mention dissolute and dear friend Eddie Goulding to direct her with, she prayed, sympathy. All her personal problems (except her fanaticism for super cleanliness everywhere on the set, which made the Barrymore brothers wild) were set aside for the duration. Billie's determination to succeed in this was, I've been told, not to be equaled again until half a dozen years later, when she was in the all-female, all-star cast of Clare Boothe Luce's *The Women* and had to work with Shearer. In spite of, or maybe because of, the experienced stellar competition she faced, the Joan

Crawford performance in *Grand Hotel* was first-class. What really put the bubbles in her champagne was that this film was a big success.

Soon after that, to her great excitement, Joe Schenck asked Mayer if he could borrow her to play Sadie Thompson in a remake of *Rain,* the classic that Gloria Swanson had made as a silent only a few years before. Like the earlier version, *Rain* was adapted from the play by John Colton and Clemence Randolph, which in turn was adapted from the short story "Miss Thompson" by W. Somerset Maugham. Most ambitious actresses dreamed of playing the role—anywhere. Billie could scarcely believe her good fortune.

In the past months Billie and I had misplaced contact with each other. We absorbed the words that each of us said, but couldn't decipher their message. I heard that she had found a hideaway for herself somewhere beyond Laguna. When I hinted that I'd look it up, she threatened to walk out on me then and there. It was becoming clear that the end of our marriage was near, though neither would go so far as to make the first move.

One day Billie hinted that we had best make our own plans and begin to think about an amicable separation. This idea came so suddenly one morning that I was momentarily stunned. And then she was off to work. Later, without pursuing her comments further, I suggested that when she had finished shooting *Rain* we should get away on our too-long-delayed honeymoon, preferably to Europe. Her reaction was a weary, condescending smile and a "Perhaps! Perhaps! We'll see."

11

Billie wanted no distractions to interfere with her concentration on *Rain* and giving her best possible performance as Sadie Thompson. Therefore, would I "and everyone else" just leave her alone on Catalina Island where the picture would be made.

I, too, wanted to get away from home life for a bit. I did not welcome Billie's preoccupation with work to the detriment of our personal life. As luck would have it, Bob Montgomery unexpectedly phoned me one day to suggest that if Larry Olivier and I were free and could find one more friend, we could charter C. B. De Mille's sailing yacht *Seaward* and split the cost four ways. That seemed a marvelous idea. I worked out the arithmetic and my share of the charter would be no more than what I would have been paying for Cielito Lindo and incidentals were I to stay home. As far as I was concerned, the deal was on.

Larry, whose own domesticity was rolling and pitching toward the rocks, was delighted and frankly relieved at an opportunity to get away from it all. He had only to finish the picture he was on, charter a putt-putt plane (about all there was in those days), and fly down to join us at a prearranged anchorage in Lower California, Mexico. Our search for a fourth shipmate was quickly ended when we asked a writer friend, Eddie Knopf, to join us. He jumped at the idea. Though he was slightly handicapped, his friends hardly noticed Eddie's disability and he would have no problems on board. Bob Montgomery did all the dirty work of negotiating the charter with C.B. himself. A shrewd New Englander, Bob managed to get a sizable reduction on everything connected with the cruise because the old man thought us "a fine, deserving group of young men." Well, at least some of our luck was turning better.

Billie and a studio maid packed for at least a month on the Catalina *Rain* location. Before she left, one could have caught a cold from the chill pervading our house. I had made a fruitless attempt to be warm and understanding. Again I brought home brochures of various Atlantic liners listing their sailing dates. (I would, like the still-to-be-invented Scarlett O'Hara, think about the costs tomorrow.) My own great excitement about the prospect of a European honeymoon was not in the least contagious. She showed a modicum of polite interest—probably to keep me quiet—and that was all. She took off on the flying boat for Catalina.

Knowing of Larry's similar domestic problems, and the fact that he would have to miss the first few days of our cruise, I decided one evening to boost his morale by telling him of a beautiful and very rich girl I knew who had seen him somewhere and had fallen head over heels for him. I made up the story out of whole cloth just for fun. But sweet, gullible Larry fell for it. "*Who* is she?" "*Where* is she?" "*When* can I meet her?"

I kept up my silly game and said that since she lived in Pasadena (Pasadenans were notoriously contemptuous of theatrical folk from Hollywood) she was never allowed "in this part of town" after five P.M. Of course, this only excited Larry's interest more. Somehow I had to produce a heretofore nonexistent girl in the flesh. How? I suddenly remembered that I knew a terribly nice, well-spoken lady who made a modest living as one of the regular dress-extras at my studio. I looked her up, told her my story, and asked if she'd like to play along with my little charade. Being good-hearted, she agreed, although she had never seen or heard of Laurence Olivier in her life.

They met—under my cagey auspices—and, to my surprise, were immediately attracted to one another. The young lady played her role perfectly, and after their third or fourth luncheon meeting, when Larry asked her to join him in a drink at the end of the day or to dine with him, she shyly protested that her family in Pasadena always insisted she be home by five P.M. This made Larry increasingly anxious to conquer this beauteous heiress. She found herself—to her own amazement—just as taken with him. Apparently I'd started something. But now what? When I heard that my uncle Bob was going to Salt Lake City on business, I asked him if I might have the loan of his Sunset Towers apartment for an afternoon during his absence. I accompanied my request with a sly "boys-will-be-boys" wink.

As usual, that darling man gave me his keys. And when he had gone I slipped them to Larry. Thus it was that on their next afternoon off, Larry and the young lady settled in for a cozy tryst in Robert Fairbanks's comfortable apartment. What neither knew was that I had another set of keys. As a kind of temporary antidote to my own domestic problems, I behaved like a delinquent teenager. I let myself in at the kitchen entrance and, after listening carefully from a concealed position and deciding that the progress of this sudden courtship had gone far enough, opened the kitchen door, rang the bell outside, and gave signals to a waiting confederate.

I had, as the double-dealing character I occasionally became, hired a huge cauliflower-eared stuntman for five dollars. His job was to burst into the apartment at my signal with my spare key, take one look at the couple, and bellow, "What're youse doin' wit my wife?" The brute did his bit to perfection. Larry jumped up from the couch, took one look at this menacing giant, and keeled over in a faint.

I then realized my childish joke had gone too far. However, when Larry came to in a few seconds and was assured it was "all in fun," he took it wonderfully. And so indeed did the girl. They both laughed uproariously. So did the stuntman. Then, last of all, me. After that we all had a drink from Uncle Bob's assortment of Scotch.

Bob, Eddie, and I went carefully about victualing the yacht and borrowing all we would need in the way of deep-sea fishing gear for our jaunt to Mexico. Before our fishing trip was to begin, I tried several times to reach Billie by phone in Catalina, but she refused to take my calls. "Miss Crawford is sorry but she's rehearsing. May I take a message?" Or "H'ya, Doug. No, Joan has gone to bed, but I'll tell her whatever you want in the morning." Only a few months before, she had answered every call from me personally or returned it very shortly after. I was angry and hurt.

Finally, after several days of this ignominious treatment, I decided to disobey her wishes and fly over to see her one afternoon. I was particularly annoyed because all my messages were left on a bulletin board for the edification of the others on the set or in the nearby hotel. Her director, "Milly" Milestone, was a good friend. Her two leading men, the great Walter Huston and Bill Gargan, were at least genial acquaintances. And, of course, I knew many of her camera crew. So her attitude to me had by now become fairly well known.

My arrival that afternoon took her by surprise. She could barely control her irritation with me for "daring" to come over when I knew she was concentrating on the challenge presented by this part. I don't recall in any detail who said or did what, but it was unquestionably a taut and emotional, very private "scene."

It was some time before they called her back to rehearsal. Milly had realized there was a serious family row going on, so he went ahead with other things for a while. When she was finally called, she advised me that as her hotel room was very small and every other room there was requisitioned by the company, and as she must have no further interference with her work, and as there was nothing more to say, it would be best if I took the next amphibious plane back to the mainland. By then I was very glad to leave, bewildered by her belligerent behavior. I decided our prospective fishing trip would be the best medicine I could take for the time being.

A few nights before we embarked, Bob, Eddie, Larry, and I decided to have a male booze-up at the Russian Club, where in a moment of alcoholic inspiration, I suggested that the Club's orchestra might enjoy a free two- or three-week holiday on a sailing boat to Mexico and back. They would be paid nothing, but on the other hand they would have nothing to do all day. Their only duties would come in the evening when, under clear Pacific skies, they would sit near the bow and play to us, lounging and dreaming on the stern. They accepted, and we instructed them precisely when to meet us at the San Pedro yacht basin.

On the great day, these particularly vivid-looking Russians carrying their instruments must have made our group a unique sight to the regulars at the docks. The size of the boat called for a crew of six or eight, but we had decided to save money and do some sailoring ourselves, keeping only three in the crew, plus one cook. Both Bob and I knew the fundamentals of navigation and piloting. We had a real skipper aboard and that was enough.

We made our way slowly out toward the breakwater breathing the fresh, clean sea air that was already beginning to rinse our various cares away. However, we hadn't reached the open sea before the musicians said they were seasick. I took the lead, as a latter-day Captain Bligh, to give them my idea of a quarter-deck tongue-lashing. It did no good at all. They went on strike. There was no choice but to turn around and put the bastards back on shore. They listened to my rantings with Slavic stoicism and disembarked. Once again we chugged past all the docked and moored boats, until we reached the open sea, and were off!

It was a blessed relief that our days were gloriously uneventful—clear, bright sun all day, brilliant stars all night, and calm seas with just enough breeze to nudge our sails along. After four or five days we decided to put into a tiny Mexican fishing village, just to look around. There was a channel through the reef outside, but the captain decided not to chance it for fear of going aground. We anchored and took our motor launch in on a rough ride.

We had been warned that this tiny village was rarely visited by anyone, let alone gringos like ourselves. The natives were known to be unfriendly, and thus it would be best not to linger too long or be too inquisitive. Such warnings were all that were needed to spur the curiosity of three young men in their early twenties. As a potential dissuader, we decided to take along a case containing the two sections of our shotgun. Eddie said he would just as soon let Bob and me inspect the village while he sat on the rickety jetty and, with the gun case in his charge, guarded the launch against any theft that would leave us unable to return to the ship.

Bob and I found little of interest in the village—just a few adobe and tin houses, a dirty shop or two, flies and dogs in the one hot, dusty street and wandering lanes behind it. Not many people were about because, as we correctly surmised, it was siesta time. We took an hour or so before returning to the launch. As we approached the land end of the jetty we saw a menacing-looking Indian, exactly like an extra in an old Western—Mexican sombrero and all. By "all," I mean he was sporting a Colt .45 in a holster, attached to a cartridge-filled belt. At the far end of the jetty, sitting on the post to which our launch was tied, was Eddie with the gun case open beside him, the gun itself still in two pieces on his lap.

The Indian exchanged fierce looks with us as we hurried past. "Thank God you're here," said Eddie. "I thought you'd never come back. I've been scared to death with that guy over there, and me not able to work this goddamn gun!" Then it struck us. We had been so accustomed to Eddie's doing everything for himself like everyone else that it didn't occur to us that he couldn't have assembled the gun, much less shot it. He had only one hand!

We commiserated quickly so as not to embarrass him with our sympathy, jumped into the launch, and putt-putted our way back over the rough and scary reef, and boarded the boat.

Two days later we reached a town near Mazatlán where Larry was supposed to meet us. It was much more respectable. It had several dusty streets and quite a number of ordinary houses, a few even of wood. We went ashore where a group of the curious, having seen our handsome sailing yacht anchor, was waiting. These people, dressed in every rumpled which way, were friendly and smiling—a relief after the episode of the other day. A great sweating man in a white suit and very old Panama hat bustled up as the others made room. Obviously he was someone of substance in the town— the mayor, as it turned out. In a mixture of Spanish, English, and gesture we made immediate friends and went with him to his modest house, where we sat on his front porch and drank tequila.

The mayor was clearly impressed by our yacht and we let him think we were a group of rich playboys on a cruise. We asked him where the local airfield was and told him we were awaiting the arrival of a great friend who was joining us shortly by plane from Los Angeles. Who was he?

"Well," said I, deciding to make poor good-natured Larry the butt of one of my stupid whimsicalities again, "he is a very important young Englishman on a visit. Let us," I added conspiratorially, "play a joke on him. Could you arrange to have him arrested—just for fun? Just for a short while? He'll wonder what on earth happened."

The mayor's big belly heaved with laughter at the idea and he immediately ordered the execution of these plans through a nearby subordinate.

Larry's rickety single-engine plane arrived, touched down on the sand-and-rock runway, bounced, and rattled. As he stepped out, he was greeted by four men, all wearing different uniforms. We watched, well hidden, from a distance and couldn't hear what was said. But we did see poor Larry being taken briskly by the arm and walked to a wood-and-plaster building next to the airport. Later, we heard that they took him to the town jail and put him behind bars. He was, he admitted, both terrified and livid with rage. "Where," he shouted, "are we going? Where's Montgomery? Knopf? Fairbanks?"

"Never heard, señor!" they replied. "But you fined five hundred pesos!"

"Why, for Christ's sake?"

"Because," said the senior policeman, "you are Englissman!"

Larry now panicked. He couldn't get any *reasonable* explanation, so in desperation he said he must contact the British consul.

"We no recognize British, señor," they told him.

Cruelly, we let poor Larry stew for a bit, and then the Mayor jovially ordered his release. There is no doubt but what Larry O. is the best sport I've ever seen. The moment he found out it was another gag at his expense, his laughter was the most raucous of all. The mayor, like a beardless, Mexican Santa Claus, stopped guffawing for only a moment to tell us our friend was lucky his "soldiers" didn't hit him on the head, because, at the time, *they didn't know it was a joke!*

Larry was all gung-ho the moment he got aboard. He asked what our daily routine was and Bob facetiously told him that, if the ship were anchored, we all began our day by diving into the water from nearly the top of the mast. Of course, none of us dreamed of jumping off anything higher than the deck or perhaps the first rung or two of the ladder up the mast.

Larry didn't hesitate. He was so keen to join in everything that, the moment he stowed his gear away and rejoined us on deck in his swimming shorts, he scampered halfway up the mast and dived into the sea. He made a bad splash that nearly knocked him out. Bob and I jumped in to help get him aboard again. Once more, he took it in the best of spirits. He always did.

As part of our morning's exercises, we all donned big boxing gloves and sparred with each other for a short while. Once Larry sustained a tiny chipped tooth. For an actor, whose face is, at the least, a valuable part of his future, this could be worrisome. But not to Larry whose sense of fun and courage have helped see him through one serious and painful illness after another in recent years. No wonder that although he is about two years older than I, I've always thought of him as younger. In fact, he once told me I had spoken "condescendingly" to him as to a child. I may have, but it was never out of anything but high admiration and fond friendship. As I write this we are, in his words, "each other's oldest surviving friends."

The cruise was the most marvelous success. We never had so much as a choppy day, never so much as a drop of rain. We returned tanned and fit, our heads clearer by far than when we set sail a few too-short weeks before.

At home Billie had finished *Rain* and had come back from "somewhere" she had gone for a week's rest. To my immense surprise, she now seemed delighted with the idea of a honeymoon in Europe—especially since our studios—for publicity purposes, naturally—would foot most of the bill. To make it even more fun, the Oliviers were leaving at the same time and we decided that the best ship for us all was the new German liner, the *Bremen,* due to leave New York soon.

I reveled in every detail of planning for the trip: the friends and plays we would see in New York, what cabin on the ship to reserve, what to do in London and Paris, and so on. My next film assignment was six weeks off, so that was about all the time allowed us, but I was delighted. The cruise had helped me to see things in what I thought was a clearer light.

New York, when we got there, was very exciting that June 1932. Billie was trying her best to make me feel the tensions were over and all was again "on the rails." She was even pleasant to Mother and Jack, whom she raved over in his show. Genie's parents entertained us warmly in their big Park Avenue apartment. In fact, Clare Chester, Genie's father, at the time Chairman of the Board of General Foods, rather lost his balance over my movie star wife and, never suspecting I'd know, sent her roses every so often with cagily written cards meant to signal his interest. I'm sure he was of the generation that thought—with occasional justice—"These actresses, you know . . .

they'll all play around . . ." Neither Billie nor I had the heart to tell Genie about her old man's carryings on.

On the night before the sailing, we went to a huge and memorable party given by my old acquaintance Barbara Hutton. It was held in the Casino in Central Park and Paul Whiteman's huge orchestra, the best dance band in the world at that time, had been engaged to play. We stayed at the St. Moritz on Central Park South, not because we had raised our sights from the Algonquin, but because that was where MGM and Warner Brothers established us.

The next morning, we were in a tailspin trying to get ready. The bags had been taken downstairs and Billie had gone ahead to face the battery of fans and photographers, when the phone began to ring—with annoying insistence. Irritated by this last-minute interruption, I answered it gruffly.

"Hello, Doug? This is Jimmy," said the voice.

"Jimmy who?" said I, annoyed.

"Jimmy! Jimmy Walker! The Mayor!"

"Oh!" said I, calming down in an effort to be polite but still worried about being late. "Hello, Mr. Mayor."

"I know you are off this morning for Europe" said the ubiquitous Jimmy, "and that you and Joan will probably be late. And I also know your ship, the *Bremen,* is leaving from Brooklyn and not Manhattan. So, m'boy, I've sent some of my gendarmes around to get you through the traffic in a hurry. Have a good trip. Call me when you get back!"—and he hung up.

When I made my way through the screaming, squealing crowd downstairs to the car where Billie sat with our company press agents, to my enormous delight, I saw two or three motorcycle cops in front just waiting for our signal to go!

Let no one ever be so blasé as to think it isn't fun to ride through the streets of a great city at considerable speed behind a phalanx of screaming police sirens clearing the way ahead. Perhaps Presidents get accustomed to it, but I like to think that perhaps they never do. I know I loved every second and can hardly imagine enjoying any trip more. (Even though very ill, I once similarly enjoyed a ride in a wailing ambulance.)

The good-byes, the crowds, photographers, whistles, the paper streamers and confetti, the gongs, the cries of "Don't forget to write" were all in the end drowned out by more bells and whistles and then, at last, we were out to sea.

The voyage over was all one—or rather two—could ask for. The weather was perfect and the ship new. The crew was anxious to disabuse foreigners of any untoward suspicions of the new German Government, about which there was so much conjecture. In fact, few of the passengers had any thought for politics. It was good to unwind for a while and enjoy the luxurious shipboard life that still existed, even if for only a few, and among those the Oliviers and us.

Billie was obviously bewildered by her first trip abroad and, I'm sure, kept thinking that the whole ship was a movie set of sorts and all the other passengers extras and bit players. Larry went on for years afterward giving imitations of Billie trying to be at her charming best most of the time, but slipping occasionally—as when she thought me too relaxed and not attentive in the way she presumed gallant husbands behaved on their honeymoons.

Larry would tell of how he and Billie competed with Jill and me in the long summer days at Ping-Pong on the afterdeck. If Billie occasionally made a particularly good shot and it got by me, and I mumbled an appropriate "Good!" or something, she called out in an irritated voice, "Douglas! You *let* me win that! Now, *don't!*" Of course, I hadn't, nor would I have been that chivalrous, and I said so. But she went on insisting until Larry was forced to intervene, "Oh, for Christ's sake, Joan, shut up and play!" The game would continue. Other games, like deck tennis, she preferred to watch, as she feared for her nails. She insisted on being the glamorous Joan for the other passengers and wouldn't just be herself.

On the last night before arrival, we four were standing on the upper deck after a dinner with the captain. It was about nine P.M. but the light was still fine and we were looking out over the sea and feeling the soft air on our faces. Suddenly Larry shouted, "Look! It's dear little England! It's home!"

Our arrival in Southampton was quite beyond even my optimistic hopes. Over and above the normal crowd greeting friends and relatives was an astonishing number of press and public, plus representatives of MGM and Warner Brothers to greet us, delaying our debarkation by about an hour. The biggest and most complete surprise was Noël Coward, who came all the way from London to meet us. He was accompanied by Heather Thatcher, the most amusing comedienne. She was ever recognizable as the only elegant woman on the stage to always wear a monocle . . . because she couldn't see without it! From there on it was, for me, one continuous, happy haze.

Children usually want others to share their pleasures—a toy, a pretty object, sounds of bells, bright colors, or a pet. That was the way I felt about London, even then. And it didn't disappoint me. We were ensconced in the old Berkeley Hotel in Piccadilly. Although it would have been wonderful to have been a couple of relatively well-to-do newlyweds on a private romantic,

sight-seeing honeymoon instead of a pair of movie star mirages, objects of
hysterical clutchings, clothes rippings, and police protection, at that time of
our lives the limelight wasn't too bad. Furthermore, it wasn't our money.

The very first night Noël arranged for us to occupy the Royal Box in the
Theatre Royal, Drury Lane, arguably the most classically beautiful big theater in the world. We were to see his sensational emotional patriotic spectacle, *Cavalcade.* For someone who has never seen Drury Lane, to be able to
see it under such circumstances was a rare theatrical treat. It was the site of
so many dramas—real and literary—from Nell Gwyn and good King
Charles to this breathtaking twentieth-century moment when we, followed
by Noël, were ushered into the Royal Box by a splendid old boy in scarlet
and gold-braided livery, knee breeches, and powdered hair. The audience
rose to its feet and applauded two absolutely numb and unprepared youngsters. The lights lowered and an unforgettable theater experience of tears,
laughter, excitement, and wonder took over the next three hours.

The next morning, I insisted that we get up and see the Changing of the
Guard in front of Buckingham Palace, the Household Cavalry, and the
magnificently caparisoned Horse and Life Guards. Then there were the
usual sights: the Abbey, the Tower and the jewels, Parliament, and St.
Paul's.

Noël had organized a very stylish and elegant cocktail party reception for
us at his house in Gerald Road, Belgravia. It was like a page out of *Vanity
Fair* or a Michael Arlen short story. The theatrical stars of the day mingled
with Mayfair's playboys and girls, and the aristocracy with the plutocracy
and politicians. Even a member of the Royal Family, the young, elegant,
and very handsome Prince George, came with the Countess of Dalkeith.
Billie had been taught how to do a small curtsy (her "bob") to royalty, and
to call him "sir"—it was all so much like a scene she might have played that
she adored it. The Prince, who reminded me of his happy visit to Pickfair a
few years earlier, was the first member of his family whom I got to know
reasonably well. He naturally took a shine to Billie, and they hit it off from
the start.

That evening a phone call came from a family friend, Margot (Lady)
Asquith, widow of the former Prime minister. She said everyone was so
anxious for us to enjoy our visit that "special strings had been pulled" at the
Lord Chamberlain's office and the American Embassy and we were to get
cards inviting us to the King's (George V) annual Garden Party at the
Palace.

The hospitality was so overwhelming we had to divide one weekend between Ivor Novello's house, Redroofs, near Maidenhead in Middlesex

County, and Noël's rambling house, Goldenhurst, deep in the lush county of Kent. Both had a typically English mixed bag of guests—not a nonentity among them.

In Paris old friend Maurice Chevalier flattered us by attending a reception given in our honor, and I was equally excited by seeing Carpentier there too. What a change—what a graduation for me only a few years after I'd been a teenager in Europe. Billie and I had our portraits painted—two huge, larger-than-life pictures by the then most fashionable artist, the Spanish Betran-Masses. The pace was exhilarating and dizzying. Not one untoward moment intruded on my long-deferred, long-planned trip. My own enthusiasm obliged me to hope it was shared by her. So how *did* she like it all? What did she think of the sounds and excitement, the beauties and friendliness of London and Paris in early summer bloom?

She hated it all! She put on a brave, well-trained smiling face, said the right words of gratitude, but she was really only peripherally interested. She felt, she confessed, like a fish out of water, gasping for breath, longing for something familiar to cling to. She would have been, she said, just as content to read about these things—and, anyway, the pictures she'd seen seemed better than the real things! She was so frightened and felt so alien, that it was like a bad dream. All she wanted to do was get home as quickly as possible—home to the United States, home to California, home *not* to Cielito Lindo, but to the Culver City and MGM studios, home to the security of what she could recognize, home to her work. So home we went—ahead of schedule. She didn't return for years.

12

I would make five more pictures within the next twelve months, but on our return I only knew of the first two. Had I thought more of my professional life, I might have welcomed the somewhat improved quality of the material in store, but I was still too let down by the anticlimactic end of my honeymoon to drive the forty-five minutes to the studio in Burbank with my accustomed energy and high spirits. My relations with the company had worsened despite their generous help in financing our trip abroad. My friend and chief booster, the real driving force of Warners, Darryl Zanuck, was leaving the company. He was a rare example of a Hollywood executive behaving with integrity. Darryl had promised that when business improved and the bosses had lifted their own salaries, everyone else would have their cuts restored as well. After a sharp rise in box office returns, the executives reinstated their own handsome stipends. But Jack Warner declined to honor Darryl's promise, so after a massive row, Darryl quit and joined forces with Joe Schenck to form a new company, 20th Century Pictures Corporation. Most of the subsequent protests, though angry, were halfhearted in effect, so fearful were most employees of Warner's infamous revenges against those who crossed him. As I recall, only Jimmy Cagney and I put up a big row. Luckily, we were in a better position than most to do so, since we were both riding high at the time. We let our agents do most of the talking, though even they were often cowed into submission if Warner threatened to bar them from the studio.

While they argued, we went ahead in order to keep our legal slates clean.

My first "punishment" was the withdrawal of the fine story I had approved and the substitution of a sub-average story called *Parachute Jumper*. I decided to be docile. Today I have no more idea of the story of *Parachute Jumper* than what anyone may guess from its title. I didn't even appreciate my new young leading lady, fresh from the stage. She was not particularly pretty; in fact, I thought her rather plain, but one didn't easily forget her unique personality. She was Bette Davis. We got on well enough, although she thought director Al Green's sense of humor as infantile as the story we were obliged to act out. She was always conscientious, serious, and seemed devoid of humor of any kind. But then, there was not much to be humorous about. It was a job and she attacked it with integrity. Our careers were to cross a couple of times many years later, but then our only interest was to get the damned thing over with.

When I first met Billie, Paul Bern was one of her favorite escorts and confidants. He was a little under forty at the time but he seemed older. I was flattered by his friendship—his other close friends were all ten or twenty years my senior. Paul was a contract producer at MGM. He was really a production supervisor whose title was upgraded by Irving Thalberg. Still, Paul's position as Thalberg's literary and cultural mentor was unique.

One day when Billie and I were quietly beginning to divide ourselves, Paul rang me to say that he was taking Jean Harlow to dinner and invited me to join them. He said he had something important to tell me. In those days Jean Harlow was a popular sex goddess who often confounded the gossips by choosing the charming intellectual, most unglamorous Paul as her escort. I was, therefore, not surprised by her presence. But what was Paul going to tell me that was so secret? Something about Billie? Or my job? I couldn't think.

We sat at a banquette in a dark corner of the restaurant—three in a row, Jean in the middle. Paul was in the most ebullient spirits. We drank a cocktail or two, ordered dinner, and exchanged stories. We were having an altogether enjoyable time, but there was no hint of what Paul was planning to tell me. Still, as we chatted, something else was happening that made whatever Paul was going to say less important by the minute. The glamorous Jean was playing very active "footsie" with me under the table. As she was vitally attractive, I first wondered if I was just flattering myself. Her very loose and revealing décolletage, though something of a professional trademark, was not wasted on me. As her foot pressed mine, I responded, timidly at first in case her pressure was not intended. But then, to my surprise, I felt her hand on my knee! There was no misunderstanding this and only with effort did I suppress a shiver. Indeed, as she kept on in this amazingly friendly fashion, I had the greatest difficulty disciplining my own reaction. I tried to respond intelligently to whatever Paul was saying, but since I could only half-hear him, and less than half-concentrate on what I could hear, it was nearly a lost cause.

I could not bring myself to reply in kind to Jean's undercover gestures, but as I was trying to think straight and neither resist nor indicate any lack of reciprocal interest, Paul suddenly beamed and said, "Now! I'll tell you—in confidence—something very important to me." His face showed that I must give him my undistracted attention, so I gently pulled my leg away from the special attention it was getting.

Paul went on, "Douglas, among my closest friends, you are fairly new and certainly the youngest. There are only about four or five of you—but you are the first to know some great news!"

I smiled gratefully and nodded encouragingly.

"Well, Jean has promised to marry me! *Me!* The old bachelor! At last, I'm getting married, and to the most witty, wonderful, and attractive girl I've ever known!"

At that, Jean pulled her hand well away and put it on top of the table to show me. "Look," she said, "the ring Paul gave me. Isn't it beautiful?"

I gulped, knowing Paul was not a prankster or one for crude jokes. Then, smiling broadly, I reached over and shook his hand warmly, kissed Jean on the cheek, pulled myself away, and ordered a bottle of champagne for the three of us.

For the rest of the evening, and indeed for the rest of the time I knew her, I kept a long distance from Jean. For Paul's sake, I was just a bit warmer and more civil to her than I felt after this experience. Inside, I was actually very shocked. And then I was angry. And I stayed that way. I was so very fond of Paul—I had such respect for everything about him—that I couldn't bring myself ever again to be honestly relaxed when she was around.

They were married not long after this episode, in July 1932. Then about a month after the wedding, sometime around Labor Day, a call came from someone early one morning, saying that Paul was dead. "Suicide," they said. I don't know where Billie was at the time. I threw on some clothes and drove as fast as I could to Paul's house in Benedict Canyon.

When I arrived, several others, like his older friends Carey Wilson, Jack Gilbert, and Doug Shearer, were there. The body had already been taken away, and there were knots of people here and there walking around dazed. I think some of the MGM big shots like Mayer and Thalberg were about, in a crowd of assistants and others. Police were guiding cars and press people somewhere. Jean, I heard later, had been at her mother's the night before to keep her company during her father's absence on a fishing trip with Clark Gable and no one was yet sure if she had even been told of the tragedy.

Paul, we were informed, had left a deeply tragic note for Jean. We later learned he had been impotent, and although Jean did know of it early on, she had grown to love him sincerely and had begun to settle down. But for Paul, the real summing-up was in his suicide note, wherein he apologized and confessed his "abject humiliation."

As I slowly walked away from the house, I glanced up and saw something I had never noticed before. The roof seemed to be supported by four gables. At the end of each, a face was carved, rather like a presentable modern gargoyle. I looked closely. They were immediately recognizable. They were Gilbert, Wilson, Shearer, and—*me!* I drove home slowly—too stunned to weep. It was my first experience with tragedy.

Jean's and my paths did not cross again.

At home, things were quite chilly. As I suspected, Billie had indeed taken a cottage in the then unspoiled seaside settlement of Malibu Beach, north of Santa Monica, but she wouldn't tell me where it was or how I could reach her for some time. She declared that she had to sort things out in absolute privacy, to be alone to read, sleep, stare at the sea, commune with nature, and study lines for *Today We Live,* her next movie, to be directed by Howard Hawks. It was meant to be an all-male picture, but Mayer insisted that a female star be written in. The principal leading man was dear "Yep-Nope" Gary Cooper, an early professional rival whose test for *The Winning of Barbara Worth* a few years back was far better than mine. He was always a charmer and a far better actor than credited. His jealous detractors saw him always as a bashful, hat-crunching, monosyllabic cowboy, and said he established "the shit-kicking school of acting," but no one else was so convincing or charming as he.

The other principals in Billie's cast were an old friend, Bob Young, and a fine actor from New York, Franchot Tone. Today we would call Tone a concerned citizen—he shocked some of the insular movie people with his outspoken and informed left-liberal politics, expressed in the cultured accents of the eastern upper-class establishment. He was really a nice, amicable guy who frankly enjoyed biting the conservative hand that fed him.

Billie had to interrupt her sabbatical occasionally when we had a long-planned dinner party or, for instance, once when one of her favorites, Clifton Webb, was in Los Angeles on a visit. I had first known him at the Algonquin. He was now an elegant Broadway musical star. Since I had to pass his Beverly Hills hotel on the way home from my studio, I offered to pick him up and drive him to Cielito Lindo for dinner.

Clifton, as his old friends will confirm, was urbane, elegant, affected, and amusingly acerbic. He would have shivered at being thought even remotely macho. Still, he was most engaging company, well traveled, and rich in international gossip. He had had a drink or two—or three—by the time I picked him up, but it didn't slur his speech or inhibit his movements. He was heartily glad to see me. As we drove along the winding, still undeveloped Sunset Boulevard, the warmth of his affection for me became embarrassing. I was, for one of the few times in my life, absolutely blank about how to respond, so I said nothing and just kept my eyes riveted to the darkening, ill-lit highway. I had, of course, known many men and women in the United States and in Europe who were homosexual and had delighted in their witty and intelligent company. But never had one ever before indicated sexual interest in me. I had never thought about how I might react. Would I become indignant and use harsh, belittling words, manfully punch his jaw or kick him in the groin? Would I get flustered and run away like a masculine vestal virgin, hysterically protecting my neo-chastity? Would I call the police? No! None of these. When my passenger gently put his hand on my thigh, as he joyfully chattered on about his feelings for me, I burst out laughing. I suddenly thought the whole thing—the time, the place, the two of us—such a funny turn that I roared. My companion quickly withdrew his hand and stopped in mid-sentence.

When I ceased my guffawing, he turned to me and coldly instructed me to stop the car at the lonely filling station we were approaching. Why? Because, he said, he would not dine with us after all. He would ring Billie from the filling station, pleading illness, and then send for a taxi back to his hotel.

I muttered something like "Aw, c'mon. Let's forget it," but did as he wished. Not another word was said.

When I got home, Billie was disappointed about poor Clifton's upset tummy and I never said a word more about it. In fact, poor, nice Clifton didn't speak to me for six months.

Many people will remember that when his beloved old clinging chatterbox mum, Mabelle, finally was gathered to her rest, Clifton went all to pieces. He rang up his old friend Noël and sobbed his heart out. His loss was irreplaceable. Finally, Noël had had enough and barked, "Oh, come on, Clifton! Pull yourself together! I know it's hell to be left an orphan like that at the age of seventy-two."

About this time I received an offer from RKO to costar with their newest "find," Katharine Hepburn. She had come out to California from a couple of solid personal successes on the New York stage to play Jack Barrymore's daughter in the movie version of Clemence Dane's *A Bill of Divorcement*.

She was an immediate success and though the studio heads thought her looks too unconventional (they could never explain clearly what they meant) for an ingenue, they decided to take the risk by giving her a most unusual part in *Morning Glory,* an unusual story. They surrounded her with two established costars: Adolphe Menjou and me. The director was the once-famous stage star Lowell Sherman (who had married Helene Costello, the object of my seventeen-year-old devotion).

The script, by Zoë Akins, called for a longish dream sequence in which Hepburn and I were to play two, possibly three, big scenes from *Romeo and Juliet.* We were both about the right age and conscientious about our work and so we carefully rehearsed these classic scenes for several weeks before they were scheduled to be shot. Costumes, wigs, and two sets (one with the famous balcony) were designed. Kate transformed her bony, strong-planed face and everyday self into the delicate, sensitive woman-child Juliet.

I, on quite another hand, had gasped myself into the tightest, sheerest green tights this side of the Ballets Russes. They stretched right up to my rib cage. I reminded myself of Barrymore's "decadent string bean." With a full blond wig, one earring, and a good deal of makeup I looked more nearly like the second-prize winner in a transvestite contest. But this is all hindsight. We were both, despite our youthful shyness, rather pleased with ourselves and particularly our readings.

And so, incidentally, were Director Sherman and Producer Pandro Berman. In fact, an audience of friends, associates, and selected outsiders was invited to watch us perform the scenes without the distraction of cameras, lights, and sound equipment. We ended up giving two "by invitation only" performances that were received with surprising enthusiasm. When the scenes were finally shot and reshot from various angles, the film was sent round to all the bigger studios and projection rooms for private viewing. I think that we were both pretty damned good, in spite of our getups. Our training and rehearsal had paid off. Kate's speech, so widely familiar, had become musical and poetic. She was feminine and frail, her voice soft, frightened, and yet eagerly passionate.

Of course, by that time my too susceptible heart had allowed itself to be captured off-stage as well as on and my sentiments for Juliet, for Eva Lovelace (her name in the picture), and for Kate herself were the same. I thought her incapable of anything but perfection—whether checking into the studio in tight blue jeans and an old shirt and smoking Parliaments or as Juliet, the epitome of romance. To me, she was wholly absorbing.

I did succeed in persuading her to dine with me once or twice, and to see a movie, but somehow I lost all poise when trying to express my growing feelings for her. I was romantically tongue-tied. For a while I hoped she suffered from too much shyness to admit a similar reaction to me. My awakening came one night when I delivered her to the house she rented in one of the Hollywood canyons. After a restrained, just-friendly good-night peck on the cheek early (we were to work next morning), I drove some fifty yards down the road in my small top-down roadster. Then I pulled over to the side to gaze at the shining night sky and sigh over the wondrous Kate. However, something in the rear-view mirror caught my eye. Across Kate's lawn was a car in the street behind her house. I suddenly saw her slim athletic figure bound out of her back door across the grass, hop into someone else's car, and drive off!

My desolation can be imagined, but even though I was stung I didn't mention the episode to her afterward. I quickly realized that I had not inspired the same reaction in her as her very existence had in me, and so rather than risk the breakup of an already valued friendship I merely "cooled" my behavior in private and became strictly a friend.

I was never quite sure who my rival was, but with hindsight it is reasonable to assume that it was Leland Hayward. But to look at it another way, I was very fortunate that we developed a solid, entertaining, and affectionate friendship in lieu of a romance. Although we see each other too seldom, we nevertheless remain the warmest and most considerate of friends.

Our big Shakespearean scene was finally cut out of the picture entirely, since the producers felt it was not only too long, but "the yokels wouldn't catch the lingo" anyway. Today, with even the negative destroyed, we have only the production stills to prove that we did it at all.

Morning Glory itself proved a smashing success—and came at a good time for me. Kate won the Academy's Oscar for the best performance by an actress that year. Although I performed my assignment as well as could be, most people have forgotten that I was even in the film. Adolphe Menjou was also swamped by the Hepburn tidal wave. I thought Kate so great in every way that I really didn't mind and was pleased to have had the experience of being in a big hit. Menjou, contrarily, was as mad as one of his elegant hatters!

The demand for the application of my time, energy, and concentration on work was again welcome. Everyone thought my next film would be a good one, despite Darryl's defection and my continuing arguments with Jack Warner over what I maintained—with no recorded effect—were cheap breaches of contract. (My rightful salary now, with the addition of some rare bonuses, just about equaled Billie's.)

The new picture had several working titles, starting with *The Kid's Last Fight* and finally ending with *The Life of Jimmy Dolan.* It was a prizefight story, with a so-called murder and a gaggle of gamblers and gangsters. The denouement of the plot depended on my being a left-handed professional boxer trying to fight as a right-hander in order to fool the police. To prepare for this, I was required to work out at the Warner Brothers' tennis court with a wise and patient ex-fighter as a coach. He bashed me about heartily but carefully. Once, though, he did slip and cut my lip and, despite the rubber guard, loosened two front teeth.

Once again, "Gretch" Young was cast as the girl, and the fine cast featured the always splendid Aline MacMahon, the lovable stock standby Guy Kibbee, and the now newly renamed bit player John Wayne. It also included Mickey Rooney, who was then, I guess, about ten undersized years of age, but already so talented and bouncy it was scary. Fat and funny Archie Mayo was the ideal director for the story—and me.

The whole package became the exciting quality melodrama that was intended. The only bad moment was when, after many careful rehearsals, I misjudged distance and caught a stiff punch smack on the button. I sank to my knees, unable to move. After stopping the cameras and giving me a bit of a rest, we went at it again and this time, thank God and my trainer, we did it right and I "won"—as planned. I gave the other fellow as clean a sock on the jaw as I could and right on cue he fell to the canvas. Archie yelled "Cut!" and the other fellow jumped happily to his feet, much to my embarrassment, quite unbruised. We were all good in this picture—properly characterizing each part, and preventing what was basically an obvious, sentimental melodrama from becoming maudlin. All in all, we deserved the success the film enjoyed. In fact, even with its 1932 sentimentality, it is quite similar to the recent film *Witness.*

Billie continued to withdraw ever more to her Malibu cottage into what she would describe as her "personal solitude." She did keep one private telephone line through which she could be reached, but only for emergency calls from the studio or her agent. If she stayed there for more than three or four days, she would ring either me, our cook, or Louis Blembel, our new family secretary-cum-chauffeur—a young, super-serious correct German.

She called to get messages, ask about our general welfare, or to give household orders.

It was hard to find time or reason to be together. We had become familiar strangers, helpless to prevent our relationship's slide from intense romance into even easy companionship. Whatever emotions or thoughts we once had in common had been fogged over and lost. While we both took serious pains to disarm the inevitable gossip, some whispers were unavoidable. I was aware that a few of her intimates did know where her hideout was and so, out of pride, I pretended to know too. I didn't really know for some time.

Meanwhile, I was not the object of anyone's pity. In fact, it looked as though I was the cheery, faithless cad who behaved as he wished within certain socially prescribed bounds of behavior. Whereas, with a poignant and resigned half smile, Joan Crawford Fairbanks seemed the dedicated, hardworking, utterly devoted, and long-suffering wife.

It is all too long ago now to recapture with reliable accuracy my own—let alone Billie's—state of mind. But I am convinced that my smoldering resentment of her behavior (no doubt reciprocated in full) led me to get away with more than my share of self-indulgence. In later years Billie would tell her interviewers that my transition from a "budding aesthete to an aspiring international sophisticate" (I could never believe she really used that phrase) had been her first clear sign that we had far less in common than she suspected. Whereas she was increasingly absorbed in improving her acting technique and furthering her career, I was more interested in developing other interests, including our social life. This was nonsense. We were both hardworking—most of the time—and whether my after-hours prurience and superficial dalliances were a statement of my equal independence or a way of getting even for something suspected but not known, I cannot honestly tell. When we had guests at home we gave a passable performance of a civilized couple.

One day Billie appeared suddenly at Cielito Lindo and, with no lead-in, confronted me in a coldly challenging way, saying that for some time she had been putting up with stories coming to her about my "carryings-on." She would not, she threatened, tolerate such humiliations any longer. This time, I was so unprepared that I was beyond even the mildest of sputters. After a long pause to be sure I'd say nothing I'd regret later, I finally said I couldn't confess anything more wicked than "third-degree guilt." This evasive rebuttal was scarcely spoken when she proclaimed that though she still hoped to save our marriage, for the time being we must consider ourselves, in effect, separated. She proposed that we say nothing to "outsiders," that we continue to share the same roof, household responsibilities and amenities, but that, with an eye to discretion, we would lead our own lives. She assured me that she was speaking only for herself, there was nobody else in her life, but that she found her work and studies too absorbing and gratifying to consider tolerating my behavior further. I seem to recall commenting about her so-called friends who, though devoted, also gossiped behind her back. I said I could recommend better ways than separation to restore conjugal compatibility. I also said something asinine about marriage needing more personal attention paid to it—and to me—less on how many times a day one scrubbed a house clean, what one's next role was to be, and reading only scripts and movie magazines.

I was, of course, speaking from weakness, though she took it as a counter-charge of her misbehavior. The fiery indignation that flashed from those famous eyes was something to make a Milquetoast quake but, at this moment, she said no more. She gulped down her words, left the room, got into her roadster, slammed the door, and drove off to her whatever-wherever hideaway. Once more the urgent and unsympathetic demands of my work precluded any further moping or wallowing in homemade dramatics.

It was too much to hope that apart from the tensions with Billie and the more familiar ones attending the start of my next picture, life would otherwise be calm. Quite suddenly, in March 1933, I was staggered by a call from my agent, Mike Levee, who said that, although the story had not yet broken in the papers, I was about to be sued for "alienation of affections" by someone called Dietz. The only Dietz I knew was Howard Dietz (the Broadway musical playwright-lyricist), then MGM's New York head of publicity and advertising. I began by giving this bit of "news" a knowing smile and shrug, but to my undisguised surprise, thinking it was a practical joke, he turned out to be a Danish citizen—Jørgen Dietz. The man's wife had apparently been one of the group of regular "dress extras" the studio favored for certain kinds of background atmosphere. She had been one of the more conspicuous types on the lot, one of those who always dressed in an extreme fashion. The fact that neither I nor any principal knew any of them beyond a nod made no difference. It turned out that my fourth-hand, supposedly sixteen-cylinder Cadillac had been seen outside Mr. and Mrs. Dietz's nearby home several times during the studio's lunch hour breaks. I couldn't imagine how that could be, as I lunched daily in the studio commissary or in my dressing room. It then took a bit of quickly commissioned and expensive private detective work to discover that my studio dresser and gofer had been in the habit of taking my car to various haunts at noon without notice, knowing I never used it then. He had himself been visiting the house.

Shortly after we learned of this, Levee and a lawyer from the District Attorney's office interviewed Jørgen Dietz in a private studio office. Dietz admitted it had been a plan to get money. If I paid a couple of thousand, he would call off the suit. The word "blackmail" was carefully suggested by Levee and the lawyer, and to the man's horror, they told him they had "bugged" the room and his own words were now "on the record." At that point, the man from the D.A.'s office took over and told the couple they would be tried and put in prison.

Instead of being shocked and upset when he was told the story, Jack Warner was delighted. "That guy Fairbanks," he said through his torpedo cigar, "has so goddamn many faggot friends that I was beginning to wonder about him too. This kinda thing is a relief and it'll prove he's no fairy. So! Let 'em print the story! I don't care!"

Neither Levee nor I thought publicity would be necessary or helpful, and I had no one "outside" I yet dared tell the story to—not for the world to Billie, or to my parents—all of whom I was sure would blow the roof off at the slightest zephyr of scandal. They had generated enough themselves in the past and the years of overblown Crawford-Fairbanks publicity were more than enough for anyone.

In a few days at a meeting in the D.A.'s downtown office, after the couple had been threatened with prison and the wife threatened to jump out the window, I was asked if I was prepared to press charges. Furious at the admittedly groundless suit and its possible fuel for the flames crackling at home, I said no—but only on condition that the couple, who were found to have been leading very permissive lives anyway, would—as non-citizens—be deported to Denmark at once. This was agreed to by all and the matter thought settled.

But a week or so later, we heard that the Dietzes maintained that the D.A.'s office had no legal right to let them off the hook regardless of my relaxing charges, especially since the D.A. himself thought them guilty. Consequently, their advisors suggested the D.A. would be threatened with exposure unless *he* persuaded *me* to "settle out-of-court"! But Levee managed to squeeze out a sort of compromise whereby Warner Brothers paid on my behalf some fraction of the Dietzes' demand "out of court"—on condition that they leave the country immediately. They did.

By that time, however, most of the damage to me—not much, as it turned out—had been done. The story got into the papers and I was almost sick with anxiety. When the press asked Billie what she felt about this mini-scandal, she, to her credit, answered that she knew all the silly details, it was an outrageous accusation without any foundation whatsoever, and that she would stick by me "100 percent"!

All the latter part of this horrid interval took place as I was scheduled to start filming an adaptation of a Somerset Maugham novel, *The Narrow Corner*. By that time my option was due to be exercised and J.L. sent word that unless I signed a new contract that did not allow for the restoration of the salary cut I had taken or for the sizable increase the old contract called for, he, Jack Warner, might have second thoughts about further dealings with me. My 1932 pictures had had mixed receptions. *Morning Glory* was not released until August 1933. The Depression was still in full flood.

Everyone was sure that *Jimmy Dolan* would be successful (and it was) but that did not materially offset the three or four indifferent films that preceded it. And now my favorite director, Al Green, was not too sure about this next one. The script was changed considerably from Maugham's story. In fact after *The Narrow Corner* was screened for Maugham, he gave me a copy of the novel, inscribed, "To my friend, young Douglas Fairbanks, from *almost* one of his authors, Willie Maugham." Still, we patched it up as best we could, and were helped by a fine cast: Ralph Bellamy (whose great voice I envied) and Dudley Digges, with whom I so appreciated working in *Outward Bound*. The girl, Patricia Ellis, was pretty enough to look at and tried hard, but she was relatively inexperienced and, with such a high-powered cast, it showed. Luckily, her part made no great demands. It proved to be a very tough picture for me, however. I had fired my studio dresser for his part in the Dietz scandal and though I'd been heartened by Billie's public support, I was not yet able to think clearly about either us or my work.

During the last fortnight or so of shooting, we were obliged to work outdoors all night on a fine mock-up of a ship, on the Warner–First National back lot in Burbank. The nearly full-sized ship was built on huge rockers and had, on each side, enormous sets of tanks that could be filled in minutes by special fire hoses. On cue, they dumped the water onto a slide that sluiced it up and over the decks. The illusion of a storm was aided by great rows of overhead pipes that poured down rain that was blown by several large wind machines. These were actually airplane engines that propelled a small gale.

The big storm sequences took three or four all-night sessions. Since the California nights can indeed be cold and damp, there was a generous tray of black coffee and Scotch whiskey inside my portable dressing room, just off the set. There was also an electric heater on the floor, a chair, a cot, some dry clothes, and tennis sneakers. A couple of sweaters and a lumber jacket to wear outside helped temporarily as I waited for rehearsals to finish before the cold, windy drenching I would shortly be getting over and over again. It was miserable for all of us in these scenes as we screamed out lines and slipped on the rocking, rolling deck, the night chill penetrating our sopping wet shirts. The coffee and Scotch were of minimal comfort but they probably did forestall pneumonia.

At one or two o'clock one morning, I was in my dressing room, drying off, warming up, my teeth chattering on the rim of my whiskey glass, when, after a brief knock, Mike Levee came in smiling. "How ya' doin', kiddo?"

"Okay so far. What are you doing up so late paying a call on a client? Do I owe you some commission? Have a drink?"

Mike declined. "I'll bet you'll be glad when this is over, eh?"

I managed an earnest response, "You're damned right I will. Even tonight, I can't wait to get into my own warm bed—and sleep till tomorrow afternoon!"

Mike smiled, then, looking away, rather mumbled his next words: "That's what I came to talk to you about. I'm sorry to bring this news . . . but . . . er . . . but you're going to stay at the Beverly Wilshire Hotel tonight, not at home."

I wasn't able to take in the full meaning of his news—not at once. I took another grateful gulp of Scotch. "What do you mean? The house burn down or something? Where's Billie?"

Mike now talked to me straight—and all too clearly. "Joan's all right. But she's had me take a double room for you at the hotel, and your German secretary, Joan's maid, and my secretary from the office have spent the whole night packing all your things in whatever we could find, moving 'em to the hotel, unpacking you and hanging up what we could. We'll arrange to move whatever we forgot or left behind tomorrow . . ." He went on, but I was no longer listening.

I'd stopped shivering, having gone numb all over. I couldn't think very clearly and it certainly wasn't the drink. I couldn't sort out what had happened or why.

Someone knocked on the door of the portable dressing room, "All ready, Mr. Fairbanks! On the set, please! We're ready to go!"

I went out, dumbly disciplined and unquestioning.

Mike shouted after me, "Don't bother to call her—she's cut off her phone and arranged a new private number. Even I don't know it."

I no longer thought about being warm or cold. What the hell had happened? Billie had thrown me out of *our* house—just like that. No warning. No discussion. No row—not recently anyway. If anything, the atmosphere at home had seemed a little more relaxed and even, at times, friendly.

I finally finished shooting in a daze, just after the first light of dawn. I was wrapped up in blankets, given a huge jug of black coffee and a mug of Scotch, put into Mike's car (he didn't trust me to drive myself that night), and taken from Burbank to Beverly Hills.

I must have looked like the Canterville ghost as Mike escorted me through the hotel lobby and up to my brand new home. I'm told I spoke hardly at all during the trip back. I was given a fistful of telephone messages. I hoped they were from Billie, a friend, or one of my parents, but they were all from newspapers. How did they know? So soon, anyway?

Mike said, "Get some sleep and I'll be back at lunchtime and tell you all the news. I've told them to cut off your phone till you ring down—and don't forget—you've got to work all night again, tomorrow night."

I plopped into the comfortable hotel bed, too weary to think or feel anything more. Mike let himself out and I fell bang off into a heavy sleep for a blank four or five hours.

I woke up, uncomprehending, in my new surroundings. I tried to galvanize my wits into clarity with a shower followed by coffee. Both morning papers were delivered and I tore open the *Examiner* first. It tended to be the more sensational of the two. There, as I feared, on the front page, was Louella Parsons's "scoop," quoting Billie's announcement of our "amicable separation."

Confirmed in print, I still found the news hard to reconcile, not only with the recent slight easing of our married misery but also with Billie's less than one-month-old assurance to the press, and to me, that she would stand "loyally" behind me in my "wicked victimization." No one rang me, as no one but Mike knew where I was. I was registered at the hotel under another name. Mike came by later and drove me slowly back to the studio. On the way he explained.

Billie, long accustomed to unburdening her innermost self to trusted journalist friends, this time chose as her confessor one of the closest and best of them, Katherine Albert, a well-known feature writer for a movie fan magazine. Some three months or more earlier she confided to Katherine that she had made up her mind that our differences were irreconcilable and, though we "remained fond of each other and respected each other greatly," it was "wiser and more honest" to separate—openly and legally. Divorce was not considered for the time being, as it was possible that an "extended vacation might help to drive us back together again." The basic idea behind giving the great scoop to Katherine for a magazine story was that magazines usually closed three months before publication, and Billie needed just about that much time to bring matters to a head with me and get everything amicably arranged before our private bubble burst publicly. But then some things happened to upset the Crawford schedule. First came the surprise of the threatened Dietz scandal, necessitating her announcement of "support and faith" in me, which she realized she would shortly have to recant. The second problem was, for her, more professionally serious: she was advised by her tyrannical boss, Mayer, and by MGM's Hollywood publicity director, Howard Strickland, that the whole idea of a breakup of her marriage would now do her more harm than the idea of our getting married in the first place. To confuse matters even more, the worst possible harm to her career would be to allow anyone but "Lolly" Parsons have the exclusive scoop on the story. Billie protested that although she might renege on her formal marriage vows, she would never go back on a personal promise to a friend—especially one like Katherine Albert. But the Big Boss's argument and her overriding apprehensions about her career decided her—the very day before the magazine story was due to appear on the newsstands.

Mike described how the night before she had telephoned Lolly and told her that her "heartbroken" decision to call an end to our marriage had been confessed to Katherine months before but she had forgotten about it until she suddenly realized it was all to come out in a magazine any day. And not wanting "dear, sweet Lolly" *ever* to be scooped, she made up her mind to beat the magazine's publication by a day and tell *her* the whole story—indeed, even before she told me.

When I arrived at the studio, I was touched by the consideration and kindness of my coworkers. Not a soul so much as hinted that a word had been heard or read. They were their usual friendly, hardworking selves. The only exception was dear Al Green. At the end of the all-night shooting he came up to me before heading for home, and mumbled, "Good night—or good morning—whatever it is. Try and get a good rest. Sorry about the news."

I thanked him, and the studio driver took me back to the hotel.

A few more days and *The Narrow Corner* was finished. The personal storms had subsided. Mike arranged for Billie and me to have a private talk —not with any thought of reconciliation, but to reduce the elements of mystery and melodrama that had arisen. When we met of course we were unnaturally agitated. Billie yawed between the teary-eyed wife bravely resigned to the bitter ending of her dreams and the firm-jawed executive of a corporation discussing financial setbacks. I protested too much in far too many ways. I muttered some "heard-saids" about the cottage in Malibu and another in the Palm Springs desert and said it had been my plan to hire private detectives to confirm them. (I made that up on the spur of the moment. She must have known it too, as she coldly dared me to "Try! Just try!") I tried to win sympathy, but that tactic only made me look more ridiculous.

I decided my best move was to withdraw with at least an illusion of dignity, intending as I did to suggest that I might win the day if I wanted to play dirty though I wouldn't. Complete silence ensued. As I left, I said I'd heard rumors that her new New York leading man, Franchot Tone, was the real reason. She answered that such an imputation was an insult to all, that *no one* was in her life and my idea of detectives was unforgivable. Our separation was, she declared, due to our increasing incompatibility, a widening divergence of interests and, most of all, to my widely rumored, deeply hurting, and intolerable "indiscretions." That was all. End of scene.

I was given a few days to take away some items I believed were mine, although a few of the things I valued most, such as two etchings given to me by Norman Lindsay, the great Australian artist, a couple of my own small statues, and a few sets of books, were denied me. By this time I had just about paid up my full share of the cost of the house, but I was asked to sign away in my wife's favor any and all claims I might ever have in the future. This I agreed to do not out of any nobility of spirit or chivalrous generosity but because I wanted to get such details out of the way with the least fuss as quickly as possible.

I moved out of the hotel to a modest apartment where few but friends would find me. Both Warner Brothers and MGM collaborated in keeping the press at a considerate distance from both Billie and me for a few days. I telephoned Mother and Jack in New York, who said all the right things and were not surprised. Nor was Genie. Or my cousins. Or other close friends. My father was away briefly, so no immediate explanation was called for in that quarter. I made a serious effort not to parade my depression or to play Pagliacci. I was very embarrassed by the "movie-biz" way in which our breakup was announced. I was pained by Billie's contemptuous scheme of secretly moving me out and then, reeking with self-righteousness, having a business associate tell me her intentions while I was hard at work in the chilly early morning hours. However, I must frankly say that although I was sad, disappointed, bruised, I was not in the least bit heartbroken.

To divert myself when the film was completed, I finished some short stories for *Esquire* and *Collier's,* and went back to a novel I'd begun a few months before. It was set in pre-World War I Berlin and the plot was shamelessly filched from Schnitzler (with a fine part for me if it ever were to be a play or a film). As I hadn't known Germany either before the Great War or

after, Louis Blembel helped out with geography and place names. The novel
was never finished, which may have been just as well.

Long before the storm broke, I had agreed to do *Captured,* another war
story. Once again I was obliged to play a Britisher. I failed to persuade Jack
Warner that I preferred the few American tough-guy parts I had been getting away with and that too many British character parts would get me
"typed." But since I was still so deeply in the company's bad books, nothing
I said got anything but the shortest shrift. However, one compensation for
being maneuvered into a so-so story was being costarred with Leslie Howard again. That good fortune brightened any dreariness I still felt and relieved my concern about making just another war picture. Leslie was bound
to raise the film's standards and I would have my work cut out just to keep
up with him in my own performance. Then, to maintain the performance
levels, Paul Lukas, the splendid Hungarian actor, was cast as a villainous
German officer.

Now Mike advised me that Warners had tried to bully him into advising
me to sign a new but less valuable contract. J.L. said the less than spectacular reception of all but one of my last three pictures obliged the Eastern
theater managers to delete my name from their marquees. This was quite
untrue. It was merely a ploy to bring me to heel. Others, Warner assured us,
had signed on the new terms—and who did *I* think *I* was. Mike wisely
suggested that since the story material I'd been given to choose from this
past year was on average only routine, I should ignore their threats, let the
contract end, and become a free lance. This was economically more risky,
but it might give me a wider choice of roles, of vehicles and better salaries.
Even Zanuck, now establishing an independent 20th Century with Schenck,
confidentially advised me that I'd do far better out than in—that Mike's
advice was good.

To my mind, to do as Mike advised was just putting a good face on what
was really a decision by Warners to make my further stay intolerable. To
add injury to insult, the sharp, unfriendly end of my unique five-year contract coincided with my receiving the first factual account of what had really
motivated Billie to rock our boat beyond any chance of steadying it again.
Three close friends—Irving Asher, Phil Holmes, and Allen Vincent—let me
know quietly what many others had known for some time but I did not: for
almost two years Billie had been having an intense and fully requited love
affair with Clark Gable, one of our friends and frequent dinner guests. Her
extra early morning departures for the studio, even when not filming, and
her late returns home were often the only times they could meet undetected

by either Ria, Clark's wife, or me. To record that I was surprised must prove one of this book's greatest understatements.

I was additionally surprised to learn that one of Joan's and Clark's favorite trysting places at the studio was the charmingly decorated, very comfortable portable dressing room I had given her as a wedding present—and had only recently finished paying for. Actually, Clark was such a nice guy that even in my private distress I couldn't blame him. Had our positions been reversed, I wasn't sure I wouldn't have been equally deceitful.

In much later years, after two or more marriages, Clark's and my paths were to cross in the unusual way of his marrying my father's widow, my second stepmother. I liked him very much, but neither of us ever so much as mentioned the name Joan or Billie to each other. He had not known me well when he and Billie began their affair and he certainly appreciated that she was as physically attractive, as dynamic to be with, even to argue with, as any of her contemporaries. Probably more so.

So Billie and I were officially separated. She would file suit for divorce on April 29, 1933, but it would not become final for another year.

13

It was decided in a hurry: Pete and I would go to Europe together. It was the first time I had ever taken a trip alone with my father. To an observer, he was still the same energetic leader of the pack, the bouncing Scout Master, but that was sheer habit. To my considerable surprise, he was becoming gradually dependent on me. He scarcely waited for answers, but he began to ask questions. What should he do about Mary? He never once mentioned her secret drinking habit, nor her disinclination to share his enthusiasm for travel and people. He had enjoyed his extended foreign jaunts and the adventures they produced, but . . . what was he to do now? He confided his wish to keep his cake and eat it as well, but he was not yet prepared for solutions.

Of course he wanted desperately to preserve his marriage and of course he was concerned about his public image. On New Year's Day of 1933 his self-esteem had a rude shock, to which I was witness. I had been invited to join him and Mary (a "let's show 'em" occasion) at the annual East-West Rose Bowl football game in Pasadena. We were driven in their Rolls-Royce by the family chauffeur. And don't think I didn't love it—at first. As we were approaching Pasadena, automobiles were bumper-to-bumper and the crowds grew enormous and packed close to the creeping cars to see whom they could recognize. It was, of course, a time when few workers could spare a dime. When they saw the fabulous Mary Pickford and Doug Fairbanks, all dolled up (I was unnoticed in front) in a shiny Rolls-Royce, their tempers bubbled over. They began to shout curses, insults, and occasional obscenities and to rock the car. Too few police failed to stop them. Mary was terrified, and even my father lost his natural bravado. Nothing really happened, but they were made intimately aware of how *gloria mundi* can and does *transit* very quickly! Mary remained shocked for days, but Pete had dismissed it from his mind by game's end.

That winter Pete didn't seem to be particularly interested in anything much—not even the details of my own marriage breaking up after so short a time. Nevertheless, for the first time he treated me as if I were his contemporary—no longer a subconscious rival, but a companion, confidant, and teammate. I wallowed happily in this long-wished-for relationship. In a strange way I was the more responsible, even mature, of the two of us. I tried to be wise enough not to allow myself airs and to show at least a modicum of filial respect.

In a few weeks we were off to New York and then, along with Dad's old secret-keeper and jester, Tom Geraghty, we set sail—again on the *Bremen*. It was mid-April 1933. Mother and Jack came down to the pier to see us off and it amused me to see how they and Pete carefully tried to avoid meeting. In the end, they all failed, but only for a brief moment of self-conscious smiles, mumbled words, and hurried backing-away.

With much hooting and tooting the great liner swung out to sea. I was as happy as that famous clam at high tide. I was reluctant to admit that I was pleased to be virtually free of my make-believe marriage and on a trip to Europe with my fine new special friend, my father. Within two days at sea I began a charming but limited shipboard romance with an American lady who possessed the German title of *Gräfin*. I had never heard the German name for countess and she was, I recall, miffed at my ignorance. But only briefly. No longer did I have to be so discreet. I could walk, stroll, swim, and dance quite openly with this graceful flirt and not feel a desperate sinner and the potential victim of somebody's gossip column. And from the start, I made the point with my father that I would pay all my own expenses.

In London, Pete took a large luxurious flat near Marble Arch on the northern border of Hyde Park. Tom was in one of its many rooms and I was in a small one at the back—out of the way. Before many days Pete was away somewhere else—in Paris, St. Moritz, or the English countryside at some great house. And before many more days, he was back again. Tom and I had fine times together in that endlessly fascinating city.

Tom was, for our family, always a joy. He originally came with us intending to be away from home no more than a few weeks. When he arrived in London he decided he liked it so much that he wrote his wife and family

Arriving in Los Angeles from New York in June 1929, just after my marriage to
Joan Crawford.

Young newlyweds, 1929.

On the beach with Billie.

With Billie and Leslie Howard at a Hollywood premiere.

Playing a gigolo, with Edward G. Robinson in the gangster classic *Little Caesar* in 1930. (WARNER BROTHERS)

With Loretta Young in *I Like Your Nerve*, 1931. (WARNER BROTHERS)

With good friend Laurence Olivier on the way to Europe, 1932.

With Katharine Hepburn and Adolphe Menjou in *Morning Glory,* 1933. (RKO RADIO PICTURES)

Sharing a backlot heater to ward off the California damp with a young Mickey Rooney while filming *The Life of Jimmy Dolan* in 1933.

Joan Crawford in front of the portable dressing room that was a wedding present from me. (DORE FREEMAN)

With Joan Gardner in *Catherine the Great,* 1934.

With my father in 1934.

Meeting my mother and stepfather, Jack Whiting, on their arrival in England for George V's Silver Jubilee in 1935.

to say that his return would be "delayed." And so it was—for seven years! Only the fear of the coming war finally drove him home—where he reentered the loyal and loving circle of his family—just as if he had never left.

Another of my father's companions on this memorable trip was the humorist and critic Robert Benchley. Bob loved his drink. When he arrived in London for the first time, he weaved unsteadily through the mass of pigeons in Trafalgar Square and, with drunken, Anglophiliac tears streaming down his cheeks, held out his hand to them and asked, "Any messages for me?" A week or so later, he disappeared altogether. Finally my worried father got a cable from him, sent from Italy. It read: "Streets of Venice flooded with water. Wire instructions (signed) Benchley." He was so pleased with his wit that years later he sent the same cable to David Niven.

Although Pete was seldom in our elegant flat, he was constantly attended by Rocher, the butler-valet whom he brought with him from Pickfair. He also had two private secretaries, assigned by United Artists.

Even away from Pickfair his days began in much the same way, with a variety of strenuous exercises and nude muscle-flexing before mirrors. If anyone else was present he covered what modesty deemed most needed covering with his left hand, leaving his right for opening doors and picking things up. It was a curious concession to convention. Then after putting on a long, light undershirt (no underpants), he always began his favorite morning ritual: with Rocher's help selecting his outfit for the day—carefully tailored Savile Row suit, Jermyn Street shirt, tie, kerchief, Bond Street shoes, and whatever other accouterments struck his fancy. This was trivial but fun. In my case it proved contagious. Though I've never acquired as vast an array of apparel as his, I still start most mornings in an abbreviated version of this sartorial nonsense myself.

When my father finally went out, his routine began with shopping, mostly for himself but sometimes with gifts for friends and companions. Then most days he drove for forty minutes out to Sunningdale Golf Club where he frequently teamed up with the Prince of Wales.

Pete found himself attracted to the wife of a popular young man about town, Tony (Lord) Ashley, the heir to the Earl of Shaftesbury. I paid little attention to this at the time—I was preoccupied with seeing favorite sights and old friends from my fizzled-out honeymoon. Indeed, at the first opportunity, I visited my old teenage crush Gertrude Lawrence. She was starring in a comedy at the Wyndham Theatre called *This Inconstancy*. I remember being absolutely recaptivated by Gertie's inescapable magic. Suddenly my personal California dramas faded and my whirling emotions flew to this great woman. I was determined to pay her court, in spite of the fact that she was ten or eleven years my senior. However, I kept the extent of my newly formed romantic plans to myself. She was not only a great international stage star but the ex-love of more than one of my father's friends and contemporaries.

I made a determined effort to sound worldly and witty and to disguise my relative inexperience in sophisticated circles. I splurged on a new wardrobe from London's then most fashionable tailor, Hawes & Curtis. (The finest tailor-made suits were then about twenty pounds, or one hundred dollars, and you got 10 percent off for paying cash, which meant you paid your bill within six months!) At a party soon after we arrived, I saw Prince George for the first time since Noël's party for Billie and me a year earlier. He was charm itself and invited me to come to St. James's Palace the next day, where he lived in apartments near those of his eldest brother, the then Prince of Wales. (Prince George would later become the Duke of Kent.) I have to admit it was a great kick walking past the scarlet-uniformed, bear-skin-hatted sentries inside the courtyard of the Palace and entering those ancient doors into a modern, modest, and very comfortable bachelor's flat.

A week later, Pete and I received a glamorous weekend invitation. It was from the Scottish Duke of Sutherland, an old friend of Pete's on both sides of the Atlantic, who was familiarly known as Gordie. He was handsome and a devastating lady-killer. One of his romances had been with Sylvia, Lady Ashley, whom Pete now fancied. He invited us both down to his magnificent Tudor country seat, Sutton Place, in Surrey. In those days Sutton Place had squads of liveried servants and consisted of perhaps more than six thousand acres of beautiful rich green country, surrounded on all sides by stone walls, with a large swimming pool, ornamental fountains and gardens, a tennis court, and a room in which the latest movies were projected. When Gordie died, the trustees of his estate sold the house to Paul Getty, who lived out his days there. It was indeed a stately home.

In addition to the great house's Tudor treasures, pictures, tapestries, and furniture, there was a strangely crafted chair in a back hall with which I was most impressed. It was outsize, with extra-large arms and places on either side to hang one's legs if one wished. What made this piece priceless was that it had been made for the greatly overweight and lecherous Henry VIII. As his immense size was said to make even his most affectionate lady friends squeal in fear of suffocation, he had this chair especially made for more comfortable dallying.

Of course, my recent well-publicized separation and imminent divorce classified me more as a notorious than famous weekend guest, but I didn't mind. Everyone was casually hospitable and my successful pose of modesty and sophistication accelerated my acceptance by the other younger members of the house party. There were at least twenty houseguests. "The young," as anyone from eighteen to mid-twenties and still unmarried was called, not only kept together most of the time but even ate in a separate dining room. These six or eight fashionable contemporaries were amusing and moderately spoiled. They were often rude to each other in a joshing way, wicked-tongued (according to my more puritanical background), and appallingly vulgar. The girls, with their delicate English pink-and-white complexions, sowed four-letter words like seeds of corn and actually shocked me. I hoped I didn't let it show. Even movie sets were not so off-color.

Meanwhile only the formalities of discretion were observed in the display of Pete's growing feelings for Sylvia Ashley, a daughter of a London bobby called Hawkes. After some modeling experience, she had become the London equivalent of a Ziegfeld Follies girl. She then married Tony (Lord) Ashley. But that marriage turned rocky when Sylvia, toasted, feted, and wooed by many, fell for a dashing society racing driver and sportsman by the name of Dunfee. Sylvia was tall, willowy, and golden-haired, with a classically fair complexion. She had a fetching gap in her front teeth, which she later had capped. I was sorry when she did, as some of her individuality disappeared. She wore clothes and jewelry beautifully, the better to match the successful exchange of her original cockney accent for more languorous Mayfair intonations. She also possessed a shrewd, quick wit that augmented her ravishing looks.

Although Pete became increasingly infatuated with Sylvia (despite the twenty-five-year difference in their ages) he managed to enchain his jealous temper most of the time. He was intensely possessive by nature, though, and once when he overstepped the bounds of public behavior, he was very lucky to escape the gossipy press. They were at a party in London's lovely Ritz dining room and Prince George asked Sylvia to dance. She accepted gracefully, making a polite little "bob" in deference to his station and custom. When the dance ended and the orchestra started a new one, P.G. (as the Prince was called behind his back) asked Sylvia to dance again. She was delighted and off they whirled. But Pete saw red. Despite the formality of the setting, the dress, and the company, he barged up to the Prince, pulled him around, and asked how he "dared" to dance twice with Sylvia. The Prince took it in humorous good heart, thinking it a joke and part of the purely American custom of "cutting in." Those dancing nearby were horrified, but the loud music and the crowded floor kept the incident less noticed than it might otherwise have been.

The most marked difference between my father's life and mine at the time was that he could afford it and I couldn't. I was living it up but was luckily usually a guest. Although I was obviously much less noted than my father, I had a more mixed and generally more interesting (I thought) set of friends.

Gee Lawrence was an effervescent personality. Although she never seemed to realize when she sang off-key (frequently), she could always carry it off with the charm of her otherwise liquid voice, her grace of movement, and the mocking sensual mouth that ignored the large, unpretty nose above it. Her lithe figure, though fashionably boyish with scarcely a real curve, remained utterly feminine. It was, I believe, for her that Noël invented the term "star quality."

At the time I came on the scene Gee was being wooed by Eric, Earl of Dudley, a handsome, charming, disturbingly rich and rather stingy older aristocrat. His stepmother had been a renowned stage figure at the turn of the century and, like all his kin, Eric loved the theater and its folk—Gee above all. Gee, for her part, found Eric pretty devastating and made few bones about how much fun it would be to be privately known as the Countess of Dudley. After her spectacular success in two of the *Charlot's Revues* and with Noël in *Private Lives,* if only Eric would propose and pay some of her mounting bills, life would be wonderful. For Gee was notoriously extravagant.

She had a sweet daughter, Pamela Howley, by her first (conveniently forgotten) marriage. Pam was sent to all the best schools but was hidden in order not to compromise her mother's glamour. Yet when it served Gee's purposes, she played a not very convincing doting mother. Poor Pam! I was always fond of her and sympathized with her. A sensitive child, she inherited few of Gee's attractions but was a far nicer character.

Gee first decided to openly respond to my courting, to "take me up" as it were, to make Eric jealous. But little by little I believe my youth and celebrity made her feel younger and I began to be a real factor in her life. For some time Eric and I were on either end of a seesaw insofar as Gee's feelings for us were concerned. I tried to determine my standing from Helen Downes, Gee's adoring and long-suffering American secretary-companion. She tended to encourage me, her compatriot.

Gee had a wide circle of friends into which I was hastily drawn. Just to give an idea of the variety of names one saw among her regular group, one might start with the Prince of Wales (the Pragger-Wagger) followed closely by my now chief royal friend Prince George, and also Larry Olivier, John Gielgud, Noël Coward, Ivor Novello, Cole Porter, Bea Lillie, Jack Buchanan, and Fred and Adele Astaire.

On the "social side," Mollie (Countess of) Dalkeith was often around, as was the frightening but attractively decadent Tallulah Bankhead and her equally unconventional admirer, "Naps" (Lord) Alington—said to be the model for the hero of one of Michael Arlen's novels. Also there was Elsa Maxwell, "Syrie" (Mrs. Somerset) Maugham, Elsie (Lady) Mendl (the decorator), Sybil (Lady) Colefax, Emerald Cunard, "Chips" Channon, and a good cross section of American and Continental devotees, most of whom were shortly to become known as "Café Society."

Through Gee I got to know the rest of Eric's very extroverted and loving family. Eric's younger twin brothers, Geordie and Eddie Ward, were so identical in their twinship that they often swapped girlfriends the very same evening without being caught out. They were both in the RAF Reserve and through them I had some hair-raising adventures. Once, for instance, on a Sunday morning, we decided to buzz very low over Noël's country house in Kent. We knew he had a lot of weekend houseguests and thought it would be fun to wake them all up early after what we assumed had been a thick night. This we did. Two RAF planes, with this American civilian aboard one of them, zoomed and swooped at rooftop height above the Coward house over and over until we could see the household, one by one, coming out on the lawn, shaking fists and making obscene gestures at us. Eventually we spotted Noël, the Master himself, giving orders to the others. Pillows were brought out and placed carefully on the lawn and the many guests arranged themselves in order to spell out, quite clearly for us to see from the air, "FUCK OFF!" We did!

That same weekend, the Ward twins took me to a reception given by a fabulously rich Parsee Indian who had become ultra-English and, with exquisite Eastern taste, had furnished and decorated three great houses—one on Park Lane in London, one well north of London called Trent Park, and this great country estate called Port Lymne in Kent. I went along not knowing a soul except the twins. I wandered about on the great terrace, among the many guests, trying to be amiable among a flock of RAF and political types. After we left, I asked one of the twins about the only other lost soul besides me that I had seen wandering around quiet and detached. He was a little fellow in an RAF uniform. I was told, with that special quality of studied British equanimity, that "he was, you fool, Lawrence of Arabia!" How the hell was I to know? Not to *know* him, not even to have said, "How d'ya do"—nothing!—was a terrible missed opportunity.

One night Gee took me to a large party at the popular Café de Paris, in Leicester Square. Various international stars and bands played in the large rotunda below street level where white tie and tails were obligatory—just as they were, in those days, for any gentleman sitting in the first ten rows of a theater. The restaurant habitually engaged four to six very pretty "dance hostesses" who were always present. No one ever suggested they were engaged for any other purpose than to be the English equivalent of geisha girls —to amuse, to encourage men to dance, to order champagne, and to dance some more. One of the Ward twins fancied one of the girls in particular— she was a most beautiful Anglo-Indian (whose Indian mother was kept disguised as her maid). She was introduced to me as Miss O'Brien-Thompson. Much later, she was one of six or eight girls selected from different sources to be screen-tested and sent to drama school by the Hungarian producer-director Alexander Korda, eventually to become part of his company's stock company of young players. To Miss O'Brien-Thompson, whose father had been a soldier in the British Army, Korda gave the name of Merle Oberon. Professionally, the rest is history. Privately, she remained a friend until her days ended. So far as I know, she never openly acknowledged her mother's identity, and when she died she buried her privately on the grounds of a Hampshire estate that belonged to friends.

There was also a business aspect to our trip to Europe. Soon after our arrival a series of meetings was set up by the United Artists office in London between my father and Alexander Korda. To my surprise and pleasure my attendance was also requested at these meetings.

Korda had been bitterly disappointed by his brief experience as a director in Hollywood, so he went to England and established himself there. He produced and directed Charles Laughton in *The Private Life of Henry VIII.* The result was the revival of his career and a lift for the lagging spirits of the British film industry. After World War I, when American film companies overwhelmed Britain and Europe, the British established a quota system under which a certain number of British-made films had to be exhibited as a balance to the preponderance of American-made films.

The United Artists management in Great Britain was in the hands of two men—George Archibald, a wiry Scotsman, and Murray Silverstone, a transplanted New Yorker. Together they persuaded my father, and through him the other UA partners, to admit to their ranks a British producer who would make high-quality quota pictures, thus increasing both the profits and the prestige of the company.

Alex Korda was very shrewd. One wouldn't say he was actually slippery, but many accused him of being just this side of it. His tremendous charm and intelligence overcame most obstacles in his pursuit of success, prestige, and power. It was here that I first experienced big-time negotiations at close quarters. The deal for Alex to become a partner in United Artists was quickly set. The cost of his partnership was then two million dollars (God knows what its equivalent would be today), but he was allowed to pay for it from the expected profits of his films. It was no surprise to those who knew Alex that in the end he managed to pay virtually nothing. The story goes that he later sold those same shares (he hadn't bought) for much more than the original two million.

As soon as the documents were signed and sealed, Alex and UA jointly announced his immediate production plans. The first film was to be an adaptation of a French play, *Catherine the Great.* The famous German actress Elisabeth Bergner would play the young Catherine and she had insisted that her husband, Paul Czinner, be the director. One of England's best young character actresses, Flora Robson, was cast as the dying old Empress Elizabeth, and one of the giants of the English-speaking theater, Sir Gerald du Maurier, agreed to play the small but excellent part of the Czar's French valet. The one remaining question was who would play the mad Czar Peter III. It was a marvelous, quasi-classic part and almost every transatlantic star of the period hoped to get the job.

At first, the Korda group considered Joseph Schildkraut the best choice—and he would have been marvelous—but both Bergner and Schildkraut spoke with German accents, and it was decided that one was enough. To everyone's surprise and my own ecstatic delight, I was the next choice. At that time Alex had no further need to do anyone any favors, particularly his new United Artists partners. He was in the catbird seat. So casting me was not even done as a favor to my father. In fact, Pete was as surprised, though surely not so pleased, as I. After several tests and interviews I had landed this plum job on my own.

Now I would have a chance to show Hollywood's producers what I could do with a real character-lead. No longer would I have to play nice young light comedies or listen to offers to ape my father's swashbuckling fantasies. I had long before decided that no one could follow in his footsteps. They were so light they left no trace.

In May 1933 I still had time to play around, since actual production was not scheduled for several months. My cautious wooing of Gee proceeded at an encouraging pace and I was, within a few weeks, almost an equal rival of Eric Dudley, though it was only natural, as Noël pointed out to me, that her long-run interests would be better served as the Countess of Dudley than as the older girlfriend of a fashionable American movie star. Meanwhile, I enjoyed the excitement.

Then one morning I was awakened by the receipt of a cable. It was from

Mike Levee, advising me that the great Ernst Lubitsch had decided I was "the only possible one" to play in the movie version of *Design for Living,* the play Noël had written for himself and the Lunts. Freddie March was to play Alfred's part and Miriam Hopkins was set for Lynn Fontanne's role. And, what was more, I was being offered two or three times what I'd been averaging under contract—and many times more than I thought I'd get, even after the success of *Morning Glory.* That day I went around, flower in buttonhole, looking for something lighter than air to walk on. My cup was indeed running over.

Before my return to the States, Noël kindly took me to lunch and gave me innumerable tips on how to play the part of Leo. He also recalled an incident involving Tallulah Bankhead. The glamorous Tallulah had been lunching with friends at a banquette near the entrance to the restaurant—exactly where we were sitting at the time. Tallulah was known for her lack of all inhibitions. Thus there was a tense moment for Tallulah-watchers when they saw a very tall and handsome man with bushy mustachios approaching the exit, accompanied by his wife. Most of those present were aware that he had only recently got to the head of the queue of Tallulah's lovers. It was quite obvious that, because of his wife's presence and Tallulah's reputation, he was going to walk right past her table pretending not to see her, though, as usual, she was the most conspicuous lady in the place. As he passed, looking straight ahead, as if on parade, she bellowed out after him in her famous husky female baritone, "Well, hello, *dahling!* What's the matter? Don't you recognize me with my clothes on?" Unfortunately, I never heard what happened next.

When my ship arrived in New York I was met not only by Paramount publicity people but by Mother and Jack. They drove me back to their apartment on East Fifty-second Street, where I'd planned to stay. It was pleasant enough, of course, as stepfather Jack was great company and Mother, if not allowed to overdo things, was sweet and helpful. Besides, it was a way of saving money. The next few days had been set aside by Paramount for interviews and pictures. I met with Louis "Doc" Shurr, the Broadway agent, who arranged a meeting with Guthrie McClintic, the producer-director husband of Katharine Cornell. Unfortunately, he was on his way to Russia on a sight-seeing tour and "had nothing in view" that was right for me. I did not know until later that Doc Shurr had sent him a telegram about me.

After all that, I was to dash out to Los Angeles where shooting was almost ready to start. Just the day before I was to leave, I dropped into

Mother's largest, deepest chair suddenly realizing that I felt absolutely awful. In fact, I suspected a temperature and my bones had the warning ache of oncoming flu. Worse, I suddenly began coughing, badly and deeply, and my chest hurt all the way back inside my shoulder blades. Mother took my temperature and, to no one's surprise, but to my own intense annoyance, it was 102°. Our old family doctor, who had delivered me into this world, was away so our friend and his protégé, Dr. Mason Hicks, came over immediately. Within minutes he sent me to Doctors Hospital, where the diagnosis was double pneumonia and pleurisy.

It had all come on within no more than a day. That night my temperature shot up to 103 1/2°. I was really very ill indeed and by the second or third night I was delirious more than half the time. This was all many years before penicillin or the sulfa drugs, so there was little that could be done beyond taking painkillers to reduce the sharp coughing agonies of pleurisy. They hoped for a crisis point to come, at which one either got better or, in those days, all too often died.

The story of my illness had got to the papers from the first night and so serious was it thought to be that bulletins on my condition were issued daily thereafter. I have often told the story of Joan sending a telegram from California offering to take the first train, but being told to wait a couple of days as I might, with luck, take a turn for the better. I also used to say that my father embarked on a fast liner immediately. I've said that by the time he arrived, I had passed the crisis point—after a temperature high of 104 1/2° —and had begun to recover slowly. However, the most touching part of my story came when I described Mother and Dad meeting, for the first time since their divorce, over my weak body. Unfortunately this was all embroidery. Joan did send me a sweet night letter that said something like, "Sorry you ill stop Hope get better soon stop love signed Billie." She couldn't have come to New York, as she was filming with Franchot Tone, her next-in-line husband, the new rival to Clark.

Apparently my father didn't even think of coming over. Mother had cabled him that I was seriously ill and he cabled back his concern and request to be kept advised of my condition. That was all. I had let romantic sentiment persuade me that a series of emotionally affecting scenes had taken place over my sickbed and had come to believe it myself.

Actually I recovered slowly. So slowly, in fact, that one day, when I was thought to be well on the mend—though many pounds lighter and still weak —I got a long-distance phone call from Mike Levee in California. After my improved condition had been confirmed, he hesitantly announced that he had to pass on some disappointing news. Paramount, realizing I must have lost a lot of weight and would require some weeks of convalescence, was obliged to exercise the "get out" clause in my contract for *Design for Living.* They had cast Gary Cooper to replace me. For the first time in a long time, I really felt sorry for myself and bitterly disappointed at losing this badly needed great plum of a part.

Then my X rays showed a new dark spot on my lung. Dr. Hicks and his colleagues said that unless I took serious precautions I would risk contracting tuberculosis. They knew I had been obliged to surrender my part in *Design for Living,* but they said I must now also get out of my commitment with Korda for *Catherine the Great.* They said I would soon be dismissed from the hospital, but after that I must have more tests and be restricted to quiet lolling-about. After that, I would have to go to a sanatorium in the Arizona desert, New York's Lake Placid, or perhaps the Swiss Alps.

These warnings and recommendations didn't disturb me, and I then proceeded to recuperate quicker than anyone predicted. However, I had won considerable sympathy for my loss of weight and pale face and I happily exploited them for some time. I answered queries about my health with wan smiles and resigned shrugs. The tubercular Chopin couldn't have done it better.

Mother doted, puttered, fussed, and smothered, begging me to follow doctor's orders, and not return to London for *Catherine.* Stepfather Jack, a few aunts and uncles, and several cousins were recruited to plead further with me. I listened to all, loyally and lovingly, and then decided. Three weeks later I set sail for England, for Korda, for *Catherine the Great* and— Gee Lawrence.

Soon after arriving back in London, a friend of my father's, Terence Phillip, rented me his tiny flat. It was in a very small building, dating back to before the Great Fire of 1666, but for me, quite marvelous. Just over Lock's, the famous hat shop in St. James's Street, it had wavy oaken floors, large uneven beams, and crooked doors. It was warmed by a working fireplace, abetted by two or three electric heaters. You entered by stumbling up rickety stairs to the floor immediately above the shop. Terence, who could easily have got quite a bit more for his place, must have heard of my true state of affairs and let me have it for less than two pounds a week. In those days this was the American equivalent of about ten dollars! I seemed to have landed on my feet once again.

I looked nothing at all like the real Peter III. Research reported that he was stubby with a puffy, pockmarked face. I wanted to create a real character in the part, but Dr. Czinner and Alex Korda insisted our story was essentially romantic. I took camera tests with white wig, plucked eyebrows, very white makeup, lipstick, and a few black beauty marks. My costumes were black or white satin suits, lace jabots, and knee britches. Had I not been so in love with my part and delighted with my good fortune in landing it, I might have been more objective and stubborn about my character, but I was afraid I would be paid off and replaced. One of our electricians described me as "beautifully tarted up!" I agreed. When Korda saw the tests, he said I looked all right, though "far too young and pretty." The real Peter III of Russia was said to be rather feminine, but it was strictly against the censorship rules of that day to even hint at homosexuality. Thus I was ordered to defy the period and cultivate my mustache—well mascaraed. The result was inauthentic but apparently satisfactory.

I had been assigned one of three star dressing rooms at the studio in Elstree, a suburb of London. Miss Bergner and Flora Robson had the other two. When I learned that my great hero, the incomparable Sir Gerald du Maurier, had been assigned one of the smaller rooms down the corridor, I was horrified. Without any ado, I quietly switched rooms and exchanged the names on our respective doors. When Sir Gerald came to the studio, he moved into the big star room without question. We became and remained good friends until he died, and I'm glad to say he never knew of my switch.

On the days when neither of us were on call, Sir Gerald sometimes dropped around to have breakfast with me in my ancient cozy flat. Usually he brought a silly little mechanical toy he had got from a hawker on Piccadilly or Pall Mall. We were both amused by toy trains and small cars and tractors. He was a joy to work with as well as to know. After he died, his faithful dresser, Mr. Buckley, joined me whenever I had a play or movie in England. Sometimes, if he was outside my dressing room in the corridor, gabbing with someone and I called out for him, he answered, "Yes, Sir Gerald—er, I mean, Mr. Fairbanks!"

In due course I reported for *Catherine* costume fittings, story and script conferences, and preliminary readings. Beginning to bounce back with recovered energy, I stayed up too late too many nights. Once we started filming, I usually had to get up before six A.M. When I felt it risky to drive myself, I wangled a studio car to pick me up along with Jimmy Barker, our imported Hollywood makeup and wig expert. We arrived at the Elstree studios after I had had a good forty-minute doze. I then plopped into the makeup department's barber chair (an idea first used by my father), leaned way back, and went to sleep again while Jimmy made me up and glued on parts of my wig. It was a grand second snooze before the awful studio coffee and buns, which served as breakfast. After clearing my head and rereading the lines I had already more or less memorized, we slid gently into walk-through rehearsals for lights and positions until we were all quite ready for more intensive work.

The film progressed excellently. The sets by Vincent Korda, Alex's brother, were superb examples of taste, imagination, and economy. A number of visual tricks, such as forced perspective and unusual angles, were employed to make them seem much larger and deeper than they were. Such techniques were well used by German filmmakers but rarely known in conventional Hollywood.

Miss Bergner was charming to work with, full of special mannerisms and meticulously honed tricks of the trade. She timed her scenes to the second. To my young taste, her accented speech was too given to gooey baby talk. But, by God, she was *good!* She was technically almost unsurpassed. Young Flora Robson, as the old empress, her first major film role, made it perfectly clear to all that she would become one of the finest actresses of the day. Du Maurier, of course, made a glistening mountain peak out of a foothill of a role as the Czar's witty French valet.

As for me, I can now see many things I might have done far better had I had more serious character actor experience. But, even so, I think I did well. I have seldom had a dramatic character part as fine as Czar Peter III and I had rarely performed any part so well. In retrospect I think some scenes were clearly but subconsciously influenced by my admiration for Jack Barrymore.

Czinner directed too gently and sympathetically. It seemed he was somewhat frightened by his star-wife and the overall caliber of the cast. Therefore it sometimes became necessary for Alex to leave his producer's office, come down to the set, and take over as director. As such, he was first-rate.

One evening I was asked by Pete to come along as an extra man to a party given very privately for Prince George and his girlfriend. P.G.'s usual "cover" was a once beauteous Australian, Winnie (Lady) Portarlington. Her husband, Lord Portarlington, was a dear old wheezing peer who was usually left behind and didn't mind a bit. When Pete and I dropped by her Belgravia town house, she suggested we interrupt her son, "Carlow," who was entertaining some "strange bookish types—his hobby is printing private Special Editions, you know." We followed tentatively, lingering in the doorway, as she kissed her son good night and made polite noises to his friends. After we had gone, I asked Winnie who that small, lonely looking man on the couch was. I was certain I had seen him before somewhere.

"Oh," she said in her flighty way, "That's that funny chap from the desert. Carlow is one of his executors and has printed one of his books—Lawrence somebody—from Egypt or Araby—somewhere like that!"

I mentally kicked myself for having missed the great T. E. Lawrence a second time! He died not long after—and Carlow was killed early in World War II.

I, of course, recognized how silly and immature these literary star-gazing quests of mine were. It was at this time that I also made the brief acquaintance of H. G. Wells and George Bernard Shaw. But they were a relatively harmless form of snobbery. I never felt ashamed of admiring achievement and saying so. And these were great literary achievers. Since my formal schooling had been so deficient, I was more than ordinarily impressed with those whose education, knowledge, and experience had been so carefully and formally acquired. Perhaps I felt that just knowing the parents of all those long admired books and plays would somehow influence my own evolving talents for the better.

With *Catherine* finally completed, edited, dubbed, and scored, I stayed on in my antique flat and plotted various futures for myself. There was never a lack of things to see or do or new people to meet. I went to weekends in the glorious green country, to houses of all kinds from huge to small. Once when I was invited to Noël's Goldenhurst for a weekend, St. James's Palace rang to say, "His Royal Highness"—Prince George—"would like to drive down with you if that is satisfactory." Of course it was. I was delighted. P.G.'s recent romances were well known in certain circles but were never mentioned in print by a discreet and loyal press. He had broken with one, then the other, and now no one lady was occupying his exclusive attention.

We drove down in my sporty, secondhand Auburn. Once out of the dreary suburbs into the gracefully curving highway leading us through the lush and rolling Kent countryside, I stepped on it. Though P.G. was as delighted with high speed as I, our pleasure was short-lived. We were stopped by a policeman. I didn't despair overmuch because I reckoned that with a popular Royal Prince as my passenger, I'd be cheerfully let off with a warning, a salute, and a wave-off. When the stern but very polite policeman walked up to me, P.G. slid down deep in his seat, turned up his coat collar, and put on sunglasses. I took my ticket for "reckless driving" without comment and continued the journey at a greatly reduced speed.

About this time, Gee had signed a contract to do a musical comedy with London's most prestigious musical producer, C. B. Cochran, familiarly known as Cocky. It was based on an amusing novel by James Laver, a witty and whimsical fellow whose profession was curator at the famous Victoria and Albert Museum. The music and lyrics for *Nymph Errant* were by Cole Porter—and though for a number of legal reasons it was never performed in New York, I still think it is one of his very best scores.

Gee's rehearsals were arduous and time-consuming. My own work on *Catherine* had been completed and I was no longer suffering any effects of pneumonia. (My X rays showed the spot on my lung nearly gone.) Thus I began to pay rather intense attention to one of the most beautiful of the post-deb ladies, Liz Paget, the youngest of a noble family, all of whom possessed, if not wealth, then wonderful looks. I criticized myself—*to* myself —for my inconstancy. I had been dizzily captivated by the toast of the theater world, had been receiving tentative but increased assurance of a reciprocal sentiment, and now I found myself nearly blinded by Liz's calm, young beauty! How could I be in love with two different women at the same time—one quite a bit older than I, the other a few years younger? One was at the very top of her profession and much more experienced than I. The other had been quietly reared in a most rarefied social stratosphere but was already a famous beauty who, I presumed, had only a greenhouse awareness of romance. At one weekend ball in the country, I was so carried away by Liz that I suggested we marry—adding, so as not to frighten her, "eventually."

Her reply was an endearing but enigmatic "possibly—eventually." In my mind, I thought myself sort of engaged to Liz, though still guiltily enraptured by Gee.

Nymph Errant had a big, ballyhooed preview at the Opera House in Manchester. It seemed to my starry eyes that much of the transatlantic theater world came up for it. As a movie figure, I created some public stir which, as it wasn't my evening, only embarrassed me, so I slunk into any crowd I could find to get out of sight.

The show was a great, cheering success. The applause resounded until the orchestra quieted everyone with a stirring brief version of the National Anthem. My old childhood friend Agnes de Mille, who had been living and struggling in England for some time, had done the lovely choreography. I was as professionally pleased by her success as I was by Gee's and Cole's triumph.

Then came the great supper afterward—Cocky had taken over the whole of the large ballroom at the Midland Hotel—and the evening went on and on. I don't recall where I spent the night except that it couldn't have been appropriate or timely to spend it in Gee's hotel suite. Still, I had a marvelous time, fell for Gee afresh, and returned to London next day, elated and smug.

14

The rest of that year, 1933, and certainly the next two or three included such a miscellany of happenings as to defy the recording of their precise dates. In fact, I recall my whole life during the thirties as one great feast of everything. People and events come in and out of focus, overlapping each other.

A month after Manchester, in October, *Nymph Errant* opened at the Adelphi Theatre in London with the most elegant-looking audience I had ever seen. Gee deservedly received probably the greatest personal ovation of her career so far—excepting, of course, those she had shared with Noël. Cole was justifiably ecstatic, as was Cocky, who beamed down from his stage-right box with equal benevolence on actors and audience. Gee's show was limited to a six-month run for reasons I've quite forgotten. I lost count of the number of times I saw it, went around backstage, often in white tie, like a cliché stage-door Johnny, and waited in Gee's dressing room before going out to supper. If, as often happened, she had other dates, I grumbled, or if, as also happened, I had to be at the studio early in the morning, I made my way back to my own place for more sleep than most eager young men in like situations usually need.

Then I accepted the only offer on my immediate horizon and started homeward again. This job was several notches below what I'd hoped for. To be called *Success at Any Price,* the film was hardly more than a fancy Hollywood potboiler. It would be saved by the immensely popular Colleen Moore.

It was raining the day I was to take the train for the port of Southampton.

Gee decided to see me off. We were well ahead of time and chose a small restaurant close to the station in which to share a pot of hot coffee and sweet parting words. Gee was in one of her assortment of moods (Noël once described her as having "twenty faces under one hat") and she became more than just sentimental. Such histrionics made my heart and head swim, but I tried to keep my own emotions from showing. I think my rejoinders must have been too florid anyway, because her next scene consisted of breaking down into conspicuously loud sobs. The tears leaped out of her eyes like dolphins. I became uncomfortably aware of others turning around to stare at Gee's gulps and heaves. It was obvious we were recognized and I tried to hush her without seeming brusque or uncaring. This only made things worse. I next pretended the time was later than it really was, paid the bill and, behaving like a big strong man going off on a dangerous trek to the dark interior, put a protective arm around her until we got to the gate. There we embraced and waved to each other piteously. As I got aboard my train, I urged her to leave ("quickly and don't look back" was the old line, but I dared not use it). She did leave and I sat down in my Pullman seat with a good quarter hour to wait before the train left. Despite the way I behaved, I was as hooked as any star-struck man could be. And who could blame me?

However, one particularly worrying aspect of our now-flowering romance was Gee's aggressive possessiveness. A few weeks earlier, when she and Eric had taken leave of each other (temporarily as it turned out), Gee surprised me by suddenly suggesting we marry. The suggestion scared me. The quickest response I could think of at the time was that my divorce from Joan was not yet legally final. Also, I needed to catch up on my finances. "But after that . . . !" Inside me was a tremor of panic. There was no question that I wanted to be the man in her life, despite the considerable difference in our age, fame, and finances. But I didn't honestly entertain any expectations of permanence about our relationship. One of my excuses for delay was real enough, but a third remained unsaid. This was my own honest self-appraisal, admitted only to myself, that however smitten I might be by the bewitching Miss L., I had not ever been strictly faithful to anyone.

My train glided out and I scribbled and rescribbled fervent romantic notes to Gee, which I mailed just before the great liner pushed out of Southampton for New York.

Neither Colleen nor I can any longer recall a single thing about the plot of *Success at Any Price,* but I do very clearly remember the many good wishes offered me for a long-contemplated campaign to find the backing

needed to form my own producing company. No one questioned my qualifi-
cations and know-how. My experience and track record were admittedly
good, and my box-office status was better than most. Even if I was not
considered a big star I was, in any case, a well-rated one. But everything
stopped right there, frozen in midair. Ever since the success of the United
Artists concept, the major studios had been joining forces in the restraint of
any challenge—real or imagined—by actors or directors (excepting, of
course, the unique C. B. De Mille) to their tyrannical hegemony. This
meant that the only professional castes reluctantly allowed to belong to their
brotherhood were either the Wall Street rescuers from suspected misman-
agement or such super-rich "angels" as Jock Whitney, old Joe Kennedy
(whose interest was more in Gloria Swanson than in movies), W. R. Hearst,
and Howard Hughes.

One of the very few really big-shot producers I knew who could read,
write, and speak the King's English, and whose brains and talent matched
his sophistication, was David O. Selznick. It was he who finally advised me
not to go on bucking a hopeless tide at home where, as an actor, unless one
was under a big studio contract, the chances for a big break were slimmer
than ever. In my case, advised David O., "Go east, young man!"—i.e., go
abroad again.

While I was in New York, "Doctor" Shurr, the Broadway agent, once
more contacted play-producer Guthrie McClintic on my behalf. He had
now returned from Russia. On being thus reminded of my availability,
Guthrie recounted how, on dashing for the night train from Moscow to
Leningrad, a messenger boy shoved a telegram at him which he hurriedly
put in his pocket. When the small, timid Guthrie discovered his compartment was shared by a huge, bearded *muzhik,* he voluntarily took the upper
berth so as not to invite a challenge. Very early the next morning he awoke
with severe stomach cramps, undoubtedly created by some strong medicine
he had been told to take the night before. It was winter, the train had no
heat, and Guthrie's only choice was to slide out of his bunk very gently so as
not to awaken the snoring giant below. He put his jacket on over his pajamas and ventured out into the frigid corridor, hoping to locate a bathroom.
His teeth were chattering with cold and no one could understand his mimed
anguished plea to be directed to "the loo." Through the train windows he
could see that it was early morning and they were going slowly through the
outer suburbs of Leningrad.

Finally, and luckily before he burst, he found an empty lavatory three
cars back. Still shivering, and fearful the trip would end before he could get
back to his compartment, he found to his horror that neither soap nor toilet

paper was in evidence. What to do? He was bone-cold. The train continued to slow down. God, what a situation! He looked through his pockets. He decided not to use his Charvet kerchief if he could help it . . . but, ah, eureka! there in his pocket was the telegram delivered as he had jumped on the train the night before. Hurriedly, he decided to read it first. It said: "Dear Guthrie—Are you sure you have nothing you can use young Doug Jr. for? Signed, Louis Shurr."

Even on his return, there was no play in preparation that had a part for which I was suitable. And so, cranking up my lagging spirits and enthusiasm, I set sail for Europe. My old friend and coplayer, Allen Vincent, came along as my secretary-companion in return for a minimum wage and board. Prior to sailing, I received a note from a friend saying that when I came over Tallulah would be very grateful for a few packs of reefers. These were marijuana-filled cigarettes, ancestors of what is today usually called pot, but since I had not yet had any urge to experiment, I was ignorant of how to go about getting them. Good friend Allen, an older and better friend of Tallulah's, knew that they could be acquired in Harlem.

Off we went one night, with a small group of friends, to the Cotton Club. I loved the nightclubs and restaurants in Harlem, and the flattering special attention I always got from Cab Calloway, Duke Ellington, the Nicholas Brothers, and Ethel Waters. However, my relationship was not close enough to ask where I might purchase reefers for a famous American stage star living in England. But Allen knew whom to ask immediately. I handed over the money on Tallu's behalf and put several packs in my suitcase. I thought nothing more about it until we were well out at sea and then I confided to Allen that I was born with a wish to at least try everything once. Allen, who was far more familiar with Bohemian excesses than I, launched into a strong, "older brother" lecture, calling me a "bloody fool" for even thinking of such a thing. Unfortunately, the effect of this was to increase the challenge.

Our third night at sea, while Allen was off playing bridge with fellow passengers, I went to my stateroom and, like a thief in the night, carefully stole a package of reefers from my own suitcase. Feeling excited and guilty, I took one and lit up. I carefully followed the way I'd heard it was done by cupping my hands over it, inhaling deeply and holding my breath for as long as possible. I repeated the process a few times. It seemed a minute or two before I felt any reaction. Then I experienced a kind of elated tingle and an upsurge of good-natured energy. My head was not cloudy as if I'd had too much to drink. I went up to the Promenade Deck. It was a balmy, moonlit night and bright little phosphorous sparklers splashed in the wake of the great liner. It occurred to me that, as exciting and wonderful as life was, death must be the ultimate adventure. I couldn't imagine any serious responsibilities that would stay my urge to jump overboard, into the mid-Atlantic. I cheerfully announced my intention to some deck-walking fellow passengers as I made my way to the rail. They were so horrified that they grabbed me and, helped by a passing steward, struggled with me for a few moments until I gave up my "gesture." When Allen found out, an hour or so later, and the ship's doctor had assured everyone that I was now back to normal, I was given angry lectures by both. I agreed that all the reefers I had could be chucked out the portholes. I had scared myself almost to death and I was not inclined to try it again. Tallulah would have to do without.

Digging back into London, I rented a small early Victorian house in Gloucester Place that belonged to an American-born friend, Chips Channon. When he had lived in it, Chips, with his ineffable taste in decoration, commissioned a mural that covered all four walls of the small dining room. The subjects were his army of friends, all in Greek costume against a temple background—a Pantheon of his personal gods.

I settled in quickly and happily. I had heard that Eric had been temporarily back in Gee's favor during my absence, but now she gave friends the clear impression that I was reinstated as number one. Our relationship, temporarily less intense than when we parted, was resumed.

Gee, her secretary, Helen Downes, and Bea Lillie came over to rearrange my furniture for me. They spent a couple of days settling me in, a task that included finding a marvelous caricature of a woman as part-time maid and cook. So special was she that Bea often got friends to telephone me when she knew I was out, just to hear the old lady answer in her uniquely accented, sliding scale "grand manner": "Oh, deah!" she would say, "Eh em seh soddy, but Mistah Fahbanks is not *hy*ah." Her "aitches" were heavily and breathily emphasized. "*H*e's fraightfully late but *h*e'll be *h*eah in tame for dinnah. W*h*o's calling, may eh a*h*sk?" Poor, dear lady, thank heaven she never knew she was being mocked.

Gee, now assuming that my bank balance had been handsomely refurbished in Hollywood, went to one of her ex-beaux, Philip Astley, to ask him to recommend a "gentleman's gentleman"—which he promptly did. I had to show off while I could, so I took Godfrey on at about four pounds a week! He was a handsome ex-Horse Guardsman, six feet four, and a classic English manservant. I thought him very upright until I caught him taking under-the-table perks from all the tradesmen we dealt with. (I hadn't realized then, as I did later, that such petty-racketeering was quite customary in London.)

At last, I started my own company, at least on paper, christened Criterion. I went ahead, helped by the better read and educated Allen, reading possible story properties in a search for our first picture. Initially it would not have done much good had we found one, since we had no financing at all. Eventually, Murray Silverstone and George Archibald offered me a United Artists distribution contract—for one picture, with options for more later. They helped me raise the seed money to start. They did insist that I share responsibility with an equal partner who would be responsible for the financial end of things. Consequently, Marcel Hellman, a Continental producer friend of Murray's, a newly arrived refugee from one of Hitler's early anti-Semitic campaigns, was made an essential "condition" of my new arrangement.

As it turned out, I was glad to have him. He was a nice little man who made many humorous mistakes in the language but none with money. On the whole, we got along quite well. I liked him personally—away from the studio more than at work, because he was a clock-watcher and a shrewd penny-pincher. I wanted a company that would rival Korda's and show my Hollywood ex-masters the mistake they had made by not backing me.

Meanwhile Pete had been cranking himself up to make a film of his own, in nominal collaboration with Korda. They had chosen a translation of a Hungarian play, *The Private Life of Don Juan.* It was an amusing yarn about the great lover growing older and trying in vain to live up to his reputation. Pete's creative flame too had been flickering lower. He still seemed unable to concentrate on work. Now he seemed willing to delegate his producer's powers and talents to Alex. Official Fairbanks approval was contractually required for everything—and was usually forthcoming for anything without even looking. Yet he appeared to be enjoying a completely free and irresponsible life, allowing his attachment to Sylvia Ashley to become a matter for gossip everywhere. Both were still married, though separated.

Sylvia had broken off her liaison with her last lover, Dunfee, the amateur racing car driver. Shortly after, Dunfee lay dying as a result of a terrible car crash. He was brought to the same private nursing home where by chance Sylvia, on another floor, was suffering from something very minor. Dunfee asked that she pay him a last visit, but since she feared this would give him false hope and distress Pete, she declined. Dunfee died, and Sylvia rejoined her old jolly crowd. They were completely new companions for Pete. Hardly any would have enjoyed his company or confidence a few years earlier. As if to emphasize the dimensions of his new life—so sadly different from the old Boy Scout image—he rented a vast medieval stately home called North

Mimms Park in South Mimms. I was told it had enough rooms to accommodate fifty or sixty houseguests. An army must have been required to staff
it.

I heard that every weekend for months dozens of his new (and a few of
his old) friends came down to visit, play golf, tennis, croquet, and, in bad
weather, cards and parlor games. He maintained a permanent suite at the
Ritz in London that served as headquarters for his visits to tailors, the
theater, and Cartier for trinkets for Sylvia. Rocher, the ever-amiable French
butler from Pickfair, who always walked as if his shoes pinched (maybe they
did), was continually whisked by car to and from London, the studio and/or
South Mimms—about forty-five minutes away.

I heard from my father very seldom during those months. I tried to ring
him every so often. Whenever I did reach him, he was unfailingly cheery,
his voice explosively bright, his words brief and preoccupied. Doggedly I
tried every subtle and blatant ruse to get myself invited to South Mimms. I
even got old Tom Geraghty to corner him alone and come out point-blank
and ask him to invite me—just for an afternoon. But nothing worked. I was
never able to see him in his role of Lord of the Manor or Master of the
Revels. I was very sorry and, though I confessed it to no one, more than a
little angry at the time. Now I'm rather glad I didn't go. I'm not sure I
would have enjoyed what I saw.

It must be clear by now that I never formed any consistent plan for my
life. I established certain objectives that suited the circumstances of the
moment on a mental map and then saw where the road toward them might
lead. As the road was unreliably signposted, I learned to keep a wary eye on
cross and side roads and to accept with only a mild curse such curves and
diversions that appeared as I drove along at varying speeds. Rarely did I use
my rear-view mirror, and then only to note what I'd just passed or was
passing me. The trouble was that, in order to approach my variety of desti-
nations, I had to take too many different routes—some great wide highways,
others narrow twisting country lanes, ill-kept roads, and byways. Then,
after arriving or even while still approaching my intended destination, I
pressed on to others. I often considered stopping to make entries in a self-
analytical logbook of my journeys, but I never did. One vital impression
remains: every mile of the road was, and continues to be, fascinating. Even
the bumps, however distressing or painful, were instructive. My route
through the thirties was the most carefree high-speed road I have traveled.

The wondrous Clemence Dane, friend, author, and artist, once critically
assessed me, saying, "The trouble with Douglas is that he likes everything

he sees, and he sees everything!" That suggests a rather pudding-headed character, but it does approximate accuracy.

Early in 1934 it was announced that Ethel Barrymore would be in Sir J. M. Barrie's one-act play *The Twelve-Pound Look* for a few weeks at the Palladium. I could hardly wait to see her first performance. She had been doing the play in vaudeville houses all over America off and on for years. When no new play for New York could be found, she fell back on this old popular favorite. Since Ethel had known and loved London from her teens (on her first trip she had nearly agreed to marry Winston Churchill), she looked forward to returning as the Queen of the American Theater in this slight but well-written vehicle.

The Barrymore clan was famous for excessive drinking. But since they were all my special theater gods, I chose to defend them. I was sure the many stories about their drinking were either exaggerated or untrue. The curtain went up that night at the Palladium and Ethel was given an immensely warm reception. But soon it was all too apparent that she was, to employ the vernacular, "pissed to the gills." She mumbled or completely muffed the lines she had so often spoken before and few could hear her behind the first few rows. English audiences are renowned for loud and emotional loyalty to their favorites. But if they detect a lack of respect for them, they let the world know it—loud and clear. Ethel, weaving unsteadily and muttering, had to struggle through occasional boos and shouted reprimands from the gallery. Her so-called performance seemed to take ages of time. When the curtain finally came down, there were whistles and catcalls and it did not rise again. The engagement was terminated by the management with the explanation that Miss Barrymore was ill and had been ordered to undergo treatment.

Several weeks later I was told that poor Ethel was still in London and virtually stranded. She was in a small but well-known hotel, had run up a big bill, and was unable to pay it. I was much saddened by the plight of this great artist. Her son, Sammy Colt, had been one of my Bovée schoolmates in New York. She was the beloved *doyenne* of the American Theater and the sister of my first idol, John. I tried to think of some way to help. I decided to go to some of her many friends in London and suggest that we all chip in whatever we could and put it into her bank account without saying a word about it.

The plan succeeded splendidly and quite a healthy sum was deposited in her name. Shortly after, she told how she had "stupidly" misunderstood her bank balance, which now turned out to be perfectly in order. Her debts were paid up and, bravely ignoring her opening night humiliation, she sailed for home and security. She was never told this story as long as she lived.

In February 1934, *Catherine the Great* was given two big Hollywood-type premieres, one in London and one in Paris. The film was well received by press and public in both capitals. Bergner was justly extolled by every top critic. Robson and Du Maurier were praised. As for my own share of the glory, it was pretty much as I had hoped. The consensus was that the role of the Czar was a spectacular change of pace for me and presaged "a classic future in more important vehicles." A few critics went so far as to say I should be nominated for one of the acting awards that year. Although some nominations and much praise came my way, there were no awards. However, I was sorry my father couldn't attend one of the opening nights.

One weekend with Gee at Shawford Park, the country house of mutual friends, we drove down to Warsash on the Solent to dine. Before dinner I was taken by our hosts on a drive all around the vast harbor area, within sight of the Isle of Wight. The day was fine and warm and spring was prematurely bursting. I was not immune to its magic and I got so full of optimistic beans that while visiting the local yacht club I decided to ask at a nearby boatyard the price of a small twenty-five-foot cabin cruiser. Although it was not much, it was more than I could sensibly afford. So I made a deal for a bit down and a certain amount to be paid over the next few years.

The boat builder made this deal in my favor on condition that I pose for pictures with him and the boat. This was not only a familiar ploy, it was expected. I remembered having to pose at the behest of film companies for Lucky Strike cigarettes—which I didn't smoke—and Jantzen bathing suits, with their obligatory tops—which I didn't wear—and getting not a dime's worth of anything from either. After I'd bought the boat, I was so elated I immediately named it *The Grateful*. I couldn't wait to take possession and assumed immediate command. All our house party of eight crowded aboard, and up the Hamble River we went to the yacht club. Unfortunately, I had not had enough practice and couldn't manage to slow, let alone stop, the damned thing. As a result, I glided past a line of moored boats, almost all of which had their booms out with skiffs attached. I cracked into three before my friends and I threw the boat engine into reverse. The shouting, cursing yacht owners were not in the least mollified by my apologies and assurance that I would make good. We decided not to stay at the club for drinks.

Hugh "Binkie" Beaumont, a brilliant theatrical producer, operated as

boss of the wide-ranging H. M. Tennent Company. He was almost too good-
looking, with pale white skin and carefully dressed blond hair, and was
elegantly tailored and just slightly feminine in speech and manner. But in
business, Binkie was a driving, shrewd, and wonderfully tasteful producer.
He had an "in" everywhere, and was not the popular idea of a show-biz
character. He was more like the young dilettante son of an idle family. Bill
Linnit, Gee's (and now my) soft-spoken agent, communicated to Binkie his
enthusiasm for putting Gee and me in a play together. The idea suggested
considerable box-office appeal, since our romance had been bruited about
fairly widely. Binkie agreed, provided a satisfactory vehicle could be found.

Meanwhile, Gee was continuing her run in *Nymph Errant* and I decided
to take my mini-yacht *Grateful* out to sea. I had not tested my seamanship
since my teens in California and Rhode Island, and I wanted to show how
tough and expert I was. (This caused a minor carfuffle with Gee, as she
insisted I had given her the boat and had no right to take it out alone
without her permission.) As a precaution, I took the boatyard's recommendation and hired an old sailor from the waterfront to help me. And off I
went, intending to sail up the Channel to the North Sea, perhaps to Scotland
—or over to France or the Netherlands—anywhere—for a week or two.

The old sailor and I set off and hadn't got much beyond the middle of the
Channel when the father and mother of all Channel storms blew up out of
nowhere. Our radio warned that "all small craft" should make for the nearest port. The waves got higher, and the wind stronger—Force 6 or 8, perhaps. The little cockleshell bounced about, rose up on its hindquarters and,
after a shudder or two, slapped down with a tooth-loosening bang. Then a
roll to either side, a pitch or two, and up we'd go again. All the while our
little dinghy was trailing us, secured by a line. I yelled through the rain and
wind to my old sailor to help me get the dinghy aboard and lash it to the
deck, else we might lose it.

As I tried holding the wheel with one hand and reaching for the dinghy's
line with the other, my sailor took out a tiny book and, waving it at me,
shouted back in a West Country accent that was barely understandable
under the best of conditions. "No, zur," he said, shaking his drenched head
and flourishing the little book, "cayn't help you none 'count 'a this 'ere
storm is the Lord's Will."

I kept on struggling, getting as angry as I dared under the circumstances.
In a flash I realized, for the first time, that my ancient mariner was an old-
time religious fanatic. "But the Lord's very busy all over," I yelled back.
"We must help him by doing something for ourselves! *C'mon, give me a
hand!*"

"No, zur! Sorry, zur!" He clutched his little book protectively. "No offense, zur—but I'll jes' leave it all in the 'ands of the Lord!"

At last, with more angry "quarterdeck" shouts from me, and with both of us now loosely lashed to the deck ourselves, I got him to help me just enough to drag the flimsy wee craft aboard and secure it well enough, I hoped, to hold for a while.

It might have been an hour or two later, though it seemed like ten, when through the driving rain and fog I detected lights. By that time, with compass broken, I had no clear idea if it was shore or even English or French. I made for it as best I could. I saw more flashing lights and discovered that the first ones had been at the end of the breakwater entrance to Dover, close by the famous White Cliffs. I had missed the lighthouse altogether and I was much nearer shore than I knew. We finally bobbed and rocked our way into the harbor and were assigned a mooring by the harbor master. After answering all official questions wearily but satisfactorily, I silently thanked my ever-helpful guardian angel and cursed my old sailor. I then put on a dry sweater and trousers and, after a strong shot of Dewar's, dropped off to a welcome sleep.

Next day I fired my old sailor, giving him enough money (not much in those days) to return to Warsash, and hired another, younger boatyard sailor. I asked him to take the boat—whenever the weather cleared—around to the enormous, fifty-mile-wide mouth of the Thames and sail it up past Gravesend and Greenwich until he reached Cadogan pier, near Chelsea, where I could make arrangements for its permanent mooring.

The young man did this in a day and a half. I never took poor little *Grateful* to sea again, but I did have several years of great fun in her—licit and illicit. I always sailed on the River Thames—way up into the freshwater part, through numberless locks by numberless pubs and inns, to the highest navigable part of the river—at Lechlade, in Gloucestershire, nearly two hundred miles away. Eventually I sold her, for a poor price. I heard that her subsequent owner took her over to help in the evacuation of Dunkirk during the early days of World War II. He came back with a small squad of soldiers, safe and sound. *Grateful*, indeed! I wonder where she is now.

In the spring of '34, on the thirteenth of May, I received a cable from Mike in California notifying me that Billie's and my divorce was now final.

Binkie submitted a play called *The Winding Journey* for Gee's and my approval. Gee and I were both so keen on doing a play together, and since this was the best of several previously submitted, we allowed our impulses to replace our sober judgment. That, however, could not excuse Binkie, who undoubtedly thought more of the box-office value of our names together than the suitability of the play.

The advance publicity linking our names as the play's stars was the most blatant and embarrassing exploitation of a private affair since MGM capitalized on my romance with Joan in *Our Modern Maidens* five years earlier. At the time, however, we were so absorbed in each other that its tastelessness made little impression. We opened with an abundance of brouhaha in Manchester. This time Gee's luxurious suite and my single bedroom at the Midland Hotel were discreetly adjacent. All during rehearsals, which were being directed by Lewis Casson, husband of Sybil Thorndike, I tried to seem poised and self-confident, to sound experienced and relaxed, none of which I was. I was nervous, dreadfully unsure, and only too shakily aware of my relative inexperience. I was not even remotely within shouting distance of Gertrude Lawrence, who was, in the mid-1930s (as she continued to be all her life) one of the very greatest stage stars. And her age was then something like thirty-six. What in the world was I doing there? Or she, for that matter?

Gee, though one who by nature took center stage wherever she was, surprised everyone by not trying to dominate me or the play. It was a grim tragedy—a bit too grim, as things turned out. Gee had a tendency to overact or change movements or words without notice unless she was carefully bullied by a director. Through fright, I was apt to be too restrained—or, as it finally turned out, too affected and mannered. The result may easily be imagined.

The play got poor reviews, but Gee and I were treated with sympathy. Binkie became understandably concerned about his investment and asked the famous novelist-playwright Clemence Dane if she would join us on tour for a few days to see if she could doctor the play. Miss Dane's real name was Winifred Ashton, and Gee and Noël and everyone except me had known her well for years. She was a huge woman, weighing, I should say, well over two hundred pounds. She ballooned in and out of rooms, accompanied by a loud but musical voice that somehow fit her angelic face. She was charming, vital, and versatile. She wrote bestselling novels and such hit plays as *A Bill of Divorcement* (Kate Hepburn's first big movie hit). She painted and sculpted splendidly and, besides, had a heart as big as she was herself. She was always bursting with new ideas.

But in the case of *The Winding Journey,* both the original author, Philip Leaver, and Winifred, as everyone called her, admitted defeat. It was beyond saving. The disappointment of all involved can be imagined. Binkie reported advance box office for the tour as wonderful, with the booking for

London equally encouraging, all of which would be canceled. Then Winifred brightly announced that she had a half-finished idea that could be worked up for us and ready for rehearsals in a month.

Binkie was courageous. He knew Winifred's talent and, after chatting with Noël and Ivor, concluded the risk was worth taking. Winifred was commissioned to write a new play—or rework an old unfinished one. Gee and I would milk this one dry by completing the provincial tour as planned.

Pete had not been able to see the play, for which I was grateful. When the tour was over, he suggested that since he was going to Spain on a holiday, he would combine my last Christmas and birthday presents in the form of a trip to Barcelona during my break between plays. I had seen hardly anything of my father since before his extravagant time in the great North Mimms Park house and the making of *Don Juan.* Gee, going ever deeper into debt, was now busy buying a lovely new house, designed by the famous architect Sir Edwin Luytens, on the Chelsea Embankment. A temporary break seemed advisable, so I accepted Pete's offer on the spot.

Our trip was short, but the company was enjoyable. Barcelona was a disappointment. It was a big, modern European industrial city with little there to remember, except for one incident.

The city's chief of police took Pete and me on a tour of the city's underworld slum quarters, the most colorful section of which was called, for no discernible reason, Chinatown. The chief and several of his stalwart bodyguards took us to a smoky dive where we stood back in the shadows of a box to avoid possible recognition. A cabaret performance was in progress and a very pretty, husky-voiced female was singing flamenco rather badly and doing a heel-stomping dance even less well. Nevertheless, she was asked up to the box to meet my father. This artiste was undeniably pretty and I could see Pete turning on the charm. But Pete was obviously embarrassed by my presence, knowing I was watching him flirt with this tarty singer. Still, his first embarrassment was nothing as compared to his second. The singer and the police chief suddenly began to bellow with laughter. The singer tore off a wig and lowered dress straps to prove that "she" was really a he. Poor Pete tried his best to laugh it off, but afterward, when we got back to the hotel, he was hopping mad. I was torn. I sympathized, but I thought it quite funny too. That spelled finis to my father's delayed present of Barcelona. He went on to Madrid and I went back to London.

Winifred had the new play ready at the time she promised. It was called *Moonlight Is Silver* and was a modern drama based on the *Othello* jealousy theme. It was not great, but a good, literate play. While auditions and negotiations proceeded for prospective new cast members, whom Gee alone had the right to approve, Binkie interviewed a keen and serious young actor for the job of my understudy. He was my coloring and about my height. His name was Alec Guinness. Binkie and Winifred heard him read a scene or two and politely told him he had not yet had enough experience and let him go. Alas.

Rehearsals were smoother than before with Winifred intelligently and forcefully directing her own play. Eventually, after a short tryout tour, we opened in London at the Queen's Theatre on Shaftesbury Avenue to good, if not great notices. Though we were not a smash hit, the audiences seemed to like the play and us. During the run, Gee and I got along well. It was surprising, because she was, like Billie, a creature of moods. She worried constantly about money, but when her secretary Helen or I pointed out some of her extravagances, she erupted in self-justification. Once, at a time when I was a temporary houseguest in her grand new Chelsea mansion, she protested loud and clear that she could not make all her loose ends meet. I must have ventured an untimely opinion. Vesuvius had no fury like Gee when crossed. She started pitching all manner of things at me and I beat the hastiest retreat I could, with Gee following me out of the house, bawling expletives like a Billingsgate fishwife.

When I reached the street I realized that I was wearing my breakfast clothes—a pair of slacks, an open sports shirt under a house jacket, and slippers. The temporarily deranged Miss L., followed by the helpless, pleading Helen, was hot on my heels, threatening me with one last dishpan. In my cowardice, I jumped on a passing bus. Gee tried to run after it in mid-morning Embankment traffic.

The British passersby paid little more than bemused attention to this scene, which must have looked like an old slapstick movie. Even the bus conductor took his time coming for my fare. By then we had crossed the Chelsea Bridge and were getting on toward Clapham. My acquaintance with the geography of the South Bank of the river was virtually nonexistent, and when I confessed I had no money, he merely shrugged, pulled the cord, and indicated I should get off. I did. Since I was totally lost, and not very anxious to return to Gee's house anyway, it was over an hour before I meandered back as if I had only been taking my regular morning constitutional. Happily, Gee was busy at something else and no more was said about the whole silly business.

Moonlight Is Silver perhaps, but certainly it isn't gold. As we neared the holidays, business slumped considerably. Then, almost as if in response to our sliding business, Gee became seriously ill with a painfully abscessed ear. She was obliged to withdraw from the play and her understudy, a very nice, inexperienced American girl, took over. She tried hard, but things were difficult because she was slightly taller than I. I stand six feet and a bit. This became something of a handicap for me when, as the jealous lover/husband, I was obliged to bully her. I always felt that if I went too far, this nice but untalented Amazon would pick me up and throw me into the orchestra pit. Also, her all-American freckles and speech made her less than convincing as the English society girl that Gee had so splendidly created. Audiences were disappointed. Box-office receipts slowed and the doctors felt Gee might be out several weeks more. (I remember cynically suspecting she was not nearly so ill as she made out and only wanted to get out of the play. She'd had enough.) Rather than lose more money, Binkie decided to close the show soon after. The run had been only four months long.

At another time, when her money problems were particularly distracting, Gee decided she would run off to Majorca for a complete rest—"alone, away from *everyone!*" I agreed she should go and determined that, if I couldn't join her, I would at least take a few days off and go as far as Barcelona with her. I would see her off on the night boat for Palma, Majorca, and return. This did not happen quite as planned.

My trip took a bit of doing, as my financial resources were limited. So that I could enjoy some extravagance without guilt, I sought out (not for the first or last time) my old Hollywood friend Irving Asher, upon whom fortune was now grinning broadly. He was producing Warner Brothers budget quota films and was their overseas representative as well. He had married the witty comedienne Laura La Plante and had settled happily in England with a fat dollar salary. He arranged to lend me more than the necessary money immediately. I wondered how and when I could repay him. He suggested, and I agreed, that if I couldn't repay him in cash, I would make a film for him with Laura "perhaps next year." If it was good, it might be shown everywhere and not limited to the quota market. Having settled that, we toured his small studio at Teddington, on the Thames. While going around, he introduced me to a very handsome, personable young Australian whom he'd seen in a provincial rep company and whom he had tested and cast in bit parts. I was asked to see his latest test. I liked it very much and said so. As my later note to Irving said, "I thought he showed not much acting ability or enough training as yet, but he has great looks, great charm, and moves easily and well." Irving, encouraged, promptly recommended him to Jack Warner in Hollywood as an actor who could be built up to take my place in some of the swashbuckler films I had turned down. Finally, Jack Warner acted on Irving's suggestion, and with a big press campaign about "his new find," Errol Flynn was launched on a career.

Most important, though, I now had just enough borrowed money. Gee and I took a train over and through the Pyrennees to Barcelona, the least Spanish-looking metropolis in Spain. Because of my brief visit with my father a few months earlier, I behaved as if I knew not just Barcelona but all that fascinating, contradictory country. We arrived in the morning and Gee's night boat to Majorca was due to sail in the early evening. Shortly after our arrival I had a stroke of luck. I ran into a fellow New Yorker who offered me two barrera seats for a bullfight that very afternoon. Neither Gee nor I had ever seen one—although I'd read and reread Hemingway and others on the subject. My friend told us that this fight would be special because Marcial Lalanda, the greatest matador of the day, would fight that very afternoon.

I was torn between my inherent love of spectacle and admiration of grace in the face of danger on the one hand and Anglo-Saxon-American sympathy for animals on the other. Nevertheless, I couldn't miss it. Lalanda, having been advised that I was in the audience, came over and, making a spirited dedication of the bull's life to me, handed his hat to us. We were to guard it until he had fought the bull. I was very, very excited. Unfortunately, this special attention to me annoyed Gee. She and I both knew that, in the eyes of our professional colleagues, she was enormously more important than I, and it irritated her that because I just happened to be in movies, I was therefore recognized by many more people than she was as a stage actress.

My New York friend, unaware of my somewhat straitened circumstances, instructed me in what was expected of one so honored by the torero. It would be incumbent on me to present Sr. Lalanda with a handsome cigarette case, a pair of cuff links (preferably from Cartier), or jeweled evening studs and buttons. I gulped, then nodded as if I knew that, and glanced at Gee, who began to snicker. My only hope was to stall. I therefore put a note on a card and put it in his hat, resting on the top of our box in front of us. It asked him to meet me for a drink later in the lounge of the Ritz Hotel. I knew this ploy would give me some time to think of something. I didn't appreciate the rest of the corrida at all, as I was too concerned with my obligations.

Gee's night boat left port soon after the fight and as soon as I'd seen her off, somewhat distractedly, I went back to the Ritz lounge. I sat, fingering my *jerez*, still wondering what to say when the great man himself strolled in. The head waiter ushered him to my inconspicuous corner banquette with all due obsequiousness.

We greeted each other warmly, and spoke in a ragged mixture of French, English, and Spanish. I could understand the latter but couldn't speak it.

After Lalanda ordered a drink and I thanked him effusively for the honor he had done me, I began slowly to explain that I had just heard of the custom of gift-giving and . . . He interrupted me with a deprecatory smile and wave. But I went on. I tried to make it clear that I lived a life financially quite independent of my father and, because of my past disappointing professional season, I just couldn't follow the custom "at the moment . . . later for sure, but not right now."

Lalanda laughed and insisted it made no difference, that he was delighted to have done it. I continued my little speech. I said that my situation had so deteriorated that actually I was not staying at the Ritz at all—I was lodged in a little pension nearby and was only in town briefly. Again, he charmingly dismissed the matter as of no moment and raised his glass to me. In raising my own to him, I confessed that there was one more "confession" I had to make. "These drinks are on *you!*"

My guest-turned-host now roared with laughter and took me out to dinner with his very nice, very dignified family. We remained "Christmas card friends" for years.

The following day, I decided in a flash of romantic impulse that, instead of returning to London immediately, I would take the next boat to Majorca, give Gee a lovely surprise, stay a few days, and then return. I figured that I'd just about make it. When the boat docked in Palma, I hired a broken-down old car and a driver to match and asked him to drive me to Formentor, on the other side of the island. In those days, it was a bumpy dirt road and took two hours or more. On arrival at the Hotel Formentor I paid off my excuse for a taxi, grateful for the weakness of the peseta as opposed to the dollar. I presented myself to the concierge and asked if he knew where Miss Gertrude Lawrence's villa might be.

"Ah, si, señor!" he answered, and then proceeded to diagram how I'd go up the hill, turn right, then down a bit, and so on, until I'd find a white house with red tiles. (Almost all the houses were white with red tiles.) I thanked him, took a small, single room to wash and clean up in (the hotel had only salt water in the bathrooms, which made the use of soap a problem), and then, spic and very span, I trudged up the hill, humming to myself in happy anticipation.

It didn't take me long to find the house. Excited as any ardent young swain can be, I rang the front doorbell. Gee answered it herself. When she saw me, she looked first startled, then horrified. She began to make frantic hand signals, then glancing over her shoulder, she turned back to me and whispered, "You can't come in! *He's* here!"

I couldn't find anything to say. She had made it so clear she planned to be alone, that to find she was deceiving me was too much to digest. How in the world did Eric get there, I wondered silently. Then of course I realized that only Eric was rich enough and interested enough to rent a villa for Gee at a time when her debts were higher than ever. My mind was in confusion and I didn't say a word. I just turned, like a dog that slinks off with his tail between his legs, and made my way back to the hotel, back to Palma, on a night boat back to Barcelona, and finally back to London, poorer and a tiny bit wiser.

By the time Gee returned, we were both so heavily involved in other activities that we kept a distance of sorts from each other for some weeks and never mentioned the Majorca incident.

More than a score of years later, I was sitting cozily in a large leather armchair in London's White's Club. Next to me was my old rival, Eric Dudley. We began to reminisce fondly about dear Gertie, what a loss to the theater and her friends her death had been, and what a mercurial and fascinating star she had been. I then recounted the sad story of my brief visit to Majorca where I found him there ahead of me. Eric listened and then turned to me with a look of utter astonishment and said, "But *I* wasn't there at all! *She* told me that *you* were there! Now the dear gel's dead and we'll *never* know who he was!" The sly thing had triple-crossed us both!

15

The year 1935 was only four or five weeks old when Gee was declared legally bankrupt. She was devastated, and her explanations to the authorities were so feeble as to give the gossip columns a huge boost in a dull season. The British press had to censor itself about the beloved Prince of Wales's indiscreet and irresponsible affair with Mrs. Simpson and it had run out of things to say about sweet but silly Barbara Hutton. So Gee's financial plight was headlined out of all proportion in what was, in the mid-thirties, the world's largest city.

Bill Linnit, Gee's, and my agent, had a senior partner named Bill O'Bryen. The two Bills were a rare breed and their list of clients was the best in Europe. A few months before Gee's financial storm broke, I went to both the Bills to suggest, quite pragmatically, that since I hadn't yet found sufficient finances or properties with which to launch my own Criterion Productions, it might be a good idea for me to take advantage of the tide of public interest and make a film with Gee. They thought it a commercial idea and proceeded to promote it. It didn't take much persuasion for Walter Mycroft, the shrewd little hunchback chief of the BIP studios, to agree. But what film to do? They had several possible treatments and outlines. The best was an adaptation of the opera *La Bohème*. I had loved the silent King Vidor production with the magnificent performances of Lillian Gish and John Gilbert. Rather foolishly, I admit, it was I who suggested that we film a "talkie" remake. I was just enough of the selfish young ham to think the role of Rodolfo would be splendid for me. Although Gee was far from the fragile figure Lillian had played so magnificently, she felt her acting would overcome the physical handicap of appearing too healthy.

The excellent cast of *Mimi* was well directed by Paul Stein. Indeed, the production was very well mounted. Only Gee's and my impulsive miscasting of ourselves were handicaps. Gee looked about as tubercular as a slim Brünnhilde and I, in a fancy beige wig, had only a faint resemblance to the dynamic Jack Gilbert. I thought everything was going well until it was all finished. Then I saw how wrong I was. The film really didn't do very well.

As soon as Gee's creditors agreed to a settlement, she threw her abundant energies into a new play. Nineteen thirty-five was celebrated as a Silver Jubilee year, commemorating old King-Emperor George V's twenty-five years on the British throne. They had been years of history's greatest wars and deepest economic collapse, years when millions of lives had been lost or broken and when the costs of victory began to cause irreparable damage to the greatest empire ever known to man. Yet George's fatherly figure still served as a flesh-and-blood rallying point. All manner of pageants and parades were planned.

Letters from Mother and Jack indicated that they might scrape up enough from Jack's recent savings and the monthly pension I sent to come over and see me and the sights.

Luckily, *Man of the Moment,* the quota film I was about to make for Irving Asher, would balance my books—more or less. Helping Gee even a little had been an additional and unexpected problem. However, I had had a windfall—actually, more of a breezefall—in the form of a trust that my father had set aside for me when he and my mother were divorced and about which I had previously been told very little—on purpose. It was in the amount of twenty-five thousand dollars and it was not to become available until I was thirty-two years old. I never did know what magic lay in the number thirty-two, but I decided that however much I prided myself on my financial independence, I would do my subtle best to persuade Pete—not directly of course—to let me have the money those few years in advance. He agreed.

Irving's wife, Laura La Plante, had been a popular star in Hollywood silents and had given up a good career to join Irving in England. She was full of odd quirks and sudden whimsies. For instance, when she was expecting their first child, they were living in a sumptuous flat in Berkeley Square. Laura was about eight months pregnant. Instead of craving weird food combinations, she liked to take midnight strolls, all by herself, through the streets of Mayfair, window-shopping. It was the end of a raw, cold winter and one night Laura bundled herself up in her best fur coat and set out on her habitual rounds. As she stopped to gaze at some expensive goodies behind glass, a night-prowling young tough saw her pretty face, sidled up to her and, touching his peaked cap, said with a big smile, "Hello, dearie! 'Aven't we met befaw somewheres?"

Laura turned, smiled in return, opened her fur coat wide to disclose her distended tummy, and replied, "Yes! And I've been looking for you!" The young man took to his heels.

Not much later, when she was returning from a weekend at Le Touquet, a fashionable French resort, His Majesty's customs officer wondered if he dared be indiscreet enough to inquire if she were "smuggling" anything beneath her coat. Again Laura opened it wide and with reassuring dignity said, "And made in England, too!" No more questions.

Professionally, *Man of the Moment* was not at all what I should have done at that period. But Irving hoped that with my name and Laura's, a good supporting cast, and direction by an ex-Hollywood comedian whimsically named Monty Banks, Warners would overlook the picture's quota category and release it in the States and Canada. Although they never did, I had the best time imaginable making the movie.

Much of the film was shot in Monte Carlo, where the casino and hotel were crucial to the plot. The company had preceded me there for the exterior location shots. They had a few days' work before they needed me and I was able to use the time to move out of Chips's Gloucester Place flat and into a far more economically feasible place in Paddington. It was very tiny and over a garage that had once served as a livery stable. It consisted of a minute entrance hall, a kitchenette, a particularly poor excuse for a bathroom, and a fairly good-sized main room that I converted into a bedroom by unfolding a couch. Allen Vincent had gone back to the States and I had dispensed with the services of Godfrey and my cook. However, I still had my old Auburn below and big ideas in my head.

Shortly after Mother and Jack arrived in London and were well settled in, I bade them and Gee a temporary good-bye and took off for Monaco and work. After crossing the Channel, I transferred to the famous Blue Train express that left Paris for various stops along the Mediterranean's Côte d'Azur. Before dinner, I stood contentedly in the passageway outside my *wagon-lit* compartment, with my head out the window. I could feel the soft air whoosh by as I stared at the early French evening unwinding before me. I remember thinking that even if my two or three professionally successful years had just been followed by something of a slump far from home, I still stood on my own two feet. Although I had energy, ambition, and confidence, I still had not rid myself of my teenage apprehension that I was destined to die young.

While I was thus ruminating, I noticed a very pretty female head at the other end of the car, also gazing out a window at the countryside. Suddenly she turned and put a hand to her eye. Obviously a cinder from the coal-burning steam engine had found a lodging there. As she was clearly in discomfort, I walked down to her end of the car and asked in French if I could help. She answered in clear, educated English, "I've got a damned cinder in my eye and it hurts like bloody hell!"

"Here," I said, pulling out a white handkerchief, "let me try to get it out for you." We did the usual thing. She pulled her lower lid down and I, locating the cinder, tried to nudge it out with the tip of my handkerchief. I succeeded, and she thanked me with the most enchanting smile. It was as hackneyed an incident as the least imaginative scenarist could devise, but we played it through with good manners. At least *she* did. I was probably about as subtle as a Sherman tank. Her now twinkling eyes signaled that even if she was on to me, she was enjoying the situation too.

We had drinks and dinner followed. It must have been excellent, since we were on an expensive French train. Strange, how quickly a superficial flirtation between mutually sympathetic people can develop into a fairly intimate but not necessarily detailed divulgence of each other's lives. I did learn that she was quite well off, of "good family," and married, though not happily. Drink was her husband's main problem. She could tell by my accent that I was American, but I decided not to proffer my name unless she specifically asked, which she didn't. Actually, I was reluctant to risk showing off in the event she, in fact, already knew it.

After dinner, more talk, and we returned to our car. We discussed, in a lovely haze as the train swayed and clickety-clacked beneath us, the fact that we were suddenly, incomprehensibly, so taken with each other. It was wonderful. No residue of Protestant conscience interrupted my natural instincts. In any case, I subconsciously reminded myself, Gee and I had gradually been loosening our bonds for the past year. I had at last discovered that girls my own age, and even those a bit younger, could sometimes be as attractive as older women.

My Lady of the Train had to get off early next morning, whereas Monte Carlo was a bit farther on. I waved out the window and we exchanged blown kisses. Our parting was rather dramatic. We spoke of our ignorance about each other, of our names, addresses, and so on. It was, she said, the right way to handle things. She had her duty to return to her husband, and neither of us must be tempted to meet again. We must just "always remember the cinder in the eye and the romantic night on the Blue Train." As, in fact, I have.

The actual filming of *Man of the Moment* was quite easy on mind and body. Unfortunately it was even easier on the exercise of talent. And the atmosphere of Monte Carlo continued to be one of benign sinfulness with profits aforethought. (I rarely gambled myself since my pleasure in winning was never as great as my pain at losing.) The company was congenial and undemanding. Perhaps that was what was wrong with the finished picture. It wasn't really bad, but it was not good enough.

It would have been hard to find an experience to compare with that delicious trip down, but that is not to say the return was without incident. This time it was a very ordinary chance meeting with a young square-jawed fellow American over a drink. We began comparing views of the French, Italians, Germans, and Europeans in general. That led to politics and to Hitler's threat, the timid, frightened democracies, and America's misguided sense of isolationism. We not only warmed to each other's company but agreed on all matters, including sports, his apparent specialty. We were both devout New Yorkers. He told me he was a newspaperman on vacation, hoping to get his own byline someday—possibly a column of some sort. He asked me what my "racket" was and I said theater and movies. He asked my name but couldn't quite figure out the Junior. He was not a great movie-goer. As we said a terse " 'night" to each other, he volunteered his own name. "Ed Sullivan," he said, as we shook hands.

In London I had taken a short lease on a small pretty house in a small pretty square in Chelsea for the Whitings. Mother settled in, as loving and demanding as usual. Whenever possible, I took the ebullient Jack on a limited sight-seeing tour (always including at least a glance at the immaculate, confident magnificence of the Guards—Foot or Horse). Being a guide to almost anywhere has always been something I thoroughly enjoy. Even if I know less about Dubuque, Iowa, or Riga, Latvia, than my guest, I invent such colorful stories that I often end up more than half-believing them myself.

These occasional idle hours were suddenly interrupted by a happy surprise for the Whitings. Jack was offered the lead in C. B. Cochran's London production of Cole Porter's Broadway hit *Anything Goes*. As everyone predicted, Cochran's production of the show was first-class and Jack was barely less than wonderful. Some critics claimed he was as good as Fred Astaire. Though this might now seem exaggerated praise, it was then very nearly true. Jack had a fine baritone voice, was an agile and graceful dancer, and was good-looking. He had almost everything—except perhaps that special magic that marks a Great Star.

Although I still lacked the capital to get my "paper" Criterion company started, I was moving ahead with the planning. The addition to the Board of Captain Alec (Bobby) Cunningham-Reid was meant to influence potential investors. Bobby, originally an impecunious country-clergyman's son, was now married to pretty Mary Ashley, Edwina Mountbatten's sister and co-heiress of grandfather Sir Ernest Cassels's absolutely immense fortune. We met during a weekend with the Mountbattens at their country house, Adsdean.

Dickie Mountbatten, besides being an avid movie fan, had always been a keen admirer of my father (even before his and Edwina's honeymoon at Pickfair in 1922) and an unswerving friend of mine. In his personal life, as the son of a famous admiral who had been politically martyred during the First World War, he had been motivated by a determination to excel. Although our circumstances were very different, Dickie said he recognized in me a "similarity of spirit." I was also the son of a once-famous world hero who was now reduced in rank. This was one of the reasons why, from the first, Dickie became almost a surrogate (though seldom seen) older brother and my own principal hero outside the theater. Likewise, his wife Edwina had always been my friend. So I suppose it was natural that they influenced their brother-in-law Bobby to join and support my new film company.

The Cunningham-Reids had a large townhouse in Mayfair, complete with swimming pool and movie projection room, where they entertained well and often. Bobby was tall, with wavy black hair and full red lips, and known to be "skirt-crazy." The idea of being chairman of even a small new movie company must have stirred up wonderfully juicy prospects of fun and games under the heading of business. He was openly delighted to join us and we were, at the time, also glad to have him.

Murray Silverstone and his chief United Artists colleague, George Archibald, now gave us a formal distribution contract for four pictures, on condition that I play in at least two of the four and that they first approve all story outlines. UA would also approve the principal players and the director. Naturally I was overjoyed. After years of trying to promote my own creativity and being kept out of the running by Hollywood's Big Company tyrannies, I was more or less my own boss.

My first vehicle had already been approved. It was an adaptation of Jeffrey Farnol's famous old novel of Regency days, *The Amateur Gentleman.* I had even won the enthusiasm of my old playwright friend Winifred (Clemence Dane), who agreed to do the screenplay. We needed a lovely-looking, experienced leading lady with a salable name. Luckily we found the much-admired Elissa Landi at liberty and eager to return to Europe. We selected the experienced American, Thornton Freeland, as director, hoping he would keep us all from becoming too arty.

In May, just before the start of actual production, King George's Silver Jubilee took place. My old governess, Dedie, retired to Ireland on the pension I sent monthly, had written, begging me to send for her. She wanted to see the "show"—not, she said, that she cared about the English, or the Scots, for that matter, but "the King and Queen are something else. They're nice people and I'd like to give them a cheer." So Dedie came over too, happy and all of a flutter, for a family reunion.

For a while, I pretended to Mother and Jack that I was so blasé that I now took all such pageantry in stride, but my pose didn't last long. The big day arrived, warm and sunny. The long colorful procession of scarlet-jacketed Guards and the jingling plumed and helmeted Household Cavalry, the horse-drawn carriages of the Royal Family, followed by dignitaries from the Empire and Commonwealth—it was a spectacle described at the time as second only to a Coronation. Colossal, but only lightly policed crowds, many of whom had slept out on the streets the night before, stood on their enthusiastic tiptoes. Finally, when the old King himself, who had presided over the disasters and triumphs of his realms for twenty-five years, rode by with stately Queen Mary at his side, the roars were thunderous. Like all such events, it was wonderfully choreographed, and the thanksgiving ceremonies in St. Paul's Cathedral afterward were more splendidly theatrical than religious.

A day or so later it was back to work for me. We didn't have a very big budget, but somehow Marcel Hellman made it stretch. He liked to annoy the hell out of us all by visiting the set periodically and conspicuously taking out his watch. I made my own relatively small additional contribution to the enterprise by dispensing with any salary and accepting (in addition to a percentage of hoped-for profits and a major share of the company's near-empty treasury) only a limited expense account.

Although the story was not really a swashbuckler, there was to be considerable physical action throughout. The most arduous—for me—would be a simulation of a nineteenth-century bare-knuckle prizefight, with a gigantic professional boxer acting as my opponent. Very early each morning, before the start of shooting, I worked out in an improvised gym. A special trainer who was an ex-fighter helped me devise our fight sequence. Every camera angle and every real, "pulled," or simulated blow was studied and rehearsed. My gentle brute of an antagonist finally joined me and together we went over a detailed blow-by-blow fight. We took good care not to land any really damaging blows, since faked ones looked just as effective when carefully photographed, especially with sound effects added later. The big bruiser kept urging me to really hit him but I held back, less from concern for him than for my already sorely bruised knuckles.

On the day of shooting the big fight scene, some friends came down to our Elstree studio to watch. It was the same studio where I had made *Catherine.* I thought they would enjoy all the excitement, the shouting crowd of extras, and what we hoped would at least look like a real fight. I had invited the Mountbattens and some of their friends, as well as Mary and Bobby Cunningham-Reid and my on-again crush, Liz Paget. Pete, but not Sylvia, had visited the studios a couple of days before to pose for press pictures and generously praised my initiative. Thus Mother and Jack, tactfully avoiding any day they thought my father might come, arrived for the fight scene. Of course the publicity boys made the most of everything.

It came time to do certain sections of the fight from different camera angles—particularly the climax when I was supposed to win by a knockout. We had no sooner begun our routine when one of us stepped just a bit out of the rehearsed position and my giant opponent's ham fist crashed into my jaw. I fell like a tree, unconscious.

Fortunately the press cameras missed the shot and our P.R. department succeeded in killing the story. I recovered a few moments later, much to the poor man's relief. We then completed the scene in just a few short shots. In the final film, artificially bloodied and bruised, I triumph over my brutish Goliath, as a good hero should.

My romance with Gee had by now almost completely petered out. The tensions, her "actressy" temperament, and the cost in money and nerves had cooled my former ardor considerably, though we still exchanged occasional fond gestures. Since I worked by day and she by night, weekends were the only times we could comfortably meet, and we did that less and less.

My trouble was I so enjoyed the fun and intrigue of romantic attachments that I now found myself making a deliberate off-stage play for my new leading lady, Elissa Landi. Usually I kept business and pleasure carefully apart. In this case, it was all more for the fun of the game than anything else. Elissa was intensely serious about almost everything—the weather, the price of eggs, her costumes. She was oppressively intellectual—a characteristic that her Hollywood colleagues reported was sometimes off-putting. Although she could be excellent company and was well informed, she lacked the sense of humor I knew and liked best. Hers could be a bit Mittel-europa; predictable and heavy.

I was actually far more taken with Coral Browne, the villainess of our picture. She was not only a beauty but the possessor of a wicked and frequently bawdy wit. She struck out at anyone with devastating and hilarious effect. She was so bright that it was sometimes difficult to accept the challenge of her very presence. She was also so good at her job that no one was surprised when, in the course of time, she became a star of the London stage. She was later happily married to that fine actor and art connoisseur Vincent Price.

The filming continued, quite arduous in the making and quite satisfactory in its end result. I admit I was pleased with *The Amateur Gentleman*—a story of high romance set in a period I particularly liked, with heroes and heroines, villains and villainesses, and good triumphing over evil without sentimentality.

Unfortunately, the gala opening night of our picture in London, scheduled for the first week of the New Year of 1936, coincided with the news that the old King was seriously ill and not expected to recover. This put a damper on all business everywhere. Though the critics were uniformly favorable to the picture and to me, we never quite gained the full momentum needed to start us off well. Fortunately, business picked up appreciably later.

During the next days, great quiet crowds began to keep round-the-clock vigils outside Buckingham Palace. A few days later the King's life was, as the royal physician announced, "moving to its close," and almost all theaters in the Commonwealth went dark for a day of mourning.

Years later, Anthony Eden, then Foreign Secretary, told me a story—perhaps apocryphal—about the King's last words. The King had been in a coma for some time and his doctors were assembled at the foot of his bed. They conferred about where to send him to recuperate, if he survived this crisis. One doctor suggested that when the King had last been ill the sea air at Bognor, on the Sussex coast, had proved most beneficial, and they should begin making arrangements. At that moment the King came groggily out of his coma, raised himself feebly on one elbow and, in a hoarse, angry whisper, said, "Bugger Bognor!" With that he fell back on his pillow and died. It is now known that the King's death was medically hastened with fatal doses of morphine and cocaine in order to assure a painless end. Other last words have been reported: "How is the Empire?" and "God damn you." I prefer Sir Anthony's version.

The new King of one quarter of the world—until now the fairy-tale Prince Charming, Prince of Wales—was proclaimed "by the Grace of God,"

Edward VIII. The British press was still loyally alone in the world in continuing its silence about his mistress, Mrs. Ernest Simpson, who, with her husband, had kept up a front of sorts by maintaining a fine house in Regent's Park where they entertained handsomely. Now what would happen? No one could guess.

After *The Amateur Gentleman* had opened, Sam Goldwyn sent me a charming and for once serious cable of congratulations and a welcome to United Artists. Soon after that I returned to Los Angeles to participate in a series of publicity photo sessions with a group of others who were producing for or releasing through United Artists. In addition to three of the original founders—Mary, Charlie, and my father (Griffith had resigned)—the others in our group included Sam Goldwyn, Ronald Colman, Vilma Banky, Rudolph Valentino, Walter Wanger, David Selznick, Walt and Roy Disney, and Alex Korda. Joe Schenck and his junior partner Darryl Zanuck had withdrawn their 20th Century company from the Goldwyn partnership when they gained control of the big Fox Films Company. They then renamed it "20th Century-Fox."

Pete preceded me to California in the hope of arranging a reconciliation with Mary even though their divorce had been declared final on January 10, 1936. He invited me to stay with him at his Santa Monica beach house—not in the main house, of course, but in the guesthouse at the rear. Pickfair continued as always to be in Mary's name.

I loved being a guest at the beach and having more or less free run of the place. With its kitchenette, small living room, and bedroom, it made for a most congenial bachelor setting.

Pete told Uncle Bob that he had "rediscovered" Mary. She was, after all, his "one and only love." He began to try desperately to win her back again. Virtually every day found him at Pickfair, taking Mary for drives in the hills and doing his romantic best to turn their clocks back. But as Mary later said, she had suffered too much public humiliation for too long from his globe-trotting escapades and public infidelities. However tenderly she recalled their life together and however deeply she had loved him, she could not continue to let her pride and heart be lacerated. She was determined not only that the divorce remain final, but also that no possibility of a reconciliation be considered. "The Great Romance" seemed ended forever.

At last, urgent business and Mary's intransigence obliged him to pack up and, as he put it, "play the Arab, fold my tent, and sneak away." He asked me to return to New York with him.

At every stop that the Super Chief made, Pete sent long, long telegrams to Mary, written in intensely romantic, desperately poetic language. Between stations he sat, most uncharacteristically alone, in his big double drawing room. I had a small connecting compartment. The still-faithful Rocher had a berth in the next car. I tried talking shop with Pete, or sports or even discussing the present state of the world, about which I now knew a little more than he, but since he didn't listen closely, it didn't matter. I quoted political pundit Walter Lippmann about the unfairness of demanding our allies' repayment of war loans. This sort of talk, so distant from his personal problems, loosened him somewhat. I even rambled on about his ex-golf partner, the new King, and, of course, Mrs. Simpson. He managed to uncork a few ready-made phrases and created a convincing portrait of being "well informed." I was accustomed to his convincing bluster and borrowed opinions and contentedly went along with them. Eventually I switched the talk around to the bawdiest new stories I could remember, which, coming from me at least, made him laugh.

Two days later, when our train reached Chicago, he inquired at the local United Artists office if there had been any message. No, there had not. He telephoned Pickfair but Albert—the old Pickfair majordomo—answered apologetically that Madame was not at home. After sending another long wire, we boarded the 20th Century Limited to New York, where his depression deepened further.

The next morning, my father went straight from Grand Central to the Waldorf Towers and I went on to the Whitings'. Mother and Jack had just returned from Jack's several successful months' run in *Anything Goes* in London to find a new offer to return to London for another musical, *On Your Toes.* At least this half of my divided family was in high spirits.

A United Artists secretary rang during that first day in New York to say that my father had been given three tickets for Bert Lahr's new musical that very evening. I knew Lahr always made him laugh so I encouraged acceptance. Tom Geraghty was in town and was invited to help us with the good spirits of the evening. Pete always bucked up and put on his best public personality when crowds recognized him. This time the Broadway theater crowd discovered us both, so there was a happy riot before the curtain rose. Lahr was his usual hilarious self and Pete was exhilarated.

The next night, almost morosely, Pete agreed to join me at the theater—this time to see the first night of Dick Barthelmess's return to the stage in *The Postman Always Rings Twice.* During the day, I had press interviews and a visit to United Artists to meet heads of departments, butter up the advertising and publicity people, and try to ingratiate myself with the company's business executives. Fortunately, one of the most important was my

late uncle Jack's brother-in-law, Harry Buckley, and another was my uncle
Norris Wilcox, my father's popular half brother.

I thoroughly enjoyed a short, hectic chat with Dick Barthelmess after his
successful opening night. Pete, however, had been terribly distraught, anxious, and quite unreceptive to the public's cheers and waves. This particular
evening he seemed almost to resent any attention and, after our congratulatory words backstage with Barthelmess, I returned him to the Waldorf. He
asked me to join him for lunch the following day. He thought Frank Case,
Tom Geraghty, and Bob Benchley would be there as well for a real "boys"
lunch. In fact, he suggested that I come over soon after breakfast so we
might discuss plans he had to produce a film with me about Marco Polo or
Lord Byron in Venice. I liked both ideas very much, particularly because
either meant we would be real working partners.

About nine the next morning I made my way from the Whitings' East
Fifty-seventh Street apartment to the Waldorf Towers. My own spirits were
so high that my feet fairly skipped across town. I arrived at the Towers desk
and was about to ask the clerk to ring my father's room when he apologetically interrupted with "Oh, Mr. Fairbanks! Your father has checked out! He
told me to tell you that he and his valet left *very* early this morning and
sailed for Europe. Mr. Frank Case took them down to the pier. Mr. Case
will call you later and tell you the name of the ship. I'm afraid I don't know
it myself."

I was speechless. What in God's name had this pseudo-thinking man, my
great hero father, gone and done now?

The clerk went on: "He also said to ask his office to send him a shore-to-
ship radiogram if any important business needed his attention—oh, and
would you please notify a Mr. Geraghty."

I must have half-turned away when the clerk called after me. "Oh, sir!"
he said. "There's something here in the box for him. None of us saw it
before Mr. Fairbanks left. It must have come late last night. Shall I give it to
you?"

I nodded and took the yellow Western Union telegram unthinkingly. I
automatically ripped open the envelope and unfolded the message. The first
thing I noticed was the signature—Hipper—his pet name for Mary. (Just as
hers for him was, for some forgotten reason, Duber.) The exact wording of
the message is lost, but I could never, ever forget its gist. It was, in effect:
"All is forgiven . . . I want us to be together again too . . . forever . . .
come back . . ." and love, and so on.

I asked the man for the key to my father's still-vacant room. I thought I
must find the name of the ship immediately and telephone him. As I was

about to go, in walked Tom Geraghty, who was also struck dumb by the news. We went up to the suite together and called Frank Case at the Algonquin. My father, according to Frank, had apparently been terribly restless and could not get to sleep. He was extremely angry and frustrated. Impulsively, with Frank's help, last-minute emergency arrangements were made to board a transatlantic liner, sailing with the tide between three and four in the morning. When I told Frank about the telegram from Mary, he said he'd come right over. Meanwhile, I would place a radio-telephone call to the ship, by now already standing well out to sea.

It took a maddeningly long hour or more to get through to the ship, and then more time to find my restless father. When I finally succeeded, his reaction to my news was not at all relief or pleasure, but rather anger at me, Tom, and Frank. He had done a complete turnabout in his attitude toward everything. We were all lying, he said, just because we didn't like or approve of Sylvia—and we had always been on Mary's side, not his! All our efforts to persuade him of the truth only enraged him more. We urged him to confirm it by calling Mary himself. He hung up on us. Efforts to get him back again failed.

Reports of what exactly happened on his arrival in England varied. No two stories were alike. Certainly, though, about a fortnight later he and Sylvia flew to Paris and there, at the American Embassy, with Ambassador Jesse Straus as his witness and mutual friend Elizabeth Govat as Sylvia's, they were married. It was March 7, 1936.

Not quite a year after my father and Sylvia married, late in '36 and early in '37, rumors surfaced of Mary's interest in Buddy Rogers, her leading man in *My Best Girl,* the movie made a couple of years before. Buddy was a handsome, charming young fellow, some ten or more years younger than Mary, who had made quite an impression in his first big part in a film called *Wings.* He had fallen hard for Mary then, but no one took him more seriously than any of the other men who fell for Mary's charm and beauty. They all wanted to "protect" her. Whether Mary reacted at all at that time, I never knew. All I did know was that her well-hidden drinking problem was still a constant worry to those close to her.

Was Mary's decision to marry Buddy revenge on Pete? Who could tell? Who could speak with real authority?

By the time I returned to London and the Criterion picture company, Marcel had successfully negotiated a small but well-equipped studio for us just outside London in Islington. Plans were made to do all Criterion productions there, unhindered by the demands and excessive overheads of other studios. Our next "approved" picture was *Accused,* a woman's story set in

France. It was a backstage murder mystery with an exciting courtroom denouement. Luckily we were able to engage Dolores Del Rio, the beautiful Mexican star for the lead, but we still had no leading man to play opposite her. I was busily planning two big specials for myself—one, *Bonnie Prince Charlie,* about the young Stuart pretender, and the other, *The Armstrong,* about the Anglo-Scottish border wars. Both would really be variations on American Westerns with different costumes. They included cattle thieves, but were played against moated and turreted castles instead of Monument Valley or the Painted Desert. Unfortunately, both projects required huge budgets for which I could not find the money. I clearly lacked Korda's persuasive charm and experience in finding financial supporters. So both stories were temporarily (I hoped) postponed and I reluctantly put myself in the not very good part opposite Del Rio.

In order to be quite correct about French law and courtroom procedures, we engaged a young English barrister who happened to know a good deal about it all. For the fun of it, I asked him to play a bit part with only a few lines as a French *Maître.* As it turned out, he had a splendid voice and presence and had been an amateur actor for years. There and then he decided to give up the law and become a professional actor. His name was Leo Genn, and he certainly made the right decision.

My stepfather Jack was about to open in another transfer to the West End from Broadway: George Abbott's production of Rodgers and Hart's *On Your Toes.* Once again he was cheered to the rafters when he joined the others in the company at the Savoy Grill for the traditional first-night celebration. But it was the glorious twenty-year-old ballerina, Vera Zorina, who made the biggest hit of the evening. She had been a member of the Ballets Russes de Monte Carlo and possessed classical beauty, magnificent technique, and a great sense of humor. I was too preoccupied with work and strangely embarrassed by the Whitings' constant presence to be more than ingratiating with this spectacular young dancer whose own mother hovered discouragingly over her.

In the midst of my efforts to make the most of my part in *Accused,* my freewheeling romantic style was undone by the accidental meeting of my "Lady-on-the-train-with-a-cinder-in-her-eye." I had not known her full name or address but vividly remembered her charm, looks, and wit. So meeting her again, out of the blue, was a happy surprise. We then met several times, but most discreetly, since she was still married, still unhappily. Her husband, the well-known scion of a great fortune, was a hopeless alcoholic and she not only felt great pity for him, but also was completely financially dependent on him and his family. Consequently our brief encounters had to cease.

16

During the '30s Marlene Dietrich was second only to Garbo in mystery, glamour, and beauty. Some thought her even sexier, though probably not so great an actress. She encouraged the legend that she was the invention of Josef von Sternberg, a most talented but moody director. Some people said he came from Brooklyn and his real name was Joe Stern. Whoever he was, he was an intelligent and cunning showman. When he made *The Blue Angel* in Germany, with Emil Jannings, he cast Maria Magdalena Dietrich in the leading female role. She was a chubby, good-looking young woman with a smoky voice. Her Prussian Junkers (i.e., military aristocrats) family, like so many other German families at the end of World War I, had fallen on impoverished days. She was always embarrassed by stories that her father had commanded the first zeppelin raid of the war over Britain. The teenaged Fräulein Dietrich got a job as a violinist in the Berlin Symphony Orchestra, hoping to supplement her earnings with occasional modeling and small parts in movies. Sternberg, a self-promoted mystery man from America, dominated the still-plump girl. He was often rude and brutal to her, but everyone assumed this was "just his way." Although she was married to Rudi Sieber, a nice young man, she gave interviewers to understand that Von Sternberg was her Svengali, hinting that she loved and feared him in a masochistic way.

She would add that she owed all her fame to his knowledge of how to photograph her to bring out her glamour. Some of this was probably true— she *did* play any part Joe wanted *and* in the manner he wanted her to play it. Still, she was really no one's puppet. She was far too intelligent and independent. Her aura of mystery, her suggestion of simultaneously sacred and profane sex, her knowing eyes in a sculptured marble face, her highly publicized perfect legs—all this was, Joe hinted, his invention. But the most important element of her public personality was that she genuinely grew to like the part. She played it perfectly.

She equally enjoyed dropping the mask to become her other unconventional offbeat self. She relished this other role too—the cultivated *Hausfrau,* who loved cooking, games, and children. Her most conspicuous frailty was extravagance—not just self-indulgence, but a positive joy in dispensing overly generous gifts to family, friends, and anyone who told her a sob story.

Marlene made little effort to hide the fact that she and her husband, a Roman Catholic, were very close and devoted friends, though they lived their lives well apart. For years Rudi shared his separate household with a good-natured German lady nicknamed Tami, short for Tamara. Marlene was more cautious about her own irregular romances, at pains to let all rumors remain unproven but constantly suspected.

At the time we met, her most publicized *grand amour* had been with the late Jack Gilbert, who had also been Garbo's ardent lover. His spectacular career began to slide with the advent of sound pictures, which coincided with the end of his big affair with Garbo. He and L. B. Mayer had a row that resulted in MGM's campaign to ruin him. It was said to have been launched by Mayer. Jack married and was quickly divorced by Ina Clare. He then took to the bottle even more devoutly, married the fair Virginia Bruce, and left her after falling harder than ever for Dietrich. At first she pitied him but then fell in love and tried to keep him away from the booze that was clearly destroying him. She failed. One night he died in a drunken convulsion. Dietrich was inconsolable, as if she and not Virginia Bruce was the real widow. She began to keep small votive candles burning constantly in front of his photograph by her bedside table wherever she went.

To escape from it all was surely one of the reasons she accepted Alexander Korda's offer to come to England, but her deep sense of loyalty made it a condition of her deal with London Films that Von Sternberg be given a job by Korda as well, though not on her movie. She had a one-picture contract for a film called *Knight Without Armour.* Another reason for Dietrich's agreeing to the deal was that though she was personally popular, her recent films had been a series of box-office slumps.

Maria, Marlene and Rudi's daughter, was with her much of the time. Marlene could be overwhelmingly maternal, unless or until she wanted to play the public part of the maddeningly aloof and untouchable Venus. The poor child could rarely appreciate who or where she was. As soon as *Knight Without Armour* was finished, Maria, with Rudi's help, was packed off to a girls' school in Switzerland.

I had met Marlene very casually once or twice before in California. When we met again in London, it was at a couple of dinner parties Alex Korda gave for her. One evening, making chitchat, I asked her to join me and other friends at a small dinner the following week. To my surprise she accepted. There was no word in any column about it afterward and all went very pleasantly. She must have been in her very early thirties at the time. I never knew her age for certain, but I had heard she was born in 1901.

My growing infatuation with Marlene soon began to show signs of reciprocation when I became her most favored companion. We spent almost all our free time in each other's company and had brief telephone chats in between. We spent weekends at various friends' country houses, most often at Dickie (Lady Morvyth) and Con (Constantine) Benson's in Shawford Park, Hampshire. There she made instant and permanent friends by donning an apron, tying her hair back with a hand towel, and preparing fabulous meals from Friday through Sunday night for whole house parties of sometimes as many as ten people. I also took her to meet the Kents, who had married in the autumn of 1934—Prince George and Princess Marina of Greece—at Coppins, their country house in Buckinghamshire. They fell for her as immediately as she did for them. Her Prussian family had brought her up to be a staunch monarchist and this new, royal connection delighted her. In our private moments, I still found it difficult to be broad-minded about the embarrassing votive candle burning in her Claridge Hotel bedroom. But I was careful to keep silent and repress my jealousy.

Since we were both anxious to soft-pedal our new relationship, I devised a plan to minimize any gossip by altering my method of leaving her suite at Claridge's in the early morning hours. Instead of taking the lift down to the lobby, I would leave unseen by the hotel fire escape that could be let down into a deserted cobblestone mews at the back of the hotel. On my first attempt at this route, I tied up my full-dress tailcoat (in those days we wore white tie to the theater and dinner almost every night). I turned up my coat collar to cover my white tie and winged collar and quietly tiptoed to the fire escape and let myself down. It was one of those deliciously fine, short summer nights and dawn was breaking as I cautiously touched the ground. I quickly turned down my collar, untied my tails, and turned around, preparing to hail the first taxi I could find. I nearly jumped out of my skin *and* tails when I saw a bobby standing before me with a broad smile on his young face.

He saluted me in a most friendly fashion and said, "Good morning, Mr. Fairbanks! Trying out a new trick for your next film? Good idea now, with nobody about! Good morning, sir!" Then he turned and strolled off in the opposite direction.

I found nothing to reply except an embarrassed "Morning . . . !" I turned in the opposite direction, hopped into a taxi, and rattled away a few hundred yards to my Grosvenor Square flat.

After a performance of Noël's *Tonight at 8:30,* in which he was costarring brilliantly with Gee, Marlene and I went backstage briefly to congratulate them. The rumors about Marlene and me had begun to circulate just enough for Gee to put on a bravura performance of exaggerated charm and bitchy cracks that made Noël dissolve into fits of laughter. I stood with a silly smile on my face, unable to think of anything to say that would deflect the wit bursting like shrapnel all around me. There was no longer any question that my liaison with Gee had ceased to be. As a matter of fact, I thought that, inarticulate as I was, I behaved in a friendlier way than she. It would be a couple of years before we met again.

Accused had a full-dress and arc-lights premiere in London in July 1936. Dolores arrived with her husband, then Cedric Gibbons, MGM's gifted art director. Marlene accompanied me and we sat with Dolores and "Gibby." I had met Marlene's husband, Rudi, and his "friend" Tamara during one of their many brief trips to Europe. He administered and invested Marlene's money for her. The urbane and cheerful way in which they all accepted each other's unconventional way of life flustered me. My hypocritical "Puritan" childhood and well-practiced habit of trying to appear as acceptable in public as possible prevented my wholehearted inner endorsement of the Dietrich-Sieber lifestyle. Yet such was my rapidly growing infatuation that I didn't really have to struggle too hard to adjust.

Marlene gradually did away with Jack Gilbert's bedside picture and the votive candle. When that gesture appeared permanent, I sensed, with pleasure, that I was now the man in Marlene's life. I tried to arm myself against future disappointment by thinking of our affair as only her passing fancy. But she gently managed to push any apprehensions out of my defensive mind. I couldn't possibly say that I was really in love at the time, but it was certainly a relationship of more sophisticated intensity than any I had so far experienced.

One day I reported to her that a flat in my new Grosvenor Square building on the floor immediately below my recently acquired penthouse was available. She dashed over to take a look and promptly took a lease on it for the duration of the filming of *Knight Without Armour.* Within a day or two her maid had moved everything of hers over to the flat I had secured in her name. It was set up as a sort of superior townhouse dressing room for her. We used both my own large living room and roof gardens above as a place to have friends for drinks and sometimes for dinners.

Knight Without Armour was a good film about the Russian Revolution. When it began shooting, Marlene was marvelously concentrated on her job —thanks, she insisted, to Von Sternberg's training and her "natural German self-discipline." She was immensely popular at the studio. Her leading man, Bob Donat, was so seriously laid up with asthma that Korda proposed to alter the script in such a way as to reduce his role to a bit part and write in another lead for someone else to play. Marlene put her foot down. She would not allow Donat to be replaced. Even if, because of the severity of his asthma, every one of his lines had to be spoken in one breath, she would give him all the time necessary and help all she could. This gesture, never publicized at the time, but much discussed in the studio, won her masses of devoted coworkers. She was that kind of woman.

Marlene had been talking for months about the charms and beauties of Austria and that summer we decided to visit one of the lakes near Salzburg where Max Reinhardt contributed greatly to that lovely city's annual *Festspiel* (largely though not exclusively devoted to its native son, Mozart). We were to stay at an Austrian chalet on a *zee,* near a quaint village. Our half-timbered chalet would be typical, the rooms large and rustic. Shopping would be done locally, near an inn where one could order huge steins of beer and drink them sitting on benches outside in the sun, listening to lilting Tyrolean music. I looked forward to this trip with the world's most desirable woman with great excitement.

The setting was even more beautiful and colorful than I had imagined. There was only one drawback. The lovely chalet, rented for a month, was to be shared! And shared, by God, by Marlene's husband, Rudi, and his mistress, Tami.

Such a real-life design for living was quite beyond my frame of reference and I protested quietly and grumbled. But it did no good and soon it became evident that Marlene and Rudi were indeed only technically married. They behaved together like old friends or siblings. And both couples made independent plans each day. Marlene had hosts of friends in that part of Austria and whenever we didn't dine in a colorful restaurant or at home—with Marlene cooking—we dressed up only a little and drove off to a *Schloss* in the area.

I spoke only a few words of "polite" German and one of them was the word *natürlich*. As may be guessed, it means "naturally" in English. Because I had a good musical ear for sounds and accents, it was quite easy to pronounce *natürlich* with no sign of a foreign accent. Furthermore, I often used the word in polite reply or in reaction to whatever anyone said to me that I didn't completely understand. If some fellow told me what was clearly either a joke or a serious account of something, I at least caught the mood of what he said and periodically interjected either a laughing *"Natürlich!"* or a more solemn *"Natürlich!"*

One night we went to a very grand *Schloss*. I seem to remember that it was Max Reinhardt's, a gift to the famed stage director from a grateful Austrian Government. It was not far from Salzburg and most impressive. It was a formal evening and luckily I knew a few people there. Marlene, of course, knew many more, and those she didn't know pretended to know *her*.

Among the guests was one spade-bearded Viennese gent whose name I never learned. He had somehow heard that in addition to my theatrical profession I had a unique *entrée* to the higher levels of the U.S. Government. Some of this was to become true a few years later, but at that time, it was quite wrong. Since my bewhiskered acquaintance believed the gossip, after dinner he signaled me to follow him to a quiet corner of another room.

When we were alone, he peered surreptitiously over his shoulder as if to make certain we could not be overheard and then he murmured something in German. I couldn't understand one single word. However, I adopted what I hoped was an expression of rapt interest. When he concluded this confidence, I smiled a knowing smile and said, *"Natürlich!"*

His eyes widened with astonishment as if to say, "Really? You know?"

I shrugged and nodded, and we returned to the party—he, impressed by my reaction, and I enjoying once again the apparent success of my nearly magical word.

Two or three years later I learned from a mutual friend what it was that I had been told. It was advance "intelligence" on the most recent discussion between Prince von Stahrenberg, the leading Austrian Nazi, and Hitler as to the best timing for *Anschluss,* the proposed Nazi takeover of Austria. It had been assumed that I would pass this bit of high-level information on to my "presumed superiors in Washington," but when the Viennese heard my reaction, they quickly gathered that Washington and I already knew all about it.

I have often wondered what would have happened had I really understood what the old boy had whispered and subsequently passed it on to high places in Washington. In retrospect, I think probably nothing. The British and French governments were still prepared to appease Hitler, believing they could eventually tame him. Under Roosevelt, we were against Hitler in theory, but disinclined at that time to do anything about him. In fact, a great many Americans, thousands of "safe" miles away, ignored or dismissed reports from Hitler's Third Reich because they believed he had brought Germany back into the comity of the Great Powers and kept the Communists out of Europe.

My Austrian vacation passed far too quickly. Typically, I had quickly acquired a fine assortment of Tyrolean getups and peacocked the lazy, sightseeing days away. Marlene was a wonderfully unconventional lover, philosopher and friend. At the end of our month we closed up the Austrian chalet and went to Paris for a few days for the big Exhibition of 1936.

Although I was on quite congenial terms with my father, we seldom saw each other now that he had married again. When we met, I made a point of being as charming as I knew how to Sylvia. But even so, he rarely included me in either his nonstop social or athletic life. He had purchased a charming Regency house with bow windows on fashionable Park Lane and, in addition, a new Rolls-Royce. It was well over a year before I was invited to see either. Even then, I was asked only for morning coffee downstairs, which is the most I ever saw of the house.

Our next Criterion project was a melodrama called *Jump for Glory*. In late September 1936 I went to see a new play in the West End called *Mademoiselle*. I was struck "all of a heap" by the personality and talent of the beautiful but then little-known leading lady, Greer Garson. Although she was quite new to important parts, my reaction to her was already shared by the critics and the public. Directly after the final curtain, I made my way backstage to her dressing room and introduced myself. She was as flustered and fluttery as a young girl at her first dance. I told her about *Jump for Glory* and said I very sincerely thought the lead would be a wonderful part in which to make her movie debut. She admitted she was tempted but had never felt that movies were her medium, as she was not, she insisted, "photogenic." I was so taken with her evident charisma that I pestered her for days.

Eventually my persistence wore her down and she came out to the studio for a test. Great care was taken with her makeup and hairdressing and our top-notch cameraman, Gunther Krampf, took infinite time with her lighting. She didn't in the least need an acting test, but she was concerned about how she photographed. We agreed on a scene she would play and I offered to play it with her—off camera. It was a thorough test, and the results were, in the view of all the experts who saw it, every bit as fine as I had predicted.

The only bit of hesitation came from United Artists authorities who said she had not yet established herself as a top-name stage star and was completely unknown in films. Therefore they thought it would be difficult to sell her to exhibitors. However, when they saw her test they grudgingly agreed she was so good, she would be worth the effort, but we had to get a "known" actor to play opposite her.

A few days later, to our enormous disappointment, Miss Garson saw the test herself and thought it absolutely dreadful! The whole experience only confirmed her belief that movies were not for her. To emphasize her reaction she wrote me the following letter:

4. 10. 36

Dear Douglas Fairbanks:

This is my first fan letter—I wanted to write it after seeing "The Amateur Gentleman" and now seeing "Accused" tonight has swept aside my last scruples. It's uncanny to watch an actor who is so natural on the screen that he makes the rest of an accomplished cast seem—well, actors doing their stuff. I enjoyed the picture immensely and so did everyone around me—a lovely job of work by all concerned.

I can't think why actresses (myself foolishly included) are so crazy to play opposite you. By now you ought to be recognized for the menace you are because you have a disarming way of seeming to leave all the glamour and whatnot to the lady, and yet modestly but firmly contrive to steal all the thunder all of the time . . .

It was so nice of you to help me through that test last Monday. I only wish the results were more gratifying. The only moment that didn't make me *prickly* with shame was when I thought they'd cut and giggled something spontaneous. I don't know what de Leon told your nice Mr. Hellman, but I rushed out of the building protesting wildly that never, no—never, unless your make-up and camera wizards could mitigate the full horror of my countenance, could I *think* of making a picture. He seemed to think I had said quite the wrong thing, so perhaps he did his diplomatic stuff and maybe it will be possible to have another try.

There was some talk of shaving my hair, and a stout cry of more and better eyelashes, and bigger and better teeth, and if the experts will wangle the angles, this honest-to-goodness face of mine may yet brazen it out.

I had a word with Jack Wilson before he sailed, and think he won't have the heart to say no mova da pic while the play lasts.

I'd ask you please to want me for another picture later on when "Mademoiselle's" finished, only that I'm afraid you might go and find some other fair [actress] in the meantime who might be pretty-and-all-that but won't be half as amusing as I am—And anyway, "Jump for Glory" *would* be fun to play . . .

This letter has grown far too long. And probably has passed through a posse of bewildered secretaries before reaching you. I almost never write and don't know when to stop politely if I do—or if you know what I mean. And I fear it is all dreadfully informal and unsuitable from a parvenue actress to a world famous star, but may I repeat how greatly I enjoyed your last film, and how very much (even if the negotiations of our official representatives go agley). I should like to be in one of your future films.

Sincerely,
Greer Garson

P.S.—
Preferably "Jump For Glory!"
G.G.

Still, I was so honestly enthusiastic that I made a virtual pest of myself and kept raising the ante. I felt like the serpent in the Garden of Eden. Presumably she got tired of my persistence and asked Binkie Beaumont, who was her play's producer, to write me a letter, so businesslike and defensive that it suggested we hardly knew each other, though of course, we were friends. It read:

28th October, 1936

My dear Douglas:

Miss Greer Garson came to see me yesterday afternoon and explained to me that your Company had made her an offer to star in a film under your management. Miss Garson was extremely anxious to accept this offer but I am afraid we have, quite firmly, had to refuse permission as it would, obviously, be quite impossible for us either to release her from the Cast of "Mademoiselle" at Wyndham's or to allow her to film in a Play at the same time. Her part there is a very strenuous one and it would be quite out of the question for her to give eight performances a week if at the same time she were playing a leading part in a Film Production.

Miss Garson was, naturally, very upset at our decision and I promised I would write to you and explain the reason she has been unable to accept your offer.

Kindest regards,
Yours sincerely,
Hugh Beaumont

With that I admitted defeat and began looking for someone else. It is, perhaps, a neat postscript to the story that probably not more than a year later the more impressive big guns of MGM, led by L. B. Mayer and Irving Thalberg, succeeded where I failed. Greer Garson *did* leave her play the following May. She signed a contract to appear in *Goodbye, Mr. Chips* with Robert Donat, was an instant hit, and never looked back. Many long and wonderfully successful years later, she married and retired to Texas.

At last we were able to engage the lovely Valerie Hobson as the frightened heroine of our movie. But we needed someone to play opposite her. We got Raoul Walsh to direct at a big price. He had worked with Pete on *Bagdad* and had done several pictures with Errol Flynn. Walsh was a dashing, devil-may-care character who had recently lost an eye when a jackrabbit, blinded by his headlights, jumped through the windshield of his speeding car one night. His use of a black eye-patch only added to his rakish appeal.

A few weeks before we began to shoot, I had another bout of pneumonia. It was not very severe, but enough to put me in the hospital for a week or so. My stay was made surprisingly agreeable by a lovely-looking night nurse. She was Scottish and I remember very well that I preferred talking to her late at night instead of sleeping. It did me no harm because I went back to work soon after. In fact, I authorized a film test of her. She ended up playing a small bit, but though she photographed well, she eventually decided she was a better nurse than actress.

Alan Hale, who had played Little John in my father's *Robin Hood,* was added to our cast, but we still had no suitable leading man. Once again, I had no choice. Under our contractual obligation to United Artists I must play the lead myself.

I was finding it increasingly difficult to get along with Marcel Hellman. He was personally as nice as could be, but our respective views of what comprised a high-quality film grew further apart daily. This affected my judgment and my performance. Nor were matters helped by studio labor troubles, which slowed us down and discouraged me even further. To make it all even more distressing, my relations with our chairman, Bobby Cunningham-Reid, deteriorated. I was becoming apprehensive about some of his slick ideas for financing the company. I began to think about detaching myself from Criterion altogether.

As autumn slid into winter, there was a good deal of work still to be done on *Jump for Glory.* But there was fun to be had, too, with good friends and country weekends with Marlene in a variety of places. Beneath the easy social banter, the latest Coward witticisms, the latest Porter, Gershwin, and Rodgers music, there was mounting tension among those in the know about the new King and his undisguised passion for Mrs. Simpson, who was still awaiting her divorce. I was as hungry for news as anyone and took every opportunity I could to get the lowdown from a stray Mountbatten, the Dalkeiths, or similar sources of court gossip.

When the Kents asked Marlene and me to Coppins for dinner or a weekend, we immediately dropped other plans because we thought we might hear something special. Our American ambassador Barry (Robert Worth) Bingham was hoping quite frankly that anyone with "reliable" news would pass it on. There was, in fact, very little "inside" gossip that wasn't openly shared.

The world's most horrible war was only eighteen years past and the giddy hopes that followed through the twenties were still unrealized because of the unprecedented worldwide depression. Now, in 1936, the fantastically popular and handsome Prince had become the cynosure of a Commonwealth of nations that numbered about five hundred million people. They hoped that just his ceremonial presence over the lot would bring a bright dawn after the long gloom. Curiously enough, the most forceful objections to the King's marriage plans came not from the people of Great Britain but from various religious groups in the Commonwealth overseas. Anthony Eden, who was in the Cabinet of the day, told me he remembered well that many indignant bodies around the world warned the U.K. Government that should the King marry twice-divorced Mrs. Simpson, they would begin a movement to secede from the Commonwealth. Yet many in England, including Winston Churchill, urged him to stay on, regardless of opinion, believing his popularity would win in the end.

During the last crisis days I spent a night or two at Coppins. Prince George and Princess Marina returned there for dinner after a day of "family talks, arguments, and rows" at Fort Belvedere, where the King was staying, and gave us a discreet summary of the day's dramatic events.

As the day of royal reckoning neared, Marlene, at Grosvenor Square, was privy to a little of the "back-stage story." She became increasingly emotional about the King's reputed defiance of his ministers' advice that disregarding the Constitution must lead to abdication or some other end to this uniquely popular monarchy. Marlene, ever a staunch supporter of the system, decided she and only she might be able to arrest history in its tracks.

She had made up her mind that if only she could see the King privately, for just half an hour, she could persuade him to alter the whole scenario. How? By her own well-proven irresistibility to men? She wouldn't say. Whether she thought she could seduce the King and thereby make him realize that Mrs. Simpson was not the only compelling woman in the world, no one will ever know. But she did put her delicious determination to work and made a notable attempt.

She summoned Bridges, her tough American chauffeur, to bring her sixteen-cylinder Cadillac limousine to wait for her in front of 20, Grosvenor Square. She put on her most seductive makeup, a fetching Aquascutum trenchcoat over her dress (which I didn't get to see) and, leaving me protesting behind, sped off into the night toward Surrey, and the King at Fort Belvedere.

Unfortunately for Marlene, but not for the ever alert press, her car was stopped by the police at the gates of the Fort. I later heard that long and desperate pleas and arguments took place between Marlene and the assembled constables. But neither her devastating looks and charm nor Bridges's threatening manner influenced the King's guardians. Press camera flash-lights popped all over the place and the next day's papers confirmed that Marlene Dietrich's brave attempt to talk the King out of what all feared would be his decision to abdicate had failed.

Thus days later, we sat misty-eyed with much of the world listening to the poignant radio broadcast—said to have been written by Churchill—in which King Edward VIII renounced his high estate and pledged allegiance to his successor, his quite unprepared but far wiser brother, Prince "Bertie," the Duke of York. "Bertie" succeeded to the job with heartbreaking reluc-tance, and chose to reign under one of his many other names—his revered father's—and so was proclaimed, the next day, George VI.

I had not forgotten the day three years earlier when I had dropped Prince George off at his brother Bertie's house at 145 Piccadilly. Prince Bertie was a charming, quiet man whose formal name then was H.R.H., the Duke of York. His wife Elizabeth was an enchanting, warm, nonroyal Scots aristo-crat, and they had two little tow-headed daughters, Elizabeth and Margaret Rose. They were playing in the garden in the back when I made my very short visit.

Now it was December 11, 1936—less than a year since his father, George V, had died and two days after my twenty-seventh birthday!

17

Jump for Glory was now ready for delivery to UA. It had some amusing "inside" moments—such as my pretending to play the violin in close-up. The instrument was held firmly under my chin while off camera someone else stroked the bow and still another man, also out of sight, fingered the strings. My job was to look idiotically soulful throughout. It was so ludicrous and I broke up so often that we finally had to play the scene in several brief shots.

Valerie Hobson was as splendid as I'd expected, and so was the rest of the cast—all virtually directing themselves because of Raoul's preoccupation with the day's racing forms. I was the only one who gave an indifferent performance. A special glamour was added to our lunch hours by the frequent visits of Paul Robeson, a real though unlikely fan of my father's and mine. He was performing in England at the time and had not yet become the center of the tragic political controversy soon to envelop him.

Curiously the film did fairly well at the box office, so I had little support in my disappointment with Criterion's record. In fact, it showed a modest profit, whereas Marlene's *Knight Without Armour,* an expensive and intelligent production, was a box-office disaster. Actually for a time it added Dietrich's name to those of Bette Davis and Kate Hepburn on the exhibitors' ignominious "box-office poison" list. My own box-office status could not be determined with any degree of accuracy, since I had mostly been working abroad. I certainly did not consider myself on a par with, say,

Colman or Gable or Cooper. Perhaps I was a notch below the newcomer Cary Grant and perhaps a notch above Freddie March.

Dushka is a Russian term of endearment. Whether Marlene first heard it in a line from her film or because it was the name of the Kents' German shepherd, I don't know, but she made it her secret romantic alias. When she left London for California, she—generous to a fault—gave me and my penthouse various gifts inscribed *"Dushka,"* behind which her identity could be hidden. For instance, a beautiful Asprey atmosphere clock that operated mysteriously without electricity and a gold wristwatch were among the farewell souvenirs she left me. Reassurances of our early reunion were made and away she sailed.

My own company and career problems resumed their usual place at the forefront of my attention. I had written a letter to my partner Hellman, with a copy to Cunningham-Reid, in which I sought to put "on the record" my dissatisfactions with Criterion's operations, adding my intention either to raise our sights and alter our policies or to resign. I stated unequivocally, on the advice of our family solicitor, F. M. Guedella, that I found my position and activities incompatible with the ideas that inspired me to organize the company in the first place. I blamed my partners' now greater production authority for my own career being "devalued beyond recognition" and recorded my wish to dissociate myself completely from the Criterion film company's future. There were no blazing rows, but everyone knew there was no way, short of a lawsuit, to stop my resignation.

Since our next picture, *Crime over London,* was to be a routine melodrama without me in the cast (it included Margot Grahame and Florence Desmond), it gave us all some space to sort out our corporate difficulties. We made a sort of financial settlement. Even though I had taken no salary from the beginning, I was unable, due to my precipitous actions, to retain an interest even in my own last two pictures. In my anxiety to settle in a hurry, it was agreed that compensation in the form of an anemic bit of the profits from *The Amateur Gentleman* would cover what I had lost on the others. After that, my resignation became final.

Whenever I saw my father, surrounded as usual by his "courtiers," I was loath to report the crumbling of my company, of which I had been so proud and after such a promising start. Even to Tom Geraghty and Irving Asher (of whom I still saw a great deal) and other cronies, I minimized my disappointment and uncertainty about the future.

My extended absence from Hollywood had made continuing representation by Mike Levee impossible. However, Marlene persuaded me that Harry Eddington, who was both her and Garbo's agent, was now the best and I should take him on. Furthermore, his partner, Frank Vincent, was equally well thought of. So when Eddington wrote, proposing his firm, I was delighted—and grateful to Marlene, who had instigated the idea.

My next difficult professional decision was not long in coming. One evening early in 1937 I had a call from David Selznick in California. He announced that he was planning to remake the old classic *The Prisoner of Zenda* with Ronnie Colman playing the star dual role. He wanted to assemble as nearly an all-star cast as he could and offered me the part of Count Rupert of Hentzau—last played in the old silent film by Ramon Novarro.

It was clear that Selznick had chosen *The Prisoner of Zenda* as a thinly disguised reference to the Duke of Windsor's abdication and the approaching coronation of George VI in June. Both situations could be related to the old *Zenda* plot.

Of course I was greatly cheered by having an offer of any kind—at this moment in particular. But I was set back on my heels at being asked to be a supporting or featured player to *anyone*—even so fine an actor as Ronald Colman. I quickly reviewed the years I had taken to become a star and recalled the long struggle to be my own boss—made possible only by going abroad. The recent setback at Criterion, though certainly disappointing, had not discouraged me. In fact I was more determined than ever to proceed as first planned. I told David all this and also assured him of my gratitude.

"Well, think about it some more, old boy," shouted David on the phone. "I won't even consider anyone else—at least for a while."

The next morning a cable from Marlene was delivered, obviously inspired by David, urging me to accept *Zenda* and hurry to California since it was "a marvelous part." But I was still resentful of what I interpreted as a demotion.

Finally I invited myself around to Park Lane to see if I could gauge an opinion from my preoccupied father. When I arrived, he was dictating notes to his secretaries, supervising Rocher's packing of huge trunks, and generally getting ready for his and Sylvia's trip to the Santa Monica beach house. Clearly it wasn't the best of times to ask for serious business advice. But I did anyway. I told him about the offer and why I was resisting. He listened attentively. When I finished, he burst out with the conviction that I *had* to accept. Why? "Because not only is *The Prisoner of Zenda* one of the best romances written in a hundred years and always a success, but Rupert of Hentzau is probably one of the best villains ever written. He is witty, irresistible, and as sly as Iago."

I was automatically suspicious and thought his enthusiasm might be just another example of his typical exaggeration, but he went on. "Whoever plays Rupert," he said forcefully, "in any stage production in any country, will always be a big hit, even though the leading part is a double role. If you play this part of Rupert, people will forget any slump you've had. You'll be on top again right away!"

Seeing that his persuasiveness was having an effect, he wound up his oration with "That part is known to be actor-proof! Nobody has ever played Rupert and failed to steal the show, on either stage or screen! It is *so* actor-proof, in fact, that Rin-Tin-Tin could play the part and walk away with it!"

That convinced me! I put a call through to Harry Eddington and asked him to give David a tentative yes to the offer. I said that in addition to an agreement on money matters (I wanted him to try for a percentage), I also wanted approval of my costumes and special billing. How could we, I asked Eddington, retain my professional status as star and still be in a featured position if I were billed below Ronnie and the recently selected leading lady Madeleine Carroll?

I suggested that as Colman and Carroll were already contractually assured of being alone together above the title, a compromise of sorts might be to leave my name off the list of featured actors that ran immediately after the title altogether and put "With Douglas Fairbanks, Jr., as Rupert of Hentzau" in big letters, right at the bottom of everything.

Within hours David agreed in another warm and friendly call. I immediately began to make preparations to return to Hollywood. In New York for a few days on my way to the coast, I stayed at company expense at the Hotel Pierre—very grand, very posh.

While I was there, Aunt Gladys came to call on me. Apparently the money I regularly gave to Mother to dispense to all the Sullys did not always reach Gladys. Mother, it seemed, passed along varying amounts of money depending on the behavior of the recipient in accordance with Mother's "rules." Poor Gladys, the best-looking of the Sullys, had had some recent very difficult times made even more difficult by her secret addiction to alcohol. Now she was broke, and Mother, still in London, declined to authorize the bank to give her sister the money *I* had provided for her. She was stony broke. While I was listening to all this in shock and anger, a knock came on the door and a man's gruff voice asked from the outside, "Mr. Fairbanks? Do you have a woman in your room?"

I replied that I did and said it was my aunt. Why?

The voice growled back, "I'm the house detective and the hotel rules state that no lady visitors may come alone to a gentleman's single room. I'm sorry, but she'll have to leave!"

I burst into a fury, told him to go to hell, and made a fool of myself with threats I knew I couldn't deliver. But he stood his ground. Poor Gladys, handsome and dignified, was pathetically embarrassed. The end of it was that I threw my things into my cases and checked out then and there. I gave Gladys another check—and promised I'd send hers to her regularly and personally from then on. I went straight to the Algonquin and ever after declined to stay at the Pierre despite many subsequent changes of ownership, management and, presumably, house detectives!

Pete had overtaken me and was already established in the Santa Monica beach house with Sylvia by the time I got out there. I settled myself in the old house I had bought for my grandparents. Billy Haines (by now retired as an actor but a most successful decorator) had redecorated it for me at a friendly cut rate—for the sake of old times with Joan, I suppose. But this was really a "cover," since most of my off-duty time was spent at Marlene's far more sumptuous house—with lovely garden and large pool in Beverly Hills. We went through the motions of secrecy, and friends were very cooperative in not making a big fuss about it. In those days, although gossip columnists like Winchell, Hedda Hopper, and Louella Parsons were given to broad hints and blunt, cruel attacks against many people, details of celebrities' addresses were never publicized.

When I was first asked down to Pete and Sylvia's house, they told me that Merle Oberon lived in the house just to the north of them. They asked if I knew her young British boyfriend who had been living with her for several months. He was recently out of the British Army, where he had been a career officer in a Scottish regiment and had come to California hoping to break into movies. His name was David Niven.

Niven and I thought we might have known each other slightly in London. We were soon to become very close friends. Pete, for his part, had been quite won over by him—as had Thalberg, Norma Shearer, Jesse Lasky, W. R. Hearst, and Marion Davies. Merle assured Niv that with her by his side he couldn't fail to get a job somewhere, sometime soon.

She was right. Niv had been a keen amateur actor for some time, and beneath his quick-witted personality, he worked hard and conscientiously at learning his craft. I was, of course, delighted when he landed the small but sympathetic part of Fritz von Tarlenheim in *Zenda*—his best break so far.

David Selznick and I got along famously—but only after I got over the first week of trying to impress him and the others with their good fortune in persuading me to give up my own company to be a featured player in support of Ronnie Colman. It took only a few days for David to patiently make it clear to me that I was not nearly as knowledgeable as I thought and that as a producer I was very small fry indeed. Furthermore, I was by no means a star of the same magnitude as Colman. In a word, I really was damn lucky to have this chance to reestablish myself at home after a spotty few years abroad.

Before shooting began, there was some discussion about my appearance. In contrast to Ronnie I decided to have curly hair (even though it meant an extra hour each morning in the makeup department having my locks "mascaraed and curled into loose ringlets" as John Cromwell, our director, disparagingly put it). I tried shaving off my mustache, but then I looked too young in contrast to Ronnie, so that stayed put. The plan for costuming was that all the men were to be dolled up in the grandest of Balkan uniforms. However, I recalled my father telling me long before never to wear anything too distracting around the neck. A loud or large-figured tie always detracted from one's facial expressions. He also thought one should be as simple and in as much contrast to others as the situation allowed.

Therefore, I pointed out that not only was Ronnie the *real* star of the story, but he had two roles—each requiring showy Balkan uniforms. And there were many elaborate characters. The splendid and ever so serious Ray Massey played the main villain; C. Aubrey Smith, the epitome of the British "Raj," played the King's faithful equerry; and also there was dear Niv. As for the women, there was gorgeous Madeleine Carroll and the great classical beauty Mary Astor. Both were fabulously gowned. The lesser parts and the crowds were so fancily costumed, it made one think this deliberately black-and-white picture was being shot in Technicolor. All this aided my pleas that I should only wear basic black uniforms with an absolute minimum of trimming. After a few camera tests, I convinced both producer and director that the relative simplicity of my dark costumes would be more menacing and also more conspicuous.

David was a great but maddening producer. Although John Balderston, author of *Berkeley Square,* had done the original adaptation and Donald Ogden Stewart, one of our best writers, had submitted an excellent screenplay, every few days a whole pile of pages, rewritten by David, would be sent to the set, and whole scenes would have to be relearned. This so angered director Cromwell that he and David had a showdown. In the end, John was relieved of his assignment and a good deal of the film was reshot with W. S. Van Dyke replacing Cromwell as director. It didn't affect anyone's part, but it did make everything go smoother.

Ray Massey worried constantly about his interpretation of his own part. One day he interrupted the aged Aubrey Smith, who was reading a fortnight-old copy of the London *Times.* "Sorry to butt in, Aubrey," said Ray, "but I just can't get under the skin of my character, Black Michael. I can't understand his *real* motivation. I thought you might advise me."

Aubrey had to turn up the power in his hearing aid first. Then he lowered his *Times,* took the monocle from his eye, and, glaring at Ray, replied, "My dear Ray, in my time I have played every part in *The Prisoner of Zenda* except Princess Flavia. And I *always* had trouble with Black Michael!" With that, Aubrey replaced his monocle, turned off his hearing aid, and picked up his *Times* again. Nevertheless Massey gave a splendid performance.

I had more days off than I had at first expected, and I spent many of them reading and scribbling in Marlene's house or, weather permitting, by her pool. On Sundays Marlene entertained a number of her European friends. Their talk was about cultural, artistic, and often political matters. They were all passionate anti-Nazis—some were socialists, and there was·an occasional half-baked communist. One of the most amusing of these intellectuals, who became my good friend, was the great German director Fritz Lang. Thank God I never worked for him. He had the reputation of being a sadistic monster on the set, and I was not temperamentally suited to take that kind of abuse. But Fritz helped me a good deal in "handling" Marlene and in reconciling my old-fashioned middle-class standards with her very liberal "Mittel-Europa" talk and actions.

I remember once being in a fury because Marlene occasionally swam in the buff. She enjoyed having her beauty appreciated. Fritz gently mocked me for my lack of sophistication and reassured me about her "basic fidelity." Sometimes Marlene asked me to drive her teenage daughter, Maria, to the Riviera Country Club stables, where she joined a sweet, energetic youngster of her own age who was equally keen about horses. Maria's friend was a child actress, not very pretty but bubbling and cute. Everyone said she had a fine voice and was doing well at MGM. Only a year or two later did I begin to appreciate the name and potential of Judy Garland.

Our "romantic attachment," as the press referred to my relationship with Marlene, settled into a comparatively prosaic one. We went out publicly together only seldom, but when we did, it caused considerable head turning. Marlene took this in her famous "world-weary" manner, and *I* took it with a mixture of embarrassment and pride.

One of the high points of *Zenda* was a long saber fight between Rassendyl (Colman) and Rupert (me). The script required a witty dialogue all through the exciting and exacting duel that carried us all over the old castle of Zenda. Selznick rewrote this sequence several times to make it as amusing and exciting as possible. Also, he engaged Ralph Faulkner, the best saber teacher in Hollywood, to train and rehearse Ronnie and me.

For the first time I had broken my antiswashbuckling rule. The circumstances of the story in which I played a villain and the fact that it had been ten years since my father had last swashed a silent movie sword, eased my apprehensions. I was intent on making the fight as realistic as possible. My early training and some fencing competitions in my youth helped, but Ronnie had little or no background in the sport. It was therefore necessary for Faulkner to double for Ronnie in most of the medium and long shots. With patient rehearsal Ronnie could manage the several brief close-up shots well, but otherwise he didn't try any sustained exchange of cuts, thrusts, and parries. In the end, the time and sweat we all expended proved worthwhile. It turned out to be one of the screen's classic sword-fight sequences.

The Prisoner of Zenda was a whopping success. Everyone gained by it, from Ronnie and everyone else in the cast to our great cameraman, James Wong Howe, the writers, Cromwell (who retained credit for direction despite the changes), and Selznick himself. As for me, although there were only about six or eight scenes for Rupert, it still proved to be almost all my father had predicted. For the first and only time in my memory I didn't get one bad or even indifferent review—nor, indeed, did Ronnie. He was truly superb. Suddenly, just as predicted, I was swamped with offers.

My lovely liaison with Dietrich was not destined to survive much longer. It was too high-powered and sophisticated for me. It was not only the more assured and intellectual German author Erich Maria Remarque who brought our relationship to an end, but my own sudden jealousy was also to blame. Quite by accident, while searching Marlene's desk for writing paper, I came across some intense love letters (from someone I'd never heard of) to Marlene. Although I had no idea of their date or any circumstances of their existence, I blew up in a jealous rage. Marlene's reaction was justifiable anger with me for going through her private papers in the first place. One word led to another, and our waning romance fizzled out then and there. After an interval, we became fond friends and still are at this moment of writing.

One of the offers that came to the offices of my new agents, Eddington and Vincent, was from Sam Goldwyn and William Wyler, one of the best directors ever. I was asked to test for the part of Heathcliff in *Wuthering Heights* opposite Merle Oberon. For me to land such a plum so soon after playing Rupert of Hentzau would be marvelous. I carefully studied the Brontë novel and the scripted scene that was to serve as my test. On the big day I was ready long before the cameraman and his crew arrived at the studio. The actual test went very quickly. After only three "takes" Wyler, who was known to make numerous shots of every scene, smiled, thanked me charmingly, and said he would call the next day. No one called me for days! It turned out the test was so very bad, in fact so *horrible,* that it was actually funny! When I finally had the courage to look at it myself, I understood only too well. Larry Olivier, thank *God* (and Willie Wyler), got the part without a test and, as every movie lover knows, was marvelous.

Despite this deserved and happily unpublicized disappointment, better luck soon followed. In fact, from that time, I began the three busiest years of my career up to then. A nationwide exhibitors' poll, published the following year in the trade papers, listed me as one of the "top ten box-office draws" among the young male stars of the day. The others were (in alphabetical order): Fred Astaire, James Cagney, Ronald Colman, Gary Cooper, Errol Flynn, Clark Gable, Cary Grant, Tyrone Power, and James Stewart. Unfortunately this rating was not reflected in my earnings for fiscal 1937–38, which ranked as twenty-first on the same list—or just under $200,000. My agents, Eddington and Vincent, were very contrite at this disclosure—and rightly so, I think.

My first movie after *Zenda* was a good change of pace. It was a screwball comedy of the kind that became so widely popular once Cary Grant and Kate Hepburn got the zany ball rolling. Its message was only of the pleasures to be derived from an undisciplined life. Its title was *The Joy of Living.* To top off my current good fortune, I played opposite one of the finest of screen actresses, Irene Dunne.

Everyone adored Irene. She had an impeccable offstage reputation—as the virtuous wife of a doctor who had encouraged her studies as a young singer (she was first noticed on the New York stage singing "Smoke Gets in Your Eyes"). She was fun to work with, yet wonderfully concentrated. Our director was Tay Garnett, my old friend with whom I'd planned some "epic films" in England that never came off. *The Joy of Living* proved an amusing time killer with a catchy theme song by Jerome Kern, "You Couldn't Be Cuter." (Most movies in those days *had* to have a theme song.)

Virtually overlapping my cinematic nonsense with Irene was a surprise offer to go over to the Universal Studios in San Fernando Valley (now known as North Hollywood) to do *The Rage of Paris,* a light sophisticated comedy. Although Universal was a company that then ranked on the less than distinguished side, this picture promised to be different. It was planned to introduce the French star Danielle Darrieux to English-speaking audiences. I had recently been much impressed by her serious performance with

Charles Boyer in *Mayerling*—a very dramatic French film—and I thought playing opposite her would be another good feather in my cap. Furthermore, it was to be directed by Henry Koster, a young German said to have much of Lubitsch's superb and witty style.

The film was very amusing, light as angel food cake, and Darrieux was a delight—when left alone by her wildly jealous husband. He, poor tortured soul, never left the set when she was working and insisted she lunch alone with him daily in her dressing room. One day he falsely suspected her of being more cordial than necessary to "outsiders" and when lunchtime came along, he got so angry that he gave her a black eye. We were deprived of her services for several days. No wonder that on her return to France she left him. I've always hoped she was consoled by the fact that the picture turned out well and proved very popular.

Then I began my next RKO obligation, this time opposite Ginger Rogers. I had known Ginger since her first days in California during her early romance with Mervyn LeRoy. Our picture was an adaptation of a stage hit called *Having Wonderful Time* and was set in a summer camp popularly frequented by Jewish residents of the New York boroughs. Both Ginger and I were reasonably adept at imitating Brooklyn-Bronx accents as well as the local slang that went with them. Unfortunately when the picture was previewed in a number of Midwestern cities, few could understand us. RKO took a deep corporate sigh and reluctantly authorized the picture to be either remade or dubbed in our own voices with nondescript Middle American accents. The finished picture did reasonably well at the box office in this country, but abroad the public was mystified by this N'Yawk pilgrimage *(hajj)* to the Adirondacks.

An interesting note about the movie is that it marked the first screen appearance of Red Skelton. Lucille Ball was an instant hit in her small supporting part, and Eve Arden did well in a less showy role. But the big bosses at the studio were unable to appreciate Skelton's broad, slapstick style and cut his part down to the barest minimum needed to hold the slender plot together.

Ginger and I got along happily and well. In fact, she got along well with everyone (although rumor had it that after so many pictures together, she and Fred Astaire were beginning to get on each other's nerves). However, I was always on my best behavior with her because she invariably reminded me of an innocent high-spirited college kid, enthusiastic about ice cream sodas, with a vocabulary dependent on "Gosh" and "Gee-whiz."

There was never anything romantic between Ginger and me. I was deflected first because she clearly was not interested in me and second because

I was very wary of her ever-present mother. Mother and daughter were both ardent Christian Scientists, and most conversations ended with efforts to recruit me. I was also aware that Ginger was keen on someone else, but I've forgotten who it was. Still, in those days rivalry was never a condition likely to put me off. It was almost a matter of self-approval to at least attempt to score with most of the attractive girls I met. And the better known they were, the more interested I became in privately listing every one. I didn't deceive myself to the extent of thinking I was irresistible. It was more probably the reverse; I really thought so little of myself that conquering the hardest-to-get boosted my self-esteem a fair amount.

Now so many good jobs came along that my growing anxieties about the affairs of the world were nudged ever more to the side. Some of the movie columnists had begun to hint that an Academy Award nomination for my performance as Rupert in *Zenda* was in the offing. Alas, as with my last prestigious part in *Catherine the Great,* much was predicted but nothing happened.

My father seemed pleased with me. He went about telling one and all that he was the one who had persuaded me to play Rupert and was proud that I had set out to do my first swashbuckler in my own fashion and style. When he learned that Marlene and I had allowed complete independence of each other to become the latest fact of our lives and I no longer had a residential "cover" (my house for my grandparents was rented), he invited me to stay in the guest house over the garage at the beach again. I jumped at the idea, not just because it was mostly free of charge (in a rash moment I had politely insisted on paying not only for all my edibles, drinks, and phone bills but also a small token rent) but because of the cheery atmosphere with which he still invested his environs.

I remember trying to analyze my father's changing personality with a certain detachment during those days. On a superficial level I could see some of the difficult readjustments he had had to make on returning to California and a retired life at the beach house. He no longer had a large studio with a great suite of offices, a gymnasium, a Turkish bath, and a lounge-dressing room; there were no more luxuriously uncultivated foothills, gardens, panoramic views, and creature comforts of Pickfair; gone too were the private screenings of new films after dinner and a domestic staff that catered to his many whims. There was no Albert as Major Domo, and even Rocher had left very soon after Pete's marriage to Sylvia. Mary still had Zorro, the yapping, snapping wire-haired terrier, but Pete had a new dog, a huge gentle bull mastiff called Polo (for Marco—because he was such a well-traveled dog).

Now a good-sized house with a saltwater pool was no doubt fine, but it was just one of several similar houses on the Santa Monica beach front. Nevertheless the new social lifestyle with Sylvia continued, as in London and New York, to bring a large new set of guests and friends into his ken. But most of them were somehow antipathetic or had nothing in common with his old familiars. Naturally Uncle Bob and other Fairbanks company chiefs, Clarence Erickson and accountant Art Fenn, came around. A few old cronies would occasionally visit and even dine, but their visits became fewer and farther between. Pete had always been early to bed and early to rise but he now sat up late most nights with Sylvia and *her* friends, learning to play cards, mixing drinks (he still abstained), and readjusting his repertoire of jokes. He overexercised to keep his figure like a Greek god's, but the strain was sadly noticeable. In addition, he continued the habit, begun in London and New York, of every so often surprising Sylvia with extravagant jewelry, a new car (preferably a Rolls), or shares of stock. His only time away from her was on his daily round or two of golf, usually with Fred Astaire or Bing Crosby or some famous pro.

I enjoyed a separate beach life. The guest house was in the back and faced the highway, so I could just barely hear the surf but couldn't see it. One of the things I liked best was that it was now easier to see more of David Niven. He was no longer living next door with Merle (that long-running romance had apparently cooled when each discovered the other's attentions were not exclusive). Niv moved up the road a few hundred yards to share a beach house with Errol Flynn that was rented from Marion Davies. Cary Grant lived farther down the beach, in the other direction, and that was pleasant too. Larry O. spent some time in Southern California as well, making things even brighter by his easygoing presence.

Whenever Pete or Sylvia invited me to the main house, either as an extra man for a dinner party or specially to meet someone, I went to great lengths to be friendly and cordial to my new stepmother. She was indeed witty and attractive. Even though she knew I was devoted to Mary, she was always very pleasantly "correct" with me. Of course I felt a little strain because, even though I recognized her attraction and was amused by her, I still disapproved of her as my father's wife. What I resented was what I took to be her schemes to get another jewel or expensive present. I had no self-interest at stake, as it had been my pride that I'd always made my own way. It was just that Sylvia was the instrument that finally broke up my father's celebrated marriage and the mirage of that love story—and also dislodged him from the pedestal on which he stood as a universally adored figure.

For a couple of months I honestly believed I had successfully disguised my hidden feelings about her for his sake. I was sure I had behaved with convincing (if simulated) warmth, family affection, and good-natured consideration.

Consequently it was with dumb horror that I listened to Pete's oldest friend, Kenneth Davenport, explain apologetically to me one afternoon that he had come to speak to me as an "emissary" of my father's. Apparently, according to a highly embarrassed Kenneth, my father had mistaken my efforts to be friendly to Sylvia as a sly way of flirting with her. Consequently I was to move out—*at once!* I was no longer welcome! Kenneth would send someone over straight away to help me pack!

I don't believe anything that was ever said or done to me in my life before shocked me so much as Kenneth's message from my father. Billie's ultimatum had been deeply upsetting in the manner it was broken to me too but had not been totally unexpected. This one was. It was a long minute before I could say anything. Then I suppose I must have sputtered something half coherent. Now, drawing in my net of memory, I can still almost feel that sudden sharp ache in my gut, followed by a wave of nausea. When, in a moment or two, I could make some sense, I asked where my father was, could I see him, talk to him?

"No," said Kenneth, "he has walked up the beach and doesn't want to discuss it." Kenneth was sympathetic, knew how I felt and why I was always so "overcharming" to Sylvia. But he also knew from their intimate life-long friendship that one of the greatest flaws in my father's character was his extreme and unreasonable jealousy. There was just nothing to do.

I rang Niv, not intending to explain but just to ask if he and Flynn had a spare room, but no one was home. I couldn't break the lease on my house bought for my grandparents. My Uncle Bill lived in too small a house for me to share. I could, of course, have rung up one of my cousins, but as Flobe had taken a "flier" in a touring company production of *Strictly Dishonorable* and as I didn't want to admit to the younger ones what had happened, I decided to take a small room at the Beverly Hills Hotel. I was not being in the least noble, but because I thought the episode made my father out such a damn fool and I was so hurt by it, I didn't want to explain anything to anyone.

A few days later I spoke to Niv. It happened that Flynn was moving out (and in with some dishy female, we assumed), so there was room for me. I wasted no time moving in. Niv had named the house "Cirrhosis-on-Sea." We even thought of ordering writing paper with that engraved on the top. I disguised my expulsion from my father's house by explaining that he had other guests coming and I would feel more independent sharing a small house with Niven than my smallish quarters over a garage with strangers.

Hearty and bawdy practical jokers all, we once persuaded Roly Young that he should meet a "lady of considerable talent." We said she was a doctor of osteopathy and that Roly's state of health (he was overworked) indicated he could do with one of her "treatments." Quite seriously, he agreed and we invited the renowned "Doctor" Corbett down to see him. A party was in full swing when the "doctor" arrived in her white uniform with a "medical kit" full of uncommon electrical gadgets. What Roly didn't know was that the doctor was a well-known, very resourceful lady of the evening! The joke was ruined when, like so many idiotic schoolboys, we sought to spy on the two of them and Bob Benchley began to choke out loud with laughter, thus giving the game away.

We happy few thoroughly enjoyed each other's companionship for months. As for relations with my father, I made considerable efforts to disguise the resentment I felt from his latest rejection. Finally, after several awkward weeks, a relationship of sorts returned to its almost speechless normalcy.

18

I had a call to return to the producing fold of David Selznick. He asked me back to play the lead in a frothy "all-star" setup, *The Young in Heart.* It was a light comedy adapted from "The Gay Banditti," a story by I. A. R. Wylie. Dear Roly Young was in it and made me laugh so often in the middle of scenes that I was frequently responsible for delaying production. I had two wonderful leading ladies—my old friend, Janet Gaynor, and Paulette Goddard, whom I had met often with Charlie before she became Mrs. Chaplin. Billie Burke (Mrs. Flo Ziegfeld) played my mother.

The great but by now very aged Maude Adams, always as reticent and mysterious a figure as Garbo, agreed to make a secret test in the leading character part, though under an assumed name. She was absolutely marvelous, but at the last moment she lost her nerve, slid back into her desired obscurity, and returned to the East Coast. The part was eventually played by Minnie Dupree, who had been the star, with my father as her juvenile lead, in a play when they were younger. The film turned out fairly well— sprightly, civilized, and agreeable. A recent re-viewing was disappointing. It now shows its age in its nice though dated technique.

At RKO I was still under contract for one more picture, but no one knew what it would be. Pandro Berman, head of production, suggested a few duds that I politely declined. Then one day Cary Grant, a remarkable guy with an agile mind (which, *he* said, was replete with complexes) and a treasure of a friend, asked me if I wanted to play in something called *Gunga Din.* He explained that such scripted plot as existed so far had been inspired by

Rudyard Kipling's "Soldiers Three." Ben Hecht and Charlie MacArthur had written the first script, but now there was a new one by Joel Sayre. Cary added that Howard Hawks—who had given me my first big break in *The Dawn Patrol*—would probably direct and that he had engaged William Faulkner to do some rewriting. I didn't quite know how to answer, as I couldn't imagine that Cary would be so magnanimous as to suggest I play a better part than *his*. So I stalled politely and said that since no script existed yet, I'd first read whatever treatment there was before I could give an answer.

A few days later I was advised that Hawks was out of the project, George Stevens, an excellent young director, was replacing him, and a new script would be written. While I wondered if that was a good or bad rumor, I heard that Victor McLaglen was also to have a major role in the picture. That set me wondering even more about where and how I could fit in. Except for those playing Hindus, I would be the only American in our otherwise all-British cast—and furthermore I would be obliged to speak with a cockney accent. I might get away with it in the United States and Canada, but not in Britain. No one except me seemed to worry about that detail.

Cary, Pan Berman and agent Frank Vincent were all equally enthusiastic about the selection of Stevens as director. Since I knew he had had long experience with silent comedies (an invaluable background for a film that would consist of movement on a large and exciting scale), I also thought him a fine choice. When I met him a few days later, I knew at once that I would like him as much as the others—that is, if I decided to do the picture. George Stevens was quite unlike the conventional, overassertive director. He appeared always to stroll about with a lazy sailor's swagger instead of walking like other people. One's first impression was that he was vague, dreamy, and inefficient, but actually this was an effective mask behind which his creative brain ticked at the speed of light. He confided his ideas in advance only to his cameraman, his scriptwriters, his first assistant, and his principal actors. His producers were often led to believe one thing when he really had something quite different in mind. He would look at you with a sort of dopey solemnity, only to break into a broad grin a moment later and call for a can of beer. He frankly tried to make his team feel they were his trusted partners rather than hired puppets, unlike such tyrannical directors as C. B. de Mille and Fritz Lang.

A few days later, Cary called me again and said he had asked Berman to send me a new, admittedly overlong, very rough draft of the script, with various notes by Stevens scribbled on the margins. This one had been written by Joel Sayre, who had been reworking still another by Fred Guiol. Cary, enthusiastic as ever, was at pains to assure me that if I joined the cast, everyone would be thrilled. As soon as it arrived, I read it. I could see at once what a boisterous, exciting, and funny picture it *could* be. Now I readily agreed that McLaglen would be ideal as the tough, experienced sergeant in the British Indian Army of the 1890s, but I still had no clue as to which of the other two younger sergeants Cary would play and which I would play. They were about equal in importance. One was the romantic who, after numerous exciting adventures, falls in love and gets the girl. This would be Joan Fontaine's first role as a leading lady. The other sergeant was his mate, an engagingly brave, funny young cockney. These two, with the older one, shared the adventures fairly equally.

When I asked Cary which part he intended to play, he answered, "Whichever one you don't want! I want us to be together in this so badly—I think the two of us, plus old McLaglen as our top sergeant, McChesny, will make this picture more than just another big special."

I have never so much as *heard* of another actor (usually considered a congenitally selfish breed) who proposed to a contemporary colleague, in some ways a rival, so unselfish a proposal. I later came to learn that such gestures were typical of Cary. He had always been most concerned with being involved in what he guessed would be a successful picture. If he proved right, he reckoned it could only rebound to his credit. I took this as a fine lesson. Even though I was more of a movie veteran than he, I had plenty more to learn. Since then, whenever possible, I've tried to apply Cary's lesson to my own decisions. We finally settled the matter by tossing a coin! That was how I became "Sergeant Ballantyne," who wants to leave the Army for Miss Fontaine, and Cary became the ebullient, funny cockney "Sergeant Cutter." Until he died, Grant and I always addressed each other as Cutter and Ballantyne—from that film of 1938!

It turned out to be a fine cast and company all around. Chief among them was Sam Jaffe, a splendid serious actor who played the title role. Another first-class addition to the cast was a close friend of all, English comedian Bob Coote, as still another sergeant, the "silly ass" one. Other important contributors to our team were Eduardo Ciannelli, the chief Hindu villain; Abner Biberman, another evil character; and old Monty Love, the colonel of our regiment.

We spent many weeks in the California desert at Lone Pine, several hours' drive from Los Angeles, close to the base of the Sierra Nevada Mountains. According to the technical directors, the setting was much like India's Northwest Frontier. It took at least a month to build a tent city for hun-

dreds of us to live in. The director, principal actors, first cameraman (the
award-winning Joe August), writer Joel Sayre, and senior technicians either
had tents of their own or shared with one another. Every day we worked in
temperatures that sometimes rose to 110° in the shade. George, Bob Coote,
Cary, Joel Sayre, and I would sit up after dinner telling stories, discussing
politics, and arguing about and/or rewriting scenes to be done the next day.
These sessions were usually enlivened by a few drinks to warm up the
chatteringly chill desert night air that followed the blistering hot days.
Drinking was clearly against regulations except for the weak beer (of which
George downed several cans a day) on sale in the commissary tent. However, we kept our smuggled booze well hidden, and I've little doubt that
many of our several hundred-strong company were doing the same and
being extra careful about it.

Cary, Bob, Vic, and I always tried to be careful with our language and
manners when Joan Fontaine was near. After all, we agreed, this was her
first important role, and she was a newcomer to both America and films. We
had many miserable daytime hours when the hot desert winds would blow
such volumes of sand and dust as to make filming temporarily impossible
and cause Joanie to suffer recurrences of severe sinus headaches and flood-
ing eyes. We all sweated like stevedores, drank gallons of bottled water, and
gulped daily rations of salt pills. Costumes were binding and hot and even
worse for the women, who had to have their makeup patched every few
minutes so they would look cool and comfortable for their scenes.

Apart from these discomforts, Joan's general manner was so shy and
maidenly that we all became models of chivalrous behavior in her presence.
It was only many years later that she confessed, and indeed recorded in her
autobiography, that while we were being so very proper and protective, she
was having an intense affair with George. In fact, when we boys had got
weary of talking and joking, had decided on the details of the next day's
shooting, and had taken ourselves back to our own tents for some sleep,
Joan would creep into George's place—or vice-versa!

In one of the picture's spectacular climactic action sequences, we three
sergeants are seen standing behind a set representing the battlements of an
old fort, trying to hold off the attack of hundreds of maddened Thugs until
we are rescued just in time by units of Scottish Highlanders and the Bengal
Lancers. (In her review of the picture, the often befuddled Louella Parsons
stated that the heroes were saved by the "Scottish Lancers" and "Bengal
Highlanders"!)

The day the scene was actually shot was even hotter than usual. The
timing of the movements of several hundreds of extras, as well as the dozen

cameras shooting from different angles with different types of lenses, took several hours of rehearsal to perfect. Our thirst was quenched by many beers, brought up to us by the prop man. Finally, Stevens announced over his mike that all was set and the scene must be shot then or the right degree of light would be gone for the day. Vic, by now tight as a tick with all inhibitions melted away, decided that as the beer had gone through him too quickly and none of us could leave our positions high up in this tower, there was no alternative to lessen his intense discomfort but to unbutton his uniform and relieve himself *during the scene!* Cary and I didn't know whether to laugh or be furious. Stevens, not knowing of our "martyrdom," later congratulated us on the spirit of furious defiance we had shown in the scene —which he could discern even from a distance.

Although we were deeper into production every day and far away on location, the terms of my contract had still not been agreed upon. Poor Frank Vincent, as agent for both Cary and me, was on an inescapable spot trying to serve both our interests equally. A big, unresolved question was whose name went where. Our salaries were never an issue. I don't know exactly how much I finally received because we went so far beyond schedule that the original guarantee no longer applied. Arguments for our getting percentages got nowhere, but I can roughly guess I made something more than $75,000. Cary, I'm sure, received more because while I had been abroad, he had had a steady stream of well-paid successes. Furthermore his bargaining position was improved because he had been chosen for the picture when it was still only an idea. Indeed it was likely that the whole package began at least partly as his idea.

Vincent's and Berman's problem of my billing was made more difficult because both Cary and I were technically classified as stars and, in the eyes of the public, virtually equal in status. The problem was further complicated by the fact that Vic McLaglen had already signed *his* contract, which called for "star billing"—i.e., his name was also to appear above the title in letters no smaller than anyone else's. Eventually I proposed something similar to the billing resolution we came to in *Zenda*. Since Cary unquestionably deserved the top position, I preferred to be featured separately at the bottom. Being deliberately last in a long list of cast names was, of course, an old trick used by my father, whose professional shrewdness was often mistaken for modesty.

After several hard slow weeks on location, Berman and his RKO colleagues nearly canceled further filming on *Gunga Din* because of its great cost. In addition, we were falling more frighteningly behind schedule each day. There were loud arguments and threats of a walkout by George (in which we supported him), but they fizzled out like damp skyrockets. Somehow we did manage to prevail. George had persuaded the company manager who represented RKO's front office that there had been a breakdown in communications and earlier warnings from studio heads had never been received.

The growing threat of war in Europe was being reported daily on every front page. The Roosevelt administration sympathized with our old allies but had established a policy of strict neutrality. Without more strength of their own and outspoken support from us, the British and French felt obliged to back down whenever Hitler screeched his new demands. It was during one of these retreats that *Gunga Din* finally opened in February 1939 at Radio City Music Hall in Manhattan. The picture's theme glorified the British "Tommy" fighting courageously against heavy odds. Despite the record-breaking crowds and the wonderful reviews, many cynical New Yorkers greeted our Kiplingesque virtues and heroics with embarrassing guffaws and loud sneers. As a result, RKO admitted to some anxiety about the overall potential of the film once it went into general release. Fortunately, the mockery was limited to famously iconoclastic New York. Even there it broke every record at Radio City Music Hall. Once the film opened elsewhere—even in the isolationist Midwest—what was originally intended as a big, exciting yarn with an exotic background became not only an enormous hit but also an effective boost for goodwill toward the British at that uncertain time in international affairs.

The picture and all of us connected with it—Stevens, Cary, Vic, Sam, and I—got marvelous reviews. It was, after all, very like a Western epic, only with good and bad *East* Indians instead of American "redskins." A small, courageous band of British Tommies was the counterpart of a gang of cowpunchers. Finally, the loyal and devoted Hindu, Gunga Din himself, was like a friendly Navajo, trying to keep the peace against a sect of religious fanatics.

Although the romantic character I played became, over the years, one of the public's three or four favorite and best-remembered of my roles, I cringed whenever anyone compared my quite routine stunts in the picture with my father's improbable athletic fantasies (he hated having them called "acrobatics"). In *Gunga Din* I probably did have a little more fist fighting and jumping about (from rooftop to rooftop and other odd places) than in other films, but reports that *Zenda* and now *Gunga Din* marked my entry into the movie swashbuckling fraternity were highly exaggerated. Nevertheless my acquisition of two broken fingers, a cracked rib, a bad twist of my already torn knee cartilege, and three knife scars in the line of duty in

Gunga Din were matters of pride. Had my parents given me another name, the inevitably odious comparisons would be as minimal as they had been for, say, Power and Flynn when they first began to make romantic costume-action pictures.

Actually I was trying to prove to others that I could play *any* kind of part in my age bracket: comedy, drama, melodrama, character or straight heroics, classical drama or farce. In fact I did all my own stunts reasonably well —after a lot of practice and several takes—and with hidden mattresses to fall on.

I was repeatedly advised that the public preferred stars to be "typed"— that professional versatility was for character actors and that I should concentrate on an always recognizable set of mannerisms in the same way that Gary Cooper, Jimmy Stewart, Clark Gable, and Jimmy Cagney did. Even the older generation—such actors as Ronald Colman, William Powell, Eddie Robinson, and the Barrymores—cultivated and exploited readily imitable mannerisms. But I preferred variety—whether it was good business or not. My greatest weakness has always been my subconscious tendency to replace originality with mimicry. If stumped for a way to do a certain scene, I would, without thinking, fall back on a vague imitation of, say, Barrymore or Colman.

I had no great hankering to be a personality like my father. Nor was I equipped to be one. I was determined to develop my potential in other ways. If my father exemplified the eternally vigorous model hero-of-heroes, I would be, if not a classic actor, then a versatile one. My father was a fine actor when he chose to be, but he preferred to project the personality that made him popular, and that was not conventional acting.

I was occasionally inspired by memories of Leslie Howard's references to acting as "a silly business for a man to be in . . . All that pretending, all that paint and posing and lights, all that buttering up to producers for jobs and the press to help persuade the public to want to see you at work! Ugh!!"

I actually never felt quite that strongly, but I don't suppose Leslie really did either.

The good serious working actor is much like an accomplished musician in an orchestra—e.g., a leading man's opposite number might be the concertmaster. A star would be a soloist. The conductor would be the director and the composer the playwright. But sometimes the whole business of entertainment, however good, seemed a trivial pursuit when compared to the grim realities from which we all sought escape. Now each day when I read the papers or spoke to someone in the know, I became more anxious to participate in at least some part of real—as opposed to fictional life.

As my interest in government, business, and world affairs grew, I received my first taste of public mocking for my naïveté and for "stepping out of line." Some of the press noted for the first time that I "consorted with" such members of the literary establishment as Bob Sherwood. In addition to playwriting, Bob was now acting as adviser and speechwriter to President Roosevelt, joining cronies like Harry Hopkins in evening sessions at the White House or weekends at the Roosevelt country estate, Hyde Park. And there was Herbert Swope, the former publisher of the New York *World,* whose nightly "gab sessions" in his Park Avenue apartment or Long Island home engendered some of the most stimulating talk on the East Coast. I "elbowed" my way among an increasing number of interested and interesting folk from many spheres.

I felt increasingly concerned about the world we were living in. We still had a Great Depression—although the New Deal disguised much of it and the fury of the dispossessed had abated. We who were the most exercised about the state of the globe were preparing to do what many theatrical professionals were always warned against—i.e., declaring ourselves informed and thoughtful citizens with the same rights to opinions as anybody else. It was thought by our employers that actors could ill afford to offend anyone—or, specifically, to be publicly identified with any controversial or partisan issue. Nevertheless, as the news grew more worrisome each month, I decided to use my celebrity value as wisely and selectively as I could in order to persuade others to share my growing anxieties. I would also try to be responsible and research my subjects thoroughly.

But I'm getting ahead of myself. It was still just past the middle of 1938 and *Gunga Din* was yet to be generally released. Inasmuch as my next picture was uncertain, I arranged to take off once again for New York and London. It was to be a fairly brief business trip—mixed, I hoped, with some pleasure. Since the end of my personal road with Marlene, I frankly missed the fun and distraction of a romance in my life, of being "attached" to someone.

I was not really the man to fall seriously for just any pretty young "ship that passed in the night," and so my overpoetic imagination kept returning to a serious but long-hidden—and, therefore, frustrating—romance with a beautiful but very married older (again) lady who lived in London. (I shall call her—just to be appropriately old-fashioned—Mme. Y.) Even in the midst of my more publicized relationships of the past, this particular lady always remained in my romantic consciousness. We had few opportunities ever to meet alone, but when we did these were moments of high romantic beauty. It was made more difficult for both of us that her husband and I had long been good friends. My Protestant ethic conscience disturbed me, but not enough to resist her or back away from the situation. I knew there was no realistic solution for us without causing great distress to others—and neither of us wanted to be responsible for anything like that. Both of us, I suppose, could be considered sophisticated, but we were not cynical. We fully realized that this situation was destined for, at best, a rueful end. Nevertheless, I had every expectation of "making contact" with my remote love during my few weeks in London.

But first there was the stop in New York, and there of course were the Whitings, now a long time back from their last London stay and anxious for a reunion.

Having completed six pictures in the past year or so, I decided I would not worry about money. Mother remained as extravagant as ever and, since Jack was out of work, needed another loan. Most of my family automatically assumed that I had such huge steady earnings that none of these "loans" would ever be noticed. To tell the truth, I was never terribly interested in money per se and always preferred to share as much as I could. I hated talking about it afterward. This attitude meant, of course, that I was usually either in debt or else just barely ahead of the game. But on *this* trip, *this* time, I thought I'd splurge a bit on myself as well.

My newest luxury was the great Emile, Pete's former valet/butler/secretary, who was Rocher's replacement. He offered his services to me after I'd left the new Fairbanks Senior household. Of course I couldn't pay him the wages he had been receiving from my father, but that didn't deter him. He wanted to retain his link with the family. He liked me and thought my life less demanding and more fun than my father's, so I now had my own Swiss equivalent of Jeeves.

One of the season's best musicals was *I Married an Angel,* by Dick Rodgers and Larry Hart. Its cast included Dennis King, Vivienne Segal, Walter Slezak, *and* the lovely ballerina, Vera Zorina, who had been so wonderful with Jack in *On Your Toes* in London. *I Married an Angel* had been directed by Josh Logan and the choreography was by George Balanchine, recently arrived from the Ballet Russe de Monte Carlo. Within a decade he would be recognized as a genius.

After renewing our acquaintanceship and attending *I Married an Angel,* numerous times, I fell all over again for Vera Zorina (more informally known as Brigitta Hartwig) in New York. And for a change I hitched my wagon to a girl who was several years younger than I! I hung around backstage almost nightly—a typical "stage-door Johnny"—quite careless that I was making a fool of myself. Gradually, I won a measure of regard from her and even from her hovering mother, who indicated with special Scandinavian wariness that perhaps she "might approve" of her daughter looking with favor on me. Fortunately my mother and Brigitta's were good friends. That helped a lot.

Once again, I was floating on the cloud that sustains young passions, but once again I failed to recognize it as a cloud I had been on before. Nevertheless I wouldn't have cared as it was so lovely.

Meanwhile, I had not in the least forgotten—and never would—my more serious secret love abroad.

Oh what a season Broadway was having this late summer of 1938! In addition to *I Married an Angel,* the luscious Lunts sweetened the year with two plays, Chekhov's *The Sea Gull,* and Giraudoux's *Amphytrion 38.* Ray Massey starred in Sherwood's *Abe Lincoln in Illinois;* there was Wilder's *Our Town, Hellzapoppin',* glorious Mary Martin's Broadway debut in *Leave It to Me* singing "My Heart Belongs to Daddy" and beloved Walter Huston in *Knickerbocker Holiday* singing Maxwell Anderson's and Kurt Weill's "September Song" (I still try to sing it myself at the drop of a reason).

On the nontheatrical front, I was in touch with Walter Wanger, one of Hollywood's few well-read and politically informed producers. He had been an aide to President Wilson at the Versailles Conference after World War I. As much as opportunity allowed I cultivated my acquaintanceship with Walter Lippmann, whose syndicated views were among those I followed most diligently.

I suppose that none of those whose brains I picked like rich fruits experienced more than a surprise *en passant* at meeting a twenty-eight-year-old actor who had traveled fairly extensively, seemed to listen to his betters and to have absorbed more than they might have expected. I was making progress in the business of informing myself about the imminent dangers from abroad to our kind of life.

I was told that Herbert Bayard Swope wanted to see me before I left New York. He wanted me to take his "very private" letter and deliver it by hand to Winston Churchill—then a very independent Conservative member of Parliament with but one supporter—Brendan Bracken. I didn't know Churchill personally, though he had once been my father's guest in Beverly Hills, but I had known his son Randolph slightly, and I'd met one or two of his four daughters. No matter, said Herbert. He knew I'd get it to him somehow. I have no idea why I suspected that the envelope given me contained *another* note—one from President Roosevelt, but I did. I never was able to find out whether my guess was right or wrong. It was probably my customary dramatic imagination.

I had been having such a stimulating time, even over and above my heady involvement with my lovely ballerina, that I was no longer so keen to get over to Europe. But I really did have business to do there, if only for a few weeks.

I was given a most *gemütlich* send-off. On the day of my departure, Mother, Jack, and others, including Genie Chester, Brigitta, and her mother, came down to the Cunard–White Star docks to see me off. There was all the same old wonderful sailing excitement I now miss so much: baggage being bustled up and down from one deck to another, the faint shipboard smell of linoleum-lined corridors, confetti, tears, cheers, and cameras snapping away.

Suddenly Brigitta asked in a whisper if we couldn't go into a nearby empty cabin for a private word before I sailed. I immediately assumed she wanted a farewell embrace. My open delight at her suggestion must have been clear for all to see. I pulled her joyfully and possessively through the door, but I immediately sensed a gentle resistance and saw a solemn face. I blurted out, "What is it? Are you all right?"

"I'm so terribly sorry—so . . . terribly . . . sorry . . . but . . ." She looked down at her right hand and slipped off the unimpressive but pretty little ring I'd given her a while back when I thought our romance was in balance. "I've tried to have things turn out differently, but they couldn't." She spoke slowly in her very slight Germanic accent. "I'm going to marry someone else!"

"Who?"

"George," she answered, simply. "George Balanchine!"

In the best tradition of nature catching up with art, our brief little scene was interrupted at that very instant by repeated gongs, loud whistles, and shouts of the stewards, *"All ashore wot's goin' ashore! All ashore, please! ALL ASHORE!"*

We both returned to my good-bye party with, I must presume, wan, unconvincing smiles. I hastily embraced everyone and herded them all out to the gangway where they disembarked. There was so much noise and bluster. More confetti. More tooting. More bells. On the pier's end, Mother and the others waved and blew kisses until we were well away. We glided down past the fairy tale sight of Lower Manhattan and out to sea. Of course my pride was bruised, but I really wasn't so distressed as I felt I should be. I wanted to wallow a bit more in the pain of unrequited love and, as a well-tutored devotee of the double standard, my misplaced faith in women. But after a breath of fresh sea air on the top deck, the look of the harbor, and a double sherry flip at the bar, I allowed the suspicion to creep up under my despondence that I was not nearly as upset as the circumstances required.

Next day I passed a few hours composing an understanding letter that I mailed to the beauteous Zorina on arrival. It must have worked because I received a heavenly and much more realistic letter from her—long since "dramatically" destroyed by me. Eventually we established a friendship that stood firm from then on. And anyway was much more fun.

19

As far as my business affairs were concerned, I found that Criterion films had done only fairly well in the European market—*The Amateur Gentleman* had done best. Neither *Zenda* nor *Gunga Din* had yet been shown in Europe because of some confusing copyright dispute. Still, United Artists and RKO organized press interviews so I at least helped prepare the way for both of these pictures whenever—or *if* ever—they should appear.

I usually found it difficult to find a female secretary who was not only reasonably cheerful and agreeable to look at and work with, but who had a talent for anticipating me, who was very quick in her work and as seemingly indefatigable as most people thought me to be. Louis Blembel had been a fairly acceptable but too serious stopgap. Allen Vincent was such a good friend that it was difficult to overwork him as I was unintentionally apt to do. But now in London I had fortunately found a pretty, happily married, tiny dynamo of a secretary, Mrs. Pat Cherry. With typical efficiency she arranged my every day.

Only one sad shock needed to be delicately broken to me on my arrival. My adored little Scottie that I'd left behind had been blown off my rooftop in a high wind and killed. Otherwise everything was fine, including the weather. Due to the efficiency of the RKO and UA publicity departments, my return was duly reported, and friends and acquaintances all but swamped me.

Between my crowded business hours, I saw the Mountbattens at Adsdean in the country with their young nephew, then known as Prince Philip of

Greece. I saw them also at a dinner party in their huge new Brook House flat with "the fastest lift in London" and walls newly painted with nautical allegories, ships, and charts by the marvelous Rex Whistler. I also attended some posh cocktail parties given by old Sybil Colefax, Chips, and other Mayfair party-givers of the thirties. I spent a couple of weekends with the Kents at Coppins, another lovely time with all the Wards and Bensons, had dinner with Winifred (Clemence Dane), Noël, and Ivor. It was all great.

One night Dickie and Con Benson included me in a theater party of six or eight. After the play we all went to supper at the Savoy Grill. We'd been there awhile when I spied an older couple entering who were escorted to the back of the Grill. I turned to Con Benson and asked, "Wasn't that Winston Churchill?"

"Yes," said Con, "Why?"

"I have a message and a note for him from a friend in the States. What kind of a fellow is he? Dare I write a note and introduce myself?"

Con laughed. "Oh, he's very easy! Quite a character in fact—but a sad one. Over the years he's had practically every job there is in the Cabinet and made a flop of each one. Now he's getting old. He's switched his political party twice, but he's in Parliament still. He makes amusing speeches as one half of a 'party of two'—he and a chap called Brendan Bracken." Con smiled in a mixture of amusement and pity, and continued, "Keeps warning everyone about Hitler and war, and he's won over quite a few new men like Anthony Eden. But though he's witty, he's washed up. Few would trust him nowadays, poor fellow. He also used to write rousing adventure books, but nowadays he's so down on his luck that your friend Korda felt sorry for him and commissioned him to write a script that he'll never film about the great Duke of Marlborough—one of his ancestors. His father was a brilliant M.P. married to an American. Winston is brilliant too, no doubt, but he has just missed everything. Life has passed him by." Con then brightened, gave my arm a gentle shove, and said, "But do go over and speak to him. He'd love it. He's one of our last eccentrics!"

So I took a chance and sent over a note of introduction to which Mr. Churchill immediately replied by inviting me to his table for a drink. I went over, shook hands with both Churchill and his wife, and explained that I was acting as "confidential postman" for Herbert Swope. Mr. Churchill mumbled affection for Herbert and gave instructions about where to bring the envelope next day. He then began a long and amusing monologue that touched on a dozen now forgotten subjects. I do remember, though, that he was fascinating—and Mrs. Churchill was charming. He would have gone on and on had I not felt it tactful to return to my hosts, the Bensons. I thanked

him, bade them both good night, and thought to myself what a shame that
this brilliant old guy had missed the bus with every chance he'd had. I now
agreed he seemed too old and politically "done for," with hardly any useful
future in sight. Even so, I was immensely glad to have met him.

Later I had reason to check the date. It was just ten months before World
War II began in England.

American Ambassador Robert Bingham's son and daughter were friends
through whom I got further impressions of how deeply divided Britain was
concerning the prospects of war. The new Chamberlain administration
seemed smugly certain that Hitler would eventually listen to reason. They
seemed sure "he wouldn't dare" attack the impregnable French or the immense Royal Navy or, by jingo, the British Empire. Opposing these views
strongly were Churchill and a tiny group of articulate supporters led by
Anthony Eden, who had resigned the foreign secretary-ship to protest the
policy of appeasement. He had begun to make a dent in the stubborn com-
placency and self-deception of the mass of British people, who were still
understandably more concerned with domestic socioeconomic problems
than with the possibility of another war only twenty years after the last in
which they lost a million young men, sometimes at the rate of ten thousand
a day! How, they reasoned, could the Germans or Russians, who had suffered even greater losses, be seriously planning to go through it all again?

Though I was astonished by the official Anglo-French devotees and their
"peace at any price" policy, their complete disbelief in the horror stories
coming from inside the Axis borders and their dismissal of a Japanese
threat, I nonetheless managed to remain discreet. After all, I was an American whose own national policy was, I felt, even more self-deceiving than
Western Europe's, but considering our vast distance from the fighting cock-
pits of Europe and Asia, perhaps understandably so.

Romantically, I managed, by lots of hook and a fair amount of crook, to
see my "Mme. Y." a few times. All sorts of surreptitious and complicated
plots were devised for our too occasional trysts—from her confidante's
Mayfair flat at odd hours, to accidentally-on-purpose meetings in the dark
"400," where our "signature songs" that I still remember so very well (such
Astaire-Rogers hits as "A Fine Romance" and "Change Partners") were
often played.

Mostly we would meet at a dinner party or in some other frustratingly
impersonal milieu. Whenever possible, we carefully exchanged notes during
a natural (we hoped) smiling handshake, or else we went for long strolls at
someone's weekend country house party. Small "thoughtful gifts" were ex-

changed via the same trusted mutual friend whose small flat occasionally served as a "safe" meeting place.

Beginning as an occasional flirtation, because we were both so happily congenial, I began squiring Dorothy Fell, a very attractive American woman. As things turned out, it also served in a cynical way, as a cover for my clandestine attachment. Dorothy's brother, Johnny, was a golfing friend I'd known originally through my newspaper pal, McClain, in New York. Dorothy was a lovely-looking blonde and fun to be with. If my deepest heart was mutely tucked away, my more open self reacted joyfully with Dorothy. Although I put in full working days, we spent so many late hours together that her starchy English aunt, Lady Granard, finally forbade her to go out with me unless I could bring her home by eleven P.M. (three or four A.M. was considered much too late!). We eased that restriction somewhat by first returning obediently at ten and waiting for the old lady to go to bed. After that, Dorothy would redress, sneak out quietly, and meet me under the gas lamp—still retained in the old section of Westminister. Nearby, Big Ben went "bonging" away through the night as off we'd go to the "400" again.

There came a time when I thought she was such fun, so pretty and companionable, that I blithely proposed to her. She said it *might* be a good idea—later. First she had to cope with her family—on *both* sides of the ocean. I couldn't avoid the caddish notion that my becoming formally engaged would divert any possible glimmer of suspicion about my illicit *affaire*.

Divorce was, of course, frowned on then by Catholic and most Protestant churches, and it was also anathema in high international social circles. My "Mme. Y." never allowed divorce or remarriage to cross her mind. As a matter of fact, neither did I. Not only had I come to dread scandal, but I knew that domesticity with an older foreign woman would be unlikely to last. The romance and adventure of the situation as it was proved quite enough to handle and, in spite of tensions, delightful. Anything more would have been unrealistic.

So Dorothy and I continued to have fun until she had to precede me back to the States. We bade each other a fond and cheery farewell, and the "engagement"—indeed the whole situation—just fizzled out. I'm glad to say we did remain friends. A few years later, she married Howell Van Gerbig. Poor dear, she died tragically before she was thirty but only after having had two sons, one of whom grew up to become my *son-in-law!*

My European sojourn had been fascinating, fun, dramatic, and, at last, frightening. It all came to an end most unexpectedly. One morning I received a message that Mme. Y.'s husband, who was—damn it—my friend, was going away for a few days of grouse shooting in Scotland. I thought this a wonderful opportunity to make some less strained, more relaxed plans to meet my love—somewhere. I therefore wrote her a very brief but affection-ate love note, asking her to suggest a specific time and place to meet. The envelope was marked "Personal" on the outside. I took the trusty Emile with me in a taxi to her house. Ordering the taxi to pull up on the opposite side of the street, I asked Emile to deliver the letter to whoever answered the door. If he was asked by a butler or maid whom the letter was from, he was to say a "Mrs. Somebody" (I've forgotten who!) and insist that the note, being important, be delivered immediately.

I watched from inside the taxi as Emile followed instructions exactly. He rang. The front door opened. A tall liveried footman took the note amiably enough, closed the door, and Emile crossed the street and re-entered the taxi. We drove away. But the lady—my own "Dark Lady of the Sonnets"—*never received the note!* She had been at the theater earlier, but on her return the footman did not mention that any note had been delivered! And I did not hear from her. I rang up our *confidante,* who then rang Mme. Y.

Panic ensued. Searches were made in every room, beneath every cushion, in every corner. It was a comfortable-sized townhouse served by a small domestic staff. Everyone in the house was questioned—in, I was assured, a very calm manner. No one admitted knowing anything! The footman denied having seen Emile. The staff said the house had been absolutely quiet, and neither doorbell nor knock had been heard.

We thought the footman, out of curiosity, must have opened the envelope and, seeing the makings of a scandal in its contents, decided to keep it hidden while deciding what to do next. When Mme. Y.'s husband returned from Scotland a few frantic days later, contrary to his original plan, he failed to ring me up. This made both Mme. Y. and me even more certain that he had been shown the note. She reported that he had said nothing out of the ordinary to her but that his manner had been unusually cold and formal.

Her confidante and I were both becoming quite terrified by what might become a serious family-destroying public scandal. But what was to be done about it? I decided the best thing I could do was get the hell out of the country as quickly as possible. The better part of valor may very well be discretion, but saving one's skin makes a lot of sense too.

I took the least expensive inside stateroom available on the *Queen Mary.* While Emile busied himself with packing and Pat Cherry settled outstand-ing bills, I phoned around to tell friends and business associates that I had received a cable from Hollywood ordering me back at once for retakes.

We never did find out what happened to the note. Either the footman decided to keep it for future blackmail or he gave it to the lady's husband, who decided to say nothing. Since my name was not on it, he may never have known who wrote it.

Once the ship was standing well out to sea and the last signs of Europe were left behind, I began to relax. To my immense pleasure I found that among my fellow passengers was the handsome and popular ex-foreign minister of His Majesty's government, Anthony Eden. He was accompanied by Ronald Tree, a Conservative member of Parliament who was Eden's parliamentary private secretary (more accurately, assistant). Another of Eden's traveling companions and parliamentary advisers was "Hinch" (Viscount) Hinchingbrooke, the heir to the Earl of Sandwich—a name I had not before believed to be real!

The purpose of Eden's trip—his first to the United States—was to address the American Manufacturers' Association. It would also be his first public speech since his famous resignation from the British Government.

In the evening I ventured to take Lady (Daphne) Straight, the wife of American-born Whitney Straight (Jock Whitney's first cousin) for a few whirls on the dance floor. Daphne was delicious company and a fine dancer (she had once studied ballet). She was on her way to visit her Yankee in-laws.

One day, with Daphne's encouragement, I mustered enough courage to ask Eden (by now we called each other "Anthony" and "Doug") if I might look at the speech they were all helping him to write. To my surprise they agreed it would be a "capital idea." I took the speech to my room that night, and the next day I brought it back all marked up with suggestions and comments written between the lines and up and down the margins. It was terrible nerve on my part, but Anthony was then such a popular political hero among anti-Nazi groups in the U.S., because of his stand against the dictators that I wanted my country to get the best possible impression of him and his views. I was naturally overjoyed that more than half my suggestions were later incorporated in the speech. I felt very proud of myself and my growing knowledge of foreign affairs.

The sea voyage, plus the diversity of charm and interest to be had in the company of tall, quiet Anthony, his wife Beatrice, and the others, did much to unwind my guilty nerves. By the time we passed the Ambrose Lightship and made our first landfall, I was still upset by the damage my overardent devotion in London might have caused, but my hypocritical conscience was subsiding little by little with each mile we got closer to home. I had been sleeping more soundly, and after five and a half days at sea my insides were returning to normal.

Outside New York harbor, the press came aboard as usual with the harbor pilot. Anthony Eden was the big news of the day. He was mobbed by reporters and photographers, even though he was protected somewhat by the ship's crew, New York City and British consular officials, and police. He handled them all with the easy charm for which he was famous. Before we went our separate ways, he asked if some night I would take Beatrice up to Harlem and show her the sights. She was a fan of American jazz and had longed to visit some of the places she had heard so much about, such as the Cotton Club, to hear Duke Ellington, Cab Calloway, or Ethel Waters, or to see the Nicholas Brothers dance. She had heard of them all. Because Anthony was in the United States on business, giving a serious message on world affairs, it would not do for him to be seen cavorting in the bright lights or nightclubs of New York. However, no one would recognize Beatrice, and if we were spotted I was to make absolutely certain she was not photographed. During these politically tense times, such a picture would be much criticized if published back in Britain.

When the night came to take Beatrice on our tour of the Great White Way and Harlem, I included some New York friends to help distract any possible notice of or queries about Beatrice. But, damn it all, the moment our party of five or six entered the Cotton Club, two or three press cameras flashed away at us. To make it worse, one of the reporters asked, "How do you like New York, Mrs. Eden?" Beatrice was taken aback and stammered politely while I wondered what on earth I could do now. Finally I decided that straight-from-the-shoulder honesty (even though I was out of practice) might help. It certainly couldn't make things worse. So I went up to the reporters, took them aside, and said in effect, "Look, fellas. You're right! This *is* Mrs. Anthony Eden, and she's never been in New York before. My friends and I have been asked to show her the town. But *Mr.* Eden is making a very important speech tonight—his first ever in the States. As you know, he has risked his career by resigning from the British Government to protest their continued appeasement of Hitler. His political enemies would just love to sneer at his wife playing in New York while all hell is apt to break loose over there. *Please,* if any of you have relatives in Germany—or England, or France, or anywhere in Europe—*please* pull those pictures. Please don't print them or say *anything!*"

And by heavens, not one of that bunch of pressmen said or reported a word! The film was exposed and thrown away, and nothing ever appeared in the papers. I had never before known a band of tough reporters to be so considerate. It was a fine demonstration of good-heartedness and political sympathy.

Meanwhile, Anthony's speech was so very moving that it was cheered to the echo and made all the front pages across the country the next day.

New York, for numberless reasons, had never looked better. The only thing to spoil my homecoming occurred just after our ship had docked. The U.S. Customs Inspector came to my bits and pieces under the "F" section, recognized me with a deprecatory sniff and a "Huh! Another movie star, eh? Well, open up everything! Let's see what *you're* trying to get away with!"

I had nothing that I considered in any way out of the ordinary—I had declared two new suits, a half dozen shirts and ties, and two pairs of Maxwell shoes. I smiled with as much professional charm as I could muster while remaining irritated as hell inside, and said, "Go ahead and take a look!"

Grumpily he went through my one trunk and the two suitcases that Emile opened for him. On top of the clothes he saw a large folder tied with a string and picked it up. It contained a gift, a set of about a dozen wonderful and only somewhat erotic pen-and-ink prints by Aubrey Beardsley. "Ah!" grumped my officious official. "Pornography, eh?!"

I was staggered and indignant. "Certainly not!" I barked back. "These are rare and expensive prints by a great artist, Aubrey Beardsley, given to me as a present!"

The gruff voice of authority spoke as from some Brooklyn Mount Olympus: "Look, sonny boy! *I* say they're pornography, and if you want to sue Uncle Sam for the return of your dirty pictures, I'll keep 'em locked up until the case comes to court. If not, then *I'll* get rid of 'em!"

I did not fancy making a front-page issue, even over such rare prints. I shrugged and held my temper. Uncle Sam's dockside not-so-civil servant then took my flat black case containing the half dozen prints and chucked them in the Hudson River.

My trip west took on a more boisterous air than usual. Two old golfing partners from London were aboard the train by coincidence. Hijinks of some sort were clearly in order. Bobby Sweeney, a transplanted American, was devastatingly handsome, the conqueror of far too many attractive females on three continents—*and* the British Open Golf Champion besides. Bobby drank just enough to enhance his reputation as a young *bon vivant.* His only other diversions were Backgammon, the bar at White's, and golf. (He had once had a fine "walkout" with my stepmother Sylvia.)

My other companion, Johnny de Forrest, was really an Englishman whose very rich father adamantly opposed paying taxes to any government. Thus he and his family were obliged to become citizens of Liechtenstein or be disinherited! The old man got the idea from Benjie Guinness, who with the introduction of income taxes became a Swiss national and stipulated in his will that none of his family would be left even a penny if they paid any income tax to anyone on their inheritance.

We three—Bobby, Johnny, and I—were delighted at the prospect of a raucous transcontinental trip aboard the Santa Fe Super Chief. Bobby and I indulged our idiocy at Johnny's expense. Our main prank was to confide in whispers to the head waiter in the dining car that Johnny had just been released from a mental home, that I was a family friend and Bobby was his paid guardian. Furthermore, we insisted we had to make sure that the one thing he never touched under any circumstances was red meat, regardless of what it was or how well cooked.

When it came time for Bobby and me to order, we invariably asked for steak, beef, liver, bacon, or some sort of red meat. Johnny would then do the same. But when Bobby and I got our order, the waiter would serve Johnny fish or chicken or an omelette—*anything* except what he'd ordered. Johnny was a high-strung fellow anyway, but this cool refusal to serve him his order of meat (without explanation), while still supplying Bobby and me with great hunks of it, drove Johnny into a furious temper. When the head waiter tried his best to calm him with great charm and politely vague excuses, Johnny got even angrier, thus confirming our warning that he *might* have to be put into a straitjacket before he got really violent. We finally gave up this charade after two days. Johnny was very nearly becoming all we said he was!

Soon after we arrived in Los Angeles, Johnny received a cable from his father ordering him to stop being a playboy and to enter *some* golf tournament—*any* tournament would do—anything rather than idleness. We searched for a fairly prestigious tournament. The best and nearest was just over the Mexican border at a new, posh spa, Agua Caliente (said to have been financed by movie tycoon Joe Schenck and a few shady gambling characters). It was very close to the sleazy honky-tonk bordertown of Tijuana.

After booking our rooms, these two really top-class amateurs went through the motions of playing. I took it upon myself to carry both their golf bags because our single caddy had to spend his time running back and forth in the blistering Mexican heat with ice-cold bottles of beer for us all.

The first evening I received a most hospitable message from a Tijuana city official inviting me and my *"inglésias amigos"* on a visit through the rougher, most colorful sections of town under his personal sponsorship. We all agreed it would be an enriching experience, provided we were not expected to do more than just look at the seamier side of bordertown life. We piled into the civic big shot's aged but adequate car, driven by a local excuse for a policeman. He asked if we would care to visit the Molino Rojo, an infamous playground for cheap gambling and liquor and the town's leading brothel, frequented by unemployed matadors and American tourists.

I was particularly careful not to be recognized and put on dark spectacles, ruffled up my jacket collar, and undid my tie as we proceeded on our tour. My companions and I were first shown through this vast conventlike layout, containing dozens of bug-infested, smelly rooms that resembled small prison cells. Each was furnished with an old brass bed, a chair, a couple of coat hooks and a hanger, and a small wash basin with a jug. Each bed was covered with dirty, rumpled sheets. Practically every room was "decorated" with some form of religious symbolism—a picture or statuette of Christ, the Virgin alone or with the Child, as well as a rosary and crucifix tacked to the wall above the bed.

If a room was temporarily engaged, the door was, of course, shut. The characters who shuffled in and out and *Las Mohairas Gusto* waiting or escorting their scruffy or anxious clientele, were both pathetic and awful at the same time. Suddenly, Johnny de Forrest, a bit ahead of us, let out a howl, *"Look inside here!"* Bobby, the City Father, and I caught up and looked inside this typically messy cell. Johnny pointed gleefully to the rusty, stinking bed. There, right above the pillow, was a large rosary nailed in a big circle to the wall with an ivory crucifix hanging down at the bottom. In the middle, as if framed by the rosary, was a "fan" picture of *me!* It was one of those small 5" × 7" photos once sent out for many actors by their studios with a stamped or printed inscription on it. This one said: "Yours sincerely, Douglas Fairbanks, Jr."

Johnny's raucous yell soon caused others to look in and a small crowd to assemble. I was obliged to scribble initials on scraps of paper and smile "graciously" for inmates, natives, and fellow nationals who clustered about. With some help from our attending *policía,* I retreated red-faced to our car, and we drove back to Agua Caliente. We returned to Los Angeles, 135 miles away, and to Beverly Hills the next morning. Johnny cabled his father that he had played in the tournament but lost his match. He received his allowance by return cable, and that was that.

One short-lived bit of pure Hollywood whimsey occurred on this trip to California. Billie and I met by accident at a Beverly Hills charity event. Her marriage to Franchot Tone was in its last months. We played an instinctive game in which we both allowed ourselves to enjoy the insubstantial idea that we could somehow "warm over" our dead-and-buried romance. We went to a lot of trouble to meet surreptitiously—and to indulge in sentimental reminiscences. We took long drives up into the hills, on obscure old roads, to try to relive our "spooning" days.

It all seemed *so* romantic, but after two or three evenings we both agreed it might make a nice scene in a movie, but it really didn't work for us. Our flame had long since flickered and died. All that was left was an inclination to giggle at our silliness.

In California it was a real stimulant to find old Tom Patten still so wise, particularly about the growing tidal wave of war that threatened every shore. Almost as a disciple, I also sought out Will and Ariel Durant. Will Durant was a vast repository of knowledge that he shared through lips that barely opened wide enough to let his soft, amused voice escape; and Ariel (or "Puck," as he called her) lovingly interrupted or contradicted him in her strident, adenoidal Bronx accent. What a gift to me their friendship and confidence was! I also rediscovered my old sailing friend, Bob Montgomery, and even earlier ones like Phil Holmes. We three shared impatient concern with the widespread American belief that all dangers would disappear if we just looked the other way.

I had joined some Eastern foreign-policy study groups and committees and now a Western one. Again I sought the views of such disparate and distinguished older people I'd known before, like Dr. Robert Milliken of Cal Tech and Professor Edwin Hubble, the famed astronomer at Mount Palomar. The heat of threatened war increased daily. I agreed passionately with many of my peers that the only way it could be avoided was if the United States came out forcefully against Hitler and the Axis. I thought we should profit by what I believed were our costly mistakes between 1914 and 1917 and from 1919 until President Wilson died and openly declare our support for France and Britain. The alternative would be to let the Fascists have their say wherever and whenever they chose, to let Europe go and be prepared for the virus subsequently to infect a completely susceptible America.

In any case, after doing some radio plays, I returned to New York. Soon after my arrival an old friend from my Central Park boyhood, young Frank Roosevelt (another "junior") showed up. Since he was immediately supportive of my still minority concern about the state of nearly everything, I went down to Washington at his suggestion. He had arranged a quick "in-and-out" meeting at the White House with his father. Under the circumstances, I was very nervous. And I was so excited—and awed—that I remember nothing of our very brief conversation except that the President was warm and pleasantly reminiscent about having met my father during the Great War, when FDR was Wilson's Assistant Secretary of the Navy.

On the same trip, I strengthened my acquaintance with the brilliant journalist Walter Lippmann, whose syndicated columns on the state of the world I thought so erudite. I casually quoted from him on more than one occasion in the hope of impressing an important listener with my advanced views of foreign affairs. At about that time I met the leading savant of the New York *Times,* the influential and arrogant Arthur Krock. Whereas Lippmann was warm, friendly, and encouraging, Krock scared the hell out of me. He treated me with the remotely polite disdain that the established intelligentsia of the eastern seaboard usually reserved for anyone suspected of living west of Virginia who was short on power, money, an Ivy League degree, or was engaged in any profession outside of government or journalism. At first encounter Krock seemed of the same iconoclastic mold as H. L. Mencken or drama critic George Jean Nathan. (Nathan seemed to dislike almost everything in the theater except Eugene O'Neill and Lillian Gish. His finely abusive prose caused many heartaches on the receiving end. My father dubbed him "George Jean Nothing.")

Nevertheless I did manage, by joining many groups at Washington's Metropolitan Club, over an extended period, to win Krock's goodwill and encouragement. He and Lippmann, as well as Cordell Hull, Harry Hopkins, Bob Sherwood (now one of the President's intimates and chief speechwriter), and my young contemporary, F.D.R. Jr., eventually became most helpful to my hesitant initial efforts to be taken seriously. We were all in our different ways trying to convert our blinkered compatriots to the concept of America as a part of the rest of the world.

In New York I received an invitation to visit my old writer-friend, John Buchan, in Ottawa where, after being elevated to the peerage as Lord Tweedsmuir, he was now ensconced as Canada's Governor-General. I had last seen him in Edinburgh, decked out in scarlet and gold with plumed hat and a variety of accoutrements as High Commissioner of the Church of Scotland.

When we had first worked together a few years back on a couple of scripts for Criterion, I knew him only as the famous author of *The Thirty-Nine Steps* and all those wonderful Greenmantle action stories. I knew he was venerated by the literati of Great Britain and had served in a high ceremonial post under the crown of Scotland. I knew him as a small, wiry man with a soft accent and an intriguing but quiet personality. I did *not* know until recently that he had been the head of Britain's secret intelligence service— the MI-5 for some time. Since I was so fond of him and his family, I would

With Gertrude Lawrence in *Mimi,* 1935.

At the theater with Marlene Dietrich, Dolores Del Rio, and Cedric Gibbons in London, attending the premiere of my Criterion film, *Accused,* in 1936.

With Ronald Colman in *The Prisoner of Zenda,* 1937. (THE MUSEUM
OF MODERN ART/FILM STILLS ARCHIVE)

In *Gunga Din,* with Cary Grant and Joan Fontaine, 1939. (RKO RADIO PICTURES)

Coming down the aisle with Mary Lee on April 22, 1939. Note Elsa Maxwell on the bride's side of the church and David Niven on the groom's side.

With Mary Lee after our wedding.

From left to right, an unidentified friend, Robert Coote, Mary Lee Fairbanks, Vivien Leigh, Laurence Olivier, and Walter Kerri-Davies on September 3, 1939, just before hearing that war had begun between England and Germany.

With Laurence Olivier aboard a chartered yacht, Labor Day, 1939.

Studying lines for *Angels Over Broadway* with Rita Hayworth in 1940. (THE MUSEUM OF MODERN ART/FILM STILLS ARCHIVE)

With Mary Lee, sharing the view of Rio de Janeiro's harbor and Sugarloaf in the background, on our goodwill trip to Latin America, April and May 1941.

A scene from the movie *The Joy of Living,* 1938. The still was printed by a pro-Nazi newspaper in Argentina with the caption "America's Unofficial Ambassador" to embarrass me during my Latin American tour. (RKO RADIO PICTURES)

Westridge, our home in Pacific Palisades, California, set on seven and a half acres, with a view of the Pacific.

Fairbanks and Fairbanks playing
identical twins in *The Corsican Brothers,* 1941.

With Captain Lord Louis (Dickie) Mountbatten (center), acting as his honorary aide-de-camp on a visit to U.S. Naval Headquarters in San Diego, September 1941. I was newly commissioned in the U.S. Naval Reserve.

have jumped at a chance to see him again in any case. But now that he turned out to be a man of many more important parts than I had suspected, I accepted without any hesitation, excitedly gathered my woolies, and took a night train to Ottawa. I was met by one of Buchan's aides-de-camp and escorted to Government House in a style that would today be called VIP. It was fun to be "behind the scenes" on the highest level in a foreign country. As on other similar occasions, I reacted as if it were all a sort of play, only half believing in the verity of where I was and what I was doing.

A Commonwealth Governor-General's job is to be in effect, the monarch's representative. As such, he is ceremonially treated almost as if he were indeed the King. Bills passed by acts of the free Commonwealth Parliaments do not become law until the Governor-General, on the monarch's behalf, "assents" to them as the symbolic head of state (not, as is the Prime Minister the head of government).

The Canadians have their "Royal Palace," a large but unimpressive Government House called Rideau Hall that would not in the United States be thought nearly grand enough for a state governor's mansion. Still, as it was all new to me, I enjoyed it. There was some sort of semiofficial reception for a few special visitors from one of the Western Provinces on the day after I arrived. As these hardy Western worthies went down the receiving line, the men, as protocol directed, gave their customary ceremonial nod from the neck and the ladies dipped their little curtsey. When the bewildered but excited visitors got all the way down the line to me, they went right ahead and gave me the same "bob and nod" greetings. I took it all in stride. No one had paid me such attention since I played Czar Peter III in *Catherine the Great.*

"His Ex," as my host was now informally known, recalled a suggestion I'd made about a year earlier to Prince George, since made Duke of Kent. It was that an official visit by the King to the States might be surprisingly well received by Americans, particularly in these worrisome days. He would be the first British monarch ever to do so. More to the point, it could suggest a cultural as well as historical affinity that just might give pause to a potential aggressor. I was told later that the King had reacted to the idea favorably but wondered if the trip might become self-defeating in the event that hardheaded international neutralists and some small but raucous anti-British groups were too unfriendly. Prime Minister Chamberlain, so I heard, was uncertain if the timing was right. On the other hand, "His Ex" thought the King's visit a fine idea and recommended it. Of course the next move would be to see if FDR's administration wanted to issue an official invitation from President to King. Perhaps naively I volunteered to discover who would be sympathetic and helpful in Washington. In fact I did manage to nudge the idea forward and upward through a few of my recently developed high-level contacts.

I was confident that my life and even my random education had provided me with a more reliable knowledge of history than many of our public servants and experts. I was at pains, however, not to let my self-assurance show, but to express modest and politely intelligent views and explanations. I dug around for a number of paraphrases of John Donne's "No man is an island . . . any man's death diminishes me . . ." I maintained that this applied to nations and communities as well as to individuals. By that token, the growing excesses we were witnessing abroad daily would inevitably be upon us in no time unless we declared common cause as soon as possible with like-minded, like-governed people abroad.

As far as politics were concerned in 1938, Americans at all levels of national life had never—even in the worst of times—fallen for Marxist cure-all theories. They feared it then (as they do now) as a danger that might, in times of paranoiac stress and anxiety, take hold by subversion or *coups d'etat*. But Nazism was different. It was neither covert nor subtle; it was overt and raw, brutal and obscene—yet many in the New World cluck-clucked their detached disapproval and couldn't bring themselves to fear it (yet).

It was clear to me that if a fanatic and militarily aggressive movement like Nazism was not checked, the other equally sinister and repressive system of the Soviets would cross oceans as easily as, say, religions. Many people of those times tolerated the ideas of Hitler not just because of his spectacular and still growing messianic hold over the great German people, but because he defied treaties and carried out his conquests with no more than terrifying bluff. He claimed that the Communists were his main and ultimate enemy, and that only he at the head of a strong Reich could dam up the poisons dripping over the Soviet borders into the rest of the Western world. The desperate wish to overcome communism bred much of the support given Hitler by many appeasers or isolationists. The British, led by a gentle, frightened Chamberlain, and the French, governed by a like-minded Edouard Daladier, convinced themselves they could assuage the Axis hunger with "understanding." Churchill's lonely warnings were scorned. And too many in all the other democracies tried, from fear and myopia, to believe Hitler. Indeed Churchill was still almost literally "a voice in the wilderness." In his elegantly phrased opposition to all dictatorships and his championing of democracies, he was far more strident and uncompromising than our own FDR.

All this should help explain why I, a rank political amateur from a "dismissable profession," was prepared to put a rising career at risk. People thought I somehow knew more than I did—that I had more influence and friends than I really had. And I made no serious efforts to alter that impression. Why should I?

At last President Roosevelt decided the time was ripe to invite King George VI and his consort, Queen Elizabeth, to visit the United States. All details of the prospective visit had been quietly cleared well in advance— despite terrified warning signals sent by our less than admirable ambassador to Britain, Joe Kennedy. He stirred the embers of terror, isolationism, and racism as did Charles Lindbergh; Colonel Robert R. McCormick, owner of the influential Chicago *Tribune* and his cousin, Captain Joseph M. Patterson, proprietor of the New York *Daily News;* a few U.S. senators; and one shockingly un-Christian priest, Father Charles E. Coughlin.

I was understandably gratified that what had been at least in some small part my doing was to come off the following June 1939.

King George VI and Queen Elizabeth accepted the President's official invitation and came over to the United States and attended the New York World's Fair. They also went to Washington and then to Hyde Park, the President's estate on the Hudson, where they had a marvelously American weekend, munching hot dogs and experiencing all that went with a big Fourth of July. The visit was an unqualified success with the American people, whose warm and admiring reception was echoed even in the usually staunchly isolationist press. I was quietly very pleased to receive in due course a note from Lord Tweedsmuir in which he wrote, "You must have been pleased at the way your plan worked out so well." I certainly was.

I was regarded by some in Washington's heirarchy as a "well-intentioned but useless pest," by others as a "fugitive from Hollywood looking for publicity," and by still others as "potentially pretty hot stuff." This latter was, I now suppose, because of the purely accidental times in the recent past when I had met and chatted with a number of diverse public characters. For example, when filming with Irving Asher and Monty Banks at the London Warner Brothers studios, Mussolini's daughter, Edda Ciano, and her ambassador husband, Count Ciano had been my guests. Count Ciano was destined to become his father-in-law's foreign minister, and I had several useful chats with them, word of which I passed on to Washington. Later suspected of treason, Ciano was executed by his father-in-law's firing squad.

I also got to know the amiable subsequent ambassador, Count Dino Grandi, who after deserting his chief, gave the Allies much useful background information on Axis personalities, secret treaties, and the like. Slip-

ping in and out of European life, I also met the German ambassador, Jo-
achim von Ribbentrop, briefly at Cliveden, the American Lady (Nancy)
Astor's great house on the Thames. Von Ribbentrop and I clearly and
almost immediately disliked each other. Often held suspect, even by Hitler,
he became the Nazi foreign minister. I had no serious or truly "useful" talks
with any of these people, nor with other less well-lit Axis characters of the
times, but the fact that I knew any of them at all helped promote me an inch
or so higher on the Administration's "shadow" list of what might have been
(but wasn't) called "Possible Useful Supporters (Foreign Affairs Section)."

Back in New York, Mother prepared my favorite dinner of nongourmet
items. It was always cream-of-corn soup (from a can), chicken à la king,
mashed or scalloped potatoes, asparagus hollandaise, and apple pie with
American cheese for dessert. "Ugh!" perhaps, but I *loved* the whole menu.

After this ample repast my family sat and listened with rapt attention to
my exposition of "the situation" as I found it in Canada. I may have been a
political curiosity to some and a useful political ally to others, but to Mother
and the family, I was Cassandra, Socrates, and Tom Jefferson rolled into
one. Consequently I "rehearsed" much of my "open" report to them, my
captive audience.

Jack's career was still sporadic. He was still highly regarded professionally, but the jobs he got were sadly either short-lived on Broadway or unnoted in national tours. When he was in New York, he would take refuge
almost daily, in the Lambs Club, where he and John Hundley and other
Lambs periodically performed in sketches for what were called "Lambs'
Gambols" and where he often drank too much. But on pain of either Mother's temper or her very hurt feelings, he was still obliged to phone her—if
not between acts, then every so often all day or evening long. Mother, for
her part, continued to act the Lady Bountiful. Though now shy of going out
in public, she would be hurt and angry if friends who got tired of her
constant turndowns neglected to go on inviting her anyway.

20

For New Year's Day 1939 I had accepted an invitation to go out to Herbert Swope's country house, Keewaydin (an Indian name meaning West Wind), on Long Island. Genie and the Chester family took me to lunch first at the Terrace Club. This was almost the first completed part of the forthcoming New York World's Fair at Flushing Meadows, due to open in the spring of 1939. The luncheon was very jolly and sweet—as it always was with the Chesters—and we had a rough preview of the great World's Fair. After lunch they drove me about forty minutes on to where the Swopes lived.

Keewayden was a thirty-seven-room mansion designed by Stanford White in the early part of the century. It was in classical Georgian-Colonial style, with huge pillars in front. An enormous house (by American standards), it could accommodate an innumerable number of house guests and glowed with the same night-and-day hospitality as the Swopes' Manhattan apartment.

It was a cold, dampish January 1 when Genie deposited me at their door just before the Swopes' tea time. The snow of a few days earlier had melted except for partly iced-over puddles. As usual I was greeted as a contemporary. Herbert was a big expansive, vociferous, and dominating talker. He had short gray hair and a red face, with pince-nez spectacles atop a longish nose. Maggie (as Mrs. Swope was to be addressed only after a trial period and then only if she permitted such intimacy) was very quiet and serious, and when she chose to, she could be far more formidable than Herbert.

Someone of the household staff took my bag, and I was asked to come and sit down. The rest of the house party were so "done in" by the previous night's carousing ("they *said* they were going to take naps . . .") that they were nowhere to be seen.

"Who's here?" I asked Herbert.

"Well, there are Will and Janet Stewart—you know them, I know." Of course I'd known Will for ages. He was one of my father's favorite people, once one of New York's most dashing and sought-after beaux, also an ex-lover of Gee's and, for good measure, my stepmother Sylvia's! Janet was always on everyone's list of the ten most beautiful blondes of the century. Together the Stewarts were models of sophistication, charm, and wit.

"Who else?" I asked.

"Well, let's see," bellowed Swope. "There's my son 'Ottie.' You've known him for ages too, and Dolly de Milo—she's always fun. And there's "Cookie" Young—Bob Young's daughter (you know Bob, owns railroads and things). She was engaged to Geordie Ward in England but broke it off just lately. And then, let's see . . . Oh, yes, there's 'Hunt' Hartford's wife —little Mary Lee. They're separated, so she's here on her own. You'll like her—lots of fun, pretty, and very bright. Mimi Baker's here too—it's mostly for the young." Herbert drew a breath, then said, "Want to get some fresh air, go for a walk? We can chat as we go." Such questions from Herbert were accepted as orders. So I got all rebundled up and ready to face the raw chill outdoors.

Suddenly into the hall bubbled a very small, brown-haired girl with large, shining dark eyes and a full, beautifully carved red mouth that seemed to smile even in repose. When it widened into a laugh or grin—which was often—she lit up her immediate vicinity with a cheery display of white-white teeth that were just uneven enough to be fetching. She was young—I guessed somewhere in her early twenties. Furthermore, she seemed to have a considerable talent for easy laughter and bright talk, with just an echo of a Southern accent. My quick summary glance noted her exceptionally tiny waist.

Herbert put on his greatcoat and introduced us. "This," he boomed pater-nally, "is young Doug Fairbanks—and" (turning to me) "this is Mary Lee Hartford. I've nicknamed her Mary-Foo after an appealing comic-strip character."

We shook hands, and I burbled something like, "I know your husband Hunt; we were in Bovée School together as kids . . ."

"Yes, I know," she interrupted. But who could mind *her* interruption?

Herbert told her we were going for a "walk-and-talk" before tea, and asked if she would like to come along.

"I've only got these silly Indian moccasins on, but I'll change them," she said and turned to go.

Herbert stopped her. "Don't bother! We're going now! They'll be all right. Come along!"

Although my new acquaintance was a minute sample of instant bewitchment, I privately preferred to be alone with Herbert. I had too many serious —to *me*—matters to talk about without being accompanied by a third party I had just met. *Especially* since she was a girl and a particularly attractive one. But she came along anyway. Herbert and I talked almost as if she weren't there.

We took long, fast strides as I rambled on about my trip abroad and my more recent one to Canada. I reported on whom I had seen, what I had said and done, how I had reacted to people I'd met and developing events, at the same time trying to answer Herbert's well-targeted questions.

Mrs. Hartford kept paddling along, about two steps to our one in her moccasins, listening attentively. Ever the inveterate strutter, I could not resist showing off a little for her—overstating everything and throwing names about like grains of rice at a wedding—trying to impress Herbert in one way and the delectable little nuisance, Mrs. Hartford, in another.

Something positive must have happened because when we returned, somewhat chilled and chattery, Herbert excused himself and left us alone together. No one else in the house had surfaced, so Mrs. H., who insisted I call her Mary Lee at once, acted the part of hostess. For my part, I felt that special dizziness that usually accompanies a case of instant crush. Such a condition is very rarely acquired at cold, damp country house parties on a New Year's Day. But this was an exception—even more of one than anybody could then have guessed.

We soon found ourselves sitting in a small library. Mary Lee was having some hot tea and I a Scotch-and-soda. I have no idea—and neither does she —what we said. At the end of an hour of behaving like a human peacock displaying its feathers in flirtatious preenings and chitchat, I had damned near overplayed my hand *(both* hands, no doubt!). Mary Lee decided that I'd gone far enough and, suggesting she had better join the others before changing for dinner, got up from the couch we had been sitting on. As gallantly as anyone I'd ever seen in the movies, I pulled myself together, straightened my tie, and went to open the door that I had surreptitiously shut when we first came in. *Most* unfortunately, the damned door was *stuck!* I had not locked it, but I might just as well have because it wouldn't open. All my then fairly rugged strength went into the effort to force it. It wouldn't budge. Panic began to set in. How would she, how *could* she, explain and expect anyone to believe her? I wouldn't normally have expected anyone to really believe *me*. But Mary Lee, beneath her lively wit had an impeccable private reputation; indeed, she could have been the reincarnation of Caesar's wife, which, thank God, she wasn't.

I alone, then both of us together tugged, pushed, and banged on the door. At first not a soul came to our rescue or even heard our shouts. Finally, the whole house party was aroused by the racket and assembled in a group outside the door. After an interminable time (we thought) and an assist from the butler, the door finally gave way and opened. The poor heroine had been saved from a fate only somewhat better than death.

The true story of the locked door and Mary Lee and I alone, our really innocent small talk (of *course,* I tried to kiss her, but then that wasn't *so* bad!), and the nonworking key were never quite swallowed by the others, nor did they let up on the teasing for years.

I persuaded Mary Lee to lunch with me the following week, then to dine, then to go to the theater, and then to accompany me to one or two dinner parties given by mutual friends. The better I got to know this small, shining girl, the more serious about her I became. However, I tried not to show it. I couldn't recall how long it had been since I'd seen Hunt, but since they had been unofficially separated for nearly three years, I wasn't of a mind to rustle up the kind of guilt feelings that under the circumstances I might have.

Although we had many New York society friends in common, we had never met before that New Year's Day. She knew very few of my European or British friends—and hardly anyone at all in the theater. Those worlds were quite alien to her—for reasons of choice rather than circumstance. This was strange because she told me she had "just for fun" invested a bit of money in a couple of Broadway shows: one produced by George Abbott, the other *Porgy and Bess.* However, she allowed that she "loved" the theater, opera, concerts, "and all that sort of thing." This statement eventually bounced back at her when I found she seldom went to the theater at all—I think I was one of the first, if not *the* first, actor she had ever exchanged more than a few pleasantries with.

Mary Lee had a very luxurious lifestyle (a splendidly useful word that was not then in vogue). She lived in a large, superbly appointed apartment uptown on Fifth Avenue, near the "Met" Museum. She was waited on tiny hand and tiny foot by an obsequious staff—and more intimately by Sophie, a devoted French maid. She went about New York in an enormous Duesenberg limousine, driven by a liveried chauffeur. I thought it had too small a passenger space, but the hood over the engine seemed to cover at least two dozen cylinders. In addition, she had been endowed with even more extravagant worldly goods. Among them was a lovely pastoral patch of Virginia in an Appalachian valley, halfway between Hot Springs and Warm Springs. Called Boxwood Farm, it was a small gem—a real Colonial showpiece of a house, presumably built in the early to mid eighteenth century. Though she herself had been born in Keystone, West Virginia, she and her family felt intensely "Southern."

Mary Lee's clothes, jewels, matrimonially shared yachts, a South Carolina plantation owned by her widowed mother-in-law, a house in Palm Beach, Florida, and another in Newport, Rhode Island—all were a part of the many material benefits accruing from the Hartford family's ownership of the great A & P chain of grocery stores—the precursors of supermarkets.

Until that fateful New Year's Day, I was able to meet my romantic attachments on fairly equal financial grounds—at least grounds not involving such a conspicuous disparity as to make me fear to appear to be a fortune hunter. In many ways I was a very old-fashioned young man. I could hold my own in almost any group from tramps on skid row to emperors to generals to geniuses—but the thought of being actually *married* to someone who could call the financial domestic tune very nearly put me off.

On the other hand, Mary Lee had little money *or* possessions on her own. Her father, to whom she had been devoted, had been a noted oral surgeon who had practiced in Bluefield, West Virginia, until his death. There he had begun the first public dental clinics in America. A distinguished lecturer, he also taught at McGill University in Montreal. In addition to her father, her two uncles, a grandfather, and her brother were all doctors.

She and Hunt had met at Harvard when she was nineteen and in defiance of parental objections had eloped. As the only son and heir on the Hartford horizon, Hunt had been greatly spoiled and indulged—particularly by a dynamic, socially ambitious mother who wasted much time trying to deny her Jewish roots for fear they would hamper her social aspirations. Though two Hartford brothers still lived and ran the company, old Mr. H., Sr., Hunt's father, had died. However, he left his widow with considerable authority concerning the disposition of his fortune.

Hunt, for his part, was a gentle and generous fellow—anxious to help art and artists, literature and authors—and to cultivate beauty everywhere, from the gardens of a great plantation to the decks of the smallest square-rigged schooner afloat—his *Joseph Conrad*. In short, he was a thoroughly altruistic fellow.

But their domesticity had become a *mariage de convenance*. Hunt, though generous and kindly, was not truly domestic by nature. Mary Lee had loyally kept up appearances that fooled no one, but there was nothing onerous or cruel about their relationship; it conformed to the social strictures of the times. Thus Hunt continued, unchallenged, his mutually understood but undisguised custom of openly wandering from the domestic base. Most of these forays were just the trivial peccadillos that most men then thought their chauvinistic prerogative, but now a deeper commitment was destined to rock Hunt's domestic boat. Hunt had been concerned not to allow a real break in his marriage up to now. Not only did he want the protection provided by the marriage state, but he was terrified of his domineering mother and his uncles, who kept a very tight rein on the family business and fortune. This spoiled but idealistic young man and his sister, Josephine, were in large measure dependent on their mother's and uncles' goodwill in order that they might live the extravagantly self-indulgent life they did— Depression or no.

Mary Lee's strict Scotch Presbyterian and "Old South" upbringing did not tend to condone such shenanigans; still, she went along with things for the time being. But on the very day that *we* met, Hunt had rung up and announced that he would now like to end their existing arrangement and have a real divorce. He very much wanted to marry someone else. Mary Lee had apparently agreed readily and cheerfully. Though she always would remain a fond friend, she was tired of "covering" for him.

The following week she wasted no time in seeking out the services of one of the most famous legal firms in New York—Cravath, de Gersdorff, Swaine and Wood. The real senior partner was the brilliant and popular Maurice (Tex) Moore. Tex warned us that in order to protect Mary Lee, we must either not go out at all or must avoid conspicuous places. As a result, we made our favorite dining—and sometimes luncheon—rendezvous at a charming, small restaurant on the East Side, the Hapsburg House. This very discreet meeting place had little booths upstairs that could be partly curtained off. The anonymity of their patrons was scrupulously respected.

Very occasionally we went to the theater, but the original fun of going in her huge Duesenberg soon evaporated as it only added to the number of turned heads greeting us as we arrived at a Broadway destination. One day Walter Winchell slipped a passing reference to us into his column after we'd mixed with others at "21" and such popular nightclubs as the Stork Club and El Morocco. That scared us more than a bit.

One would naturally assume that since I had only recently got into and out of a variety of complicated romances, I would not be so foolish as to become involved again quite so soon! This time I *knew* it was solid and realistic. This time I *knew* I was really and truly in love. And head over heels at that. There was no theatrical resonance because Mary Lee was so patently *un*theatrical in looks, manner, and views. Also, here was that rare someone who needed nothing material whatever. She seemed in all ways self-reliant, with no affectations, a heretofore unknown kind of woman whom I knew *I* needed for my life. Now all that was required was to persuade her that she felt the same—or at least nearly the same as I.

Sometimes when we found absolutely no place to meet alone and unobserved, we took what now seem very embarrassing steps to amend the situation. I would ask Mother if we could meet for a "private chat" in a back room of the Whitings' apartment. Mother, of course, had always adored being privy to secrets, and she quickly sympathized with this situation—especially since she took a fancy to Mary Lee right from the moment they met. This situation was *almost* as "close to home" as one could get.

Here is a letter that Mary Lee wrote to her best friend that gives her version of the early days of this lovely new year.

Darling Tucky:

I hated missing your party, but I must bring you up to date on my life that has taken a most agreeable turn. You know all the part of darling Maggie Swope scooping me up and forcing me to go to Port Washington for New Year's and how I met "you know who" and all the romantic interlude that had to come to a nasty halt when G.H.H. demanded a divorce. Well, it was one of the hardest things I've ever done, refusing to give my address and telephone number to "Dazzler" but for once I felt first things first and put the episode in its proper perspective. HE is a notorious flirt and I'd better keep my head! Now here comes my old philosophy, Tucky, that I've told you so often—it's being at the right place at the right time, but always cautious while opening that gate and walking down that path . . . but walk away everytime!! If I ever have children I'd drum that into their heads—anyway I knew when to turn around and walk out of that gate. Oh heartbreak!! Now here's the fates part I always bang on about. Frances Brooks telephoned and said she was having a welcome home dinner for Douglas and Sylvia Fairbanks and she asked me—I refused with some lame excuses, but she, as dear Maggie, knew I was having a crisis (& my 4 wisdom teeth removed), and I must say the older ladies were so sweet and attentive—anyway the long and short of it, a No Will Power of it, I said yes. She said, "I'll send a ravishing man to fetch you." I quite expected Serge or Joe or that age group, and being quite numb by the coming weeks and facing issues that only you and I know, I said okay, and who, sweet dearest friend, should walk in to pick me up (let in by John & Lesley shown up to the living room, what he must have thought!). Joe announced him, starry eyed, and I was overcome by sheer panic! I practically knocked Sophie down getting out of the room, climbed the stairs that seemed like the Empire State, and Tuck, there, HE was—I muttered Kismet or some fool thing and he held out his arms, I flew into them—golly July 4 seemed like Macy's basement! You know I'm haunted by the fact that, as you know, that floor is terraced all around and I fear the staff were so flabbergasted they assembled to watch me—anyway *that's* fate. The other thing that's quite outlandish is when I entered the room with HIM, his father was talking to Will & Janet and said, "Who is that girl with Jayar? They told him. He said, "He will marry that girl." Isn't it fantastic. Now you are up to date.

I leave for Palm Beach in a couple of weeks, depending on G.H.H. as he's calling the dances, as we say down South. It's all his doing and I feel desperately sorry for him. Even his family and Tex don't know all the story, nor will they ever from me—but I like keeping you in the picture as I need an ear as well as your heart and soul.

I will expect you . . .

Frances (Mrs. Harold) Brooks was one of New York's most famous and insistent hostesses. She was a most generous older lady, whose unprotesting (and nearly humorless) husband seemed to be quietly resigned to Frances's insatiable appetite for social prestige. A *very* plain-looking woman, she was nonetheless vital and charming. Wherever she was in the world in whatever social season, her invitations were rarely declined. She *could* be rather tough and normally popular guests could be, on her say-so, "dropped" from nearly every list.

Another of our friends was the best professional party-giver, the most fun, the poorest lady, everybody's friend and name-dropper, Elsa Maxwell. She learned through the grapevine of our budding romance, but because she was already so devoted to Mary Lee and had also known me for many years, she too loyally kept our secret.

The more I got to know Mary Lee, the more deeply, seriously, happily entranced I became. To be so completely carried away was new to me. No past experience of romance compared to it. But we both agreed that marriage was an embittering experience. We thought we should not entertain such a future for ourselves. Indeed, we should not even mention marriage in discussing future plans. It came to pass, however, that when such a nondiscussable future seemed virtually inevitable, we could—in our still young and silly way—say, "When do you think would be a good time for us *not* to marry?" or "Let's *not* get married in April; let's wait till June *not* to be married."

I made a great effort to stay well out of the whole Hartford legal business involving the upcoming divorce. Tex decided, with Hunt's lawyer's concurrence, that the case should be heard with the least possible publicity somewhere very far away. Thus they decided to file suit at Lake Okeechobee in Florida. The Hartfords had a house and a small yacht in Palm Beach, and few would notice what went on elsewhere in the state.

By now I was beginning to overcome my fear of actual marriage, to try to truly settle down and give up my comparatively irresponsible personal life for good. I had just about decided that at age twenty-nine it was time to plant my feet firmly on the ground and devote my thoughts and energies to *caring* for one person—for the rest of my days.

The time was fast approaching for me to be back in California to start a new film, *Rulers of the Sea*. In early February still only a handful of our most intimate friends knew there was a romance of any kind going on. None so much as dreamed that the young Hartfords would ever divorce or that the effervescent but "sensible" Mary Lee would find my hodgepodge existence of more than transient interest—an amusing change to add background drama. How could anyone guess that such a deceptively delicate, though really strong-willed lady would give up so much easy security for a thoroughly unpredictable life with me?

I went to great and honest lengths to disabuse her of any ideas that my name and family connections were in any way synonymous with wealth or social position. In fact, I made a particular point of painting as gray a picture of my life as I could. A congenital exaggerator, for once I just told the truth, but she remained uninfluenced. She seemed to find my dullest word pictures exciting, and as she made no effort to disguise her interest, I began to alter the course of my revelations and put odd sparkles to them here and there.

All my anxieties about Mary Lee's money became exacerbated as Tex Moore announced every fresh detail of the settlement that Hunt was hurriedly making. First of all, Hunt decided to make a settlement of more than a million dollars on Mary Lee—at a time when a dollar was worth several times what it is nowadays. He had already given the tiny square-rigger *Joseph Conrad* to the U.S. Coast Guard as a training ship, but he also owned a seventy-five-foot inland water yacht called *Wando* (after his Carolina plantation), and this he gave to Mary Lee. Lovely Boxwood Farm and its herd of black-faced Hampshire sheep had already been a gift a few years back, so that was not counted as part of the settlement. Several fine works of art were likewise made over, together with jewels, fine furniture, and on to dizzying further on that had already been outright gifts.

It was all too much for me, and I very nearly convinced myself that I just could not emotionally handle the fact of a wife having all these advantages. Mary Lee thought me silly to set such store by material things. She felt Hunt's generosity was, in effect, a special gesture of gratitude for her "loyal years."

However, we did both feel some guilt as Tex Moore announced the long list of Hunt's settlements because at this time it was doubtful that Hunt knew of *our* romance. There was no reason to think he would really have cared since he was too anxious to follow his own romantic destiny, but Tex thought it might give the Hartford family and their legal advisers reason to balk.

I still couldn't tolerate even the appearance (let alone the reality) of being a "kept" man. It was too un-American! Finally I told Mary Lee that if and when we seriously decided to live together, there must be both a personal and a legal separation of our finances and possessions. I made it clear that I could not be dependent on a rich wife or lover. She would have to live within my means, not hers. Should she wish to spend her money, she must do so on and for herself alone—not me. Furthermore, I said that if we ever made our relationship legal and had children, she must make all her money over to them. We could, if she insisted, share certain of our household expenses, but never on other than a fifty-fifty basis.

Mary Lee was as intrigued hearing about the movie world as she was ignorant of it. In fact, she blushed and said she felt "obliged to confess" that she had never seen me in a movie. This was a cue for me to swagger a bit, so I suggested that I would arrange a small private screening of one of my films. She jumped at the idea. She had never heard of small screening rooms and she admitted she didn't know the names of any of my pictures. What would I suggest? I proposed the now two-year-old *Prisoner of Zenda.* It had proved a very exciting romance, and women seemed to like it better than the more masculine *Gunga Din.*

Mary Lee was delighted. At my suggestion she invited eight or ten chums to come along to a United Artists screening room on upper Broadway. On the day of the screening, several of her bubbly friends trooped in and sat down in the great, stuffed leather chairs. Mary Lee was shaking with excitement at this facet of her newly discovered, and possibly *next,* life. The room darkened and the picture began.

I was nervous as well—hoping to show my wares to best advantage in this setting. The film had been running for about fifteen minutes; Ronald Colman, Madeleine Carroll, Ray Massey, Aubrey Smith, and I had all established our characters, and the plot was clearly on its way. I had just finished a long and amusing scene in which I first encounter Colman when Mary Lee grabbed my hand and whispered in a very distressed voice, "Oh, dear! Isn't it *terrible!* I hate to admit it, but I've just now realized *I've seen this before—* and *loved* it! *I just forgot you were in it!"*

Though not an auspicious way to flatter a not yet fully trapped lover, I got over it in time, and it has been a favorite family yarn ever since.

Bob Sherwood had always idolized my father. He wrote whole critical essays on what a great artist he was. This near hero worship never faltered and Pete became ever more flattered by Sherwood. When I came on the scene and my father heard that I had some entrée to the inner workings of power and that my ideas were considered by those who ran the country, he could barely credit his ears. Best of all, when he heard serious words of praise from Sherwood, he began to see me in a new (only partly understood) light.

Mother, on the other hand, had always been certain beyond question that I was capable of doing anything I set my mind to (there were moments when I believed there might be a grain of truth in that). Some suspected that I was probably a benevolent Machiavelli. Fortunately for me and the world, no one in Washington or any other center of influence had heard that I had any talent for influencing the mighty.

Still I worked on in a minor but intense way to persuade the hesitant to see what was going on in Europe. Although it was to be some time before the world knew of Nazi concentration camps and the many devices by which they would exterminate millions of Jews, Hitler's early speeches were beginning to horrify the Western world. At about this time several thousand Jews were, surprisingly, promised safe exit visas from Nazi-occupied territories to the United States or somewhere in the British Commonwealth. Even though we prefer to deny or even forget it today, the fact remains that the United States, Britain, and France were guilty of undercurrents of anti-Semitism. As a result we contented ourselves with strong disapproving public statements. One overloaded shipload of desperate Jews sailed from one country to another and was never allowed to disembark anywhere. It sailed back "home." Surely our leaders were not heartless or cynical, and no doubt a decision to welcome them would have begun a flood of refugees that we really couldn't cope with at that time. Nevertheless it was a *profoundly* disturbing decision.

Harry Hopkins, the President's *éminence grise,* asked me "off the record" what propaganda support for a stronger anti-Axis position I thought could be expected from the film industry. I admitted I was not privy to the deliberations of most movie producers, but I did suppose that since so many were Jewish, they would be enthusiastic in supporting any strong anti-Nazi campaign. However, except for a few, like the great David Selznick and the bright clown Jack Warner (Darryl Zanuck, a great anti-Nazi supporter, was not Jewish), the others were being very cautious. Because all the operations of big film companies involved enormous expenditures of money and the public's tastes were famously inconsistent and unreliable, the movie moguls tried to keep a policy of strict neutrality by not producing anything seriously provocative or controversial. There were shockingly few exceptions to this policy, I was sorry to say. I told of my own low-level efforts to insert anti-Nazi and anti-Communist "messages" in my films and what a difficult time I usually encountered. Bob Montgomery and I almost alone made any effort at all. Even such huge radio sponsors and advertisers as Lever Brothers (Lux soap), Shell Oil, and other commercial giants with British or European bases forbade any hint of opposition to Fascism. They feared antagonizing some section of the public or inviting the wrath of the federal government for contravening some article in the newly approved Neutrality Act.

I returned to California, and when I let cousins Flobe and Shirl Burden in on my secret, they burbled with pleasure. Mary Lee and I communicated as often as discretion allowed. I had taken on Uncle Bill Sully at a very nominal salary as a sort of assistant or superior "gofer." With his help I rented a charming, not very big, California-Spanish house from Charles Boyer. It was in Pacific Palisades, about fifteen or twenty minutes' drive from Beverly Hills. The two-story house had a small but pretty garden and a modest swimming pool. Pat Boyer, Charles's pretty English wife, had bought and decorated it as an investment.

Although Mary Lee and I still clung to our little game of never openly discussing marriage, we had gone ahead with transcontinental telephone plans for such an event anyway. Somehow, without actually using the word, we managed to agree that a ceremony could take place in California as soon as (a) she had obtained the divorce and (b) I had located a Protestant church that would agree to marry two divorced people.

Throughout my life I have been involved in several totally disparate matters at the same time. This period was typical in the variety of things that demanded my attention but unique in that now each was somewhat related to the others. Perhaps my life was at last becoming coherent.

One day I had to go through the touchy business of being presented by telephone to Mary Lee's mother (her father had died a few years previously). This lady's Southern accent was to prove a constant joy. Then I had to confirm our very probable forthcoming plans to Genie and Flobe, to Mother and Jack, and to the rest of my family and close friends. Most nerve-wracking of all was breaking the news to my father and Sylvia, and then to Mary and Buddy. No one seemed in the least surprised—and yet not a word, not even a *whisper,* had been leaked to the press.

Meanwhile I had begun conferences with Frank Lloyd, one of the best of Hollywood's directors and, as a Scot, a perfect choice to guide me through

Rulers of the Sea, in which I had to speak with a hint of a Scottish accent. It was the story of the building, in Greenock on the River Clyde, of the first steamship to cross the Atlantic under its own power, without sails. My leading lady was the lovely "Maggie" Lockwood, whom I had last worked with when she played my very young sister in *The Amateur Gentleman,* five or six years before. The costar and main character part was played by the inimitable Scottish music hall singer and actor, Will Fyffe, who turned out to be perfectly wonderful.

A great deal of planning had to be done well in advance. Much of the film would actually be shot at sea. Some of it (the closeups in heavy storm scenes) would be faked in the studio where the desired effects could be controlled. Costume and set designs took more days of conferences before we could reach unanimous approval. To make matters even more complicated, it was necessary (because of other cast commitments) to start the film several weeks before Mary Lee and I could even hope to be married—and we could not safely schedule or predict when the whole thing would be finished.

After a number of dead-end inquiries, Uncle Bill and I finally found a charming Spanish-style church on Wilshire Boulevard, just beyond Beverly Hills, the Westwood Methodist-Episcopal Church. The rector was very nice, young, and agreeable to tying our matrimonial knot. Mary Lee was still a Presbyterian, and I was technically an Anglican-Episcopalian, but very far indeed from being a reliable or devout one.

Our next step, after a few weeks of continued secrecy, was very confidentially to "warn" a handful of other friends who were in Los Angeles at the time. The most devoted and loyal to us both was old Elsa Maxwell.

For the first time in my life I engaged a personal public-relations expert, colloquially called a press agent. He was Russell Birdwell, said at the time to be Hollywood's best. I had known him for some time since he was responsible for all the David Selznick Company's publicity. His services were undisputedly the most effective and always the most expensive in the movie business. My professional reputation had already profited from some of his subtly aggressive campaigns while I was working for David. In fact, the first big theatrical award I ever received for "Outstanding Romantic Character Star of the Year 1938," was presented by a New York University drama class in 1940, and I had good reason to suspect that Birdwell had promoted it. But that was still to come, and now Birdwell wanted to keep Mary Lee's and my name *out* of the news as long as possible. He succeeded handsomely. Only one very vague hint of my being "attached" to someone back east was heard in a radio broadcast by the local gossiper, Jimmie Fidler. Except for that, there was nothing until a week after Mary Lee's quiet divorce decree had been handed down by an incurious judge in Okeechobee. Then someone like Winchell squeezed a tiny item in a column to the effect that rumors were rife that the Hartfords were "not getting along." The only other comment was one by Maury Paul (whose *nom de plume* was "Cholly Knicker-bocker"). A good ten days following the divorce, he hinted slyly that I had been trying to break up the Hartfords' marriage. But not even Hearst's powerful, not very bright though dangerous Louella Parsons nor her bright and also dangerous rival, Hedda Hopper, ever printed a word. No more public hints appeared until *"the* Day."

I gave Mother and Jack a trip out on the Santa Fe Super Chief (Mother would never go near an airplane) and arranged rooms for them at the Beverly Hills Hotel. Grandmother Munnie still lived on the coast after grandfather Dan'l's death nearly nine years ago. Despite old age, she busied herself with charities and bringing up Uncle Bill's pretty daughter, Patsy Sully.

Naturally, Pete and Sylvia were invited, but I worried (needlessly as it turned out) whether either of my parents minded the other being there. Luckily not, but we were spared an extra possible embarrassment by the fact that dear ex-stepmother Mary was back east on a business tour with Buddy and couldn't come anyway.

I went over the list of my closest pals in a vain effort to decide whom I should ask to be my best man. I had no single friend who was really any closer than three or four others. I had always had a number of chums with whom to share a laugh, a trip, an evening, or an occasional confidence, but my own life was too peripatetic for any single close friend. In later years, Johnny McClain and Niv were closest and, on occasion, Larry, but he was too far away most of the time. One of my oldest friends from Laguna days (Bobby Gillette had died and I had lost track of Freddy Anderson) was Phil Holmes. He would have been a fine choice, but he had gone to Europe and was jailed in Rome because, so I'd heard, he had expressed his disapproval of Mussolini and his Nazi guest Joseph Goebbels by relieving himself from a balcony onto their procession during a state visit. It was a heroic gesture but not appreciated by the Carabinieri, who put him in a Roman slammer until he was sober. After this he returned to New York, lived with and broke up with Libby Holman, the torch singer, and I couldn't find him. That ruled Phil out. Gene Markey was, I then thought, too old . . . dear Tom Geraghty was even older.

No one really fit the part on conventional lines. I was an unintentional loner. I was a good and trusted friend to several, but few ever got very close to me. I wasn't distant or aloof but I was unable to completely confide in any single person. Perhaps Veda Buckland, Genie Chester, and Flobe knew me best—and were in their own special ways really closer than anyone else. Still, none could be cast as best man.

Finally I thought of asking my father if he would mind the unconventional duty of being his son's best man. To my surprise and pleasure, he agreed and *seemed* pleased. When people asked him about it, he said all the right things and at least behaved as if he was happy at the prospect. He must have been, though, more than a bit self-conscious.

Mary Lee, for her part, had no one to "give her away"—like me, no one conventionally suitable. For a couple who wanted as traditional a (second) wedding as possible, we lacked important elements. In the end we decided to stretch convention even more by asking her mother (whom I now called Nancy) to perform that usually male ceremonial function.

All these arrangements—plus countless others—had to be planned at night at home or during lunch hours at the studio. Free time was rare. I was up by six-thirty each morning and would start work before eight. I would be lucky to get home by seven-thirty P.M. After dinner and a massage at ten by old Fernando Miron, I was fast asleep before he could finish. Fortunately, Emile—the great, irreplaceable Emile—arranged most of the details. Uncle Bill also helped. Finally, Mary Lee rang me from New York to say she was leaving by train with Nancy in order to arrive in Los Angeles on the fifteenth of April—one week before the Day, the twenty-second.

It suddenly occurred to me that if a horrible catastrophe like war should engulf the United States, then the added factor of domestic responsibility would likely become a brake on whatever action I might feel I must take. Why was I now so happy to surrender my enjoyable selfish, freewheeling life to the bonds of marriage?

I never seriously thought that war would develop. It was my conviction that we should immediately present a solid front with the British and the French in opposition to Nazism, Fascism, and communism. My prospective bride did not, I regret to record, always see eye to eye with me on either domestic or foreign policy. Most of those in the circles she had frequented were devout anti-Roosevelt, super-protective Tories—those who felt their favored world would be endangered by a war that they persisted in saying didn't concern us. Of course I was as familiar as I was angry with that and other copouts.

Before we met, Mary Lee had traveled abroad a few times but only to fashionable places "in season": London in June for the Derby and Ascot Week, Paris for the *haute couture* collections and Longchamps, and finally the Côte d'Azur or Italy in July. And why not? I readily understood how hard it was for those floating in such paradisiacal settings to worry over-much about a remote world filled with argumentative foreigners they might have mingled with on visits but now only read about.

Tradition stated that a wedding should, for best luck, begin at half *after* any hour so that the clock's minute hand would be on the way up, rather than *on* the hour when the minute hand is on the way down. Thus ours was planned for two-thirty P.M.

"The Day" threatened to be a problem—even before it arrived. To begin with, Mary Lee had brought her devoted maid Sophie with her—but I had not been warned, and no provision had been made for her at my newly rented house. Fortunately Emile, the resourceful, who lived nearby at his own home, did some room juggling so that Sophie could be suitably accommodated.

Thus Mary Lee, Nancy, and Sophie chuffed into California, and I (trying again to act the "easygoing big shot") hired a grand car to meet them at Pasadena where they disembarked and were driven to the hotel.

I had naturally been obliged to let my director Frank Lloyd in on our secret some time before. We were already many weeks behind on our long and expensive picture when friends and family began to converge on us from all directions for the ceremony. The studio's production department promised me faithfully that all would be well for the Big Day when they would shoot around me.

Finally the press was officially tipped off by Birdwell about the details of the ceremony. Then, out of the blue, director Lloyd sadly warned me that because we were so terribly behind schedule, I *might have to work the whole day of the ceremony!* I got angry. After all, I *had* fixed the date only after much prior discussion and firm promises.

"Sorry!" they said, adding in an offhand way the slim consolation that they would do their best. After a few throat clearings, they then added that in order to have any chance, I might have to work on Wedding Day morning, possibly through the lunch hour—or else Paramount would have to pay the crew overtime. With luck, they mumbled, I might get off before two P.M. —reasoning that if the wedding was at two-thirty I might not have time to change clothes but at least I'd get to the church on time. I fussed and fumed, threatened and cajoled. Frank Lloyd was sympathetic but helpless to do more. I didn't dare tell Mary Lee.

Bill and Emile went right ahead with preparations, ordering flowers, sending telegrams, and wrapping my jeweled wedding present to Mary Lee. (I received a beautiful set of ruby and diamond evening-shirt, waistcoat, and cuff buttons from her. Unfortunately, they were, at a later date, all stolen

without a trace.) A driver from the studio was hired to drive my newly
polished old Cadillac touring car. Emile, typically efficient, had brought
back from London my no longer new but still well-fitting "swallowtail"
morning coat and striped trousers. The possibility of a semiformal wedding
ceremony in Southern California had never occurred to either of us, but
Emile was, as usual, prepared for any emergency within his bailiwick—my
clothes certainly qualified. "Who knows," he explained, "you might have
had to go to a formal funeral, *n'est pas?* Or," he added a bit snootily, "an
eastern wedding!"

I did buy the ring myself. Even so, the jeweler was obliged to come to the
studio at "lunch break" one day as it was the only time I could see him.

My father had been showing signs of nervousness himself. He was fidgety
and didn't look forward to seeing Beth. He was nevertheless always sartori-
ally well prepared for any occasion. In fact, he kept one set of every kind of
outfit on both sides of the ocean—formal, very formal, business, and lounge
suits, country clothes, sportswear—for every climate and season. I dared
not criticize or tease him much about this indulgence (his wardrobe included hundreds of shirts and ties, dozens of shoes, hats, and walking
sticks), because I, too, in my comparatively minute way (all I could afford)
enjoyed this form of peacocking.

At last April 22 arrived, and the studio advised me that my only hope was
to begin shooting at seven-thirty or eight that morning. I *had* been allowed
to leave early the night before for a stag party with pals at my house. Their
jolly jest was to present me with a rolling pin, with all their signatures—my
best-man father sent word he "couldn't make it." Everyone was careful to
confine their rowdiness to one large room and the garden in the back. As
most all present were also working the next day, no one stayed late and I
plopped woozily into my new large bed for all too few hours. I had made up
my mind that if there was to be any insistence by Lloyd and Paramount that
I work past one P.M. I would just be unprofessional and walk out. If they
wanted to sue me, let 'em!

I appeared on the set properly costumed and accoutred (I seldom used
makeup) several minutes ahead of time. Emile had brought all my formal
clothes to my studio dressing room in order to lessen the time needed to
shower and change. Mary Lee, her mother, and Sophie were all at the
Beverly Hills Hotel. They began to get ready hours ahead of time.

I worked poorly all morning. I had a dreadful time remembering my lines
—and when I did, I'd forget my Scottish accent or my interpretation. At
ten-thirty, Lloyd came up with a broad grin to tell me what a "good sport" I
was—and then to announce that the threat of working after lunch was all

just a hoax. Shooting had always been scheduled so that I could leave before noon on this day. I tried my best to take it as the big joke they intended, to be a sport and to laugh at it all, but it was a struggle. I was damned irritated. The company then gathered around and presented me with a scroll that included all their signatures wishing the happy couple whatever it is people wish. I dashed off to my dressing room, where Emile waited with conventional Swiss stoicism and all my clothes carefully laid out.

The right side of the church held my family and friends—a surprising number showed up. The left side was for the bride. Unfortunately, everything had been kept so very secret until the last few days and the trip from the East Coast was so long and expensive for an afternoon's event, that Elsa Maxwell (who happened to be in Southern California anyway) was Mary Lee's only real guest.

While waiting for the show to begin in the vestry behind the altar, Pete and I stood, sat, paced, leaned, giggled, and rehearsed the things we were to do—he making sure he still had the ring in his little waistcoat pocket and I hoping I wouldn't choke on the words I had memorized so well.

Like so many other grooms before me, I went through most of the ceremony in a sort of daze. My most vivid recollection is that my voice sounded detached, as though it belonged to someone else, like a recording emanating from a remote source. Mary Lee's voice was strong and clear. And why not? She was a strong and clear girl. At the time I barely noticed what she wore (she couldn't wear white at a second wedding). The photographs bore out the press description of a "short beige draped silk dress." She also wore the silliest little hat, with funny little flowers and stems that shot upward. It was wonderfully attractive.

Pete, always conscious of being shorter than I (I didn't realize that it was one of the reasons he usually preferred me at a distance), stretched himself to the limit all day. But he remained in fine spirits, even if they were artificial. Mother was at her most appealing: warm, plumply pretty, and dripping with the charm she could always bring out in abundance.

No bells pealed as we came out of the church since it had none. This was a romantic disappointment, and I promised the minister that as a gesture of gratitude I'd make him a gift of some bells. I added the phrase "in due course" to my promise because I had no idea how expensive church bells might be. It was a good many years before I managed to buy even one bell for his bell-ringer to toll in summoning parishioners. But the friendly greetings awaiting us outside from the sightseers made a pleasant start to our new life. A battery of cameras clicked and flashed, and newsreel cameras whirred—all recording our unspectacular but widely reported wedding.

Another group of well-wishing tourists waited for us as we drove up to the Monaco Drive house. Sophie had long since finished unpacking trunks and repacking Mary Lee's small bags for our honeymoon. Our destination was not just a secret from all family and friends; I didn't even tell Mary Lee what plans I had made. Only Emile knew. We went outside and then in, posing for "official" wedding pictures—the two of us alone, then with our mothers and then with my father, in a variety of conventional groupings. My mother and Sylvia were understandably embarrassed by each other and tried to avoid being caught together, playing an elaborate game of "guest go round" in the crowded room. This was also frustrating to the two or three photographers allowed in for just a short time who naturally wanted to get the most "newsworthy" shots they could. By the time that routine was over, the small house was jammed with friends happily drinking and nibbling. Toasts were made—and answered—and finally we were able to move slowly toward the stairs. Once she got halfway up, Mary Lee turned, blew a kiss to Nancy, then to Beth and to her new friend, dearest Veda Buckland. Then she turned to the side and threw her wedding bouquet to Genie, who was smiling broadly from her wheelchair below.

After changing into light sport clothes, we ran through a veritable air raid of rice and confetti, jumped in the "Cad," and drove away. There were the usual "Just Married" signs, tin cans, cowbells, and other nonsense tied to the back of the car, and after a few blocks I stopped and cut them all off. We whirled onward up the beautiful coast road.

Mary Lee asked where we were going.

"Toward Santa Barbara," I replied as enigmatically as I could. After forty-five more minutes of driving and enthusiastically reliving the day's adventures, I stopped and telephoned Emile back at the house. Mary Lee couldn't restrain her curiosity.

I told her I wanted to know if everyone had left by now. Emile had said, "Yes—even the two mothers," and added, "and all will be ready on time!"

"Why? What for?" Mary Lee asked, still bursting with curiosity.

"You'll see," I replied, a bit mysteriously.

Then, giving her my most deliberately sly, conspiratorial look, I said, "Everyone—particularly the press—is trying to find out where we're going for the first night of our honeymoon. And I decided on the nicest place— that no one will have thought of. *We're going back home.*"

Mary Lee gasped and no doubt wondered if I was starting our married life with some silly schoolboy joke. But I meant it. No one would ever have guessed.

By the time we got back, everyone had indeed gone, except Emile and

Sophie. They had followed my orders precisely—and then some. All was tidy except for the mass of presents laid out on two large tables in the hall. It was dark by now, but the house was lit only by candles. Mary Lee seemed delighted. We each took a small glass of champagne (which I actually dislike but do just sip when the occasion makes it too awkward to refuse). We had another after that. Then another! Then a fine candlelit dinner of I don't remember what. Records played soft *gemütlich* music from the next room. It was wonderfully corny, but grand—the lovely, deliberately sentimental, penultimate moment of a near perfect day. We oohed and aahed over wedding presents, and then, after some sheepish, self-conscious jokes, went upstairs.

What a beautiful day and evening it had been. I was not at all sure I merited the rewards of that memorable day and the ones we planned to accrue, with luck, in days and years to come. I did remember Mrs. Pat Campbell's oft-quoted comment after her own wedding day: She was said to glow as she purred about the "peace and quiet of the marriage bed after the hurly-burly of the *chaise longue!*" We happily identified with the sentiment.

21

Our only break that even vaguely resembled a honeymoon was when the *Rulers of the Sea* company, with an excellent replica of the first transatlantic steamship, went on location to Catalina Island. That small island, about twenty-five miles or so from San Pedro, the port of Los Angeles, had been owned by the Wrigley (chewing gum) family for as long as anyone could remember. It was not just the nearest place with acceptable amenities for shooting semitropical island pictures but also a vacation spot for regular tourists and yachtsmen. Many pictures were shot there—e.g., *Mutiny on the Bounty* and *Rain*. Here I'd had that dreadful row with Billie seven years ago. How very different it was to be here now.

Our big storm scenes had already been done in a huge studio tank with wave makers and wind machines. We were all handsomely put up in the local hotel. Each night Frank Lloyd, Mr. and Mrs. Will Fyffe, Maggie Lockwood and her mother, George Bancroft, and Mary Lee and I dined together in the hotel dining room. The weather was chamber-of-commerce lovely. One night, outdoors and near the water, feeling I must impress my bride, I began to describe how I felt and how she looked in the balmy moonlight. It was a rather good and, I thought, persuasive declaration. But after at first seeming impressed by my ardent words, Mary Lee suddenly stood back and laughed. "Oh, darling," she said, "you said all that to me before—word for word the same! Where did you get it from?"

I was caught out. I had stupidly thought I had been getting away with it. "From Noël Coward's *Private Lives,*" I answered sheepishly.

She said, "But you speak it so well—so convincingly! Why's that?"

I replied with a modest smile and a shrug. Actually the fact was that as it was such a very good speech, and as she *did* look lovely in the damned moonlight, I said so. I knew it well because I had made the same speech—with minor and less sincere adjustments—to other girls several times before! Instead of getting angry, she went into peals of laughter and has been telling the story of that night ever since.

The picture was finally completed. The reviews and box office business were good but no more than that. Although the public found it an agreeable romance, there was no storming of the theater doors. One would think people were surely hungry for entertainment to take their minds off the ever worsening news from abroad.

Both the German and Italian military dictatorships had been trying out their latest weapons and training their troops by backing General Franco in the still blood-flooded Spanish Civil War. And that agonizing conflict was made even worse by Moscow's support of the leftist government. It was a hideous out-of-town tryout of the Big Show to come soon to your favorite Theater of War.

If my next film couldn't be the best I'd ever made, then it somehow seemed fitting that it be about the worst. It was called *Green Hell.* Harry Eddington, senior partner of Frank Vincent in their prestigious agency, had long wanted to be a producer. As he was personally popular, he prevailed on several of his most amenable free-lance clients to play in his own first production. No one who was free had the heart to turn him down. Joan Bennett was the leading lady, George Sanders was the villain (naturally), and John Howard was the second male lead in a cast that also included the distinguished Vincent Price (before he specialized in spooks), jovial Alan Hale, and serious George Bancroft.

The setting was a jungle, presumably somewhere in the Amazon. The long establishing shots of rain forests and rivers were probably purchased from a travelogue documentary company. The sets for the rest of the film, jungle and all, were built on one of the Universal Studio soundstages. The only thing any of us thought *might* have resembled reality was the horribly close, humid heat on the set (this was still before air conditioning).

George Sanders, every bit as sardonic and caddish as one would imagine, was nevertheless witty and amusing company. I had first known him in England where he sang as one of the Regency Rakes quartet in Noël's musical *Conversation Piece.* However, I remember being very politically put off by his laughingly telling us that he "couldn't care less if Hitler took over everything. . . ." He agreed, he said, with Errol Flynn in that he wasn't going to fight or lift a finger to stop the Germans. I felt it was a tasteless and unattractive thing for him to say. Many of his family and friends were "over there" under the gun.

The picture, when released, did, in spite of everything, achieve a certain distinction. It was voted the worst picture of the year 1940 by the students of Harvard University.

I knew I could not continue to ride high on the strength of past successes if I didn't stop making indifferent, "easy" pictures. At the same time I wanted to be assured of the money *and* keep up my extracurricular political activities. These two concerns just couldn't be made to jibe, at least in my case. Bob Montgomery felt much the same as I but was protected by his MGM contract. I was free-lancing and had no consistent backing from anyone.

Hollywood was, on the whole, enjoying a return to prosperity with a number of successful pictures. *Gone With the Wind* was a great money maker. John Ford's *Stagecoach* was one of the best Westerns ever—and brought my old football "protégé," John Wayne, to the fore, where he began his climb to the top without stopping for many years. There was also *Wuthering Heights,* with Larry and Merle (and Niv in support), and Larry again and Joanie Fontaine helping Hitchcock and author Daphne Du Maurier make a hit of *Rebecca.* In addition there was Clare Boothe Luce's *The Women,* Jimmy (the Great) Stewart in *Mr. Smith Goes to Washington,* and Bob Donat and Greer Garson in the imported *Goodbye, Mr. Chips.* A fine new list of pictures to which, alas, not a single opus of mine was rated an equal. My scattered attention and conscious distractions were largely to blame.

When Mary Lee and I finished settling down, we went east for a bit, staying with Mother and Jack and attending as many new Broadway shows as possible. Somehow we thought it might prove embarrassing to go see Gee Lawrence in *Skylark.* We didn't miss much else.

On the way back, there was the usual few hours' stopover in Chicago. I had seen in the paper that my old idol, Jack Barrymore, was in town appearing in a play called *My Dear Children.* Poor Jack was now sadly and infamously on the alcoholic skids and had been making things even worse for himself by his fourth marriage to a very young woman stage-named Elaine Barrie. I thought her singularly untalented. Still, I wanted to see the Great Man (always remaining so in my forgiving, long-memoried eyes) and introduce my bride of a few weeks. Luckily, there was a matinee that day so I got two tickets and transmitted my excitement to Mary Lee, to whom the theater world was still a fabulous wonderland. She had heard, of course, about Barrymore's triumphs, his voice and his profile, and I fed her excitement with varnished tales of our old friendship, of his being like an older brother, and his touching orders to his then manager never to let me see him drunk so I wouldn't be disillusioned.

My Dear Children was a stupid play, carelessly designed to exploit Barrymore's autumn-spring romance with Miss Barrie, to give him some moments to dress up as a pathetically decayed Hamlet and to ham through a couple of that play's more familiar soliloquies. But as embarrassingly bad as it was, I allowed my happier memories to put a scrim over the performance.

At one point, however, he astonished his cast by ad-libbing the non sequitur announcement, "When young Doug Fairbanks was a boy, he loved to see me make faces from *Dr. Jekyll and Mr. Hyde*—like this . . . !" Whereupon he crouched over, pulled his hair over his eyes, and screwed his face into the most malevolent weird shape imaginable. The cast was stunned by this flagrant departure from the script, but the audience roared with laughter. He then returned to what had sadly become his "normal self," descended to the footlights, and addressed the audience with the announcement that his old friend, young Doug, the son of his *older* friend, *old* Doug, was in the audience. I broke into a cold sweat of embarrassment and slumped deep into my seat (Mary Lee said my hand got suddenly cold and clammy). The audience applauded and peered around until they discovered me doing my best to hide. I was finally obliged to stand up, bow, and then sit down as quickly as I could. The play was never the same after that— which may or may not have been a good thing!

However, Mary Lee was thrilled by this particular first and couldn't contain her anticipation of meeting the fabulous man afterward. By the time we went through the pass door to get backstage, I'd recovered some of my poise and was able to show Mary Lee what a stage set looked like from behind and how the curtains, ropes, and lights were controlled. An emissary of sorts came up and announced that he would take us to Mr. Barrymore's dressing room. I was so anxious for Jack to be on his best and most charming behavior and for him to be captivated by the effervescent charm of my beautiful Virginia bride that I'm sure my hands shook and my heart pumped faster—although I made every effort to appear calm, if not blasé!

As we approached Jack's dressing room, we saw it was guarded by a menacing mountain of a man who, by the disfigurement of his ears, gave evidence of an earlier career as a boxer. I had heard that Jack was nursed nowadays by a so-called bodyguard who was charged with keeping his public behavior tolerable, limiting his access to drink, and getting him to and from the theater on time. He told us to wait.

This monster opened the door of the star dressing room and announced us to the Boss in hoarse Brooklynese. With the door now open, we could see the star himself sitting at his dressing table, staring in the mirror and making a series of grotesque faces at himself. First he filled his cheeks and blew a few times, and then he did a series of push-ups with his eyebrows, growling and mumbling the while and sipping from a tall glass that appeared to contain whiskey.

We were told to go in and sit down on the couch beside the dressing table. Finally Jack mumbled, "Hello, old man! Who you got with you?"

I introduced my new wife, explaining that this was her first time ever backstage meeting someone like him. He appeared not to hear me and went on grimacing at himself. Finally, to break the embarrassed silence, I burst out with forced jollity, "Well, Jack, a lot of water has passed under the bridge since the last time we met."

In answer he scowled and, with a croaking laugh, using brusque Anglo-Saxon, likened the time passed as more like what filled our sewers. I didn't doubt that Mary Lee had heard the four-letter words that decorated his conversation before, but I was nevertheless embarrassed that this was her first experience with a celebrated artist and boyhood hero of mine.

Trying quickly to change the subject, I asked him what he planned to do next. This caused him to put on his "thinking face," which changed shortly to bleary-eyed pleasure as he announced, "Macbeth!" Then, coughing with laughter, he described in detail the hidden anatomical delights to be considered "with all those great hulking Scotsmen in their medieval kilts. . . ."

I'm sure I blushed and dared not look at Mary Lee, but I interrupted his graphic conversation by asking who he'd want for Lady Macbeth.

He shrugged as if he hadn't an idea.

I tried to keep the ball rolling by asking, "What about Kit Cornell?"

Our foremost theatrical legend looked horrified at the very suggestion, wheeled toward me, and barked his disapproval, "No *tits,* old man! *No tits!*"

With that, I suddenly pretended we were late for our train, hurriedly thanked him, hoped we would see him again soon, and whisked the bewildered Mary Lee out of the dressing room, past the hulk outside, into the street, back to the hotel, picked up our bags, made for Union Station, and got aboard the train!

It was good to return to our little stucco and red tile house. I was feeling truly domesticated for the first time in my life—and liking it. It was all just what I'd imagined from books and movies. The heavy welcome from my huge dog Sahib added to my warm feelings. A couple of years earlier, my father had two great bull mastiffs, known as Mr. and Mrs. Marco Polo because they had traveled so widely. I was making *Gunga Din* when I was given one of their pups, so it seemed appropriate that I name him Sahib. He was an adorable, hearty, but gentle and affectionate slob, and it was a relief that he and Mary Lee took to each other on first sight.

Mary Lee slipped easily and happily into our new life. She agreed that one should avoid cliques in a small community like ours where silly rows are apt to start over trivia and people invariably take temporary sides. Fortunately, all my favorite friends fell for her immediately. And it was mutual. She thought them very interesting or good fun. Some, like Merle, she had known before. Others, like my cousins—and most particularly Genie, Flobe and Veda Buckland—became completely devoted in no time.

Mary invited us to Pickfair, and Mary Lee took even that occasion, usually daunting to newcomers, in stride. Mary and Buddy were wonderfully warm and welcoming. We also ventured away from the glamour scene so that I could introduce Mary Lee to such disparate academic friends as Will and Ariel Durant, Dr. Robert Milliken, and Dr. Edwin Hubble at his famous Palomar astronomical headquarters. These men and I first became friends because of our common concern for the world's affairs.

The first all-star celebrity Hollywood party in our honor was given by Basil and Ouida Rathbone. Contrary to his theatrical image of strength and purpose, Basil was a sweet pussycat of a man. He was obliged to play in too many pictures he hated because his wife, Ouida, a writer but not a great one, frightened all resistance out of him. She was a character with cultivated uniquely bright red hair. It was said she was a *femme fatale* when young, but by this time she was round and fully packed. Nevertheless, she *was,* to her many friends and guests, a pleasant and expansive hostess. She was so extravagant as well that poor Basil had to work constantly at anything to pay the bills for her numerous parties.

My better-heeled friends and such producers as the Zanucks and the Goldwyns and fellow actors like the Boyers made efforts for which I was grateful to make the new little outsider feel at home. Thus it was that our marriage got off to a flying start.

I had no picture contracted for until the next November, still some four or five months away. So I dived into all sorts of energy-absorbing activities. I wrote a few more articles on public affairs, maintained a large, private correspondence (handled mostly by Emile and an ex–studio secretary), and exercised as much as time allowed—swimming in our small pool or in the rolling, cold Pacific, playing tennis and golf, and hacking through the hills on horseback with friends.

I also decided it was a good time to get back to some sketching and sculpting, and that a small statue might be a nice Christmas present for Mary Lee. I wanted it to be a semi-impressionist, partly undraped female figure with a scarf over her head, a long, rough skirt draped around her, and an infant child in her arms. My beautiful cousin Letitia seemed an ideal model. Two or three times a week we would repair to the attic that Emile had cleared for a studio. It finally turned out acceptably well, and I named it (pretentiously) *Peasant Madonna*.

I also read scripts, plays, and treatments for scenarios. Mary Lee took on the job of acknowledging every present and telegram in longhand—very polite but, oh God, how onerous. We had sweet messages from Billie and Marlene, who still signed herself "Dushka," but none from Gee. In our early weeks I made a big thing out of destroying piles of old photos and letters of Billie, Gee, Marlene, and others. I even had inscriptions taken off watches and other gifts. I've regretted such impulsiveness ever since. I didn't admit for years that one of my better statuettes was an undraped and possibly idealized torso of Marlene.

The only small cloud on our domestic horizon was that Emile and Sophie did not get along as well as we had hoped. Sophie clearly didn't like the established masculinity of the atmosphere. Back east, Mary Lee had lived virtually on her own, and Sophie was accustomed to having all domestic matters subject only to Mary Lee's approval. Emile's sense of proprietary interest in me seemed equally strong. There were several tight-lipped domestic sparring rounds: One night Emile had decorated the dinner table with red flowers. Mary Lee came in, saw them, and having had a blue color scheme in mind for that evening, told Emile to change them to blue—from our garden. Emile, rather arrogantly told her, "Mr. Fairbanks prefers *red* flowers!" When my firm-minded lady made the point that *she* was now the mistress of the house and wanted *blue* flowers, Emile drew a deep sigh of resignation, shook his head, and then took a very long time to change them. He was never able to be so happy in my employ again as he had been since he left Pete.

Mary Lee noted that I tried to send Mother a message of sorts almost daily. I didn't really want to be tied to this duty and I privately bridled at it. In fact I was embarrassed by Mother's hurt feelings and self-pity that required such hours of reassurance. Mary Lee was more outspoken about all this since *her* mother was so easygoing in her relationships with her children. After giving me a few lectures, she pointed out to Emile one day that I seemed to send Mother many expensive, unimportant telegrams and phone calls instead of writing letters and notes. She gently suggested that perhaps Emile might try to persuade me to write or dictate letters instead of sending so very many telegrams and cables. Emile drew himself up to regimental attention, smiled coldly, and, speaking respectfully, replied, "Yes, madame, but after all, poor Mr. Fairbanks has such *few* pleasures nowadays!"

Mary Lee wasn't quite sure whether to be angry or to laugh. But the answers to the almost daily frictions and staff jealousies were resolved when Sophie became suddenly and utterly fed up. She disliked California and her new life (which was less luxurious than that in big, well-organized New York City), and she couldn't stand Emile a moment longer. In a moderate fit of Gallic fury, she resigned her post amid floods of tears and took the next train back east.

Emile, for his part, felt his Swiss stubbornness had won the day—which indeed it had. But only temporarily. It wasn't long before he, too, resigned his post as my guardian Jeeves. He frankly couldn't stand the competition he faced, now that I was married and settled down with one lady. The last I heard of him he had become the postmaster of a tiny U.S. post office in the village of Pacific Palisades and had renewed his relationship with his own family, who lived nearby but whom he rarely, until now, had had time to visit.

Now it was my turn to meet the rest of Mary Lee's immediate family, the very Southern Epling clan in West Virginia. First there was her elder sister Louise, and her husband Charlie Burress—a combination of a First Family of Virginia gent and an almost unintelligibly accented "good ole boy." They had no children because mother Nancy had frightened both her daughters about the dangers of childbirth. Anyway, Louise said she was just as glad because the whole begetting process was "disgustin', painful, and ah'm shuah it must look downright silly!" Then there was brother Harold, the only son and the pet of the family. Like most of the male Eplings before him, he became a doctor—a very serious and dedicated physician.

Shortly thereafter we descended on Newport, Rhode Island. It had been my bride's former summer headquarters when she was Mrs. Hartford, and of course I had known it as a boy, sailing there across Block Island Sound from Watch Hill.

From Newport we made our way to Mary Lee's pride and joy—her Boxwood Farm—midway between the villages of Hot Springs and Warm Springs, Virginia, deep in the Appalachians (I had hoped it would be in the Blue Ridge Mountains as I loved the name!). We stopped off en route at the Eplings' hometown—Bluefield, West (thank Gawd!) Virginia, about ninety miles to the southwest. Next day the local newspaper headlined the news: MARY LEE RETURNS HOME WITH NEW HUSBAND! That quickly let me know how I rated in that part of our occasionally united states.

Boxwood Farm was an absolute gem, built in 1740 or thereabouts. The boxwood was brought over from England in little bushes two or three inches high that now stood in great clumps ten feet tall. The gardens with their hollyhocks and phlox and the lilac and dogwood surrounding the place were so seductive that I said I had married the farm, and Mary Lee had come with it!

It really was gentle enchantment. About ninety acres were set in a long green valley at the foot of one long heavily forested hill, with several other small but charmingly proportioned Colonial farms dotted along the way. Boxwood Farm kept a few black-face Hampshire sheep, and after a bit of expert advice from the splendid old local caretaker, I quietly recommended an increase in the flock—to be sold, not for quantity but for quality and breeding.

The Virginia mountain climate and grazing land, though good, were not superior, and we were advised that to maintain the flock's standards and fetch good prices, a fresh new ram from England should be imported after about every third generation. This advice was acted upon, and in the course of time we developed such a profitable flock that, small as it was, it paid for the farm's upkeep.

From time to time I did get a very *bourgeois* conscience about being the newly appointed—just by virtue of marriage—unofficial "Squire of Boxwood," a property originally paid for by my no longer interested predecessor and grammar schoolmate, Hunt. I tried to be sophisticated about it and finally was able to remind myself that all I was doing really was putting on a tweed jacket and striding about playing a part. I told myself that everyone knew I was just the owner's new husband and that it was also well known that I had no need to be a fortune hunter and indeed had my own, far better known career and family heritage, which most people thought every bit the equal of my bride's—*and* of Hunt's!

Our stay was brief but heavenly and included daily visits to Warm Springs —an old, quite round clapboard house that encompassed a natural spring of very warm, but not hot water. It had been well known to the Indians and later boasted the custom of British Colonial Army Colonel G. Washington. By this century it had become a fine meeting place for a limited number of exclusively male local landowners and visiting diplomats (the District of Columbia was a mere five-hour automobile drive away!). One would begin shoulder or chest high in the 95° pool while a wonderfully good-natured old local attendant would place lovely mint juleps on a cork tray and float them out to the gossiping bathers.

After an hour or so of the warm springs and the juleps, I and the others would drive very cautiously back to our various farms. I managed to adjust myself with no trouble to this daily ceremony of local VIPs. I always got home in a lovely glow—crediting the waters for their apparently magic powers. Mary Lee was skeptical. Ah well was all the profound thought I would give it before nodding off for a brief preluncheon nap. All too soon we had to go back to California. We returned via Washington where I checked with the State Department and telephoned others for the latest high-level views on events abroad.

Tom Geraghty, now no longer one of Pete's closest friends but shunted aside in favor of Sylvia's favorites, had attached himself anew to me. He had got the wind up and left a young mistress behind in London because, as he was humorously frank to admit, he listened to that shamefully frightened American ambassador, Joe Kennedy, advising all Americans to get home as quickly as possible. By the time we returned from the South, my sweet old Tom was waiting for us—his all-too-familiar, smelly cigar in hand. It was good to see him and get a picture of what the tensions were like "over there."

It was August 1939 now, and Hitler and Stalin announced the Nazi-Soviet peace pact to a staggered world. Less than a month before, such a thing would have been inconceivable. Sworn opponents—both real tyrants in the classic mold—had now suddenly become friends? The hearts of the Western world sank deeper in dismay while they beat faster in fear. It was hard to credit this Dark Ages alliance that so cynically ignored the free world's views in our modern age.

Within our more personal world, there was surprising but happy news that blotted out any other worries—for the moment anyway. Mary Lee confided that she had taken a test and learned to her delight (not unleavened by natural apprehension) that she was pregnant. I suppose I reacted like any other young father-to-be. I must have taken a gulp to swallow my heart, which was trying to escape through my throat. Almost certainly it would not have been me if I did not suddenly "tear up." But having been taught since childhood that it was unmanly to blub even a little, I hid my head behind Mary Lee's as I embraced her.

We telephoned our mothers with the news, swearing them to temporary secrecy. *My* mother gushed like a Yellowstone geyser. Nancy was, to my mind (but not to Mary Lee's), something less than sympathetic. I would say she was more pitying and regretful. I remembered, when my initial shock had turned to irritation, that dear Nancy had always discouraged her daughters from having children. Our greatest anxiety, however, was about breaking the news to my father. He who had swathed himself in the mantle of perpetual youth, whose outlook and living patterns constituted strenuous denials of time, could hardly be expected to welcome being a grandfather.

Nevertheless on one afternoon's visit to the beach house, we found him in an unusually quiet, almost reflective mood. I began by asking him how he would feel if . . . we were to . . . have . . . We stumbled on. He replied with his favorite old Teddy Rooseveltian, "Bully!"

"Well," one of us said, "that's just what's happened!"

He grinned broadly, jumped up and embraced Mary Lee, and said and did all the exactly right, though totally unexpected (from him) things.

In sharp contrast to our predictions, the succeeding weeks found him surprisingly affectionate and, curiously, proud. I had *never* seen him that way before. He even began to insist on taking Mary Lee out himself on occasional afternoons and driving just the two of them, chatting happily about who knows what. Sometimes he would be most "un-senior-like" (Uncle Bob's phrase). They would go to some drive-in for a hot dog, a hamburger or an ice-cream cone. He seemed to take a sudden proprietary interest—to find a new part to play (a "character part" of course!)—and he wallowed in it. I don't think I ever noticed how Sylvia felt. When ex-stepmother Mary heard, she bubbled over in sentimental anticipation of "genetic continuity."

This was a time when with a new wife, a child on the way, an imminent new movie, and some quality radio jobs to take care of current expenses, I nonetheless felt I could devote even more time to writing and speaking against the spreading threat of militarism and the lack of an effective political or economic antedote. My greatest failing has been to bite off a greater variety of things than I can possibly chew and I was now becoming conspicuously noted for it. I was immodestly but silently confident that my versatility and ability as an actor was as good as any of my contemporaries. I certainly did not want a political career. I far preferred being a voice, an influence, however limited; an attentive supernumerary in the halls of the mighty instead of being one of their number.

Each day's news made us all so tense that Mary Lee and I decided to charter a fair-sized but not luxurious yacht, get a few pals to share the cost and take the forthcoming Labor Day weekend as an excuse to sail over to Catalina. (We had decided to give the *Wando*—part of Mary Lee's divorce settlement—to the Coast Guard since no one wanted to buy it.) Whoever could afford to share did, and those who couldn't didn't. In addition to

Mary Lee and me, our passenger list included Larry and Vivien, and as they weren't yet married and needed to make a hypocritical nod in the direction of morality for the sake of the Hollywood gossips, Vivien's boring, troublesome mother came along to chaperone. Others aboard were Niv, Bob Coote, Willie Bruce, and Walter Kerri-Davies, a writer. The mood was one of somewhat forced merriment. Although it was a national holiday weekend, it was almost a case of "I've brought you here to enjoy myself and enjoy myself you're going to!"

Washington was quiet. The world seemed hushed in dread anticipation. Hitler had again disavowed an older nonaggressor pact, this time with Poland. Suddenly he blasted his way through that country's western front, while his new strange bedfellow, Stalin, by prearrangement rolled over Poland's eastern front. Great Britain and France warned them both that they would honor their guarantees to Poland unless the invaders withdrew immediately. An answer was expected by the morning of the third of September. On that day our little yachting party had slowly been gathering on deck in silence, grouped around the radio, spirits cringing.

The radio suddenly broadcast Big Ben's deep chimes. Then a solemn BBC voice announced, "The Prime Minister, the Right Honorable Neville Chamberlain." Chamberlain calmly and briefly reported the situation and said that by the deadline a reply from Herr Hitler had not been received. Therefore, as of 11:15, Greenwich Mean Time, "This country is at war with Germany."

No one spoke. No one could. However apocalyptic our thoughts might have been, we could not have envisaged that the next five years would record the most awesome, horrible, and obscene indulgence in human fratricide since mammals first evolved from the primeval sludge. Over *forty million* human beings would lose their lives as a result of the next five years of World War II.

We began to drink—lightly. Then more. A very stupid way to cope. But we were fairly young—and probably stupid too. Within a couple of hours we were hiding our utter despondency behind brave talk. Larry, however, was the only one who got really and truly drunk. More than that, he was plainly *pissed!* No longer mixing with the rest of us, he lowered himself over the side into our dinghy and began to row under the bows of the larger and grander yachts anchored in the Yacht Club basin where we were only weekend guests. All had passengers sitting on their boats' afterdecks, presumably as stunned as we. Larry had now cast himself as Cassandra crossed with Henry V. He stood up, a bit wobbly, in his little cockleshell and shouted up, "You're all finished! Done! Drink up! You've had it! *This is the end!*"

He then sat down and rowed over to the next yacht at anchor and repeated his proclamation. This clarion call from the future giant of the theater was repeated several times.

It so happened that Larry, obliged by the demands of whatever film he was in at the time, had a small line of mustache and closely resembled (at a quick glance) the older, very correct Ronnie Colman, whose own sailboat was peacefully anchored a bit farther out. In an hour or two a small motor launch came out from the clubhouse to the Colman yacht. After a few minutes this same boat came over to us. Our skipper was handed the following note, which he passed on to me and which I then read aloud. It was addressed to the "owner" and it read: "The commodore's office has received numerous reports within the last hour that Mr. Ronald Colman has been rowing around several members' anchored yachts calling out loud and abusive language. The commodore insists that an immediate apology be forthcoming, followed by a formal letter of explanation to this office at the earliest convenience." After an abashed guffaw at this release from the general tension, we weighed anchor and quietly slipped out of the harbor. It was some time before Ronnie found out who his "double" was.

The Russians had moved in on the Finns and got bogged down, so they took over some Baltic lands in the meantime. In the west there seemed a weird silence, a strange lack of movement by anyone. The French, now fully mobilized, sat confidently behind their massive in-depth fortifications—the Maginot Line—that ran the whole length of the French-German border. The British were at last mobilizing and training, filling sandbags and raising dirigible-shaped balloons to considerable heights, intending to discourage low-flying enemy bombers. Otherwise, all was indeed "quiet on the western front."

The French and British residents of the Hollywood film community swamped their respective local consulates and Washington embassies with requests for advice. They were all told to stay put, that the lack of any real effort being made by either side (not counting occasional reconnaissance flights of aircraft by both sides) had caused the world to call it "the phony war." Furthermore, they were told that there was no need for additional manpower yet and that British and French artists, authors, entertainers, and performers in the United States were best serving their countries by remaining here, making friends, and helping to win the goodwill and support of the American people. For a time they all did as they were told. No one left except Niv. He was the only well-known British actor who not only had been to Sandhurst Military College (the British equivalent of our West

Point), but had for a short time been a serving "professional career officer" in the Highland Light Infantry. As such and proud of it (he'd only left because he was broke and had other ideas for his future), he announced that he was determined to get Goldwyn to agree to his return as soon as he could rejoin his outfit. Right then and there I decided I would throw a Farewell and Strictly Stag Party for him. I did and it was a whopper.

I ordered corny life-sized posters with stupid-looking burlesque queens on them and a live second-rate semistripteaser. I then collected a roundtable of mutually favorite chums who were in town. After some funny and sentimental toasts, followed by Niv's witty reply, in through the garden doors marched a small band of wailing Scottish pipers, who circled the table, went out on the lawn, and played some more. This proved very moving—particularly because so many goblets had been quaffed. It was a fine send-off.

Larry seemed at first to be dragging his feet about going home. He couldn't bring himself to leave Viv, and she couldn't let him go either—so besotted with each other were they. It was a matter of classic animal passion for both. They seemed to be constantly impatient to get the trivialities of everyday life over with so they could just rush madly back to bed. Or anywhere else handy and preferably private. The possessor of delicate beauty and sharp intellect, Vivien was apparently extremely libidinous. Larry's own brand of prurience, though more disciplined, was no less keen. So Larry, as patriotic as the next one, deferred his return while he and Vivien stayed on awhile and gathered up some quick bucks by touring the United States in their own production of *Romeo and Juliet.* To Larry's permanent credit, he did do something quite splendid. Quietly, in fact almost secretly, he rose very early every morning for the next few months. Not telling anyone but Viv, he went to a nearby airfield to learn to fly, even though he feared and detested flying. Eventually, after their none too successful tour, he and Viv did return to England, where Larry presented himself to the Royal Navy. He was shortly commissioned as sublieutenant and pilot-instructor in the Fleet Air Arm. It was typical of the kind of guts that marked every facet of Larry's life.

Among other prominent British friends who soon made their way into the war were Dick Greene (in tanks) and Bob Coote (in the Royal Canadian Air Force). It must have been a hard decision for them all to leave promising careers and very good money to drop it all and go off—not knowing when or if they would return.

Many of my old French and British friends began to write wonderful and often very amusing letters about what was happening during these days.

Among the first to write was Dickie Mountbatten. He was already well out at sea in his destroyer, H.M.S. *Kelly.* Edwina (Lady Louis) Mountbatten had given up her playgirl image to devote all her remarkable energy and intelligence to the philanthropic Order of St. John (allied with the Red Cross in wartime) and later headed up the women's section of the St. John's Ambulance Brigade. My old friend-with-the-cinder-in-her-eye had joined up as the equivalent of a private in the WAAF (the women's branch of the RAF).

Niven began writing me from the moment he arrived back in England. His letters were gems of hilarious exaggeration and occasional fabrications, and were carefully kept by every lucky recipient. To the Hollywood columnists, he shrewdly wrote regular but funny reports—many of which were reprinted. To others he would often make wickedly funny jokes at the expense of his "boss," Sam Goldwyn, adding that Sam was so angry with him for leaving that he cut his salary off completely. Actually, few believed this because Sam, infuriating monster that he so often was, was really very fond of Niv and kept him on a retainer "for the duration." Still, the letters were great.

By late November 1939, it seemed to some as if the war would just peter out with a negotiated peace. Even I breathed somewhat easier as I began shooting *Safari,* a routine program picture wherein I (and not Colman this time) had lovely Madeleine Carroll for a leading lady, and Tullio Carminati, a good but somewhat sissified Italian actor, played the villain. It was a part he hated because, as he never ceased reminding us, he had been Eleanora Duse's leading man for some years. As I recall, I was the brave white hunter in Africa who foils Fascist plans to do some damn thing or other to impede Allied interests.

As our lease on the Boyer house would expire in three or four months, Mary Lee and I began to go about the business of looking for another house —preferably a larger one. Since I was at the studio most days, she and Uncle Bill were deputed to check with various real-estate agents for preliminary look-sees. One day she and Bill both rang me in a state of excitement. A big rambling house had just come on the market, and Mary Lee thought it could be made over into something very special. It was almost around the corner from where we lived. Apparently it had belonged to Elissa Landi, my leading lady from *The Amateur Gentleman.* I was told she was now virtually penniless. The bank was putting the house on the market for what was still owed them on the mortgage. It came to about $25,000!

When I went to see it on my one day of the week off (Sunday), my enthusiasm equalled theirs. It was a rambling Spanish mansion, set on the crest of a hill, overlooking a small valley with a tiny river below. From where we stood, the Pacific Ocean was clearly in view five miles away. Although the property was measured as something like seven acres, it had the advantage of appearing to be many hundreds more because it looked out on California state parkland that could never be developed.

We decided then and there to nab it before anyone else. (The purchase cost was divided equally between us.) Neither of us was all that keen on California-Spanish architecture, so I got in touch with Wallace Neff, the famous architect who had converted Pickfair into a showplace for my father and Mary. Neff shared our enthusiasm and went to work almost immediately on plans for changes inside and out. Meanwhile, though we would not move in until the spring of 1940, it was wonderfully exciting, particularly as it was going to be so inexpensive.

When Thanksgiving Day was imminent, Mary Lee and I planned a family dinner (though it was incomplete) at last. It was really a good excuse to have Pete and Sylvia as our guests—the first time since our wedding day that they had been in our home. We had had a very severe heat wave shortly before and as this was pre–air conditioning, everyone suffered and lost sleep in the unremitting scorching weather. Pete rang us to advise an old relief idea: get all beds, sheets, lights, and so forth down to the cellar, attach all the electric fans available, and let them blow over great blocks of ice (it was "pre-fridge" days as well).

It was a fine idea, one I'd recalled from East Coast summers as a child, but forgotten. It was a small but ingratiating gesture, indicating without embarrassment, a wish to be close, noncompetitive friends—*real* friends. He even hinted again at our often planned, and as often deferred, professional partnership.

A few childish gags were prepared. One was to get a live turkey to come through the kitchen door, squawking and flapping, as the cook chased it around the dining room and then back into the kitchen. A moment later, a huge *cooked* turkey was brought in on a big platter. (Ha-ha!) Another so-called joke was devised by Pete to tease Sylvia and her staunch British patriotism: He had me engage a tiny, wizened skeleton of a man—normally employed in a movie as an atmosphere extra. He might have been an aged cockney jockey. He was actually bright and healthy but looked neither. When our party of twelve sat down to dinner, an extra place was hurriedly set next to Sylvia. This bedraggled character, looking half-starved, in a dirty, rumpled linen suit, wearing a pith helmet, was given no introduction to anyone. Sylvia looked both astonished and scared. No one else knew how to react. Suddenly, the "jockey" stood up rather shakily, raised his glass of wine and solemnly toasted, in broad cockney, "Victory for the bulldog breed!" Anything less "bulldog" than this chap could hardly have been envisaged. He did his part splendidly, but it was a feeble joke that got feeble laughs, though applause for the skinny old man.

December 9 was not only my birthday but Shirl Burden's as well. Even though the date was close to Thanksgiving, another party was planned—this one by Flobe and Shirl, to be in honor of "the twins," Shirl and me. As so many others in our family were also Sagittarians—Sissy, and her Hank, Flobe, and now Mary Lee—for years we kept on trying to have one big birthday bash in our own common honor. Pete and Sylvia came to this one —held in the Burden's large house in Beverly Hills.

We all determined in advance to forget every serious concern and be thoroughly cheery and festive for the evening. Everyone succeeded in giving amusing or moderately sentimental toasts. When my turn came, I impulsively broke my lifelong habit of manly undemonstrativeness toward my father. This time, after a few light quips, I directed a brief, but affectionate toast "to Dad." Everyone appeared to be rather touched, but he most of all. I was happy I had done so then and even happier I had said all I had when two nights later he died.

The day after the party he suffered what he thought was a bout of indigestion that a hurriedly summoned doctor diagnosed as a strained heart. The word went out: "Senior has had a serious heart attack." The restrictions imposed by the doctor depressed him beyond belief: "Stay in bed for some weeks."

He had often been warned that his excessive exercising, golfing (often thirty-six holes in a day), swimming, business board meetings—*and* staying up late to please Sylvia—would take its toll. Though he still did not drink, few things would be worse for him than his almost constant smoking—from wake up to lights out at night.

The next night Dad had a word with my Uncle Bob and told him he dreaded the idea of being an invalid far more than death. Indeed, I remembered that on his fiftieth birthday six years earlier, he said he hoped "to die soon—but violently, in an accident of some kind." He added that he had done just about everything he had wanted to do in life at least twice, that now when he woke in the morning he couldn't think of anything new to do. He was bored with life and prepared to die, but not to linger. I was shocked by this statement—even allowing for the probability that it was said for melodramatic effect. Still, I could certainly sympathize with his fearing a long illness. Dad's oldest brother, Uncle Jack, had had a stroke and had lived on, his wits as keen as ever, but was unable to move or speak for the last years of his life.

On this night there was a tone of urgency in Dad's voice as he enjoined his brother to ring Mary if anything should happen and simply say to her, "By the clock." Nothing else!

Bob remembered the origin and meaning of the message: The story dated back some twenty-four years, to the end of 1916, when we were on our way back east after one of our trips to the coast. The discord between Mother and Tu-Tu had not healed despite Dad's unreasoned hope that his wife and his mother would somehow magically become friends without his mediation. A short time before leaving California, he had arranged to deposit a healthy amount of money in his mother's account, hoping it might somehow pacify the situation—smooth out some of her persisting anger with and jealousy of my mother. But then suddenly, on the twenty-third of December, just two days before the family's elaborate Christmas plans could materialize, Tu-Tu died.

I still remember Tu-Tu fairly well, although I can't recall her death. My father remembered her death vividly and guiltily, right up to the day of his own death. When she died, he had been nearly inconsolable with grief, though everyone did their helpless best to ease his pain. Mary, tenderhearted and thoughtful, dropped him a brief note of condolence. He had known her for about a year, and in the emotional flood of the moment he found himself turning to her more than to my mother.

One evening he furtively managed to drive around Central Park with Mary in her limousine. They pulled over somewhere and stopped, and then, for the first time since Tu-Tu died, Mary said he went completely to pieces and sobbed convulsively. Mary sympathized, and after he had more or less pulled himself together, they prepared to drive on. But first they both happened to look at the car's clock at the same time. It had stopped at what they agreed was the moment he had begun to break down. This coincidence became a superstition of sorts between them—a symbolic bond linking them in the most emotional moments of their lives together. At such times they admitted that they conjured up, almost as an incantation, ". . . by the clock!" And the link between them would, by the very repetition of the words, be restrengthened.

Uncle Bob carried out Dad's request the next morning, as promised. He telephoned Mary, who was in Chicago, and reported, "Late yesterday Douglas told me to tell you—'by the clock!' " Mary was silent. Later she made a lovely statement: "He passed from our mortal life quickly and spontaneously as he did everything in life, but it is impossible to believe that vibrant and gay spirit could ever perish."

Although I appeared to be well controlled, I had not been able to talk coherently to Mother. Mary Lee was obliged to break the news to her. She was silent for some time. Then, very quietly, she said, "He was a fine man. God will bless him . . ." Then silence. She said no more but wrote most sisterly letters to Mary and Sylvia and a lovely letter to me.

As for Sylvia, she was inconsolable, but I did my self-conscious best to say something, God knows what. My mind kept reiterating like a broken record that I had spent most of my life hoping to be worthy of my name and to win Dad's approbation. When at long last we seemed to have a more relaxed and fraternal relationship than ever—it had *almost* always been an enjoyable one—his vital spirit had taken flight. Except in a good print of one of his pictures, he has been from then on, a memory.

22

Paramount and my director, Edward H. Griffith, generously rearranged the *Safari* schedule to allow me a few days off while they proceeded with sequences in which I didn't appear. The world's press carried the story of Pete's death on their front pages in huge black headlines—London's *Evening-Standard* actually put out one of their big posters with just the solemn shock printed on it: DOUGLAS FAIRBANKS DEAD. Many movie and Broadway theater lights dimmed for a few moments of tribute.

The funeral service was at the Forest Lawn Cemetery, and Mary Lee and I accompanied Sylvia. Charlie Chaplin came—a small stooping figure—alone. A huge crowd of the curious ogled and muttered as family and friends entered listening to the organ playing slowly and softly his favorite, but probably inappropriate songs: the Mexican ballad "Cielito Lindo" and "La Paloma."

I returned to the studio the next day. I was grateful to my fellow workers that little was said and we went right to work.

It had been difficult to guess the assessment of my father's estate in advance. It is doubtful even if he knew its worth in any detail. Money had never been a worry to him. His credit rating was A-1 throughout his life. It seemed always to be there when needed—even though he usually needed a great deal. When he and my mother were divorced, he did complain loudly that the settlement of half a million dollars he made on her was all he had. This was true, but that was in 1918. He told friends he would be obliged to "start all over."

All of the cousins had often been told of Pete's immense losses during the Depression—not only from the stock market but from severe depreciation of great hunks of real estate that had to be dumped. Still he never appeared to worry. The prevailing gossip was that his estimated ten or twelve million dollars had fallen to three million. He may have greatly exaggerated his losses; at the time it was the "in" thing to do among the wealthy. Undeterred, he made more than ever. Nor was this gain just from his phenomenally successful films or the new United Artists Company, but from the acquisition of good land and generally profitable investments. Furthermore, he went on spending as if there would be no tomorrow. His high standards of living always included yachting trips, extravagant gifts to friends and acquaintances, and very generous ones to others. When Sylvia entered his life, he showered her with every kind of bangle and bauble, cars, and a London townhouse.

Pete's money only crossed my mind when a little "borrowed" help would have come in handy. I had made such a frequently publicized boast that I would never, *never* lean on him and would always proudly make my own way unassisted that I didn't expect anything from his will, except perhaps some personal items. I rarely thought about it at all until after he had died, and Clarence Erickson, the Fairbanks Company general manager, told us that the Trustees would advise all who were mentioned in the will of its contents.

There was no formal gathering in a book-lined room or even a lawyer's office for a solemn recitation of the will's terms. Everyone was informed more or less separately. The results were certainly surprising. His total cash estate was now down to an estimated four million dollars. Although it was certainly more than I guessed, it was much less than others expected.

I later learned that I had once been his chief beneficiary, but Sylvia kept after him to substitute her name for mine in the final testament. Thus half the total estate went to Sylvia—as, in fact, it would have done under California law in any case. I inherited "twelve fortieths," Uncle Bob received "two fortieths" and Uncle Norris (Wilcox, Dad's half-brother) "one fortieth." My four cousins—Uncle Jack's and Uncle Bob's daughters Flobe, Sissy, Tish, and Lucile—also got "one fortieth" in trusts of some kind. Then he left another fortieth with a note that instructed me to distribute it in different amounts to such various old friends and sidekicks as Tom Geraghty, Chuck Lewis, Kenneth Davenport, Earle Brown, Clarence Erickson, and to a list of his favorite charities.

There were also a number of immediately available items that were left to the Trustees' discretion: such things as a marvelous set of Purdey sporting guns (from a .22 rifle to an elephant gun); some beautifully carved bulls by Herbert Hazeltine (one in red marble and one in black); illustrated letters from C. M. Russell, the great cowboy artist; some paintings of the Old West by Russell *and* by Remington. Some of the latter my mother had given him before they married when she paid about two hundred dollars for each— since then they were worth many hundreds of thousands.

Most of these tangible assets were set aside for Sylvia's first choice. Some, like the marble bulls, "disappeared" for years and finally showed up mysteriously in Sylvia's possession. When I wanted to buy them from her, she said she'd given them first to her sister, Vera, and then to Vera's son, her nephew —a fine, bright, and charming boy in his teens who had been badly hurt in a car accident and lived ever after in an iron lung. Obviously, I could no longer express a desire for them and dropped my quest. But when, in time, the poor boy died, they were put on the auction block at Sotheby's and sold to the sculptor's son before I even knew about it.

I decided that since I might soon be short of ready cash, I would take that instead of the Purdey guns that were offered me. This was a foolish decision because Purdey guns came to be worth fortunes. So it went with the pictures and books—all declined in favor of cash. I did keep an interest in the studio and in United Artists, both of which I later sold for much less than I should have because—once again—I badly needed ready money.

Mary Lee sweetly bought from the estate one very fine Russell picture of some Navajo Indians riding along the desert at sunset. It was, I believe, one of those Mother had given Dad, but I could never find out for sure. I loved it. Alas, I've since sold it (for a *very* hefty price). Mary Lee also bought a shamelessly extravagant large alligator-skin suitcase that stepmother Mary had commissioned from Asprey's in London as a present for my father years earlier. It was all fitted out with a gold dresser set: shoehorn, jewel boxes, cups, combs, brushes, and a mirror with a small family crest on each. It was quite out of keeping with the times but nevertheless beautiful, and I surely would have regretted some outsider having it. The price paid for both these items was, of course, deducted from my share of the inheritance.

Next, and most complicated, was the disposition of Rancho Zorro, the big three-thousand-acre citrus and cattle ranch Dad loved and that Uncle Bob supervised. The ranch manager's fine Spanish-style home, a pump house, an office, and a large kitchen building were among the structures built on the property. I never pretended to understand the confusing ramifications in connection with this part of the estate beyond the fact that it gave us all— particularly Uncle Bob—masses of trouble for several years to come.

Negotiations with Sylvia and the Bank of America—acting as trustees—

lasted for years. After the war the value of the ranch slumped severely. There were no calls for large tracts of prime real estate. Subsequently Sylvia, after two failed marriages—one to Lord Stanley of Alderly and one to Clark Gable—offered the estate $365,000 for the ranch. The bank, eager to be rid of its responsibility, accepted this extremely low bid for the entire property, including the mineral rights.

Matters were not helped by the fact that the state of California had imposed the Common Law on the "Napoleonic Code," which these western territories had inherited from their Spanish and Mexican colonial past. This meant that widows could keep on drawing an amount of money roughly equivalent to their standard of living before their husbands' deaths until the will's final settlement. In this case Sylvia's lawyers persuaded the court and the trustees that she should have at least three thousand dollars a month— an enormous sum for 1940. Indeed, the total amount paid out from the estate over the next several years became a considerable drain on its resources. Although Uncle Bob influenced the bank's main decisions, Sylvia also had the legal right to draw on a revolving fund up to the time of the final settlement—something she continued to do for several years and through at least two of her succeeding marriages. After more than two years, the court cut her "allowance" in half. But after complaining to everyone, including the press, she managed to delay settlement even further, running up even more court costs and legal fees.

Although my feelings fluctuated between first disapproving of Sylvia as a stepmother and then becoming mollified when I saw how well she succeeded in making my father happy (though other closer members of the family felt that he *never* really "got over his great love" for Mary), I had now come (very privately) to actively dislike her. I and all the rest of the family thought her money-grubbing behavior most unbecoming. We disliked her aggressive, mercenary attitude and her disregard for others in our family who could usefully use every penny due them.

It was particularly upsetting to me when old friends, like Benita (Mrs. Ronald) Colman, rang up Mary Lee and me to say, in effect, that she never wished to speak to us again after the way I had "mistreated" and "abused poor Sylvia," my father's "grief-stricken" widow! Still, Sylvia successfully clung to the London house on Park Lane, the Santa Monica beach house, practically all their contents, the Rolls in London, and a couple of other cars in California.

I thought it best to keep silent and refrain from adding fuel to the flames by replying, either publicly or privately. Such insults were alleviated in time as I was away from California for long periods. Sometimes I wouldn't even know what was happening and depended on notes from Uncle Bob.

We *all* came to know, however, that when the final settlements were at long last made, in the early fifties, many heirs received a great deal less than predicted.

My first domestic Christmas with Mary Lee produced new emotions, interests, and concerns that tugged and pulled. First of all, my father's absence from our world emptied it more than I would have imagined. I must have loved Pete, but for few reasons that I could name. Yet now, even though I was at last "my own man," oddly freer, no longer a shadow, I missed knowing that he was alive—here, there, somewhere.

Outweighing not my grief but my sadness and regret for so many things was my undisguised pleasure at the positive fact of being joyfully and truly married in a most beautifully conventional way. What was more, I was going to be a father in about four months, and I behaved just like every corny one had done before me.

As if to provide a setting for this kind of normality, the new house was progressing rapidly. We were certain that architect Wallace Neff would become more famous than ever when he completed remodeling our gem of a (medium-sized) mansion. At our suggestion, he had designed a gracefully winding stairway, a long elegant dining room, and a comfortable-sized living room—one of the few then equipped with full-sized movie projectors, discreetly hidden behind hinged panels in the wall. And a splendid-looking paneled library was taking shape, crammed to the ceiling with shelves housing all the fine sets of books I had inherited from Old Dan Sully and many more that Mary Lee contributed. I had one of these bookcases built as a secret door that swung out to disclose circular stairs, leading up to my own sleeping quarters. It was secret in name only as I was so pleased with it that I showed everyone how it worked, as if it were a toy. Mary Lee, with a renowned talent for interior decoration, had a marvelous sense of color and design. As a touching gesture, she commissioned a posthumous portrait of my father that we hung over the library fireplace. Together with Neff, she worked out a marvelous suite of rooms upstairs for us both—plus an enchanting nursery for however many children the future might endow. A charming lady who was a German refugee was commissioned to paint wonderful scenes from Mother Goose on the walls in pastel colors.

In my own ample suite, adjoining Mary Lee's, I had a fine, big dressing-bedroom with large picture windows looking out over our valley below and onto the Pacific Ocean, about five miles away. And since costs were so much less than they are today, the installation of a modest steam room (Turkish bath) as part of my bathroom was no great extravagance but marvelous fun.

The old Spanish exterior of the house had been so modified that it now had only a little ethnic identity left. Next to the existing tennis court, a fine swimming pool with diving board, slide, and dressing rooms was installed close by on the northern edge of our hill. Gardens and lawns around the front and sides, a cypress walk leading to a folly down the hill at the back, and fruit trees of all kinds surrounded this exquisite property. Everything was developing wonderfully, and there were many times when I felt guilty because my appreciation of it all came so soon after my father's death.

As the property faced west and was perched above a canyon, we agreed that the house should be named Westridge—a name also evoked by the Sully family's Watch Hill summer house, Kenneth Ridge.

Another sobering counterpoint to all this enchantment was the daily news of war in Europe—and the growing intensity of America's divided reactions to it. The phony war in the West did not begin to boil over until the ninth of April 1940, when Hitler's hordes began to invade the kingdoms of Norway and Denmark. Early in May, in a brutal but brilliant offensive, they also invaded the kingdoms of Belgium, the Netherlands, and the Grand Duchy of Luxembourg. By mid-May the French Republic was also invaded when the Germans glibly swept around the outside of the Maginot Line. Less than a month later, the French army was in full retreat from the Blitzkrieg; some of them did, however, manage to escape a great German pincers movement and join many thousands of the British Expeditionary Force in their heroic evacuation from the beaches at Dunkirk.

Hitler's original mentor, the buffoon Mussolini, took quick advantage of the imminent French collapse by joining his colleague's declared war on both France and Great Britain. A few days after that, Winston Churchill—having replaced the ailing Chamberlain as Prime Minister—received the King's authority to offer France a full partnership, involving a common citizenship and parliament. But the French, having declared Paris an "open city" (hence not to be defended) and groggy from the sudden defeats on all fronts, declined the British offer and surrendered to Hitler. On condition that France remain "a friendly neutral," the Nazis let them keep nominal charge of about half their country and permitted an obedient government, under the elderly doddering Marshal Petain, to operate from the new French capital of Vichy. Meanwhile, Hitler marched down the Champs Élysées and made a sightseeing tour of the rest of Paris.

All these—and more—bloody devastating events were to leave the British Isles stubbornly alone without defending allies. They were bombed; their merchant, passenger, and naval ships were sunk with ruthless equality, and vast areas of their beautiful cities suffered the destructive effects of the swarms of Luftwaffe bombers that randomly blew them about, taking thousands of civilian lives.

In the United States, Roosevelt carefully tried to send as much assistance to Britain as politics and an argumentative Congress would allow. Part of the country became very loud in its support of isolationism and a small but still surprising number of groups declared themselves for Hitler as the "sole savior from communism" and ". . . from the worldwide conspiracy of international Jewry." When the Vichy government turned over thousands of helpless French Jews to the Germans, there were, shamefully, a few sizable groups in America that applauded this act.

The year 1940 did bring some private exaltation. One happy event was the Academy Awards ceremony for the achievements of 1939, the symbols for which were presented in 1940.

My father was widely acknowledged to have shared with Louis B. Mayer the original idea of an academy for the arts and sciences of the cinema. They intended it to be a serious academy; a place for study, research, training in the creative and performing arts, and technical developments, among other things. When it was fully organized, they made my father the Academy's first president in 1927. He was reelected president each year for the first five years! No one since has come close to winning such administrative confidence. The only thing he came to quibble about was the evolving method of presenting the annual awards. He wanted to give serious and tangible recognition each year by investing the money derived from the tickets for the ceremony in further motion picture research and development. When the annual events began to show signs of becoming vaudeville shows that encouraged rival film companies to lobby for votes for their own products, he objected. This competition was not always above board or free of arm twisting and even bribing the local press.

As these practices became more widely known, Pete protested but to no avail. He then ceased trying and retired to a comparative back seat. However, it didn't appear to occur to those who ran the Academy that his spectacular record and worldwide recognition in the motion picture industry were sufficient to qualify *him* for his peers' symbolic recognition. Other less notable figures were honored—actors, producers, writers, cameramen, and others, but not my father. Nor indeed until many years later were his superlative partners, Mary Pickford, Charlie Chaplin, or D. W. Griffith, so honored. Nor were Garbo, John Barrymore, or many others *ever* recognized by the Academy's members. But very soon after my father's death (actually less than three months after) he was at last unanimously voted a posthumous Oscar, with the inscribed legend on its base: "Commemorative Award Recognizing the Unique and Outstanding Contribution of DOUGLAS FAIRBANKS—First President of the Academy—To the International Development of the Motion Picture—1939."

It was not just because I privately thought the inscribed citation was grossly inadequate and far beneath what the body of his work deserved that I bridled at the advance descriptive press release, but more importantly because it was considered only *after his death!*

In those days the ceremonies were held in the large dining and dancing restaurant, the Cocoanut Grove of the Ambassador Hotel, and were broadcast over the radio. At the time I was also miffed because the Academy had formally invited not me but Sylvia to accept the honor. I suppose, with hindsight, it was natural enough to invite his widow to receive it, but all the rest of our family bit its collective tongue and said nothing.

As it turned out, Sylvia came down with flu and a high temperature on the morning of the big day, and her sister Vera rang to ask if I would substitute for her. I was remarkably civil; and "modestly" accepted her invitation. By some presumed oversight, Mary Lee and I had not even been invited to attend the awards. Nevertheless, we dolled ourselves up and went along. I was very moved by Walter Wanger's eulogizing speech of presentation. I tried to say something brief but appropriate and walked quietly away with the famous statuette. Next morning, Sylvia sent word she would like me to send the Oscar around to her at the beach house. I did so.

Fade out. Fade in. Scene: About two years later. Someone—I never knew who—prevailed on Sylvia after she had remarried (Lord Stanley of Alderley) to send the statuette to me. It still stands on a table in my New York apartment.

Looking back on that evening, I think I must have stubbed my toe (or my tongue), because in all the years since then I've only been invited to participate in—or even to attend the Academy Awards—twice. The first of these times was after World War II, when I was asked to present a small technical award, one usually unnoticed by the public, early in the program. The second time I appeared was when I was asked to present the special Jean Hersholt Award (for long and distinguished service to the motion picture industry) to the widow of a fine old friend and former codirector of the later United Artists Company, Bob Benjamin. This pleasant duty was not the Academy's idea but rather came as a result of a request of Mrs. Benjamin and Bob's partner (and another old friend), Arthur Krim—now the head of the Orion Pictures Corporation. As the official recognition of my father by his colleagues did not come until after his death, it didn't require a poke in the eye with a branding iron to persuade me that I was something less than the Academy's favorite son.

My next job turned out to be both necessary and stimulating. The offer came from Ben Hecht, who was of course a brilliant playwright (e.g., *The Front Page* with coauthor Charles MacArthur). I didn't even try to disguise my delight. I had long admired Hecht's colorful command of "big city" language and his priceless inventory of offbeat characters.

The screenplay was called *Angels over Broadway* and I thought it a gem. It was another gangster-gambler story, but this time a fantasy, not at all cast from the well-worn mold of most Hollywood films. In fact, after reading it, I couldn't wait to ring Ben (we were "first-naming" each other right off the bat!) to accept his offer.

There were, however, one or two potential problems lurking in the studio shadows: one was the studio itself—Columbia. It was no longer the Poverty Row company it had been when I first worked there with Capra in the silent days, but it wasn't among the top prestige companies either. Columbia turned out a few good pictures annually, but its reputation was for second-rate pictures that were just generally on the cheap side. Presumably they were successful. The studio's big boss, Harry Cohn, was a vulgar, ill-tempered, loudmouthed bully.

Even so, Cohn was very anxious to have Hecht make a picture for him and thought the combination of the two of us—plus one of the best of all cameramen of his day, Lee Garmes—would make a fine package. Hence the more Hecht—followed later by myself and then by Garmes—kept raising the ante for our services, the quicker Cohn agreed. Finally Hecht (who despite his superb writing talents had very little knowledge of movie making) insisted that he and I should be coproducers of the picture, Garmes the codirector—and, most important, insisted that after the budget and other details were agreed upon, we were to be left completely alone. No interference whatsoever from Mr. Cohn would be allowed until the picture was cut, scored, and delivered. Cohn astonished us by agreeing to everything.

The other principal male part was to be played by the fine character actor Thomas Mitchell. His mellifluous voice perfectly matched the character of a down-at-heels, alcoholic, out-of-work Broadway ham. I, for my part, brushed up my easy-to-speak, native N'Yawk-ese and now planned to enjoy every syllable of it. For the leading lady we decided on a very new, young girl whom Cohn had recently put under contract after changing her original Latin name to Rita Hayworth. All she had to commend her till then was her beauty and dancing talent, learned from her professional dancer parents.

It was a lucky choice for all concerned. Even though I had been fooled by the seeming naïveté of Joan Fontaine when making *Gunga Din,* I was sure that this time I was right about Rita's innocence. She was *so* new and *so* shy that even such naturally uninhibited talkers as Hecht and I hesitated to use any expletive more earthy than "darn" or "gosh," in her presence.

After tests for costumes and hair-dos, the makeup people decided that Rita's natural hairline was too low, so they shaved her brow to where they thought her hairline should have been in the first place. When later a "shadow" began to show, the poor girl submitted to electrolysis to make the new hairline permanent. The wardrobe department tried to improve her bust line but finally decided God's design was best after all and gave up the idea. Offstage, she rarely spoke, and when she did, it was just in a bit more than a whisper. But Rita took direction very well. She had been studying hard and seriously for some time, and we all agreed that she deserved the success first predicted by this picture. But all this was not to happen for several weeks. In the meantime, we concentrated on the details of production, set designs, schedules, the casting of other parts, and so on.

My finances were as usual something that, for reasons of pride, I kept hidden. Now, trying to sort out present and future, I calculated that all my recently earned money was allocated. It would not carry us for very long, but who knew how long the war would last? My inheritance from my father —the original total was about four hundred thousand dollars—had been severely eaten into by lawyers, accountants, and taxes, but whatever was left would surely be enough for a while. Of course Mary Lee was taking over a good deal with the income from her capital—which I still insisted I wouldn't touch because it should be willed to whatever children we had.

The new job was a stimulating, professional break—being able to star in and coproduce an unusual movie about the back streets of Broadway, its gamblers, racketeers, and typically unemployed actors.

I always felt that if I were to put my heart, mind, and muscle to *almost* anything, I could achieve it. I didn't give my mental powers any abnormally high marks, but I was at least partly convinced that, given the time, I could become the ablest of statesmen, the most sensitive of artists, the most prolific of writers, an actor with few limitations, a better than average athlete, an all-round sportsman and even an inventor of sorts! Because of my fragile early years, my alarmist family, and my father's brief candle, I still feared my life would end soon.

Yet in quite another section of my ego there lurked a young man who was at all times thoroughly uncertain, shy, supersensitive—even cowardly— cowardly both physically and morally—and limited in every boasted field of endeavor. But in recognizing my deficiencies, my pride made me hide them to convince others of virtues that I feared I did not possess.

Sometime late in the day, on April 7, Mary Lee calmly announced that she had every reason to believe the baby would arrive within the next twenty-four hours. That night she woke up with the calm declaration that there was no further doubt about her increasing "discomfort" (Mary Lee's word for "pain"). I checked with her physician, Dr. Williams, and confirmed reservations of her room at the Good Samaritan Hospital in Los Angeles. When the predicted signs of a miracle were imminent, I bundled the glowing mistress of ceremonies into the car (still my old half-breed Cad), and we whizzed toward downtown Los Angeles and the "Good Sam" hospital—just a bit off the ground. We seemed to zip along on an air-cushioned roadway. Despite my breaking every traffic rule in the book, no traffic cop stopped me. The normal fifty-minute drive from Pacific Palisades into Los Angeles proper took about twenty-five minutes.

After we had been officially checked in and over, Mary Lee was told she would not have her big moment for some hours yet and Dr. Williams was so advised by telephone. Therefore she was encouraged to doze as best she could, and I flopped into a chair. She was in labor for about twelve hours. By then it was near noon on the eighth of April.

As Dr. Williams gave her a somewhat strong sedative and she seemed more relaxed, I asked if I might witness the birth of our child.

"Of course!" was the answer. And so I was prepped, gowned, hooded, and masked, and directed to a sort of bleacher seat in a theater operating room. Mary Lee was wheeled in under a display of white sheets. My heart stopped—or seemed to—because she was so very tiny and peaceful and yet was about to do something I couldn't really believe. I felt an urge to cry out, "Don't let anything happen! Turn the calendar back to last year! Don't let her have pain. Don't take any risks!" But she was surrounded by nurses, anesthetists, and others I couldn't recognize—and I had to assume Dr. Williams was among them.

There was a lot of fumbling beneath the sheets, a crowding around, so I could not (mercifully, I suppose) really see anything. Then suddenly there were noises from the white huddle around Mary Lee. Dr. Williams reached for something and gave the something I couldn't see a slap that brought forth a wonderfully reassuring cry. Then, turning to me, and holding up a red, squalling *wonder thing,* said in a voice that smiled, "Look! A lovely baby girl! And everybody is fine!"

I suddenly, unashamedly, teared up to overflowing. God knows what I did next. I was in a daze. All I know was that a bit later on—by minutes, I suppose—I was in another room, mask and gown still on, and was led in to Mary Lee, who seemed half asleep. Then I was given a close look at the fine, funny, wrinkled baby and was told that she weighed seven and a half pounds.

Shortly after, when Mary Lee came around to full consciousness and was told it was all over and that she and her baby were fine, she too beamed, and when I went to hold her hand, she teared up too.

"It's a perfectly lovely girl," I told her, showing off my temporarily superior knowledge, "and she weighs seven and a half pounds! And *here she is!*" That moment was a timeless exquisite interlude of sheer loving and grateful joy. When the baby was put in her arms, she looked so proud, almost arrogant. She beamed and quietly, happily wept, holding her sleeping bundle very gently, very closely.

I must say that even though I had seen all manner of infants before, and had glanced through masses of books about them recently, I still marveled that this tiny creature actually had fingernails so small and neat that they could serve as hilltops for Queen Mab ("the fairies' midwife," as Mercutio reminded Romeo). She even had eyelashes all in place, as they should be— on her eyelids! It was remarkable!

Mary Lee had said that since my father had died she had become very "dynastically" conscious and therefore had hoped for a boy. She even hoped to name him "Douglas III." Of course I was holding fire and not arguing yet, but had the issue actually arisen, I would have protested burdening any child with the same problems I had had to cope with. While I admit the sharing of my father's name had certain advantages at certain times, it also had an equal number of disadvantages. I would have matured with far fewer hang-ups and complexes and even smelled as sweet had I been given another name. We nevertheless prepared in advance for any eventuality by ordering "D.F." to be put on everything that could use initials. Had it been a boy, we could argue whether the "D" was for Douglas or David or Donald or whatever. As it was a girl, there was Deirdre, Danielle, Deborah, Daphne, and others to choose from.

In the end, because Mary Lee loved daffodils, the mythological Daphne had been a romantic Greek goddess, and because we both liked that name best anyway, Daphne was the one we chose. For middle names, both grandmothers rather hoped to be somewhat immortalized. To keep them happy, we compromised and gave our darling Daphne a hyphenated middle name: Nancy-Beth, after both grandmothers.

In those days, the mother of a new baby was not encouraged to get up as soon as possible after the Big Event, and so, even though everyone involved in this delicious drama was healthy and well, it was about three weeks before they could come home—to Westridge, to the new nursery, to all the "oohs" and "aahs" of grannies, friends, cousins, and everyone else.

Then came the arrangements for getting Daphne (soon to be nicknamed "Dabby") christened. We decided that lovely old Tom Geraghty should be one godfather and Gene Markey the other. Either was almost old enough to be her grandfather, but both were outrageously young in spirit. As for godmothers, the first chosen was one of Mary Lee's best friends, Ellen Tuck (Tucky) Astor. We both agreed that enthusiastic and ageless Veda Buckland should be another. We also chose two English honorary godparents—both "Dickies": one Dickie (Lady Morvyth) Benson and the other Dickie Mountbatten. The actual christening took place in the church where we were married. Dabby behaved in exemplary fashion—as did Mary Lee and I —even at the reception afterward back at Westridge, despite all the popping corks and flashbulbs.

Now, with Hecht, I devoted my time to helping tidy up the loose ends of *Angels over Broadway:* the final editing, sound effects, musical scoring, and so forth. At our previews the audiences were warmly approving. Both Ben and I were satisfied that it was a very good picture, and when it was released, most of the critics seemed to agree. Unfortunately these press laurels were written on wet paper. The public stayed away in disappointing droves. Looking at the film again after many years, I can see why. It had some fine but perhaps overstylized Hechtian dialogue; both Tommy Mitchell and I greatly overacted; dear Rita, though very pretty, was very inexperienced; the photography by Lee Garmes was fine; but the whole thing was just too fanciful and, aside from a few melodramatic instances, too fey.

23

The closer to home big impersonal events thundered, and the louder and fiercer these war sounds from Europe became, the angrier grew the debate in the United States. Polls showed that eighty percent of our population wanted the Allies to win. But ninety percent said they wanted America to stay out of any conflict. A shrill nationwide isolationist organization of some eight hundred thousand members that called itself America First was formed. One felt they didn't care if both American coastlines were invaded as long as our great midwestern heartland remained inviolate.

To give voice to the growing sentiments of antiisolationists, a group of liberal Republicans and conservative and middle-of-the-road Democrats (led by Bob Sherwood, the brave Chicagoan Adlai Stevenson, and others) approached William Allen White in Kansas. White was the nationally respected owner-editor of a small paper in his deep midwestern town of Emporia. His profoundly wise yet homespun phrases urging Americans to support the Allies with all the means at their disposal (short of actual war) were quoted in the Congress and throughout the nation. The William Allen White Committee to Defend America by Aiding the Allies (an acknowledged mouthful of a title) was an openly political pressure group designed to negate the effects of the richly supported isolationist America First Committee.

Bob Sherwood invited me to be the head of the committee's Southern California branch (it would be one of more than three hundred throughout the country) and one of its national vice presidents. He said that because mine had been a prominent national voice and name in support of the Allied cause and because I enjoyed the President's personal confidence and good-will, he would like me to accept the offer. *Would* I? I was only too pleased and accepted almost before Bob finished his invitation.

The Aid the Allies Committee's technique of swamping the Congress and the White House with letters, telegrams, and telephone calls urging this or that pro-Allied support was not new, but it was more effectively executed than the opposition's.

Little by little, public opinion moved to our side. The President urged us to put even more public, media, and congressional pressure on him to "push" him into more support and aid to Britain—to become, in his famous phrase, "the arsenal of Democracy."

In this context, I recalled a former visit to the White House when I was among a small, informal group venturing to discuss related matters. The President was expounding the techniques of political leadership. "A leader in a democracy," he said, "must never let himself get too far ahead of his constituents, or else he loses contact with them. Like a military leader, he can't get so far in front of those he leads that they can no longer hear him. What you and your committee—or anyone urging governmental action—must do is to first build up huge public support for a particular bill or law, and that will 'push' the leader. He then advances a little until his followers catch up. After that, with more support, he advances a bit again, until once more his followers join him. So that's what you've got to do. Because even a President of the United States can only go so far without the majority of the whole nation—not just his own party—supporting him. Now, go out and get the public to *push* me!"

The White Committee soon won tens of thousands of supporters and the President agreed as much as he dared with most of our proposals. Quietly, unnoted by the press, I now traveled to Washington and met with FDR and Secretary of State Cordell Hull quite a few times. Under Bob Sherwood's guidance, I even suggested a phrase here and there for a presidential speech. I made some nationwide broadcasts backing the White Committee and the urgent need to support Allied defenses. We urged a deal under which we would exchange two hundred elderly U.S. destroyers (which were desper-ately needed because of the many sinkings in the North Atlantic suffered by the Royal Navy) for the "loan" of a number of permanent bases for the U.S. Navy on British-owned islands in the Bahamas and the Caribbean.

The public support for this plan was stupendous, but canny FDR, sup-ported by his wise and wily Secretary of State Hull, had to bargain with Churchill, who in desperation was obliged to agree. The White Committee's administrative head, Clark Eichelberger, appealed to the famous legal eagle Benjamin Cohen for an opinion on how, legally, the President could transfer the destroyers to Britain quickly without waiting for the possibly interminable time it would take to pass an authorization bill through Congress. He came up with a plan virtually overnight that was then publicly approved and put forward by our committee's leading lawyer-statesman, Dean Acheson (later to become President Truman's Secretary of State). The date was August 23, 1940. The President signed the order for the ships to go to Britain on September 5.

One of the angriest arguments of the isolationists was that the Allies had not yet paid up the debts incurred during the Great War, so why help them until they did? I collected reams of solid rebuttals to these protests and wrote and published a widely circulated pamphlet on the fallacy of those arguments, proving how rich *we* had become from the last .war, even as others had lost nearly everything. Although haughtily disdained by those who deplored my even commenting on economics, it did have a salutary effect and was entered in the Congressional Record.

When Lord Lothian was replaced as ambassador by Lord Halifax, I recognized an old acquaintance in a new guise. I don't believe he ever remembered that in the early thirties, when he was known as Lord Irwin and before he was made a Viceroy of India (and the Earl of Halifax), he had been the disapproving father of one of my great crushes, the lovely Lady Anne Wood. She was now happily married to a gallant and handsome Yorkshireman, the Earl of Faversham. I never wanted to remind this unassuming gentleman of his former disapproval because we soon became good friends and remained so for many years. It was a most useful connection because I was permitted to quote to an appreciative President and Secretary of State (in confidence of course) his and his government's private views. Part of our "Aid the Allies" Committee's job was to learn both what was needed to further the anti-Axis cause and what the President was prepared or *wanted* to do.

Very privately, in response to a suggestion from Dickie and Con Benson, my beloved old friends in England, I arranged (somehow, by a fiddle with my accountant and by using some savings from my last picture) to support and maintain with small-installment contributions three small voluntary hospitals for the RAF in Hampshire, to augment their big official ones. They were called the Douglas Voluntary Hospitals, and no one knew I was their "angel" until well after the war. They were administered by the British Red Cross and the Order of St. John's Ambulance Corps. I also joined a large Hollywood group in a short theatrical run of some of Noël Coward's one-act plays, with the profits going to British War Relief.

At this time, Bob Montgomery had come back from an unpublicized visit to France where, in defiance of MGM's order to stay put in California, he volunteered to drive an ambulance for the still uninvaded French for several weeks. I applauded his splendid spirit while envying his experience. Together we decided we would see what we could do about volunteering in one of our own military services very quietly, without any publicity whatsoever. My old friend Phil Holmes had left his love, blues singer Libby Holman, for his brother Ralph to marry and had joined up with the Royal Canadian Air Force—but, damn it, he got himself killed within months. And what were *we* doing except talking?

And talk *I* did—for certain! I made a number of "cheer up, we're behind you" broadcasts to Britain and other Commonwealth nations. They were gratifyingly received by immense audiences. I also made several local and many national broadcasts on one or another of the American radio networks.

When the President's reelection campaign went into high gear and it was clear that his Republican opponent, Wendell Willkie, although domestically conservative, was in substantial agreement on foreign policy, I called on Willkie and we had a short private talk. I told him that he was, in my amateur's opinion, making several good points as an opponent of the Democratic Party's New Deal with which I could agree, but that if he were elected and Roosevelt defeated, the outside world might take it as disapproval of FDR's foreign policy. To his great credit, Willkie admitted (privately) that this was a matter of concern to several of his advisers and he quite understood why I, for one, would continue to support the President.

My own personal "campaigning" had certainly done me much professional harm. I received hundreds of abusive and threatening letters. A few were anonymous. And there was a handful of film exhibitors who spread the word that they would no longer show my films. There was a marked decrease in new offers from any of the film companies. Then I learned to my anger that Joe Kennedy, fresh from our London embassy, had gone out to Hollywood to advise the studio bosses that they should refrain from making pro-Allied, anti-Nazi films because people would say it was because of the Jews! I wrote Washington about it and the President was reportedly furious. Though I was very upset by this at the time, an inner voice reminded me of the spot most American Jews were in. If they supported anti-Nazi movements, they would, of course, risk being attacked as warmongers anxious for America to go to war on their behalf. If they did nothing, they were criticized for turning their backs on Jews in Europe. The whole pushing, shoving, and shouting homefront confirmed my old disinclination to go into party politics. My skin was still much too thin for their everyday rough and tumble.

It was upsetting enough to read snide syndicated criticisms, but now my frequent support of our government's pro-Allied, anti-Nazi, anti-Fascist (and, up to then at least, anti-Soviet) policies alienated people in other ways. One small example involved nice old Harold Brooks, the very sedate husband of Frances, the New York hostess who had so warmly encouraged my romance with Mary Lee in its early days. Harold had proposed me for membership in New York's elegant and expensive Racquet and Tennis Club. All had gone well—at first. Seconders and letters of support were flatteringly forthcoming. But then, suddenly, the club received a rash of letters from a group of members protesting in the strongest terms any membership for an "open supporter of Roosevelt, that notorious left-wing traitor to his class, that warmonger." In the end a very embarrassed Harold Brooks was regretfully obliged to withdraw my name in order to avoid a rumpus that might get into the papers. More than forty-five years later I still resist the proposals of friends kind enough to want to revive the idea. The snub still rankles.

The White Committee organized a rally of several thousand people in Chicago for September 18, 1940. I was asked to speak on the same platform with the influential and articulate Senator Claude Pepper and the widely syndicated political columnist Dorothy Thompson. (Miss Thompson—Mrs. Sinclair Lewis in private life—was so forceful and unrelenting in her championing of the Allied cause that she had been nicknamed "Perpetual Emotion" by her mockers.) I feared I would be in far too high-powered company, speaking alongside widely accepted authorities on foreign affairs. But I relished the chance to be with them, so I wrote and rewrote my speech weeks ahead of time. When Mary Lee and I finally got to Chicago, I was more nervous than I would have been on an opening night playing *Hamlet* —and, in retrospect, with good reason.

Our welcome to Chicago, the heart of the "America First Committee," included a couple of rather off-putting threats to bomb us if I went ahead with my speech at the meeting the next night. Although I turned this and a few other inhospitable messages over to the police, I remained in a fairly well-disguised shaky condition. Later, facing a capacity crowd of more than sixteen thousand, in addition to another incalculable number of listeners to a national radio hookup, I felt my knees banging together like loose crackers in a tin. My throat was as dry as the Sahara. Both the senator and Dorothy Thompson were enthusiastically received, and when it was my turn I began my oration with as much composure as I could. This pose was made more difficult by a sudden urge to throw up right there on the platform. Somehow I managed not to and began to speak.

Now, I am frankly pro-British. But only because I am radically pro-American . . . The question posed by some of our diehards as to what we have in common with Britain is the easiest of all to answer. The first and very important reason is that we have in common the language of Chaucer, Shakespeare, Milton, and the King James version of the Scriptures, of Keats, of Byron, and of Shelley. We have in common a tradition of representative government dating from the time of the Druids—more than two thousand years ago. We share the history of an idea which men wrote of, thought of, shouted and fought for. An idea which will allow us to say what we please, think what we please, write what we please, and do what we please—within the limits of the laws which our elected representatives legislate on our behalf. An idea that gave us the Magna Carta, the Bill of Rights, and the Common Law. That idea, in the face of seemingly insurmountable obstacles, has never died.

I then added a footnote dating from a conversation with Ribbentrop, Ciano, and Count Grandi in London:

Prominent Nazi officials, as long as two years ago said, in my presence, that a military invasion of the Western Hemisphere "may not be necessary" to bring the U.S. within the Nazi-Fascist orbit. They had other methods equally effective. Their organization has already been so thorough that Central and South America are wincing under their pressure. Dr. Goebbels, the notorious director of "Fifth" Columns, said, no longer than thirteen months ago, to a personal friend of mine—"I'll see you in America within eighteen months."

This remark had been made to my father in Venice just before he left Europe for the last time.

After it was all over, I was told my speech had won "thunderous" applause. I hadn't noticed it, however, as with Mary Lee beside me I made my way shakily down the steps and beneath the platform, where I took some deep breaths before others came and escorted us out to cars and back to the guarded hotel for some round-robin congratulations.

Our committee's widely acknowledged success in the opposition's heartland spurred a vicious series of angry rebuttals. I was, of course, the easiest target. One of my most important assailants was a respected member of the America First group, a former government administrator and Army officer, General Hugh Johnson. He wrote to the press:

We have been harangued by several eminent breast-beating war-criers . . . We were advised on this serious strategical question by a movie he-vamp from Hollywood, young Douglas Fairbanks. He, as everybody knows, has a long, heroic, and varied celluloid military and diplomatic experience—in all parts of the world that can profitably be imitated on photographic film in Hollywood . . .

Like the inexperienced fool I was, I took immediate exception to the general's putdown and wrote him so. His answer, which I have preserved in the family archives, outdid the first slaps. It read in part as follows:

Dear Douglas: When you are as old as I am, and my friend your father was, you won't take yourself so damned seriously. You may know a lot besides acting—although I am not so sure you know that very well—but I don't think you know very much about strategy, defense, politics—and especially fighting Britain's wars. I know the latter even if not the former. You are being a propagandist's little agent—and the direction of that propaganda is disaster. When you call me an isolationist, you are calling names. It isn't isolation to prepare to defend—and get ready to defend—half a world. I don't know what you would call protagonists for our involvement from Singapore to Aden and dear old Baghdad—except silly suckerism. Forget it, kid—I neither meant not did you any harm, but you can't get down into the arena without getting sawdust or tanbark on your shoes . . .

After I had read his hand-delivered letter, I would gladly have punched the old poop on the nose had he been handy. But I kept my temper—at least for the time being. In so doing, I was undeniably calmed by the enormous number of congratulatory letters and telegrams, telephone calls, and press reports I received from other more sympathetic areas as well as, predictably, from British, Canadian, and other Commonwealth newspaper accounts. Nevertheless the Chicago police did not relax their protection until we left town.

The weekend after the Chicago experience, Mary Lee and I were invited to the Roosevelts' big country estate, Hyde Park, on the banks of the Hudson. It was fun and fascinating to be with the Roosevelt family informally on their home ground. The only ones present besides FDR were Eleanor, the President's lovely-looking but domineering mother (of whom everyone —including her son and daughter-in-law—was afraid), young Frank Jr., and Harry Hopkins.

Both Mary Lee and I found it particularly hard to leave the new baby so soon after she had been born. Not that Mary Lee was nursing, but Daphne was so adorable and at that time of her life, such a uniquely personal possession, we didn't want to be away from each stage of her growth for a minute. Also, there had been problems in settling on just the right nurse. But it did seem important for *me* to go at least, and I was relieved that Mary Lee felt, as I did, that it was essential in those troubled days for us to be with each other. Luck being on our side, a new nurse was found and, with Bill Sully on a retainer to keep watch, we'd gone off for just a few weeks. Dabby, I must sadly record, minded not one bit.

After Chicago and Hyde Park, we stole a quick but wonderful few days of rest in Virginia at Boxwood Farm. Then, after a trip to New York, we headed home to our huge-eyed Dabby. That was more than good; it was delicious.

The best reports of life in Britain came from Niv. After one of my transatlantic broadcasts had been reported in the British press, he cabled: "Speech perfectly grand . . . papers reported [it] in full . . . Have been in London last six weeks—Bang, bang. [Signed] Niv."

Instead of rejoining his old regiment, the Highland Light Infantry, the Army put him into the Rifle Brigade—the "Green Jackets," as they were popularly known. Niv reported that he had been selected to train with a new special, still secret kind of outfit—a motorized reconnaissance group designed to dash to and fro, acting as liaison between forward infantry units and field command headquarters to the rear. These functions were once performed by the horse cavalry! The group was called Phantom, and its uses were kept very hush-hush.

Niv, as a former regular career soldier, reveled in his new assignment and had a typically hard time remaining quiet about it. He often joked that the phrase "to keep mum" had something to do with his mother's expense allowances. But he managed to write yards of letters to friends in the States. Of course, I was delighted to be number one on his lively mailing list. What he probably didn't know at the time was that mail from the U.K. to America passed through Bermuda where it was censored by masses of WRENS, the women's division of the Royal Navy. Or, now that I think of it, perhaps he *did* know! In any case, one time Niv wrote me an *eight*-page letter—all crowded in a small but clear hand. The missive described in hilarious detail a surprisingly uninhibited amorous adventure he had recently experienced in a car, at night, in blacked-out London, during a heavy bombing raid, with a mutual female acquaintance of ours. She was a most attractive lady we had once thought to be far removed from carnal fun-and-games. Niv left nothing out. Every detail of every moment of their mutual lechery was carefully noted. But the primary and naughty fun of the letter was in contemplating the reactions of all those giggling blue-jacketed WRENS in Bermuda gathering around to read aloud a letter from Major David Niven in England to his friend Doug Fairbanks, in Hollywood, and splitting their sides with laughter—or *shock!*

I read on. After omitting absolutely nothing, Niv ended his report by writing, ". . . and at that precise moment a large bomb dropped in . . ." and some dear, sweet WREN, anxious to deny the enemy any knowledge of the Luftwaffe's accuracy, had carefully cut out where the bomb had dropped!

Not all my British mail was so cheerful. I also received a note, after a long, disturbing silence, from my old friend and colleague at Criterion, Harold French. He finally got around to painfully reporting one dreadful night of blitzing when a fire bomb landed on his St. John's Wood house and his sweet wife, Phil, was destroyed with it. A year or so later, I had another shock when I heard from the husband of my pretty long-time British secretary, Mrs. Pat Cherry, that she had been another of those blown up one night during a heavy raid.

It was undeniably enjoyable to be invited to the White House from time to time and to have at least limited access to the President on a personal and private level. FDR always seemed relaxed in spite of the constant pressures of his high office, finding many moments in the day to banter and discuss trivia. Frank Jr. was the one son I knew best, and he was able to wangle invitations for me and Mary Lee. We would be asked to come to our national "palace" for an occasional cocktail or even more occasionally to stay overnight *or,* once in a rare while, even for a weekend! During these latter times the First Lady was the most considerate of hostesses. Mrs. Roosevelt would usually come up to our room on the third floor, sit on the end of Mary Lee's bed, and chat with the two of us.

On rarer occasions we were asked to spend the weekend at Hyde Park with what seemed the special permission of the ever-present matriarchal Mrs. James Roosevelt, who presided over a room filled with family, and such intimates as Harry Hopkins, Bob Sherwood, Averell Harriman, and Joe Lash. The President would dominate the room by habit and personality, quite apart from rank and title. Sometimes he would tease me about movies, or politics, or public affairs. During some of these easy times in the afternoon at tea or after dinner, the President, encouraged by Hopkins, would make suggestions as to what we in the White Committee might do to help his campaign by stimulating national interest and sympathy for the Allied cause. Occasionally I would be asked my opinion on something or other. Always very self-conscious and anxious to appear better informed than I was, I sometimes detected a good-natured condescension, or patronization if you will, of a young and (probably) helpful public supporter.

Once, when an opening gave me the opportunity to speak of something besides politics or war, I decided to champion the cause of my professional colleagues in all the arts. "Why," I asked, "couldn't professional artists of *all* kinds be taxed as are oil wells and other limited natural resources? We, like other natural resources, have some boom times when we're taxed to the maximum extent; then the next year, when we might have no job at all, we should be taxed just as oil wells and other resources are taxed on their *average* production over a period of years."

The lion would not be bearded in his den. The presidential answer to my standard bearing was a laugh. "Sorry, Doug," he said, "but the arts—splendid as they are—are just not as necessary to the national welfare as are such natural resources as oil and minerals!"

I tried my best to cultivate the confidence of Harry Hopkins, presidential intimate and *éminence grise.* I tried largely because I suspected that he did not really like me in the first place, that he would distrust anyone of my profession. He always looked terribly frail, pale and wan, with a lopsided face and a strong, almost raspy voice. He nevertheless traveled the world at his master's order, was a tough negotiator and finally the husband of a much younger and attractive woman. Hopkins made *me* edgy because I thought he made slightly snide remarks or else talked down to me. Young Frank finally put in a word with Hopkins, after which he apparently spoke very cordially about me. But I didn't know about it for some time.

My insecure feelings came to the fore when I had made an informal proposal that the United States should encourage the British to create a new order of some kind—such as the Crusader Knight Templars of the Middle Ages, to be conferred as an honor on both Commonwealth and American citizens equally—since we came from roughly the same cultural and political environment. We could request the King to be its nominal head.

Hopkins, quite rightly, blew his touchy top at this hint that anyone could be even ceremonially higher than the President. I blushed at my own tactlessness and quickly withdrew the idea with a feeble laugh and a rapid change of subject to baseball.

The President's polio, which paralyzed him from the waist down, was never discussed. When he had to be lifted into or out of cars or into his wheelchair, one left the room or else carefully turned away. Outdoors the Secret Service men were careful to see that no one photographed him. It is another sorry comment on our own "up-to-date" time when too many media editors have disavowed any semblance of taste by giving the public every icky detail about a President's innards—plumbing and all. In FDR's day no one, not even his enemies, referred to his disability. Everyone, including his family, stood whenever he was wheeled into a room. Even his mother was at pains to tell Mary Lee and me that she always did so, even when they were alone, because, she said, "He is the President of the United States, and the office itself deserves everyone's gesture of respect."

At other times, however, she would tease him in ways that neither Eleanor nor any of his children, not even his intimates, would venture to try. For instance, she would "playfully" tilt his chair back, as if to upset it, until the President in a semiexaggerated panic would call out, "Mother! For God's sake, *stop* it!" Whereupon, with what she presumably thought was a reassuring smile, she would obey. Eleanor, at such times, would look fearful but helpless to dare impose herself on her mother-in-law's first-claim possession.

From the waist up, the President was a very muscular man with enormous shoulders and strong forearms, though his hands were very soft and gentle, fleshy and sensuous. His manner in private was just as winning, as even his opponents conceded. I personally was intrigued by his eyes. They were very small, slightly askew, and too close together. I wondered if others noted this as well. They almost served to contradict or modify his engaging smile, velvety voice, and cultivated Groton-Harvard speech. His wife and cousin, the plain, gangling, gentle Eleanor, was his constant strength and brace. Few knew at the time whether she alone was unaware of his flirtatious peccadilloes and more serious attachments. The details of his intimate relationships, with his secretary Missy Le Hand, and later with Lucy Mercer, have been amply recorded elsewhere.

Many people in high-level public life develop some form of megalomania. It is as if it is a necessity to maintain a power position and the confidence of supporters. Roosevelt was no exception. Still, his contagious charm, which he could turn on and off like tap water, neutralized a good deal of the bitterness that many of his policies engendered—particularly among those of his own upper-class background.

One afternoon at Hyde Park, the President asked me if I would care to drive up to a small lodge he had had built at the top of the hill behind the main estate. He had a specially equipped little Jeep that he could drive using only his arms, having had it so designed that it needed no foot pedals. A Secret Service man accompanied us in the back seat, and *his* backup followed at a discreet distance in another Jeep. The "lodge" was, the President told me, where he would go from time to time, either alone or perhaps with an aide, to read and look over his estate out to the great lazy Hudson just beyond and below. The lodge was bare of luxuries but well stocked with books and equipped with a few comfortable chairs and a couch.

The afternoon I went up there with him was lovely and warm, and we sat talking for a spell outside in the Jeep. Suddenly he interrupted himself to gesture at the view and points of interest nearby. He seemed particularly relaxed that afternoon, and as we watched the ships passing up and down the great river beyond, he said, as if speaking only to himself, "Just think, there well may be a time in the future when ships passing this part of the Hudson might dip their flags as they go by."

There are other vignettes that suddenly flash to mind. FDR was known to share most of Secretary of State Hull's views on foreign affairs, including a far from cordial dislike of the intemperate and arrogant attitude of General Charles de Gaulle. Roosevelt always admitted to a strong admiration for the British, but he could also be suspicious and jealous of them for reasons that even his confidants disputed among themselves. He admired French culture but was far from a Francophile. He was proud of his partly Dutch, partly Scottish ancestry. Along with the chief of naval operations, Admiral Ernest King, Roosevelt believed that the approaching years might very well find the United States heir to Britain's mantle of world policeman, of becoming the Great Power influence that the British Empire had been for so long.

It is an amusing sidelight to the Roosevelt character that he resisted believing that Churchill wrote his own speeches. Although he had a fondness and admiration for Churchill, he was also jealous of him in many ways. When Bob Sherwood and I both insisted that Churchill *always* wrote his own speeches, FDR became indignant. Even when Harry Hopkins, after a visit to wartime London, reported that he too knew Winston was his own speechwriter, FDR was quoted as saying, "You've all been taken in by the redcoats again! After all, Winston has to debate in Parliament, answer questions, and administer the nation as well—he *couldn't* also have the time to write his own speeches! *I* don't have a spare minute to write a speech. How can Winston?"

I wished to join the Navy before the war actually began, when I thought we might eventually be involved. I was discouraged, at first, however, because getting a naval commission in those days normally meant one had to have a degree from a recognized university, and of course I had no such thing. By any formal standards, my academic record was not only lopsided but virtually nonexistent.

All my life I had loved the lore of the sea, adventure stories of the bounding main, and almost everything to do with ships. I was amused by the seriousness with which the world's navies clung to old traditions and designations: for example, "ladder-ways" instead of stairs; bow and stern, forward and aft, "sharp" and "blunt" ends instead of front and rear; port and starboard instead of left and right; bulkheads and poopdecks, and always decks in lieu of floors, bos'ns "piping the brass aboard over the side"; for meals or announcements, "Now hear this . . . !"; gigs, barges, launches, "aye, aye, sir!" and "eight and lesser bells"; "ruffles and flourishes," with drums and bugles; "side-boys"—and all the other carefully preserved nautical romance.

I did not fancy starting as a regular "bluejacket," possibly stuck way below decks in the engine room or somewhere similarly claustrophobic. In Britain's Royal Navy, the volunteer reservist—whether son of butcher or duke—*had* to begin at the lowest rank. In the States, only a very few ordinary sailors were given commissions. When they were, they were almost always originally "regulars" or "career" men who, even so, wore the dark red service ribbons indicating they had come up from the bottom, had *not* gone to Annapolis, and were slangily, sometimes admiringly (and sometimes snootily) called "mustangs."

I resisted suggestions to join the Army Air Corps because I knew next to nothing about flying and wasn't particularly anxious to learn. I politely declined to accept some relatively easy-to-get commissions in the Army— first because I suspected I'd be given too cushy an appointment for Army public relations purposes or else the other extreme—a foot-slogging, parade-ground bashing, wet, dirty, cold infantryman's job of being shot at from close range. Furthermore, I remembered too well my time in military schools and how much I hated having to walk. I *did* think the Marines might be for me. They were at least a part of the naval establishment, often part of a ship's company, and had the best-looking uniforms. But then I learned that as a Marine, I would very likely have as much walking and close combat as I would in the Army, so I dropped that idea, too.

I made some private inquiries about joining the Canadian Navy. This just *might* have been possible. Many Yanks were joining the Canadian forces—as my mourned old pal, Phillips Holmes, had joined the RCAF, but I really preferred to get into the American forces if I could. The chance of being drafted after the age of thirty was, at least for the immediate future, most unlikely. But finally Bob Montgomery and I arranged an interview with the commander of the 11th Naval District in San Diego. Bob already had a university degree and I was allowed at least to apply. I would have to pass a number of fairly complicated exams in Navy regulations, which I would have to learn by correspondence courses. Also I would have to attend a certain number of drill sessions, take courses in navigation and gunnery, and then present a responsible person's signed assurance that my educational standards were equivalent to two or three years of college or university. Then it would be *possible* to get a regular "deck officer" (as opposed to a "specialist") commission.

As things turned out, neither Bob nor I had the time off to go down to San Pedro for all the required drills and other training. After his early ambulance stint in France, Bob had to return to work at MGM. Although I had no good job offers at all after *Angels over Broadway,* I was very busy. My continuing activities with others in Hollywood on behalf of war charities, boosting public political support for the Allies and campaigning for the President's reelection had inspired so much public controversy that even after a fine three-year roll of hits, there was suddenly almost nothing on the horizon worth considering. I was not box-office poison (indeed my exhibitor's rating was quite high, and I was listed near the top), but they said I was becoming too controversial and an unacknowledged boycott appeared to be in effect.

With the help of Gene Markey, a naval reservist of many years standing, I made some progress in my obligatory written exams, and on occasion managed to get in some of the other training classes as well. As there was a strict clamp on any publicity, there was no great pressure or distraction to deter me.

When Election Day 1940 was almost upon us, my heretofore docile bride began to rebel. She was not going to vote for FDR under any circumstances. She admitted she liked the President personally, had been thrilled to be his guest, and was "absolutely devoted" to Mrs. Roosevelt. However, she just could not bring herself ("Southerner" though she stubbornly insisted she was) to alter the conservative Republican influences of a lifetime. Furthermore, all her friends back east had firmly convinced her that FDR was a "rabid socialist." Furthermore, she was privately not even so sure as I that the United States was potentially threatened by the spreading dictatorship virus. Regardless of my own beliefs Mary Lee firmly decided she would vote for Willkie!

I had been called to join a big, nationwide network broadcast in support of FDR the evening before Election Day. I had taken a lot of trouble over my speech, not just because I believed in what I had to say, but because I was so pleased to be asked to give one under such impressive auspices. Before we turned in that night, I convinced the poor trusting mother of our firstborn, that her vote for Willkie and mine for Roosevelt would cancel each other's out. Therefore, I said we should agree to sleep late the next morning and not go to the trouble of voting at all!

Bless her sweet, sort of innocent heart, she agreed. But I, a sinister cad, got quietly out of bed early the next morning. I drove into the village of Pacific Palisades, some five or so miles away, voted for the President as planned, and got back to my room and back into my pajamas before Mary Lee awoke. And what's more, I didn't tell her of my dirty trick till the next day! She was—understandably—livid. However, as it turned out, the President's majority was enormous, and (I was sharply reminded) he had not needed my deceitful vote anyway!

The only sop to my guilt was that shortly thereafter I was deluged with letters, telephone calls, wires, and back slappings, mostly congratulating my broadcast. As a topper to that came congratulations from the President himself, wishing to "felicitate" me on my "fine performance over the radio on election eve" and adding he was sure Secretary Hull would keep my offer of service in mind.

Another pleasant result of my efforts was an invitation to stay with President and Mrs. Roosevelt for a few days during the inauguration in January and to attend the small (by Washington standards) dinner at the White House that the President would give before the two or three big Inaugural Balls to be held that night. It pleased us mightily to learn that Bob Sherwood would be there acting as the official master of ceremonies and making the dedication speech to be broadcast at the start of the festivities.

On *the* evening, the President was as outgoing as ever—perhaps even more so—although he had been heard to complain of fatigue after such a long day of standing in his leg braces for the ceremonies. He must have stood for hours as he reviewed a long parade of armed forces.

The formally dressed White House party of course happily sampled a plain supper of scrambled eggs, sausages, and bacon that began early. About halfway through, a Marine presidential aide, resplendent in full-dress uniform, delivered a note to the President. We all wondered anxiously what had happened. The President then said to us all, "Bob Sherwood has suddenly been taken ill. He's had a dreadfully painful attack of *tic douloureux*. His cheek is paralyzed. He can't speak! He arrived at Constitution Hall all right but he's now been obliged to go home."

The sympathetic mutterings down the table were shortly interrupted by the President calling out, "Hey, Doug!" and beckoning me to come to him. "Will you do me a favor?"

Of course I would.

"Will you skip the rest of your snack and run over and take Bob's place?" They'll take you over there in one of our cars and brief you on the way. Good luck!"

There was just no ready way I could think of to decline such a request.

I think I managed a wan smile, hurried over to assure Mary Lee that another car would bring her on with the others, and in a kind of daze was off to the ball! It was a stupendous evening. I somehow managed to rise above my anxieties.

The next day the press, while commiserating with poor Bob Sherwood's painful illness, was unusually complimentary to his last-minute substitute. The only real giggle occurred at the final run-through, when Irving Berlin sang his own "God Bless America." The conductor had borrowed Irving's personal copy of the song, on which was written at the top: "Dedicated to the Republican Party!" This *faux-pas* was never mentioned.

Soon after 1941 began, we were back in California. Even with a new nurse engaged for Daphne, Mary Lee was more reluctant than ever to leave her again so soon—and in fact, she didn't!

At the President's request, the Aid the Allies Committee plunged into its next campaign—one that history would refer to as the "Lend-Lease Bill" and early in February I was down in Miami speaking at a rally of twenty-five thousand people to another nationwide radio audience. My zealous forays away from motion pictures and into the ruthless arena of foreign affairs continued to bruise my career. That I managed to be heard in the disputatious life of national affairs did not fool me into thinking I was God's next gift to American politics. I never considered elective office—as did my supremely successful former colleague President Reagan—because I knew I was too thin-skinned to enter that often muddy arena. The more I got to know some of the inner workings of party politics, the more disillusioned in them I became. I felt like Jimmy Stewart in *Mr. Smith Goes to Washington,* but I had no wish to emulate that character and dive headlong into the arena only to be wasted by the lions. A good many politicians were, and of course are, honest and hard-working, but I suspected they were in the minority. A modern example is the large number of senators and congressmen who are vehement supporters of small-arms and gun control *in private,* but who are obliged to admit dependence on the financial support they get at election time from the rich and powerful gun lobby. Many don't dare vote as they believe—nor *even* as their constituents urge!

I did once think that part-time "behind-the-scenes" assignments in foreign affairs would be a fascinating avocation, provided I was given a position of some responsibility and influence. But I knew my own limitations better than anyone. To ease into the rarified atmosphere where great decisions affecting our nation were made and, to a different extent, be a trusted friend and diplomatic confidant of older and wiser foreign officials would be fascinating. But I did not have anything like the amount of money necessary to be an ambassador to one of the better posts (e.g., London, Paris, Moscow, or Rome) and I wouldn't want a lesser one. Even in those prewar days when ambassadors had more real political responsibility than they do now, I didn't try to be more than I was already. I had no illusions of being a modern Metternich, but I did frankly enjoy being a fly on the wall in the corridors of power.

24

The American government had been noting the deterioration of pro-democratic sympathies in many parts of Latin America for some time. Despite our long-term efforts to improve capital investment there, encourage more and better education, and provide some defense matériel, a growing admiration for (or fear of) German leadership was becoming apparent. Up to that time the British had been the largest long-term investors in South America, building and developing great seaports, vast long-range railroads, Argentine forests, Brazilian rubber plantations, and establishing huge cattle ranches and meat-packing companies. Many of these once friendly Latin American countries suspected that their bread might not be buttered much longer by Britain and that taking her side openly, now that she seemed "done for," could be dangerous. Brazil and Argentina began "requisitioning" many British investments—sometimes by bargain-basement purchase and sometimes by outright condemnation and takeover.

In the 1940s there were nearly two million people in South America who had recently come from Germany. Most were in Brazil and Chile. In the Argentine, however, they estimated the greatest ethnic majority was of Italian descent. Many of the international upper-class society in Argentina stated that since France had fallen, the West no longer had a cultural center; that both the British and North Americans were uncouth, like Napoleon's description of the English as "a nation of shopkeepers," interested only in money and undeserving of Argentinian support.

There was nevertheless in those days one great solitary Argentine voice that carried the banner of democracy and anti-Axis resistance—the most influential Buenos Aires paper, *La Prensa*. Fortunately its influence was still great enough to encourage those who were our and Britain's champions. Meanwhile, Nazi agents managed to encourage their fellow Germans to form Fascist-like organizations. Some of these posed such problems that some Latin governments expressed fear of a *coup d'etat*. Resistance to growing pro-Axis sentiments (passively aided by local Soviet supporters) was growing harder to maintain than ever.

Thus the general mood of the subcontinent did disturb the United States. (Their once friendly reception of our movies, for instance, was noticeably changing.) There were some panicky predictions that if nothing was done to counter this volatile mood, almost all of the more unstable or authoritarian Latin American countries would give way. So serious had the situation become that the President created a special department to concentrate its attention on financial, cultural, and political cooperation and assistance to Latin America. He named the energetic and well-informed young Nelson Rockefeller to head it up.

My venerable and warmly admired "champion," Secretary of State Cordell Hull, arranged for me to have a talk with Sumner Welles, the Under-Secretary of State. I knew that Hull disliked Welles intensely, but FDR, an "old school friend," insisted on keeping him on the job. Welles had a fine, trained diplomatic mind, but his detractors called him too suave, too slick for his chief, Cordell Hull. In any case, Welles repeated my wish to be "of service in any capacity" the Administration thought fit in a memo to FDR. He briefly reviewed his special concern about the state of our relations with Latin America, concluding with a suggestion that I might be appointed to help "combat this [pro-Fascist] trend." The President scribbled his "very good idea" approval on the paper and returned it.

Soon after, I received an invitation from Welles, on behalf of the President, to undertake a mission "at the end of April" in certain Latin American countries. The "mission would ostensibly be to investigate" the effects on Latin American public opinion of American motion pictures. The *real* objective, however, was to get in touch with certain influential national groups who "are now believed to be veering toward Nazi ideology." I was to submit an analysis of their current and potential influence—in addition to proposals of what we could do about it. I was also to make public addresses (to be arranged by our embassies), ostensibly to boost our own American cultural policy sympathetic to the Allied cause. Welles's letter concluded with his hope that I would "find it possible to accept this invitation."

I was not just flattered by this request—I was thrilled! I realized, of course, that it was a sort of payoff for my public support of the Administration over the past two years or so. I wasted not a moment in wiring my acceptance and proposing an early visit to Washington to discuss details. Mary Lee, quite understandably, voiced a high-pitched protest against another trip!

I had been fretting at the slowness with which the Navy was considering my application for a commission in spite of the fact that I'd passed my exams and had some "half-assed" training. Now I was more anxious about it than ever. I had done as much "regular" Navy training as my busy life allowed (admittedly not enough), but was there no way I could get in under the wire before leaving the country?

To my delighted surprise, an old retired admiral tipped me off to an idea. He said if Bob Montgomery and I would apply, as a first step, for a commission in naval intelligence *only,* we probably wouldn't be required to finish all the rest of our regular training until later. I had already passed (after months of study) the unexpectedly hard course in naval regulations, as well as a few lesser exams. I wouldn't have to worry too much about simple navigation—I remembered enough to squeeze by—but I feared I couldn't cope with all the up-to-date electronics and mathematical gadgetry of ships and weapons. I would, however, still have to get some equivalent of a college degree.

I settled on the proposed "naval intelligence" idea, mostly because of assurance that once *in,* I could be sent out on regular sea duty and, with some help, learn the position of deck officer on the job.

As dear Tom Patten had died a year or so earlier, I turned now to his widow, who wrote a most laudatory account of my education under her late husband's tutorial guidance. Then I sought out my old friend and first Parisian tutor, "Hookie" (Carlton Hoekstra, now Charlie Farrell's executive secretary and assistant at the Palm Springs Racquet Club). He made my haphazard, unbalanced education sound almost as though it deserved honorary degrees from Harvard, Oxford, and MIT. I managed also to get a passing grade for a degree of some modest kind from a correspondence course sponsored by the state of California. I then mustered a flock of recommendations from a few learned pedants, some old retired admirals, and the like. Finally on April 10, Secretary of the Navy Frank Knox signed my commission as a lieutenant (j.g.) in the U.S. Naval Reserve.

I received it shortly after Mary Lee and I, with Dabby, had spent a few weeks in New York, where I daily attended the Berlitz School of Languages to learn a smattering of Spanish and Portuguese in preparation for my trip south. Being still fluent in French (practically bilingual), having picked up odd bits of Latin along the way, and having an actor's ear for accents, I caught on to the rough edges of these languages fairly quickly. Every day I shared my class with a polite, rather toothy young fellow, about twenty-three or twenty-four years old. He was modest and charmingly impressed to be as he said "in a language class with a movie star!" Months later I found the same engaging young fellow sitting next to me in a plane returning to the United States from Panama. I had, I confessed, forgotten those past meetings until years later he reminded me of them. I was in his office on the day John Glenn first orbited the earth in 1962 and he asked how my Spanish and Portuguese was. I mumbled something about being "very rusty" and looked, I'm sure, quite blank, so he recalled our first meeting at Berlitz. By this time he was President John F. Kennedy.

After a few days at the farm in Virginia, where we deposited Daphne in the care of mother-in-law Nancy and a nurse, we drove to Washington for a final high-level briefing at the State Department. It was there I learned for the first time that Nelson Rockefeller had been quite indignant that I was not going on this mission in connection with *his* newly organized Latin America relations section. As Coordinator of Inter-American Affairs, he was piqued that I, a personal envoy of the President, with the title special representative, was expected to report my findings to *no one except the President, the Secretary, and/or the Under-Secretary of State!*

It was, I later learned, unwise to confide to the Rockefeller group that my job in Latin America was *not* to be, as advertised, just a "cultural goodwill" trip, but rather one that concerned itself with certain facets of "strategic geopolitics."

There is no use pretending I wasn't impressed myself. I was told "State" would do as much as possible to support our official "line," that I was in South America to "further develop cultural relations" between the United States and Latin America; "to meet and exchange views with painters, sculptors, writers, theater and film people." However, whenever I spoke in public I was to emphasize (as subtly as possible) America's anti-Fascist, pro-Allied policy. I was to ascertain, in whatever offhand manner I could, whether each country I visited would be sympathetic to us if we were attacked and/or actively involved in the war. And most important I was to find out if we would be welcome in that country if we needed to use its ports as possible emergency repair bases for our navy.

It was emphasized that for security reasons I was *not* to confide these additional "suggested" activities to *any* of our ambassadors! However, I would be expected to share confidences with and follow the advice of Hutchinson Robbins, an experienced young fellow who would be assigned as my "assistant" and who would with his wife Louise travel with Mary Lee and me. Robbins, who was aiming at a foreign-service career, was detached from the Rockefeller group and assigned to "State." He had been thoroughly briefed and was from a diplomatic family (distantly related to the Delano branch of the Roosevelt clan). His mother, Argentine-born, was the official State Department decorator for all our embassies and legations abroad.

I could also, if need be, confide certain *"purely military matters"* (e.g., having to do with ports, repair facilities, possible armed support, and intelligence) to the U.S. Naval attachés who would be receiving special information about my mission. I could also send my own necessarily vague reports directly to Secretary Hull or Under-Secretary Welles, for the President's information, *without* ambassadorial approval, *and* in the embassy's or the naval attaché's code, or by the air-mailed diplomatic pouch.

My affected nonchalance made it obvious that I was excited as "all hell." Before the Robbinses and Mary Lee and I took off, supplied with official diplomatic passports, two important last-day developments took place. The first was that British Ambassador (Lord) Halifax asked me privately if I could get official State Department permission to make a general "observation report" on matters affecting the British war effort which would, of course, first be approved by our State Department. Permission, via Welles and the Navy Department, was promptly granted.

The second development, more welcome than I openly acknowledged at the time, was an offer to play in a motion picture adaptation of a short story by Alexandre Dumas, "The Corsican Brothers," soon after my mission was completed.

As international night flights had not yet been authorized, our Pan Am plane trip from Washington to Rio took several days. A big government publicity blast was arranged for our first overnight stop in Miami on April 22, our second wedding anniversary. The next night we stopped off in Trinidad and flew on to Brazil.

It would be not only boring but false to report our South American mission in excessively modest terms. It soon became obvious that Fairbanks was almost literally a household name. For more than a score of years my father's films had been the unequaled favorites of many millions throughout the world—not the least in all the Latin countries. In fact, many of these countries invented stories claiming that he had been born in one or another of them. Then I came along—*quite* different of course, but not so different as to be unrecognizable. To their tradition-trained eyes I was the next in line of succession. I managed to win over the goodwill of the loyal elders of the public, and I also had a loud and cheery following from my own generation. The results, insofar as getting the attention our state department hoped for, were very gratifying indeed.

Well before we arrived, President Getulio Vargas had issued formal invitations to senior government officials, Rio "society," Brazilian business and cultural VIPs, and the diplomatic corps to attend a banquet and ball in my honor. I was not so naive as to misinterpret this extravagant gesture as literally being made for me personally. I was quite clearly President Roosevelt's cultural envoy and nothing else! The very friendly, very pro-American Foreign Minister, Sr. Oswaldo Aranha, made this charmingly clear in a most helpful interview I had with him soon after we'd settled in. The presidential ball was beautifully done, although the evening was, as the climate continued to be through our visit, steamy and hot. The large fans in the ceiling were insufficiently effective. At the head table I was seated next to Vargas's daughter; Mary Lee sat next to Vargas himself (he was a widower).

Earlier that day, I had been taken to meet Heitor Villa-Lobos, an exceptionally gifted musician who had, I was told, just composed a new dance rhythm about which all who had heard it privately were very excited. When he played it for me that morning, I—confessing I knew next to nothing about such things—heartily agreed it was "very catching."

Now at the banquet, Señorita Vargas told me that the orchestra was going to play—for, so I understood, *the first time ever in public*—a new Brazilian dance rhythm. Would I, when the time came, take her out on the floor and dance around—just the two of us—before the others joined in? She would teach me its simple steps as we went along. I accepted the invitation with as much amiability as I could muster while warning her that I was not really a good dancer at all. (When I said I was just average, she thought I was being modest. *I* knew I was boasting.) I tried to wiggle out of it by admitting I'd be very shy trying out a brand-new dance for the first time with so many people watching. The señorita reassured me it was really quite simple and that I'd catch on "immediately."

We took the floor to polite, good-natured applause. As it turned out, it was indeed a very contagious rhythm, and dancing to it was really not all that difficult—so long as one was free to laugh openly at oneself. When others finally joined us on the floor and began trying out the new steps, we returned to our seats to Vargas's approving smile and polite clapping. Mary Lee then took the floor with the President.

That's all there was to it, but I was told I could say ever after that we were at the first public playing of what became an enormously popular new song, rhythm, and dance—the samba.

We stayed in Brazil for a little over a crowded fortnight. Between the many formally scheduled events I had a few unexpected opportunities to wander into more sensitive areas of political finagling. My pursuit of confidential objectives was surprisingly successful. I was, though, annoyingly hindered by my omnipresent bodyguards. As an "honored guest of the country" and because of "a good deal of pro-German sentiment," the Brazilian Government had decided I needed this protection. Whether I actually did or not was, I later learned, immaterial. More to the point, according to one of our own American intelligence officers, Sr. Lorival Fontes, the Minister of Education, Arts, and Propaganda, was suspected of being a Nazi sympathizer. He had apparently made little secret of his admiration for the sinister talents of Hitler's propaganda chief, Herr Doktor Goebbels. Furthermore my two human watchdogs seemed to Hutch and me not truly bodyguards, but spies themselves who shadowed us everywhere. In fact, whenever I had cause to speak to someone in confidence, one of them could usually be found hovering about and seeming to eavesdrop. On the surface at least, Fontes was always very agreeable. I thought he did have a somewhat sinister mien, possibly suggested by a slightly wayward cast of one eye.

Nevertheless, everything I learned helped to confirm that if it was discreetly negotiated, our navy could expect to have the help and the use of Brazilian bases should the needs of war ever require them.

My report back to Washington said:

Much of the German strength in Brazil is due to a growing defeatism on the part of responsible officials and society leaders. To counter this I invented out of thin air more terrifying statistics of our rearmament program and of growing British strength than the legendary Munchausen could have conceived. I seriously feel that it did have some effect, as before I left I had repeated to me rumors of a great mysterious power which I myself had started on the way. In short, it had gone the rounds and had come back. Even the pro-Nazis admitted that perhaps Brazil's place was in line with the States, although it was really "too bad."

A few days before our time in Brazil ended, Lorival Fontes sent Mary Lee, on behalf of the Brazilian Government, a large and beautiful pot in which a number of different species of orchids was growing. It was a beautiful arrangement that the embassy staff said they could package for us to take along.

Mary Lee wasted no time in ringing up Fontes's office to thank him for the unusual and exquisite gift. He muttered the equivalent of "Not at all" or "You're welcome," and then added, "But did you look at it *thoroughly?*"

Mary Lee said she had.

"But," persisted Fontes, "did you *really* look *everywhere?*"

Yes, she had, and they were the most "beautiful things" she'd ever seen. Even this answer failed to satisfy him. "But did you dig *under* the plants —into the dirt?"

"No, I hadn't thought of that! Should I?"

"Yes," said Fontes, "please do!"

Mary Lee dug her newly manicured nails deep into the dirt. Suddenly she felt something—a long black box! She opened it and was stunned to find nine large semiprecious stones—all native to Brazil. There was an amethyst, two aquamarines, two topazes, and four other large stones.

What *could* one say? Mary Lee, no more nor less than the Robbinses or I standing next to her, was staggered—wordless. When she pulled herself together, she burbled her thanks so effusively that I was certain Fontes wished he had never asked her.

Before we left, President Getulio Vargas awarded me the Republican Order of the Southern Cross of Brazil in the degree of officer, as recognition for special "outstanding" diplomatic services. It was the first official decoration I ever received—and I was very pleased.

In sum, the Brazilian visit provided the local leaders with a chance to say things to me informally that would have been awkward to express through regular channels. We also ascertained, in very general terms, the considerable assistance our navy might expect regarding bases, supplies, and refitting facilities.

Next stop Argentina, the second largest country in South America (after Brazil). I grumbled to Hutch that all our visits were far too rigidly programmed. Fortunately our ambassador in B.A. (we were told we must always call Buenos Aires just "B.A.") was about the best and most experienced of all our career diplomats at the time—the charming and wise Norman Armour, wonderfully helped by his aristocratic Russian wife, Myra.

The press, however, was not so welcoming. One of the lesser but more spectacular B.A. papers called me a "spy extraordinary," further suggesting that Argentina should send an Argentinian crooner named Antonio Caggiano ("among the worst in the country") to the United States as a fair exchange for me. Once, as I was entering a radio station, a loud firecracker went off, and my first startled reaction was that a bomb had exploded. *El Pampero* was the main anti-American paper; its headline the next day read: *Hero of a Hundred Films Almost Dies of Fright.*

The same paper later put a picture of me on its front page taken from *The*

Joy of Living, made with Irene Dunne a couple of years before, showing me in a scene in which I was supposed to be recovering from a late-night binge, lying on a couch in my underwear, with Irene's hat on my head and her fur coat thrown over my middle—with hairy legs and sloppy socks visible below. A sign propped beside me read: "Keep Off the Grass." The picture's caption was: "America's Unofficial Ambassador to Argentina."

We were most elegantly and frequently entertained by the chic, rich, young Argentinians, and our cultural and naval attachés saw to it that our daily schedules were filled with hours equally divided with matters of interest, boredom, usefulness—and speeches everywhere!

Ambassador Armour was anxious for me to make a dent of sorts on the rich and influential younger set and planned two or three big parties in our honor, at which the young would be more prominently represented than usual. Also included was an Army officer who was being noted as a possible future political figure. His name was Colonel Juan Perón and in that crowd of new people I fear he didn't make a great impression. (Of course it was among the working classes of Argentina that Perón and his wife, Evita, inspired such hopeless passion.)

The British ambassador, who was about to retire, was a sweet, doddering old pro named Sir Esmond Overy. He and his nice French wife were so personally popular that he stayed on—and on. His "number one" was Robert Hadow, nicknamed "Shadow," the minister and first secretary. Hadow, a great light-blond bellowing giant of a Scot, was actually the driving force of British diplomatic representation in Argentina. Though seemingly outspoken and indiscreet, he was in fact one of the shrewdest diplomats I came to know. One day, when we were having a private chat, he casually asked me about our mission in Brazil. My reply was honest but cautious—hence rather vague. I did mildly complain that the bodyguard assigned to me by the Brazilian Ministry of Propaganda was like a leech and, try as I would, I couldn't shake the s.o.b. off.

Shadow smiled understandingly and, seeming to switch the subject, proceeded to tell *me* about some of the meetings I had had, more or less what I'd said to whom and when, and so forth. Stuttering with astonishment, I asked how he knew all that. He roared with laughter and explained, "That Brazilian government bodyguard you suspected of being a Nazi spy was one of *our* chaps, and he gave Ambassador Armour here the same full report of all your doings he gave me! We were very impressed!"

So was I.

One day, Shadow asked me to pass on, very delicately, a British request to the United States—to cease supplying oil to Japanese ships. Indeed we still were doing this even though the coalition of states known as the Axis, headed by Germany, Italy and Japan, had been formed in 1936. It was one of the leaks in the otherwise successful British blockade of Axis powers. Although it was out of his bailiwick, Armour was glad to pass the request on to Washington.

We next made a quick trip across the Río de la Plata to Montevideo, the capital of Uruguay. Uruguay is, of course, a very small country but in a wonderfully strategic position between Brazil and Argentina where the Plata (which Argentinians just across it have sometimes thought was theirs) meets the South Atlantic.

A huge meeting was arranged of tens of thousands of members of Uruguayan labor and trade unions that filled their football stadium. I spoke in slow, carefully rehearsed and enunciated Spanish, and was often interrupted by well-orchestrated cheers. Next day, the effulgent press called me *"El Ambajador de la Sonrisa!"*—the ambassador of the smile!

Our trip over and back was most luxurious. We traveled as guests of a fabulously rich Argentinian and his glamorous wife on their large yacht. They were both very kind and attentive. But what impressed me most was my hosts' rather original bathroom quarters. Most of the big room itself was marble with gold-plated fittings. There were two tubs, side by side, a two-in-one shower, two side-by-side washbasins, and *two side-by-side toilets!* I have spent many a happy moment since then contemplating the domestic tranquility of this very advantaged couple, sharing a magazine or the latest newspaper before sailing and discussing their forthcoming social season in such amiable circumstances.

We left Argentina after three weeks and were sorry to do so. Norman and Myra Armour had been dreams—both as tutors and as what they became and remained ever after: our close friends. I was really very moved when, many years after this tour, I was allowed to see the glowing report that Norman had sent Cordell Hull about me. It was so encouraging that I often wished (just to myself) when I was being particularly roughly criticized or attacked by someone in a position to be heard, that this "report" could have been made public.

The next place on our schedule was Chile—that long sliver of a country, on the continent's west coast. Getting to Santiago from B.A. by air was still a unique adventure. A slow, winding up-and-down train and a thousand-hairpin-curves car trip were both contemplated but dismissed as too time consuming. Anyway, Pan Am had regular daily flights that wove their way between mountain peaks with occasional wind-induced zooms up and down valleys until they reached the other side. We were dispatched with the usual ceremony, and with unspoken trepidation we took off, climbed up as high as planned (so the captain said), and were then told to begin taking oxygen by sucking through the tubes supplied next to our seats.

None of us was particularly happy with these arrangements. The aircraft pitched and yawed and bumped and swayed its way between and around the great Andean peaks. At times it seemed as if our wings were going to scrape the mountains on either side. When we reached the midway point and were shown the huge marble statue *Christ of the Andes,* there could be no doubt that every trip made new or confirmed old believers! It was not really a long flight, and we all behaved very well, smiling wanly at each other as we descended into Santiago on the Pacific Coast.

There was no time for the women to do more than a cursory touch-up to their makeup or for Hutch and me to wipe the sweat off our brows. A great crowd had assembled at the airport. We put on the best show of phony nonchalance we could muster as we stood in the airplane door, pale but smiling bravely (and gratefully) at the mob behind the police and the cameras. They had surged toward us—pushing our kindly ambassador, Claude Bowers, and the first secretary of the embassy, Cecil Lyons, before them.

The greeting we got was loud and good-natured, but it was difficult to decide whether the enthusiasm was for the living evidence that movie actors at least looked like real people and could be touched and heard to speak, or for America, *la democracia,* and pro-Allied support. Hutch thought it might be a crowd gathered by the authorities and paid a pittance to smile and shout, *"Viva—allo Doogla Fye-bucks!"* (Sometimes a few risk-takers added "Hoonier.")

While smiling dignitaries shook our hands, I wondered in an aside to Hutch whether the same bewildered-looking little girls always met all planes everywhere and presented Mary Lee and Louise (and other female VIPs) with bouquets of flowers. As he was about to reply, the grubbiest-looking, stalest-smelling tramp I ever saw broke through the amiable police line. This smelly, unshaven old man with matted hair and stained broken teeth rushed up to me with hand extended, his evident goodwill exuding from long-blocked pores, and shouted, "I yam *Alfredo Delano!* I you Presidenta Rosa-belte cousine—*Alfredo Delano!* Gie my Presidente cousine my loff—I come to Yewn-eye-ta Stayse!" An alert constable gently pulled him away, still announcing his kinship to our chief.

A long time later, when the opportunity arose, I reported this unusual reception in Santiago to the President. He laughed heartily and said, "The old boy may well have been right! One of our 19th-century Delano forebears was a sea captain who was said to have a wife—or at least a lady friend—in most every port! No doubt you'll find lots of our Delano 'cousins' all over the place."

The State Department had surmised that I would be exhausted by the strain of my delicate duties and so had planned that the last leg of our mission would be interrupted by a pleasant break on board a big cruise ship, sailing from Santiago to Lima, Peru. We made no bones about being absolutely delighted at the prospect of a few lazy days at sea.

We were seen off with almost too much kindness from our hosts and, for a change, a thoroughly friendly press and high Chilean officials. Many years later, almost as an afterthought, the Chilean Government decided to award me one of their highest honors for public services further cementing Chilean-U.S. relations during a very threatening period . . . It was the Order of the Chilean Eagle, in the degree of Knight Commander.

Just as we were leaving Chile, I received a very long cable from Uncle Bob in California. Its message stunned me. I suddenly felt we were so far away we might have been on Mars. He advised me that stepmother Sylvia had decided, completely on her own, to move my father's body from the Forest Lawn Cemetery, closer to "home" in the Hollywood Cemetery. With the Bank of America Trustees' approval and the estate's money, she had, quite on her own, commissioned a striking classical marble monument with a bronze bust of Pete on a sort of plinth in its center, to be set at the end of a long, ornamented, lagoonlike pool. Uncle Bob said that earlier information about this had somehow failed to reach me. Now the ceremony was to be held in about a week. He asked if I could be home in time for it!

Naturally this news upset me terribly! My official mission still had at least another couple of weeks to go. Cutting it short for personal reasons was out of the question. I tried to telephone Uncle Bob without success and finally cabled to ask why, under the circumstances, the ceremony couldn't be postponed for a few weeks. I added a direct, personal plea to Sylvia, to please reconsider and postpone the date, as I had not previously heard anything at all about her plans and wanted very much to be there.

The answer to this was a short and infuriating radiogram. Uncle Bob, clearly disheartened, admitted defeat. Sylvia declined to answer my message and claimed that all invitations had been mailed, preparations were complete and . . . "Therefore am advised impossible to postpone."

Everything about the rest of our trip now became largely unmemorable. An emotional fog beclouded my brain. Mary Lee, equally incensed on my account, tried to console me but was reluctant to probe too deeply into my new and painful wound. "That bitch!" was all I could think of saying. And repeating. How did she dare go so far with her plans and not only fail to talk to Uncle Bob, but let no one of our immediate family know until it was too late to stop her? And why, if it was a "simple" ceremony, could it not have been postponed? We might have agreed if we had been consulted, but we weren't and that made us all furious—me especially.

Our mission to Peru was ill-timed not only because I allowed my personal problems to preoccupy me, but also because that fascinating country was in one of its periodic "let's hate the U.S." moods. Anti-Americanism was and still is, despite everything we have ever tried, endemic throughout much of Latin America.

Subsequently, after roughly two and a half months (April to the end of June 1941) of an odyssey that took us to just five of our twenty-one Latin American neighbors, we stopped for more refueling on a tarmac in Miami. After countless interviews, meetings, broadcasts, and several dozen speeches we arrived home, safe but barely sound. The mission undertaken for President and country was over.

World events kept getting hotter on *all* burners, front and back. FDR announced the nation's dedication to the four freedoms and the Lend-Lease Act providing credit to Britain was signed. The Axis extended their bloody writ to the conquest of the Balkans, to Greece, Cyprus, and Crete—where Dickie Mountbatten was as always in the thick of the action. From his reconditioned battle-scarred ship, H.M.S. *Kelly,* he commanded a destroyer squadron. During the Cretan battle, he was blown into the sea as his gallant ship was torpedoed, bombed from the air, and sank, her guns still blazing away till the sea drowned them, though not him. Rommel's first-rate Afrika Korps had supplanted Mussolini's weakened Fascists and had driven the British back almost to the Egyptian border.

In June, before I got back from South America, the almost unbelievable happened: Hitler did the big twist on his erstwhile supporter, Stalin, and with three million troops invaded the colossal Soviet Union. It was among history's rankest double-crosses, so sudden that the Russians became, virtually overnight, Britain's only cobelligerent ally.

FDR extended the restrictions of Lend-Lease to include the Soviets, and by July our neutrality zone (some called it our sanitation area) in the Atlantic extended to a line drawn downward a little east of Iceland. The British immediately occupied that ancient northern land, in order to deny it to the Germans, who were on the verge of moving some troops there from Norway and Denmark. By July the U.S. joined the British and sent some ships to join their Home Fleet and Army troops (most of them brand-new, barely trained draftees) to set up a base in Iceland. In August, Churchill and

Roosevelt met aboard a warship off Canada and signed a joint Declaration of Principles, to be called the Atlantic Charter.

In spite of all this ever more deafening thunder, the war seemed so very far away to most Americans it was almost as if it were just a movie. The baseball season went on its merry way. Patriotic parades, the "boys" called up and joining up—it was all exciting and not very real.

Immediately on our return we flew to Washington to report on my mission to the President, Hull and Welles. I still had not quite done with my assignment; I had to make verbal and, with Hutch's help, more detailed written reports than we could give during this quick Washington check-in or could have cabled in code from our South American embassies. To do this, even with the help of government typists with security clearance, took several days.

I paid a long call on Under-Secretary Welles. He expressed what I interpreted as sincere interest in a proposal of mine that the U.S. create an executive department of information to counter the effective propaganda of Dr. Goebbels and his imitators. (I pointed out that "Comrade" Stalin, for one, was a practicing believer in such an idea.) The British too had learned that wartime pressures required a ministry of information. Nothing happened except agreement in principle, but later it was very satisfying to feel when the Office of War Information came into being (and many old associates from the Aid the Allies White Committee were recruited for it), that at least one of the seeds of the idea had been planted by my suggestion to Welles—and later by notes to Bob Sherwood and Secretary Hull. Who knows? Meanwhile I enjoy taking a little private bow, anyway.

Welles told a press conference that my mission to South America had been "eminently successful in every way" and that he couldn't "speak in terms sufficiently high on the admirable work and excellent impression" I had created. The President wrote me, "From every source I have heard nothing but praise and commendation." I was very pleased indeed and wondered, "What next?"

Secretary Hull soon asked me to his office. On the day of my appointment, Hull was his usual genial Southern self. He never seemed rushed when I visited him, nor in my view very "security-minded." Once on a visit to his office, I couldn't help seeing a private memo from him to the President. It was lying upside down on his desk. Being naturally devious (provided the chances are good that I can get away with it), I didn't even try *not* to read it. I could see it was a classified memo from the Secretary of State to the President. About all I could make out of the typing from my angle was that it was a question about something General de Gaulle was "demanding" for France. FDR had scribbled his reply to Hull right across the memo with a great big blue pencil. I could make this out more clearly. It said simply, *"To hell with de Gaulle!"*

As I left, Mr. Hull asked in passing if I minded these terribly hot muggy summer days in Washington. I shrugged and said something about the sleepless, restless nights of my New York boyhood, particularly when one lived near the El. He interrupted with, "Well, bah Gawd, when ah was a boay growin' up in Tennessee, the summahs were hot as the hinges o' hell. We didn't have any goddamn aiah-conditionin' an' we grew up all rot. *No,* suh! None of that will be put in this depahtmint whal ah'm heah!"

Nor was there, by God!

While still in Washington, I reported to the Navy Department, where as a newly commissioned (but deliberately unpublicized) naval reserve officer I was warmly received by some of my superiors. I inquired when I could go on active duty and was told, "No hurry!"

25

After a few wonderfully bucolic days at the farm, collecting Daphne—who was in bubbling good health—and another few days in New York recounting and exaggerating our South American adventures to family and friends, we went back to the glory of Westridge and California.

As we chugged west by train, I marveled anew at the vastness of my country, which in spite of its human and physical variety was all of a piece —many millions of people agreeing peaceably to live under one extraordinarily permissive system of government, where no one was supposed to be bound, unwillingly, to anything or anyone. What a marvel—and how fragile it could become if those in power, or those sometimes incognito, faceless institutions that helped to make it tick, looked the other way for just a moment. Who *dared* say, "No need to worry"?

A boost to my diluted energies awaited me that summer of 1941. It was beginning work on *The Corsican Brothers*. I was still anxious to resuscitate my neglected career. Negotiations had begun with Gregory Ratoff as director. I had known Grisha—Ratoff's nickname—for ages and was fond of him. He had an amusing personality, enhanced by a broad Russian accent. He was a good character actor and comedian, with early experience in the Moscow Art Theater, and a friend and jester to Darryl Zanuck at 20th Century, who had given him his first break as a director.

The war on the Eastern Front between the Nazis and the Soviets created a new wave of emotional excitement in this country that was particularly intense in Hollywood circles, where a number of anticommunist White Russian emigrés regained overnight an apolitical pride in the resistance shown by their kin back in Mother Russia. Now, all the closet pinks, reds, and variations thereof doffed their disguises and cheered mightily for the unsurpassable bravery being shown by the poor and bleeding Russian people.

Grisha Ratoff began wearing a lapel button which, instead of the Churchill-inspired *V* for Victory, was a small, gold *W*. When someone inquired what it meant, he replied, "Is a *WEE* for *WEEKTORY!*"

All of us in the film community were soon begged to give money for the various "Bundles for Russia" and similar charities that sprang up overnight. As usual I had to be in the middle of such a good cause, so despite my usual drained finances, I lent my name to the growing list of Russian Relief Committees and gave them whatever I could afford.

Unfortunately that gesture of the moment, shared by many thousands everywhere, came back to haunt me more than a quarter of a century later. During both the Truman and the Eisenhower presidencies, I was asked if I would accept an important government appointment. I never knew for certain whether it was to be an under-secretaryship or an ambassadorship because whenever such an idea was proposed I knew if it was to be a first-class post, I probably couldn't afford it—and wherever I could afford one, it was most unlikely to be offered to me. Then, when the recommendation for my advancement in the naval reserve was passed over, I demanded to see *all* my records from every file, under the Freedom of Information Act. When a couple of reports continued to be denied me despite the law, I made a fuss. I couldn't imagine what could be said against me of any *real* importance. The most I ever learned was that my name was on a list of those who contributed to the Russian War Relief and that as I backed FDR, I was "probably a leftist!" Also it was hinted that at an earlier time I led a less than Puritanical personal life. What this meant, no one would ever disclose exactly. But the reason given for forbidding me access to the file was that the informant agreed to tell about me, *provided* his or her identity was kept secret. I'm still curious—and still furious!

Naturally I had, in the course of time, been involved in many top-secret goings-on, but there was nothing I could remember that could not in later years be made known to everyone. If *I* had no knowledge of anything derogatory about myself—even my old unquenchable admiration for pretty faces or figures was never a state secret—then I couldn't think what it was. Finally a good and true friend "in the know" told me that the black mark against me was a check I had written to some Russian relief or charity organization in 1941.

Now in the summer of 1941, I settled down to my *Corsican Brothers* job, conscientiously working ten and sometimes twelve long, hot wearying hours a day.

One morning Mother's old Algonquin friend, now the powerful Hollywood gossip columnist, Hedda Hopper, decided, after hearing one of my recent Aid the Allies broadcasts, soon after my return from South America, to turn on me with a vengeance. She set down for her millions of readers of the prominently isolationist Chicago Tribune Syndicate her regret that I had been so conspicuously a fool in the alien world of foreign affairs. She said, "The great senior Fairbanks must be turning in his grave in shame as his son plays at sending our young American boys to war while he, being an over-age father [I *was* at the time thirty-one] stayed safely at home making movies" or (as another columnist put it) "gallivanting to Washington and fashionable New York, and taking a jaunt to South America at the public's expense, hoping to help push us into other people's wars."

These and a few similar comments appeared just a few days after a special hand-delivered envelope came to me on the set. It was an official confidential letter from naval headquarters, notifying me that as soon as I could complete my current business and professional obligations, I was *to report for active duty*.

I said nothing about this notification for a few days, though I wanted to tell everyone—particularly Hedda, the old cow! I immediately broke the news to Mary Lee, who had in any case been expecting just such a word for quite a while. I also wrote to Gene Markey, who had now been called up himself. He was an old reservist—having served in the first war—now with the rank of lieutenant commander and already on duty on some small, smelly minesweeper near the Panama Canal. I knew that he, as my chief naval mentor, would be pleased.

The family duly kept my secret. (I dared not tell Mother yet as she would tell everyone she knew!) It was only several weeks after I left California that the press caught on. Even then it was, thanks to naval policy, little noted.

Early that fall, before I left for the East, I learned that the Mountbattens had arrived in New York. Edwina, with their very pretty teenage daughter Patricia, in tow (the younger Pamela was left behind as too young for the trip), was about to begin a trans–U.S. and Canada tour on behalf of the British Red Cross and its companion organization, the St. John's Ambulance Brigade. Dickie was to assume command of one of the Royal Navy's biggest and best aircraft carriers, H.M.S. *Illustrious,* then undergoing a refit and some patching in Newport News, Virginia. Mary Lee and I were inspired to invite the three of them to stay with us at Westridge for whatever respite they could manage. The glamorous Edwina, the ex–society playgirl, had now become a dedicated saint to bombed-out victims in England and was badly in need of some unwinding. Dickie also deserved whatever break he could get after sea battles and frequent near-death experiences from bombs and torpedoes before taking over the huge aircraft carrier. The visit would have the further advantage that the U.S. Navy had invited him to Hawaii to lecture senior staff officers at Pearl Harbor on recent antiaircraft developments. The idea of stopping on the way in a big, comfortable house in California seemed a great idea!

The Mountbattens arrived and couldn't have been cozier or more fun. Mary Lee and Edwina sat about, sunning and swimming. My cousins took "sub-deb" Patricia in hand for a bit of sightseeing while I took Dickie alone on a tour of some of our Southern California aircraft factories where they—like everyone else—rolled out their own version of a red carpet. Always a keen film fan, Dickie particularly loved visiting the movie studios. He had been the prime mover behind getting movies shown on his navy's ships. He was having a real ball—even though both he and Edwina often found it difficult to believe the contrast between where they had been and what they had been through, and now—lolling among the lotus-eaters and honeybees. One night, for example, he fell in with my suggestion that we visit the long-established carnival of Ferris wheels, Dodge-'ems, merry-go-rounds, roller coasters, Big Dippers, and fun houses on the finger piers of Venice and Santa Monica. Dickie literally *loved* the biggest and scariest of the roller coasters. We must have gone on at least three rides that night, and each time we came to the biggest and steepest dip, Dickie would hold on to the bar in front of him, stand up, and laugh and shout like a boy all the way down—and up the other side again.

I never knew anyone who disliked Dickie. He had a most engaging personality and an energetic, vital attitude about nearly everything. His enthusiasms were contagious; his loyalty to friends and shipmates was famous. Nearly everyone by now knows how he relished strewing the names of his royal friends and relatives around as if sowing seeds of grain in a furrowed farmland—but nevertheless with an air of seeming to share them with you as he talked. Although mocked for this, I never found these quirks in the least offensive. In fact, I usually thought them interesting—part real, part fantasy. He had a way of making you think you were his most intimate confidant—when, in fact, you were no such thing. He was just enjoying to the full the almost true fact that he was who and what he was—and liked sharing it with you.

I found his feeling for the individual members of his family truly touching and not, as some said, embarrassing. Nor did I think his penchant for ceremony and dressing up a target for criticism. I suppose, in a totally different and less important context, I shared them vicariously.

Dickie, who frankly loved all forms of royal and ordinary theater, was certainly a member of my pantheon of heroes. However, I think the real bond was not his glamorous presence, not his warmth and loyalty as a friend, but an ever-present though dimly sensed need we shared in common: to be the kind of sons we felt our fathers wanted us to be. Although Dickie's older brother, Georgie, was the more intellectual of the two (both brothers went to the Royal Naval College), Dickie was the one most bitterly affected by his father's fate.

The elder Mountbatten, Prince Louis of Battenberg, had been a German-born princeling married to Queen Victoria's granddaughter, Princess Victoria, and naturalized British. He rose in the British Navy to the highest rank —first sea lord. But during World War I, the public's anti-German passions grew to such nearly hysterical proportions that he was virtually hounded from office and forced to resign. It was a heartbreaker for the old man, who never got over the pain of it. Dickie swore he would make his father proud. He began early to develop a climber's spirit, to be a go-getter in order to win his idea of his father's approval.

Edwina was a sharp contrast to Dickie in many ways. She was strikingly beautiful and rich almost beyond measure. Dickie, despite his semiroyal status, was virtually penniless. More cynical, more sophisticated, more spoiled than Dickie, Edwina was nonetheless a loyal and true friend (virtues that did not always obtain in her capacity as a wife). With the coming of war and its gruesome opportunities to get a firsthand view of how the rest of the world outside her own goldfish bowl lived, suffered, and died, she became a near angel of mercy—hard-working, untiring, and utterly dedicated. They both identified themselves loosely (though not very convincingly) with the British political left, but it was unlikely that either ever seriously considered adjusting their very privileged private lives to the levels of a truly socialist society.

I was told that once when she had publicly supported a socialist government, the late King privately warned her that she must either give up all her associations with the royal family (as a cousin by marriage) or detach herself from all partisan politics. Edwina gave up her open espousal of leftist politics.

We gave a large party for the Mountbattens at Westridge soon after they arrived. A temporary dance floor was laid down outdoors in the patio. A long guest list was filled out with the many famous movie names they said they wanted to meet. Then we added a sprinkling of well-known directors, producers, local industrialists, socialites from Los Angeles, Santa Barbara, and Pasadena (normally a no-go mixture). We also invited two or three of the more senior naval and military officers of the district.

A night or two before the dance, we had a phone call from the great blues singer Ethel Waters. She told us that she was an admirer of the British because of their whole year of "fighting this here great war alone" and because they were "great champions of democracy." ("You know, honey, that they got rid of slavery *long* before we did!") She then asked if we "minded" if she came along to the party, bringing her own small orchestra and choral group to sing her most popular songs and some "Negra spirituals" for us and the Mountbattens. I could hardly credit my ears! I thanked her effusively, and on the appointed night, she was as good as and better than her word. She and her group sang and sang. The party wept and cheered and applauded and listened for over an hour. It was marvelous.

Then the dancing. Edwina whirled about like a deb, (in fact, as it was Patricia's first-ever grown-up dance, we have ever since called it *her* "coming-out party!"). And Dickie, all thoughts of war and devastation put away for the night, had an equal whirl. He made no bones about developing an instant crush on Rita Hayworth and was unashamedly persistent about wanting to dance with her as often as possible! The night—balmy and pleasant—ended at about four A.M.

On first arriving in California, Dickie had accepted an invitation to pay a formal visit to the U.S. Naval Headquarters and its commanding officer, in San Diego. He then thought it would be appropriate to ask our naval authorities if his host might be ordered to temporary duty to act as his aide just for that day. Approval was immediately forthcoming, and I, pleased as Punch, donned my brand-new uniform, flew down to San Diego with Dickie in the admiral's private plane, and stood as a silent, dumb shadow behind him all day.

A few days later Dickie flew off to Hawaii for his lecture, leaving Edwina and Patricia with us for a day or so. While Dickie was away, I was surprised and pleased to receive a cable from P.G. (the Duke of Kent by then), saying he was due to make an official Royal Air Force inspection trip across Canada. He asked if I would like him to request that I be his honorary aide—or, as he put it, his American "A.D.C." I was privately happier to hear from him than I let on because I had not heard a peep out of him for some time, and I feared I was for some reason in his "bad books." But this gesture indicated that if I once had been, I was no longer. However, I phrased a long, friendly, and grateful reply of regret, letting him know I was on the verge of reporting for active duty, but hoping to see him sometime soon "over there."

Dickie returned from Hawaii, pleased with the hospitality shown him but privately expressing concern that the American armed services seemed over-confident. Then a decoded message was received from Prime Minister Chur-chill that clearly distressed him. He was told he was not, after all, to com-mand his "dream ship"—the carrier H.M.S. *Illustrious*. Instead, he was being recalled to replace Admiral of the Fleet Sir Roger Keyes as Chief of Combined Operations. This was meant to be a great opportunity for him to be in charge of all amphibious training and development of early plans for what would be the eventual invasion of Hitler's "Fortress Europe." He would also expand the operations of the tough special amphibious raiding "dirty tricksters" who came to be called Commandos. They developed and experimented with new weapons, vehicles, forms of camouflage, invasion tricks, plans, diversionary operations, and amphibious hit-and-run raids. Dickie would be given honorary two-star rank in all services, enabling him as "the chief" to cope. One night in New York a few weeks later, he and I walked for hours, up and down and around Manhattan until late, while he used me for a sounding board, rambling on about whether he could or should decline Churchill's appointment.

In the end, of course, he went back to England as ordered, and I began to hope that one day he might request (and the U.S. Navy might approve) my becoming attached to his new command in some capacity. Edwina, together with Patricia, returned to her St. John's and Red Cross North American tours.

Our charmed life at Westridge made my going on active duty suddenly seem an impetuous bit of bravado! Who was I impressing? Was I going to win the war single-handedly even though we weren't legally in it—and might never be? Well, I'd decided on it months ago and it was too late now.

Before leaving California for the duration, we decided that Mary Lee and Daphne would stay with me as much as possible, but if I were sent away, they would settle at Boxwood Farm. We were lucky to arrange a rental for Westridge right away. Even more luckily, we rented it to Barbara Hutton and her new husband—my movie sidekick and always friend, Cary Grant. Cary was not as settled then as he later became, but he always seemed bright and cheery to me, and I never found him to be other than charming. Bar-bara had the better of this deal, as Cary was literally the only one of her attachments who neither wanted nor took anything from her. She was such a silly, affected girl—but so sweet in many ways—that I suspected Cary just felt sorry for her and thought he could bring her down to earth. He failed, but Barbara was the loser, not Cary.

We thought we were lucky to rent to friends. Any number of people would have been glad to take it since Westridge was one of the most beautifully decorated comfortable big houses in Southern California. But we were so anxious to have someone there who would take good care of it that we did not (considering the Hutton resources) make very much out of the deal. Barbara never knew exactly what money was except that people wanted it, and she had so much that she didn't mind getting rid of a lot. Cary was just about the shrewdest businessman I ever knew in movies (Charlie Chaplin, Harold Lloyd, and stepmother Mary excepted). Frank Vincent, Cary's agent and mine, arranged for Mr. and Mrs. Grant to pay us six hundred dollars a month, with options every six months. I knew it was far less than the house would have fetched if we had had it on the rental market longer for just any tenants. But we were naturally in a hurry.

We later heard a likely story that Barbara (contrary to Cary's wishes) engaged three shifts of servants: one for day, one for night, and one to wait on the other two! At first we wondered where she would house them. We later heard that she rented cottages and rooms nearby and supplied them with transportation. They agreed to keep on our dear fat old Finnish cook Eva and Nestor, her husband of similar dimensions, who served as night watchman—a community necessity even then. One of sweet befuddled Barbara's contributions to the war effort was having our lovely front lawn with its fruit trees and bushes dug up and replanted with potatoes. Early in October with no public fanfare or formal farewells, Mary Lee, Dabby, a nurse, and I headed east. I was ready to report to the Navy Department, willing to end the war.

I collected some naval papers from a building in Lower Manhattan and proceeded to the Navy Department in Washington. Sir Galahad had arrived. Hitler wouldn't sleep well now! But the Navy Department hardly heard me. In fact, I barely had time to exercise my most professionally ingratiating charm before I was subjected to a tough lecture. Because of my incomplete training, the priggish young regular lieutenant told me, I should by rights be assigned to a minor job in Navy Public Relations or shuffling papers in the Office of Naval Intelligence.

My boss of the immediate moment turned out to be a snotty lieutenant commander from the Bureau of Naval Personnel who went on in boring, patronizing detail to explain that if I expected any publicity from my service I could forget it! I interrupted him (not quite as respectfully as I very shortly learned how to be) to say that I had taken considerable trouble to avoid any publicity so far. Had I wanted any, I would have volunteered for a less silent service. My interviewer interrupted my interruption to say that Lieutenant Robert Montgomery—"an old movie actor sidekick of yours, I guess"—had been too much in the press to please the Navy ever since he was sent to our Intelligence Section in the map room of the U.S. Naval Attaché's offices in London; they weren't going to make the same mistake again. "So, Fairbanks, the brass has decided the quickest way for you to be a seagoing "deck officer" is to go to sea and learn on the job. We're sending you to a supply ship in Boston." I think he was a bit surprised that I was so obviously pleased with the prospect.

The next day we were surprised and delighted to be asked by Mrs. Roosevelt's office to spend the night at the White House before leaving Washington. The presence of Bob Sherwood, and even the ghoulish Harry Hopkins, made for a fascinating informal night. There was a moment's embarrassment during dinner, when the President mentioned that a certain Scandinavian princess was coming to the U.S. and would be visiting the White House for a couple of days. As the Royal Highness in question was young and attractive, and the President had been suspected of being susceptible to her on a previous visit, Mrs. R. made a rather sharp comment, clearly intimating she was less than pleased at the prospect.

Just before the President went upstairs to his papers and bed, he wished me well and expressed the hope that I would soon be promoted to "Captain of the Head." I was too new and nervous to get the point of his joke about the shipboard slang for "toilet," but I faked an embarrassed laugh. As we said our respectful good nights, Mrs. R. escorted us to our bedroom. There were twin beds in the large room, and Mrs. R. sat herself on one of them. This was her way of putting us both at our ease. She was also trying to assuage what she correctly guessed was Mary Lee's concern about my going to sea—that I was "so insufficiently trained."

This prompted Mary Lee to refer to Mrs. R.'s four sons (all in one or another of the armed services by now) and one daughter. Mary Lee, who earlier had glibly said she'd like "lots of children," then began to talk about "favorite children." She asked our hostess if she'd ever had a favorite child —and added (very tactlessly, I thought) that if so, "which one would it be?"

Mrs. R. thought but a moment and then, with her sweet and very bucktoothed smile, answered, "Oh, I suppose the one who's most in trouble at the time." Adding a good night, a wish for pleasant dreams, and "Breakfast in your room if you like, but downstairs starts at seven!" she left us.

Our last night together was spent in New York with Mother and Jack. We all went to see Gee Lawrence in *Lady in the Dark*. It was a bit awkward trying to shrug off the teasing I received from Mary Lee about my former liaison with the star. But the big impression of the evening was the birth of another great star—Danny Kaye. What a brilliant comet on the Broadway scene he was!

With Mary Lee still in tow, and Daphne safe in Nancy's grandmotherly hands in Virginia, I arrived in Boston, donned my uniform with its one-and-a-half stripes, and reported for duty at Boston's Charlestown Navy Yard. There to my grateful surprise was my old friend, F.D.R. Jr., already on active duty but only an ensign as he was younger than I. Frank knew, from his similar point of view, what it was like to be overnoticed and have to surmount the junior tag. Thus his support was gratefully received when he accompanied me to check in at the Navy's Boston headquarters office. Orders were all written out in officialese, together with any number of copies destined for various official paper collectors along the way.

I was to report the very next morning for duty aboard an old Navy supply ship, for training as a "deck officer under instruction." I was in fact hardly more than a passenger, until the ship put in to the big Royal Canadian Navy Base in Argentia, Newfoundland, where I was to transfer and report for duty aboard the U.S.S. *Ludlow,* a middle-aged destroyer, at which time I was "to perform such duties as I would be assigned by the ship's captain." I was then to report to the commander of U.S. Task Force 99, aboard the U.S.S. *Mississippi,* the flagship, based in Reykjavík, Iceland. It was a brand-new base for us as we had just joined the limeys in occupying the country. After that . . . ? No one—least of all I—knew.

Mary Lee and I tried not to be dramatic or sloppy about my last night ashore and stiff-upper-lipped-it all evening, helped by the presence of Frank. The next morning, in gray damp and cold, I phoned Mother and Genie, both in New York, to hint at goodbye. We then trotted down to the Navy Yard's dockside with all my gear—three kinds of uniforms for different occasions, extra white cap covers, gloves, raincoat, shoes, and a ceremonial sword with my name etched on it (a present from M.L.), a scabbard, and sword belt. Mary Lee waved and presumably shed a dutiful tear as I clambered, with about half a dozen others, aboard a launch and hove out to our anchored ship.

Once alongside, we mounted the gangway, saluted the quarterdeck and the waiting officer of the deck, looking very officious with his necessary badge of authority, a dummy telescope under his arm. An attentive bos'n's mate stood beside him, his pipe hanging around his neck, though none of us was important enough for him to pipe aboard. The officer returned my salute, and I solemnly rattled off the regulation "Request permission to

come aboard . . ." Permission was granted. I gave my name and outlined
the orders I was to give to the executive officer about joining my ship in
Newfoundland.

"Very well. You'll find the exec on the bridge." He instructed the bos'n to
escort me. As we left, I gave one last glance shoreward to see Mary Lee still
waving. I dared not really wave back—I just lifted a gloved hand as if to
adjust my cap.

It was only now beginning to sink in that all this was real. The early
training was over. Conventional comforts, the attention of family and
friends, the illusions of security—these and other ordinary activities were
rapidly fading behind the gray mist of the sea. I looked at the shore one last
time and tried to smile as for a camera. My face wouldn't move. As the ship
noisily weighed anchor and hooted and groaned its way off to sea, I could
still see the tiny figure of Mary Lee waving on the quayside. I damn near
blubbered. What *the hell* had I got myself into?

The Films of
Douglas Fairbanks, Jr.
1923–1941

1923

Stephen Steps Out. Famous Players/Lasky. Released by Paramount. Dir. by Joseph Henabery. D.F. Jr., Theodore Roberts, Noah Beery, Harry Myers, Fannie Midgley.

1924

The Air Mail. Famous Players/Lasky. March. Dir. by Irvin Willat. Warner Baxter, Billie Dove, Mary Brian, D.F. Jr.

1925

The American Venus. Famous Players/Lasky. Dir. by Frank Tuttle. Esther Ralston, Lawrence Gray, Ford Sterling, Fay Lamphier, Louise Brooks, Edna May Oliver, Kenneth MacKenna, William B. Mack, George De-Carlton, W. T. Benda, Ernest Torrence, D.F. Jr. (who plays Triton in Miss America sequence).
Wild Horse Mesa. Famous Players/Lasky. Dir. by George B. Seitz. Jack Holt, Noah Beery, Billie Dove, D.F. Jr.

1926

Padlocked. Famous Players/Lasky. Dir. by Allan Dwan. Lois Moran, Noah Beery, Louise Dresser, Helen Jerome Eddy, D.F. Jr.
Broken Hearts of Hollywood. Warner Bros. Dir. by Lloyd Bacon. Patsy Ruth Miller, Louise Dresser, D.F. Jr., Jerry Miley, Barbara Worth.
Stella Dallas. Samuel Goldwyn, Inc. Dir. by Henry King. Ronald Colman, Belle Bennett, Alice Joyce, Jean Hersholt, Lois Moran, D.F. Jr.

Man Bait. Metropolitan Pictures. Released by P.D.C. Dir. by Donald Crisp. Marie Prevost, Kenneth Thomson, D.F. Jr., Louis Natheaux, Sally Rand.

1927
Women Love Diamonds. MGM. Dir. by Edmund Goulding. Pauline Starke, Owen Moore, Lionel Barrymore, Cissy Fitzgerald, Gwen Lee, D.F. Jr.
Is Zat So? Fox Film Corp. Dir. by Alfred E. Green. With George O'Brien, Edmund Lowe, Kathryn Perry, Cyril Chadwick, Doris Lloyd, Dione Ellis, D.F. Jr.
A Texas Steer. Sam E. Rork Prod. Released by First National. Dir. by Richard Wallace. Will Rogers, Louise Fazenda, Sam Hardy, Ann Rork, D.F. Jr.

1928
Dead Man's Curve. FBO Pictures. Dir. by Richard Rosson. D.F. Jr., Sally Blane, Charles Byer, Arthur Metcalf, Joel McCrea.
Modern Mothers. Columbia. Dir. by Philip Rosen. Helene Chadwick, D.F. Jr., Ethel Grey Terry, Barbara Kent.
The Toilers. Tiffany-Stahl Prod. Music and sound effects. Dir. by Reginald Barker. D.F. Jr., Jobyna Ralston, Harvey Clark, Wade Boteler, Robert Ryan. One song dubbed for D.F. Jr.
The Power of the Press. Columbia. Dir. by Frank Capra. D.F. Jr., Jobyna Ralston, Mildred Harris, Philo McCullough, Wheeler Oakman.
A Woman of Affairs. MGM. Music and sound effects. Dir. by Clarence Brown. Greta Garbo, John Gilbert, Lewis Stone, John Mack Brown, D.F. Jr.
The Barker. First National. Part-talkie. Dir. by George Fitzmaurice. Milton Sills, Dorothy Mackaill, Betty Compson, D.F. Jr., George Cooper, John Erwin.

1929
The Jazz Age. FBO Pictures. Part-talkie and musical score. Dir. by Lynn Shores. D.F. Jr., Marceline Day, Henry B. Walthall, Myrtle Stedman, Joel McCrea.
Fast Life. First National. Full sound. Dir. by John Francis Dillon. D.F. Jr., Loretta Young, William Holden, Chester Morris, Frank Sheridan.
Our Modern Maidens. MGM. Sound effects and musical score. Dir. by Jack Conway. Joan Crawford, Rod LaRocque, D.F. Jr., Anita Page, Edward Nugent.
The Careless Age. First National. Full sound, as are all films hereafter. Dir.

by John Griffith Wray. D.F. Jr., Carmel Myers, Holmes Herbert, Kenneth Thompson, Loretta Young, Ilka Chase.

The Forward Pass. First National. Dir. by Eddie Cline. D.F. Jr., Loretta Young, Guinn Williams, Marion Byron, Phyllis Crane.

The Show of Shows. Warner Bros. Dir. by John G. Adolfi. A revue with many stars. Master of ceremonies, Frank Fay. Frame story stars William Courtenay, H. B. Warner, Hobart Bosworth, John Barrymore. D.F. Jr. appears in "Bicycle Built for Two" sequence, with Chester Conklin, Lois Wilson, and others.

1930

Party Girl. Victory Pictures. Released by Tiffany. Dir. by Victor Halperin. D.F. Jr., Jeanette Loff, Judith Barrie, Marie Prevost.

Loose Ankles. First National. Dir. by Ted Wilde. D.F. Jr., Loretta Young, Louise Fazenda, Ethel Wales, Otis Harlan, Daphne Pollard.

Dawn Patrol. First National. Dir. by Howard Hawks. Richard Barthelmess, Neil Hamilton, D.F. Jr., William Janney, James Finlayson.

The Little Accident. Universal. Dir. by William James Craft. D.F. Jr., Anita Page, Sally Blane, ZaSu Pitts, Roscoe Karns, Slim Summerville.

Outward Bound. Warner Bros. Released by First National. Dir. by Robert Milton. Leslie Howard, D.F. Jr., Helen Chandler, Beryl Mercer, Alison Skipworth, Montagu Love, Dudley Digges, Lyonel Watts.

The Way of All Men. First National. Remake of 1922 film, *The Sin Flood.* Dir. by Frank Lloyd. D.F. Jr., Dorothy Revier, Robert Edeson, Anders Randolf, Noah Beery.

One Night at Susie's. First National. Dir. by John Francis Dillon. Billie Dove, D.F. Jr., Helen Ware, Tully Marshall, Jame Crane, John Loder.

1931

Little Caesar. Warner Bros. Released by First National. Dir. by Mervyn LeRoy. Edward G. Robinson, D.F. Jr., Glenda Farrell, Sidney Blackmer, George E. Stone.

Chances. Warner Bros. Released by First National. Dir. by Allan Dwan. D.F. Jr., Anthony Bushell, Rose Hobart, Mary Forbestein.

I Like Your Nerve. Warner Bros. Released by First National. Dir. by William McGann. D.F. Jr., Loretta Young, Henry Kolker, Boris Karloff, Claude Allister.

Union Depot. Warner Bros. Released by First National. Dir. by Alfred E. Green. D.F. Jr., Joan Blondell, Guy Kibbee, Alan Hale, Frank McHugh.

It's Tough to Be Famous! Warner Bros. Released by First National. Dir. by

Alfred E. Green. D.F. Jr., Mary Brian, Lillian Bond, Walter Catlett, Louise Beavers.

Love Is a Racket. Warner Bros. Released by First National. Dir. by William A. Wellman. D.F. Jr., Frances Dee, Lee Tracy, Lyle Talbot, Ann Dvorak.

1932

Scarlet Dawn. Warner Bros. Released by First National. Dir. by William Dieterle. D.F. Jr., Nancy Carroll, Lilyan Tashman, Guy Kibbee.

Le Plombier Amoureux. MGM. French version of *The Passionate Plumber.* Dir. by Claude Autant-Lara. Buster Keaton, Jeanette Ferney, D.F. Jr.

L'Athlete Malgre Lui. Warner Bros. Dir. by William McGann.

L'Aviateur. Warner Bros. Dir. by William McGann.

1933

Parachute Jumper. Warner Bros. Dir. by Alfred E. Green. D.F. Jr., Bette Davis, Leo Carillo, Frank McHugh, Claire Dodd.

The Life of Jimmy Dolan. Warner Bros. Dir. by Archie Mayo. D.F. Jr., Loretta Young, Aline MacMahon, Lyle Talbot, Mickey Rooney, John Wayne, Guy Kibbee.

The Narrow Corner. Warner Bros. Dir. by Alfred E. Green. D.F. Jr., Patricia Ellis, Ralph Bellamy, Dudley Digges, Sidney Toler.

Captured. Warner Bros. Dir. by Roy Del Ruth. Leslie Howard, D.F. Jr., Paul Lukas, Margaret Lindsay, J. Carroll Naish.

Morning Glory. RKO. Dir. by Lowell Sherman. Katharine Hepburn, D.F. Jr., Adolphe Menjou, Mary Duncan, C. Aubrey Smith.

1934

Catherine the Great. London Films. Distributed by United Artists. Dir. by Paul Czinner. D.F. Jr., Elisabeth Bergner, Flora Robson, Sir Gerald DuMaurier.

Success at Any Price (Success Story). RKO. Dir. by J. Walter Ruben. Colleen Moore, D.F. Jr., Genevieve Tobin, Frank Morgan, Edward Everett Horton, Allen Vincent.

1935

Mimi. B.I.P. (British). Released in U.K. by Wardour, in U.S. by United Artists. Dir. by Paul Stein. D.F. Jr., Gertrude Lawrence, Diana Napier, Harold Warrender, Carol Goodner.

Man of the Moment. Warner Bros. (British). Dir. by Monty Banks. D.F. Jr., Laura La Plante, Margaret Lockwood, Claude Hulbert, Donald Calthrop.

1936

The Amateur Gentleman. Criterion Films (Prod. by D.F. Jr. and Marcel Hellman). U.S. release by United Artists. Dir. by Thornton Freeland. Screenplay by Clemence Dane. D.F. Jr., Elissa Landi, Gordon Harker, Margaret Lockwood, Hugh Williams, Basil Sydney, Irene Brown, Coral Browne, Athol Stewart, Esme Percy.

Accused. Criterion Films (Prod. by D.F. Jr. and Marcel Hellman). U.S. release by United Artists. Dir. by Thornton Freeland. D.F. Jr., Dolores del Rio, Florence Desmond, Basil Sydney, Cecil Humphreys, Esme Percy, Googie Withers, Roland Culver. Leo Genn.

1937

When Thief Meets Thief. Criterion Films (Prod. by D.F. Jr. and Marcel Hellman). U.K. release as *Jump for Glory.* U.S. release by United Artists. Dir. by Raoul Walsh. Based on novel *Jump for Glory.* D.F. Jr., Valerie Hobson, Alan Hale, Jack Melford, Esme Percy, Leo Genn, Basil Radford.

The Prisoner of Zenda. Selznick International. Released by United Artists. Dir. by John Cromwell. Ronald Colman, Madeleine Carroll, D.F. Jr., Mary Astor, C. Aubrey Smith, Raymond Massey, David Niven.

1938

The Joy of Living. RKO. Dir. by Tay Garnett. Irene Dunne, D.F. Jr., Alice Brady, Guy Kibbee, Jean Dixon, Eric Blore, Billy Gilbert, Franklin Pangborn, Lucille Ball.

The Rage of Paris. Universal. Dir. by Henry Koster. D.F. Jr., Danielle Darrieux, Mischa Auer, Helen Broderick, Louis Hayward.

Having Wonderful Time. RKO. Dir. by Alfred Santell. Ginger Rogers, D.F. Jr., Red Skelton, Lucille Ball, Eve Arden, Jack Carson, Donald Meek, Grady Sutton.

The Young in Heart. United Artists. Prod. by Selznick International. Dir. by Richard Wallace. D.F. Jr., Janet Gaynor, Paulette Goddard, Roland Young, Billie Burke, Richard Carlson.

1939

Gunga Din. RKO. Prod. and dir. by George Stevens. Cary Grant, Victor McLaglen, D.F. Jr., Sam Jaffe, Eduardo Cianelli, Joan Fontaine, Robert Coote, Montagu Love.

The Sun Never Sets. Universal. Prod. and dir. by Rowland V. Lee. D.F. Jr., Basil Rathbone, Virginia Field, Lionel Atwill, Barbara O'Neil, C. Aubrey Smith.

Rulers of the Sea. Paramount. Prod. and dir. by Frank Lloyd. D.F. Jr., Margaret Lockwood, Will Fyffe, George Bancroft, Montagu Love.

1940

Green Hell. Universal. Dir. by James Whale. D.F. Jr., Joan Bennett, John Howard, George Sanders, Vincent Price, Alan Hale, George Bancroft.
Safari. Paramount. Dir. by Edward H. Griffith. D.F. Jr., Madeleine Carroll, Tullio Carminati, Muriel Angelus, Lynne Overman, Billy Gilbert.
Angels Over Broadway. Columbia. Prod. by Ben Hecht and D.F. Jr. Dir. by Ben Hecht and Lee Garmes. Written by Ben Hecht. D.F. Jr., Rita Hayworth, Thomas Mitchell, John Qualen, George Watts.

1941

The Corsican Brothers. Edward Small Productions. Released by United Artists. Dir. by Gregory Ratoff. D.F. Jr., Akim Tamiroff, Ruth Warrick, J. Carroll Naish, H. B. Warner, John Emery, Henry Wilcoxon.

(Further films, for 1942 and thereafter, will be listed in the second volume of this autobiography.)

Index